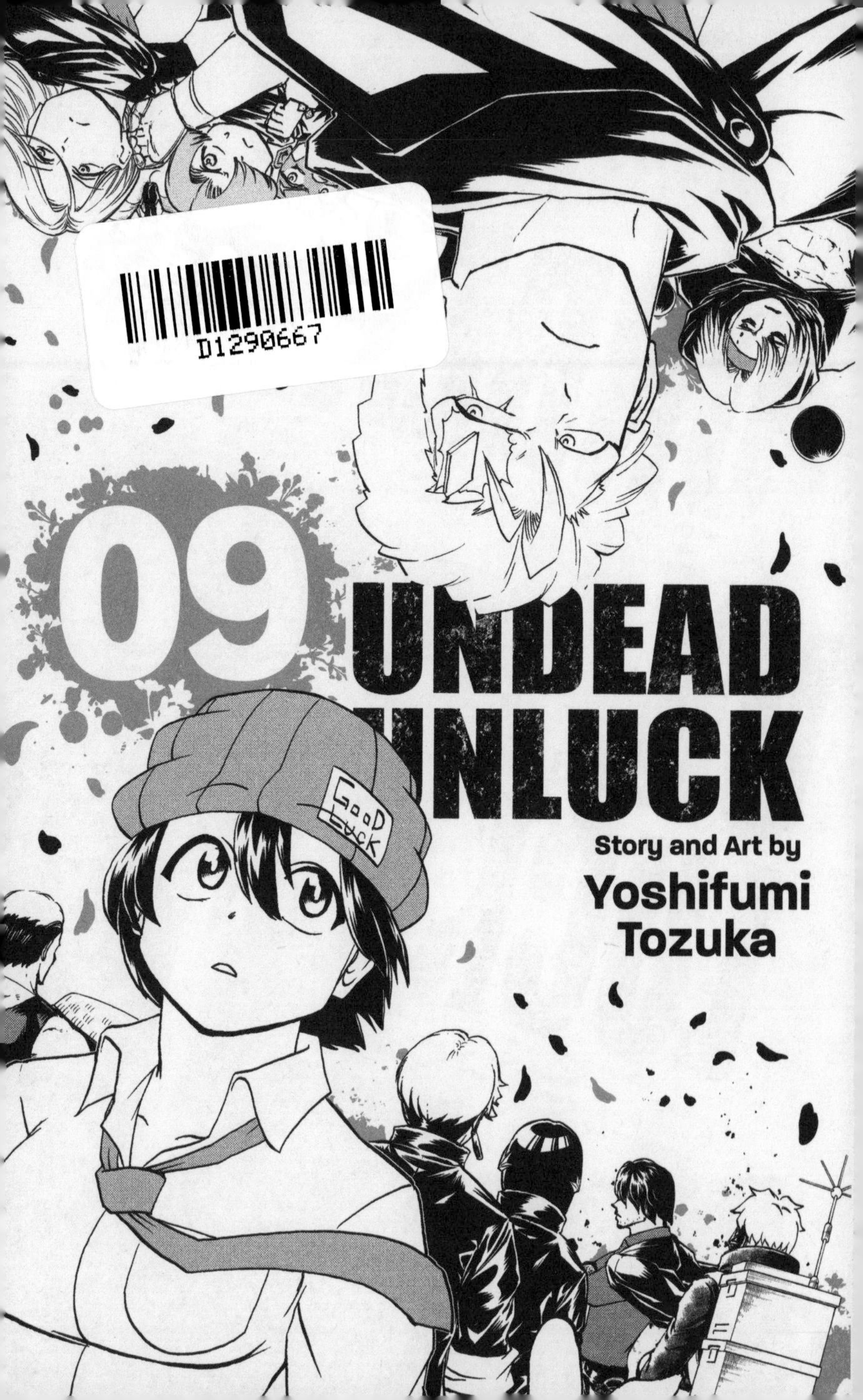
09
UNDEAD UNLUCK
Story and Art by
Yoshifumi Tozuka
GOOD LUCK

UNDEAD UNLUCK

CHARACTER

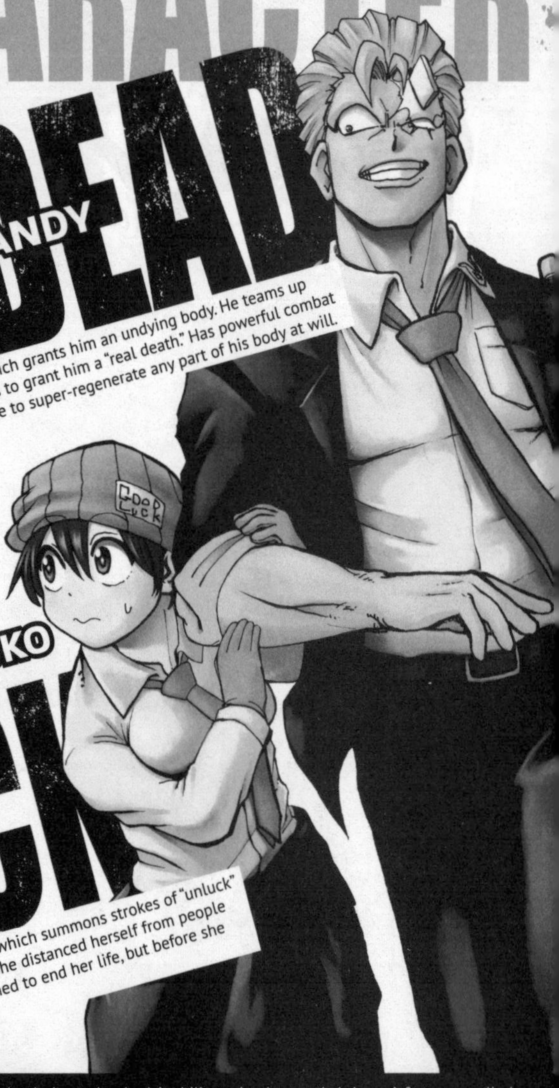

UNDEAD
ANDY

User of the Undead ability, which grants him an undying body. He teams up with Fuuko to use her powers to grant him a "real death." Has powerful combat capabilities due to being able to super-regenerate any part of his body at will.

UNLUCK
FUUKO

User of the Unluck ability, which summons strokes of "unluck" upon those she touches. She distanced herself from people for a long time and planned to end her life, but before she could, she met Andy.

STORY

Fuuko consigned herself to death due to her body's ability to inadvertently bring misfortune—called "unluck"—to those she touches. However, after meeting Andy, a mysterious man with an undying body, she gained the will to live. During their journey, they learn about the Union, an organization that polices UMA (unidentified mysterious animals) and unexplainable phenomena. After defeating enough of the Union's members to join their ranks, Andy and Fuuko discover the true purpose for the organization's existence—to rebel against God and overcome his quests. Summer has been successfully slain, but at the cost of throwing the Earth's climate off balance, leading to an extreme cold snap. As a stipulation to get Under to neutralize Winter, Fuuko surrenders herself to Under. The only quest that remains is neutralizing Spring, but how will that turn out?!

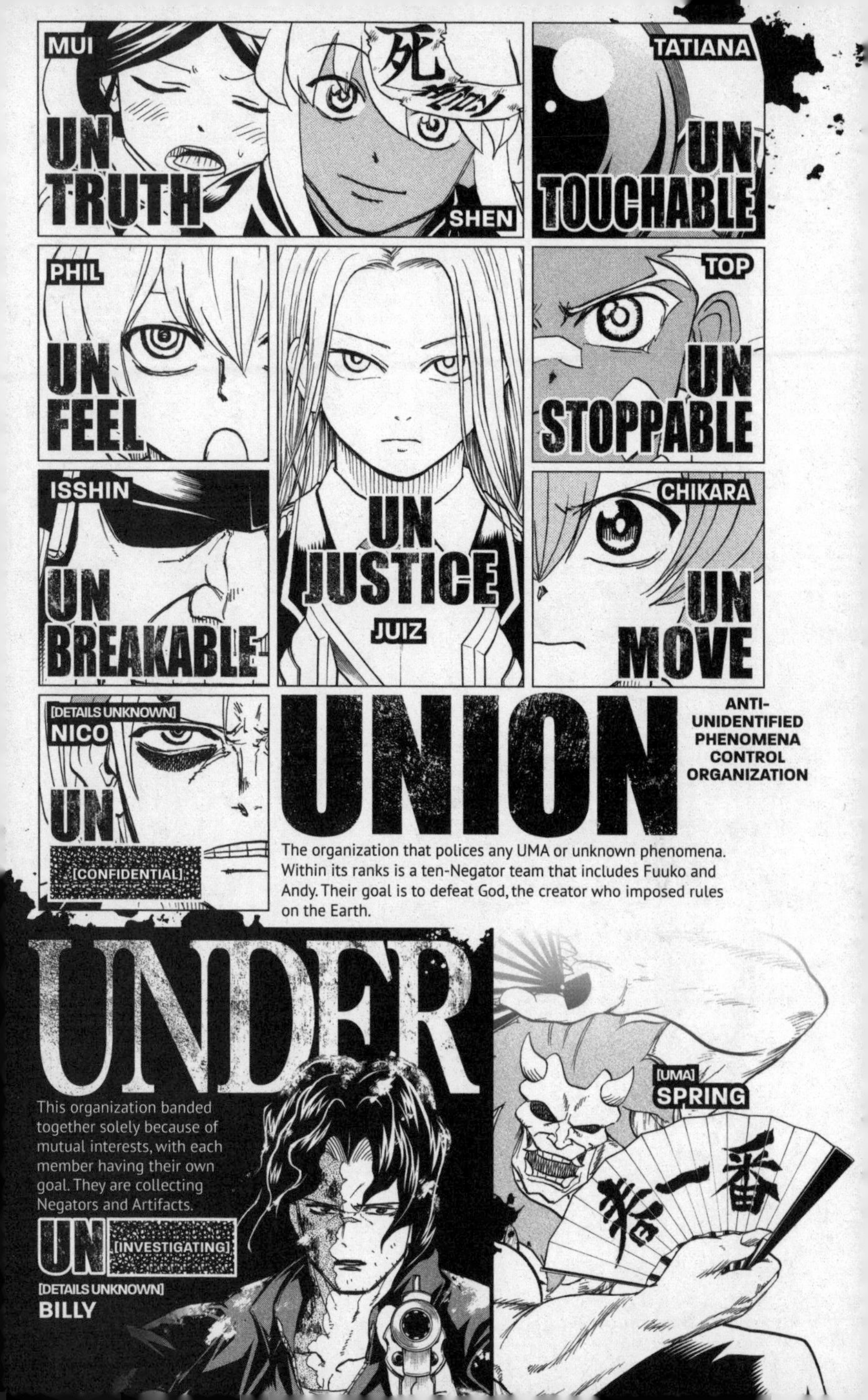
TATIANA
UN TOUCHABLE
SHEN
MUI
UN TRUTH
TOP
UN STOPPABLE
CHIKARA
UN MOVE
UN JUSTICE
JUIZ
PHIL
UN FEEL
ISSHIN
UN BREAKABLE
[DETAILS UNKNOWN]
NICO
UN
[CONFIDENTIAL]
UNION
ANTI-UNIDENTIFIED PHENOMENA CONTROL ORGANIZATION
The organization that polices any UMA or unknown phenomena. Within its ranks is a ten-Negator team that includes Fuuko and Andy. Their goal is to defeat God, the creator who imposed rules on the Earth.
[UMA]
SPRING
UNDER
This organization banded together solely because of mutual interests, with each member having their own goal. They are collecting Negators and Artifacts.
UN
[INVESTIGATING]
[DETAILS UNKNOWN]
BILLY

UNDEAD UNLUCK

09

No. 071 To Love

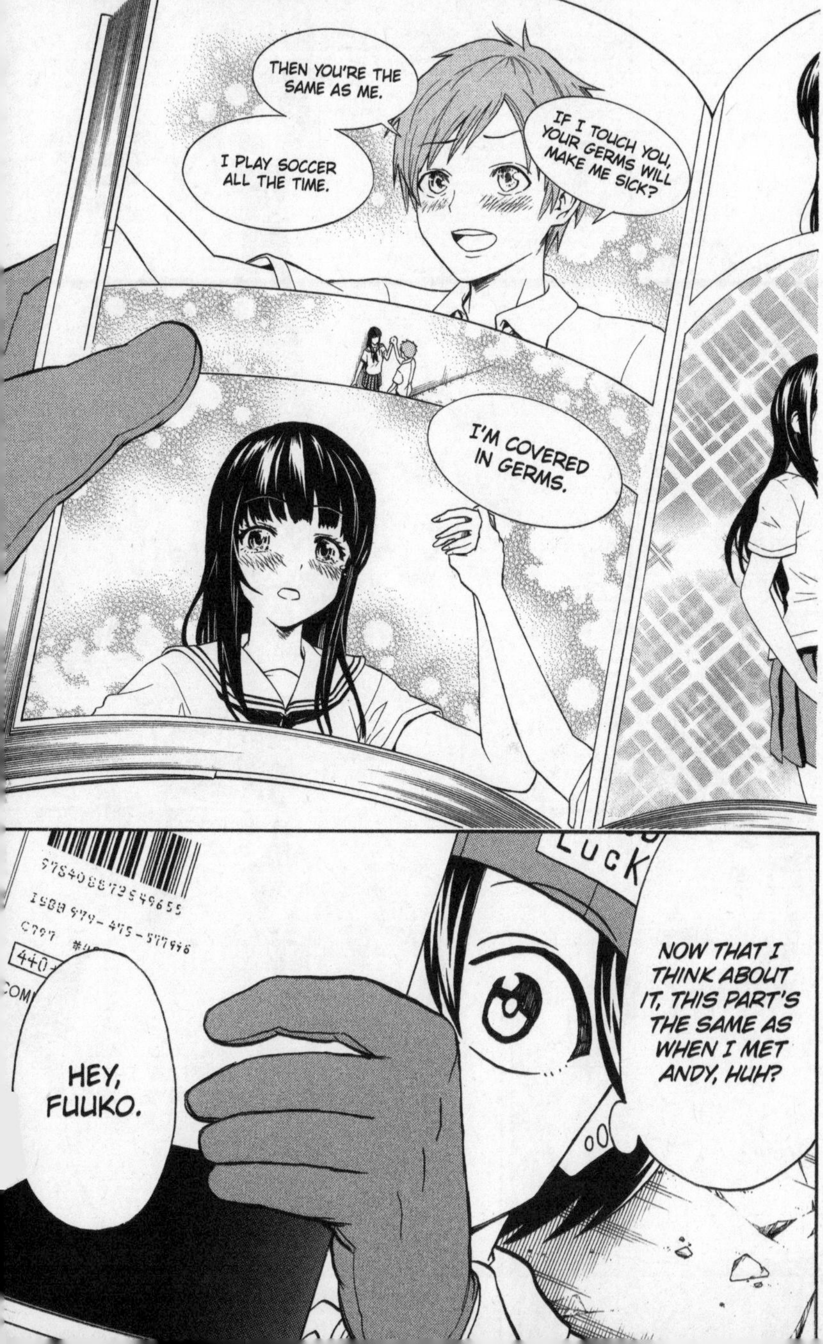
IF I TOUCH YOU, YOUR GERMS WILL MAKE ME SICK?
THEN YOU'RE THE SAME AS ME.
I PLAY SOCCER ALL THE TIME.
I'M COVERED IN GERMS.
LUCK
NOW THAT I THINK ABOUT IT, THIS PART'S THE SAME AS WHEN I MET ANDY, HUH?
HEY, FUUKO.

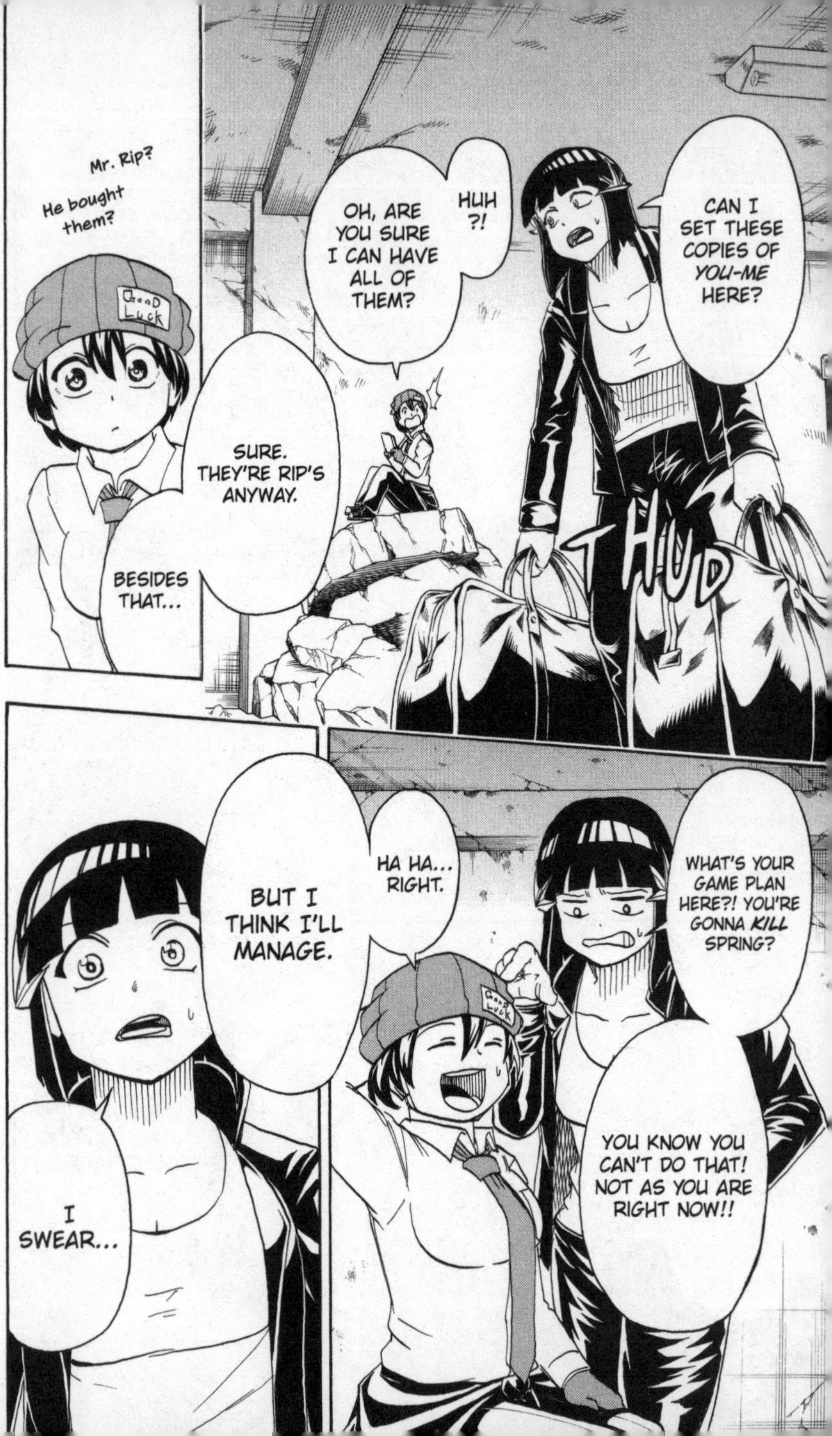
CAN I SET THESE COPIES OF *YOU-ME* HERE?
THUD
HUH ?!
OH, ARE YOU SURE I CAN HAVE ALL OF THEM?
SURE. THEY'RE RIP'S ANYWAY.
BESIDES THAT...
Mr. Rip?
He bought them?
WHAT'S YOUR GAME PLAN HERE?! YOU'RE GONNA *KILL* SPRING?
YOU KNOW YOU CAN'T DO THAT! NOT AS YOU ARE RIGHT NOW!!
HA HA... RIGHT.
BUT I THINK I'LL MANAGE.
I SWEAR...

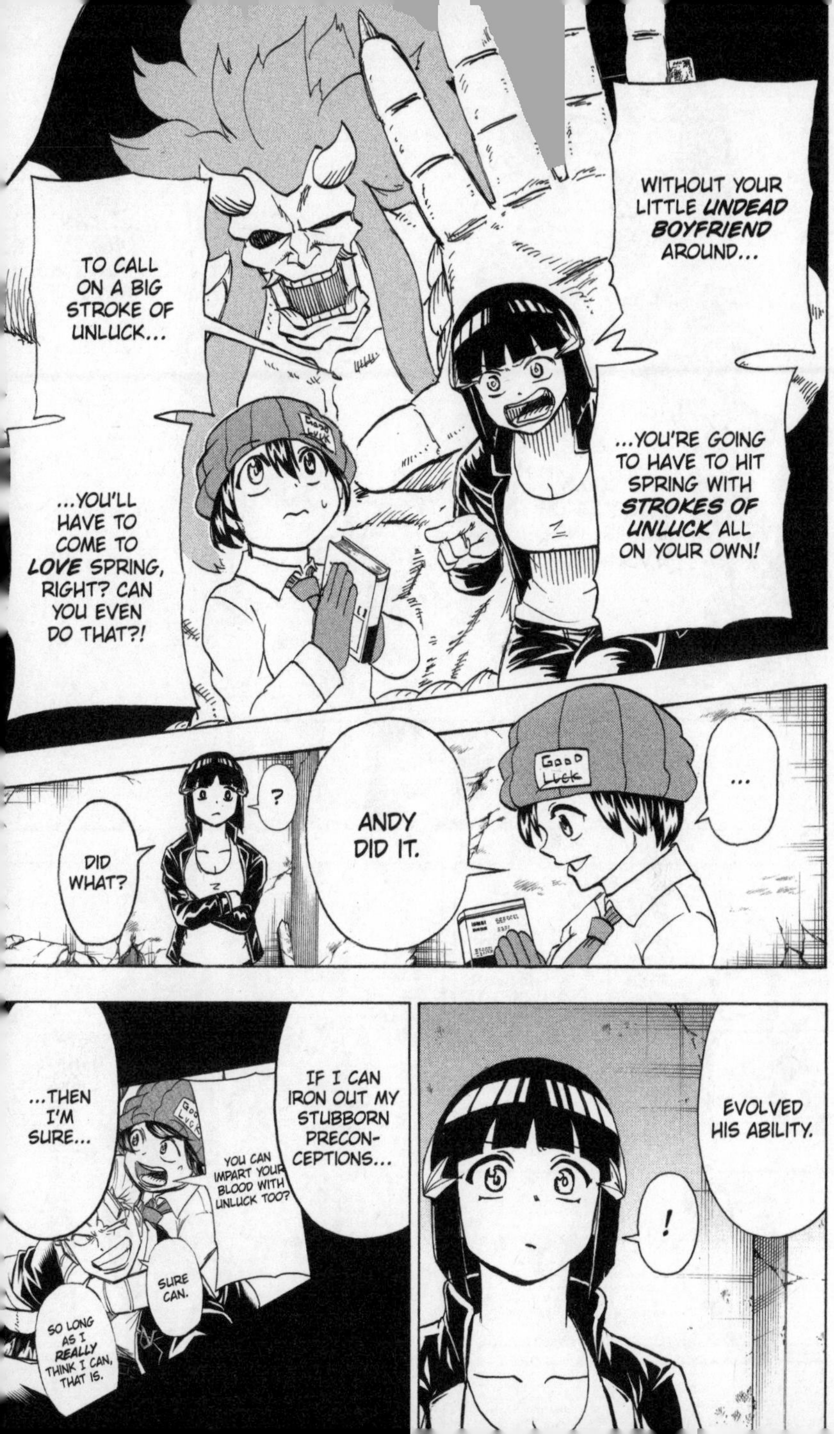

WITHOUT YOUR LITTLE *UNDEAD BOYFRIEND* AROUND...
...YOU'RE GOING TO HAVE TO HIT SPRING WITH *STROKES OF UNLUCK* ALL ON YOUR OWN!
TO CALL ON A BIG STROKE OF UNLUCK...
...YOU'LL HAVE TO COME TO *LOVE* SPRING, RIGHT? CAN YOU EVEN DO THAT?!
...
GOOD LUCK
ANDY DID IT.
?
DID WHAT?
EVOLVED HIS ABILITY.
!
IF I CAN IRON OUT MY STUBBORN PRECONCEPTIONS...
...THEN I'M SURE...
YOU CAN IMPART YOUR BLOOD WITH UNLUCK TOO?
SURE CAN.
SO LONG AS I *REALLY* THINK I CAN, THAT IS.

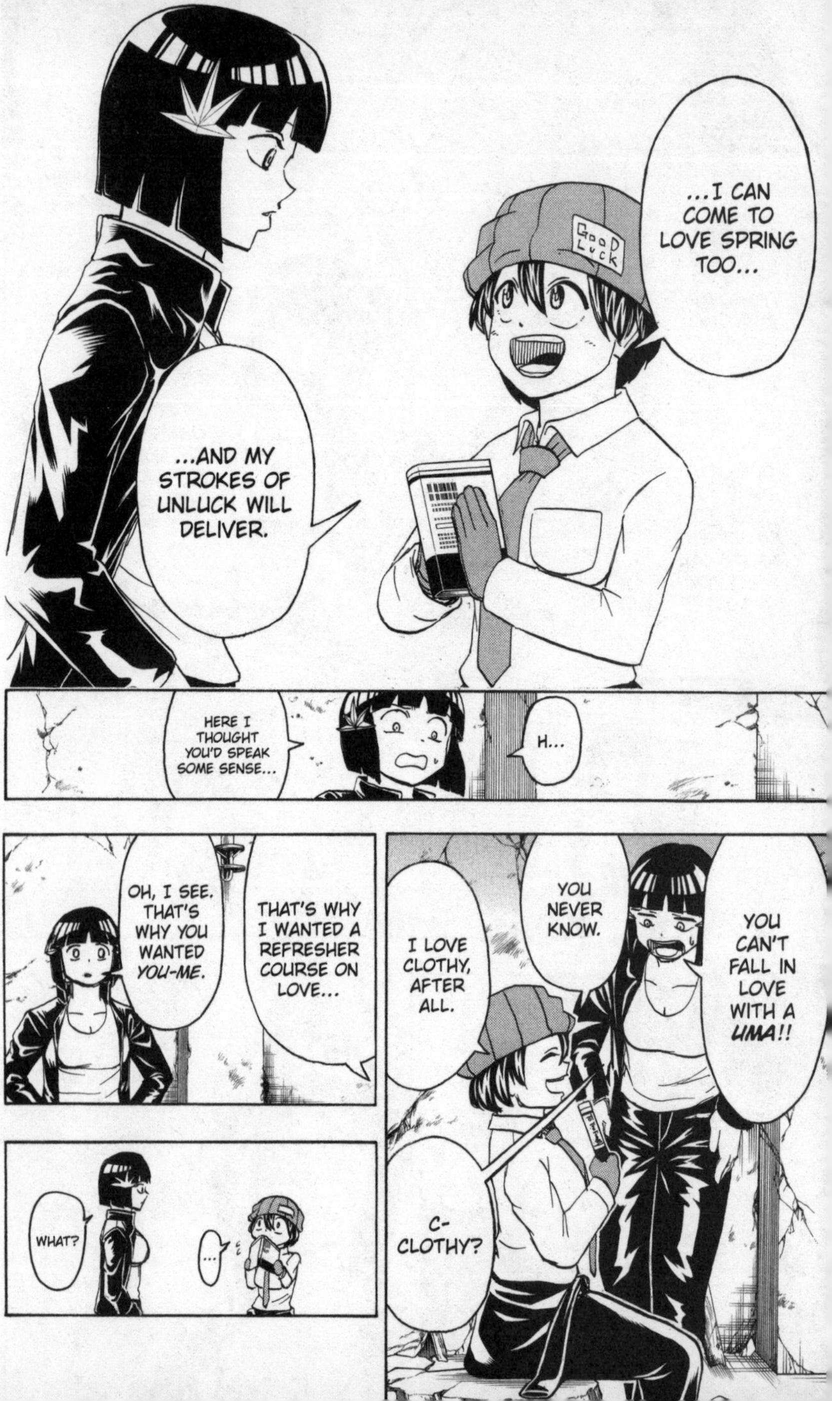
...I CAN COME TO LOVE SPRING TOO...
...AND MY STROKES OF UNLUCK WILL DELIVER.
H...
HERE I THOUGHT YOU'D SPEAK SOME SENSE...
YOU CAN'T FALL IN LOVE WITH A *UMA*!!
YOU NEVER KNOW.
I LOVE CLOTHY, AFTER ALL.
C- CLOTHY?
THAT'S WHY I WANTED A REFRESHER COURSE ON LOVE...
OH, I SEE. THAT'S WHY YOU WANTED *YOU-ME*.
...
WHAT?

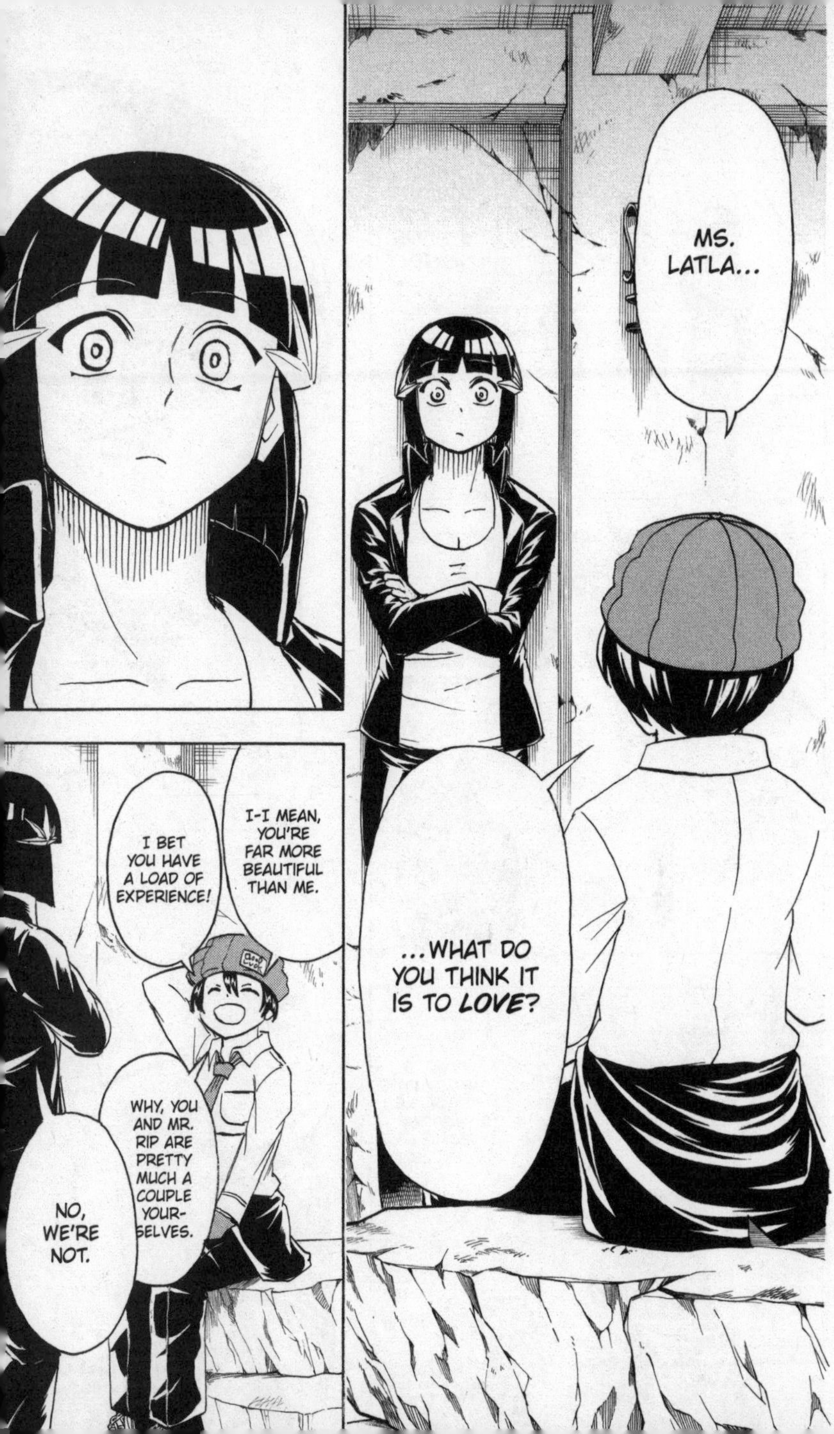
MS. LATLA...
...WHAT DO YOU THINK IT IS TO *LOVE*?
I-I MEAN, YOU'RE FAR MORE BEAUTIFUL THAN ME.
I BET YOU HAVE A LOAD OF EXPERIENCE!
WHY, YOU AND MR. RIP ARE PRETTY MUCH A COUPLE YOUR-SELVES.
NO, WE'RE NOT.

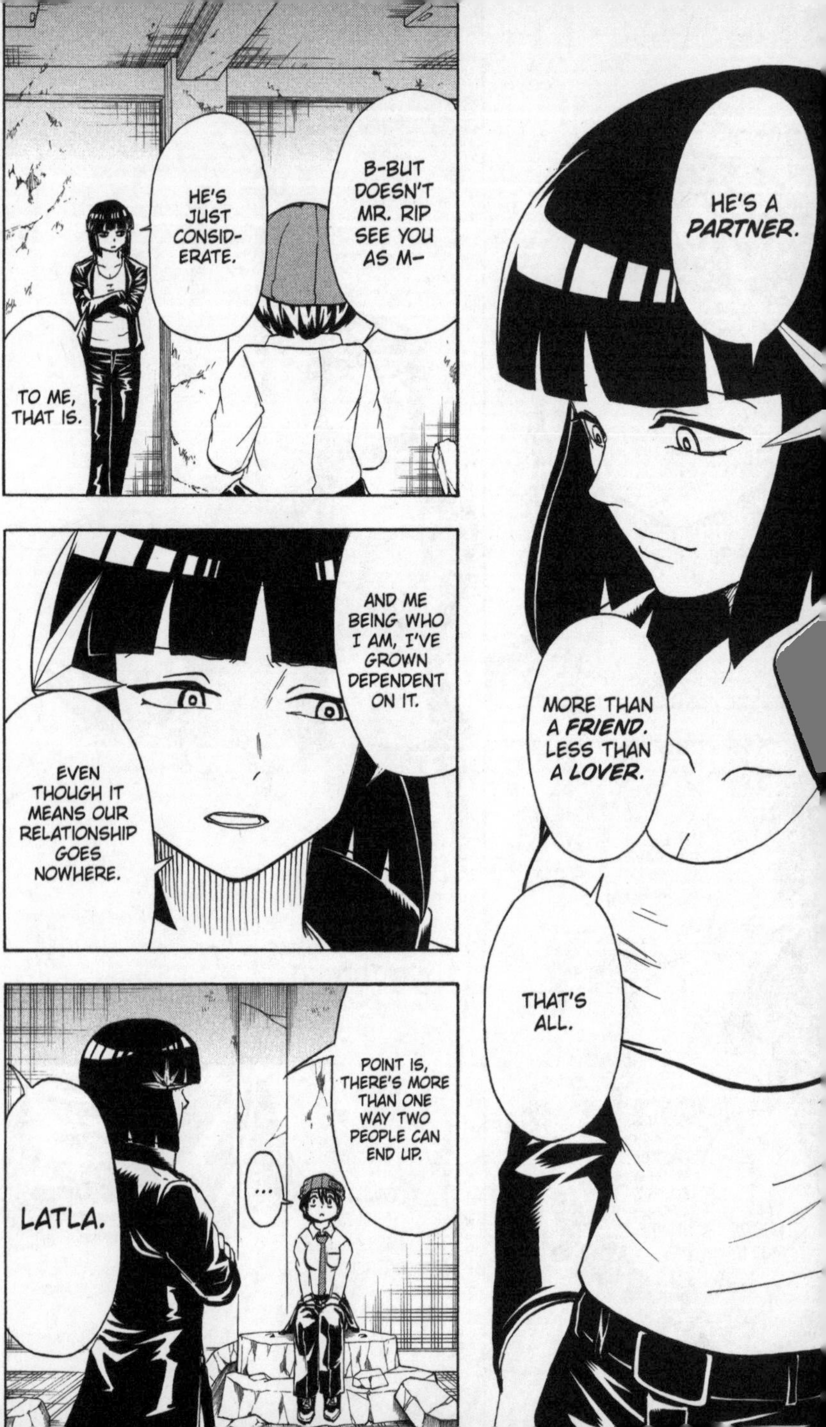
HE'S A *PARTNER.*
MORE THAN A *FRIEND.* LESS THAN A *LOVER.*
THAT'S ALL.
B-BUT DOESN'T MR. RIP SEE YOU AS M-
HE'S JUST CONSIDERATE.
TO ME, THAT IS.
AND ME BEING WHO I AM, I'VE GROWN DEPENDENT ON IT.
EVEN THOUGH IT MEANS OUR RELATIONSHIP GOES NOWHERE.
POINT IS, THERE'S MORE THAN ONE WAY TWO PEOPLE CAN END UP.
...
LATLA.

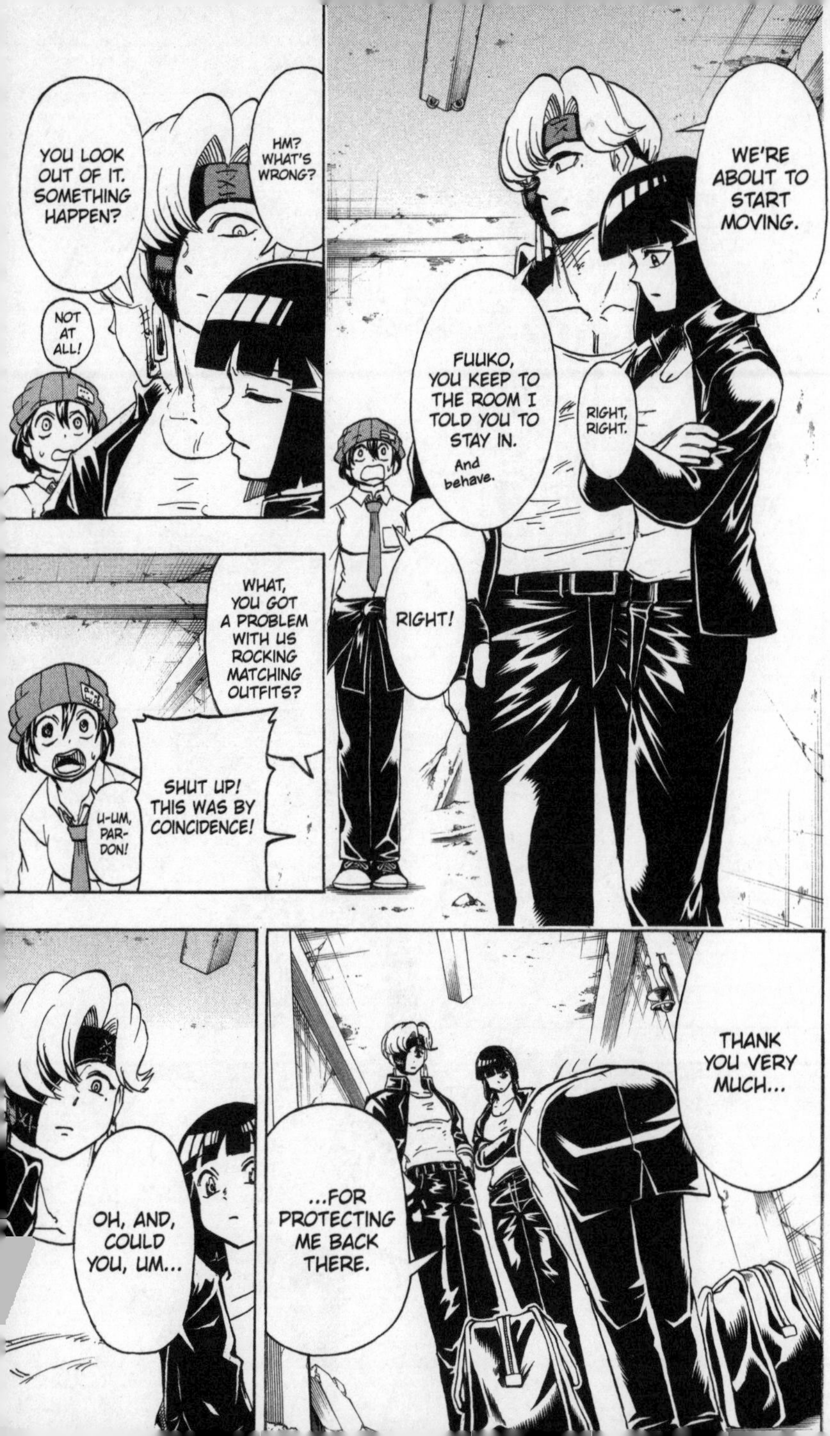
WE'RE ABOUT TO START MOVING.
RIGHT, RIGHT.
FUUKO, YOU KEEP TO THE ROOM I TOLD YOU TO STAY IN.
And behave.
RIGHT!
HM? WHAT'S WRONG?
YOU LOOK OUT OF IT. SOMETHING HAPPEN?
NOT AT ALL!
WHAT, YOU GOT A PROBLEM WITH US ROCKING MATCHING OUTFITS?
SHUT UP! THIS WAS BY COINCIDENCE!
U-UM, PAR-DON!
THANK YOU VERY MUCH...
...FOR PROTECTING ME BACK THERE.
OH, AND, COULD YOU, UM...

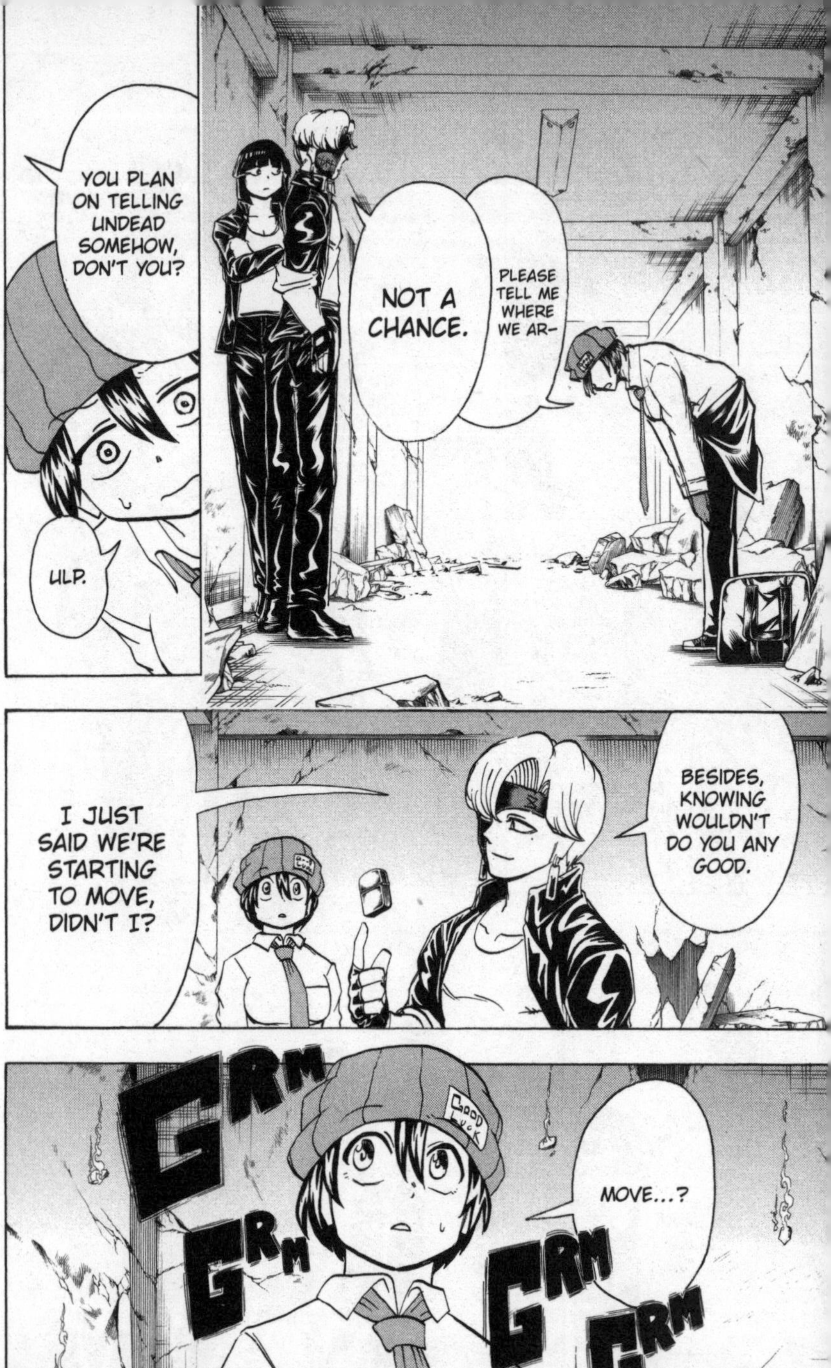
PLEASE TELL ME WHERE WE AR-
NOT A CHANCE.
YOU PLAN ON TELLING UNDEAD SOMEHOW, DON'T YOU?
ULP.
BESIDES, KNOWING WOULDN'T DO YOU ANY GOOD.
I JUST SAID WE'RE STARTING TO MOVE, DIDN'T I?
MOVE...?
GOOD LUCK
GRM
GRM
GRM
GRM

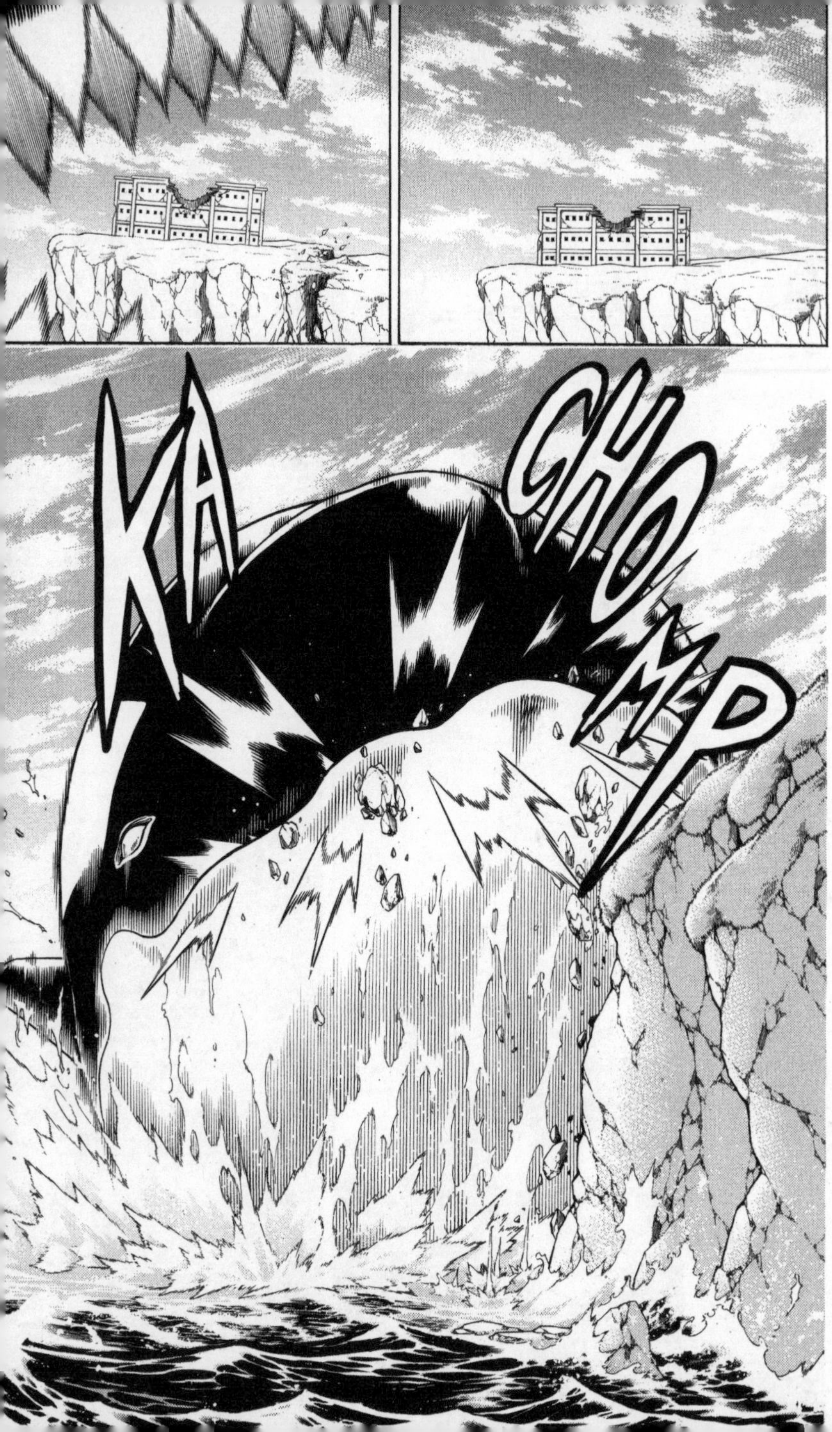
KA
CHOMP

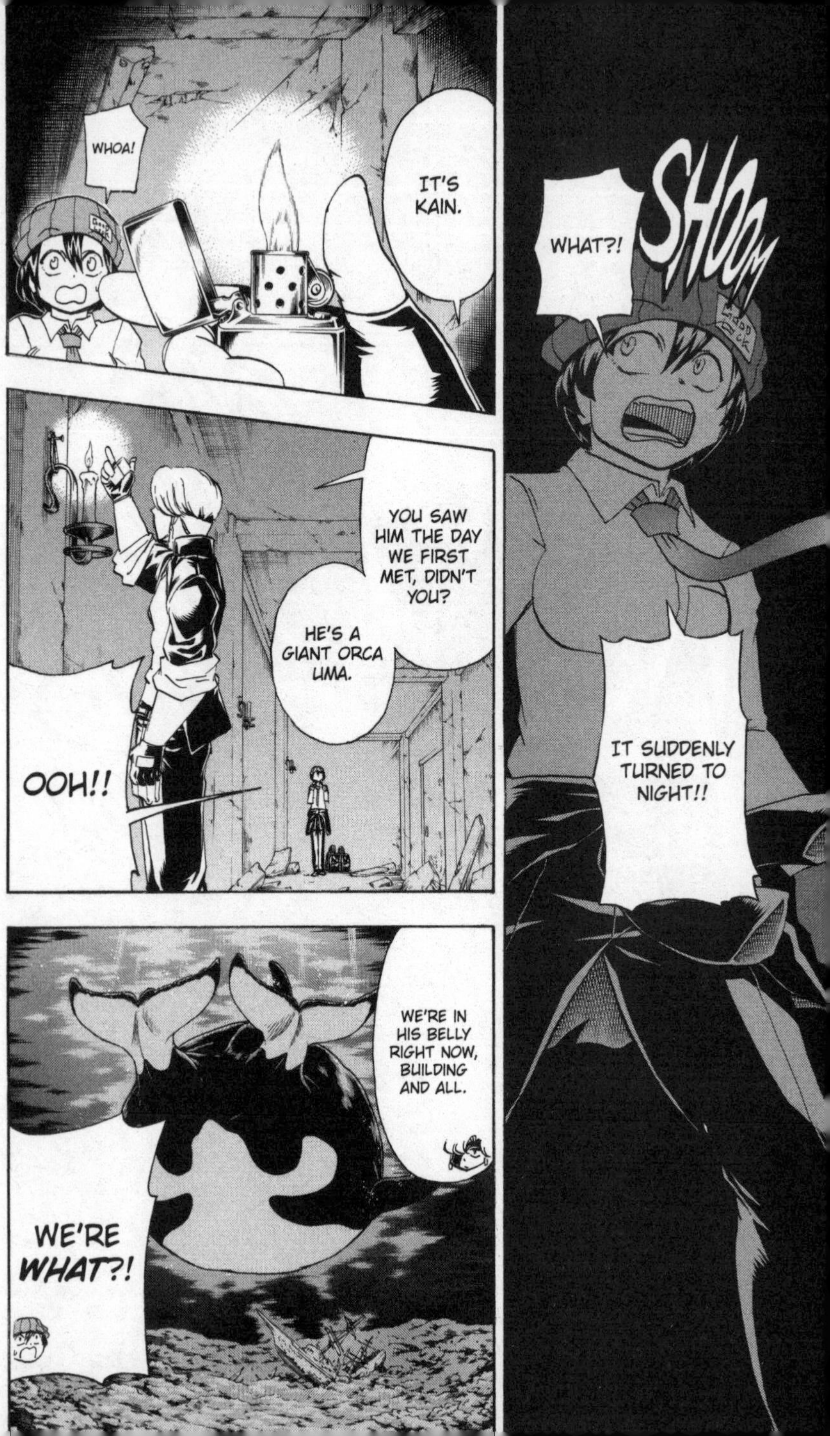
WHAT?!
SHOOM
IT SUDDENLY TURNED TO NIGHT!!
IT'S KAIN.
WHOA!
YOU SAW HIM THE DAY WE FIRST MET, DIDN'T YOU?
HE'S A GIANT ORCA UMA.
OOH!!
WE'RE IN HIS BELLY RIGHT NOW, BUILDING AND ALL.
WE'RE WHAT?!

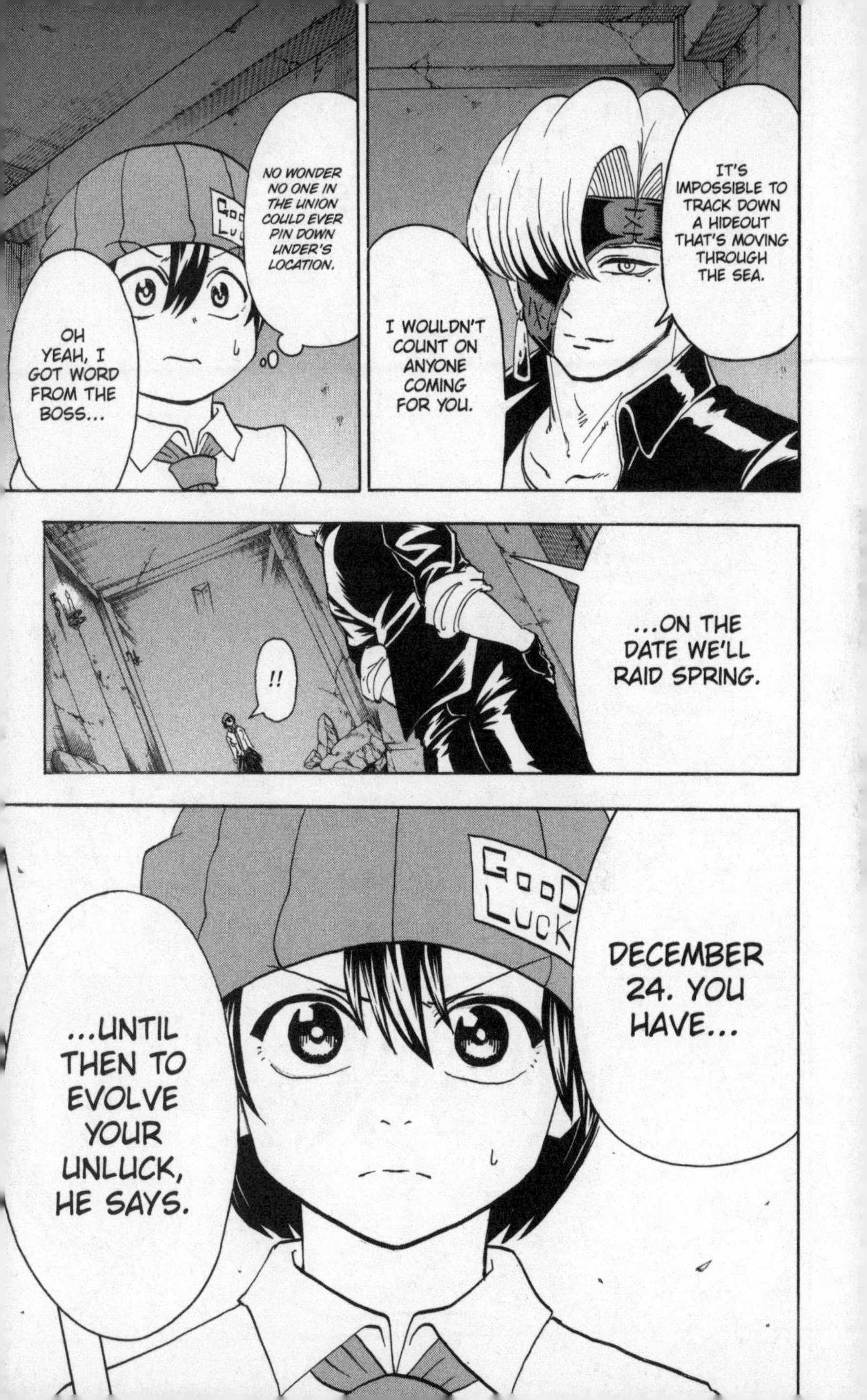
IT'S IMPOSSIBLE TO TRACK DOWN A HIDEOUT THAT'S MOVING THROUGH THE SEA.
I WOULDN'T COUNT ON ANYONE COMING FOR YOU.
NO WONDER NO ONE IN THE UNION COULD EVER PIN DOWN UNDER'S LOCATION.
OH YEAH, I GOT WORD FROM THE BOSS...
...ON THE DATE WE'LL RAID SPRING.
!!
GOOD LUCK
DECEMBER 24. YOU HAVE...
...UNTIL THEN TO EVOLVE YOUR UNLUCK, HE SAYS.

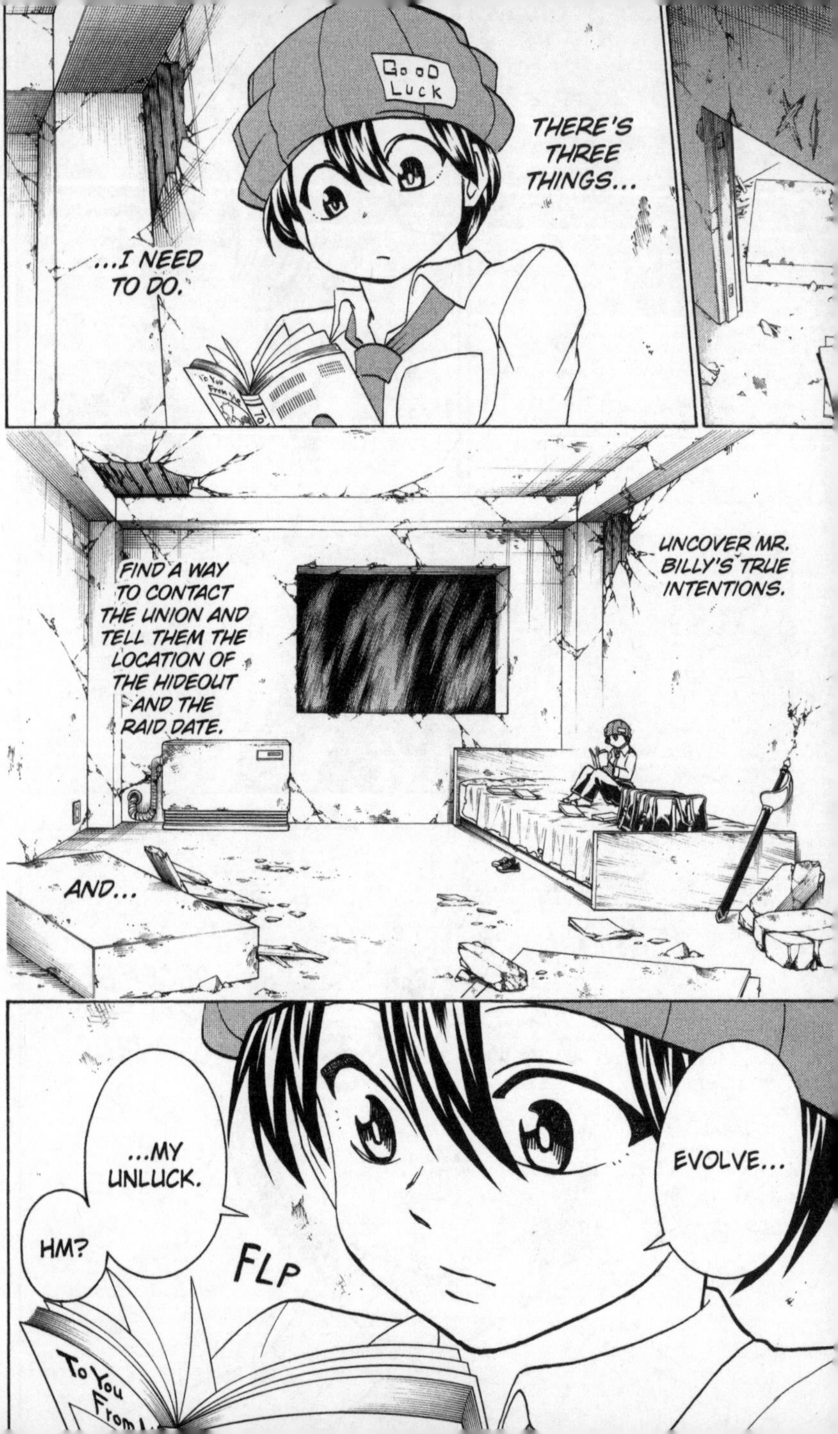
GOOD LUCK
THERE'S THREE THINGS...
...I NEED TO DO.
UNCOVER MR. BILLY'S TRUE INTENTIONS.
FIND A WAY TO CONTACT THE UNION AND TELL THEM THE LOCATION OF THE HIDEOUT AND THE RAID DATE.
AND...
EVOLVE...
...MY UNLUCK.
FLP
HM?

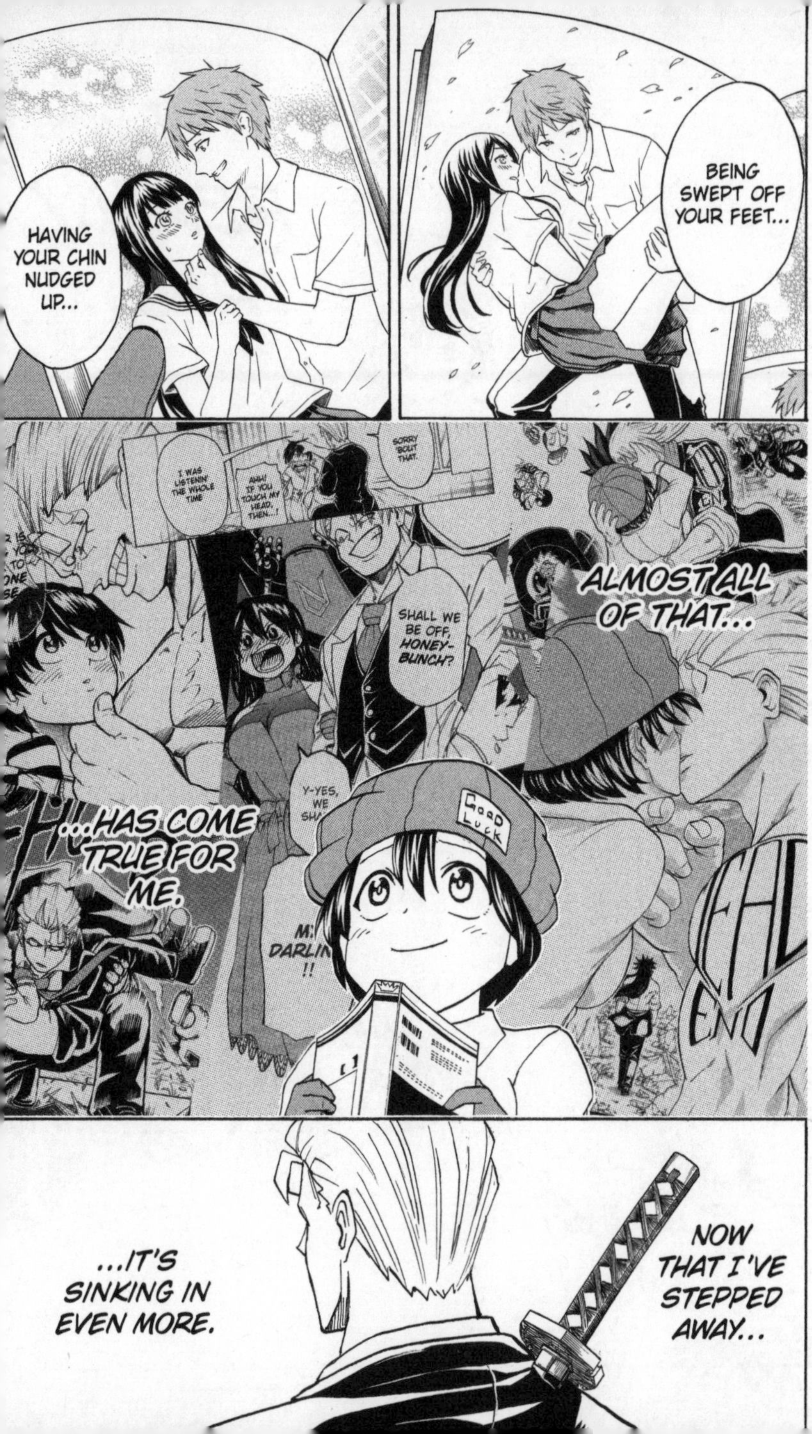
BEING SWEPT OFF YOUR FEET...
HAVING YOUR CHIN NUDGED UP...
SORRY 'BOUT THAT.
AHH! IF YOU TOUCH MY HEAD, THEN...!
I WAS LISTENIN' THE WHOLE TIME
ALMOST ALL OF THAT...
SHALL WE BE OFF, HONEY-BUNCH?
GOOD LUCK
...HAS COME TRUE FOR ME.
NOW THAT I'VE STEPPED AWAY...
...IT'S SINKING IN EVEN MORE.

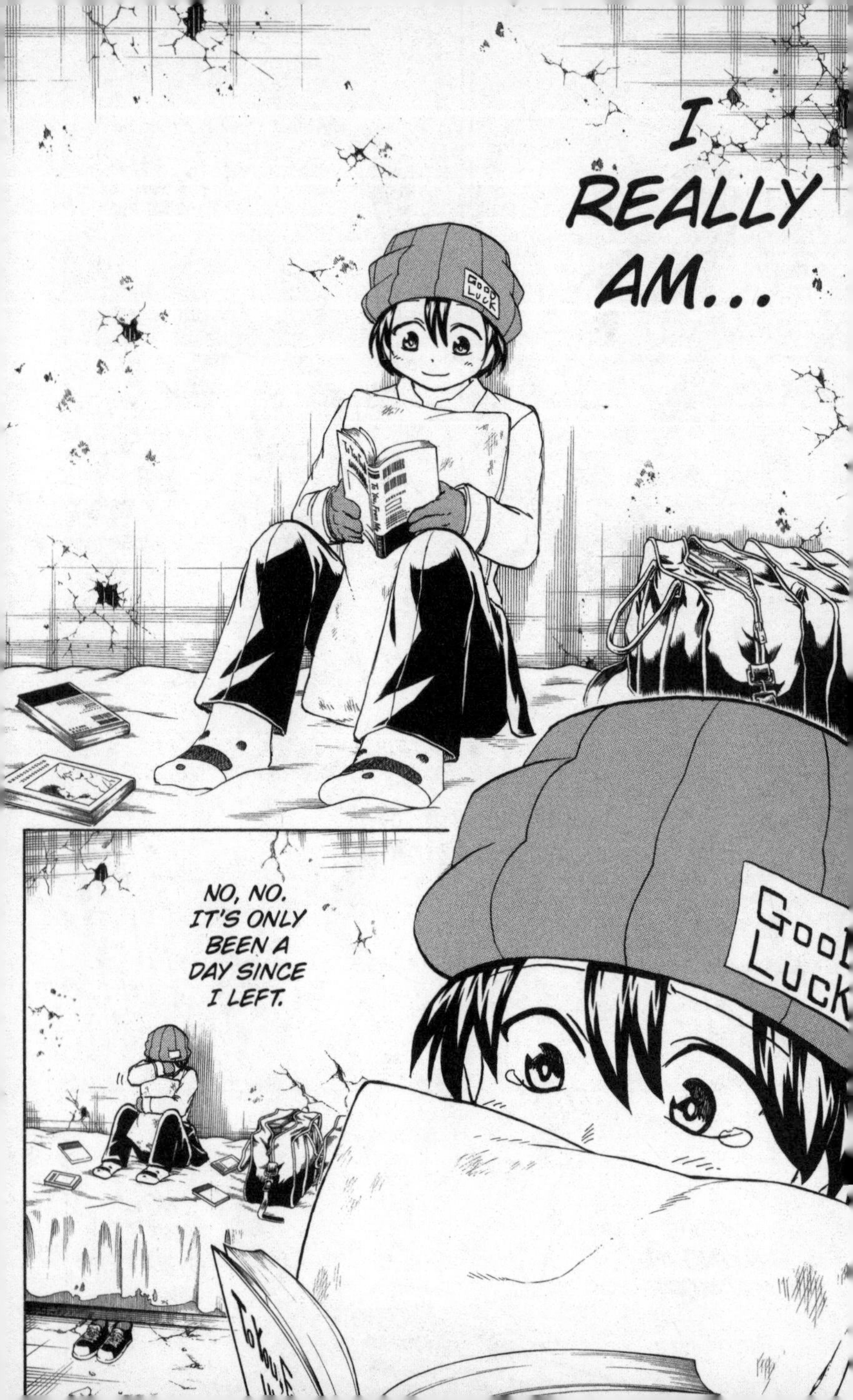
I REALLY AM...
NO, NO. IT'S ONLY BEEN A DAY SINCE I LEFT.

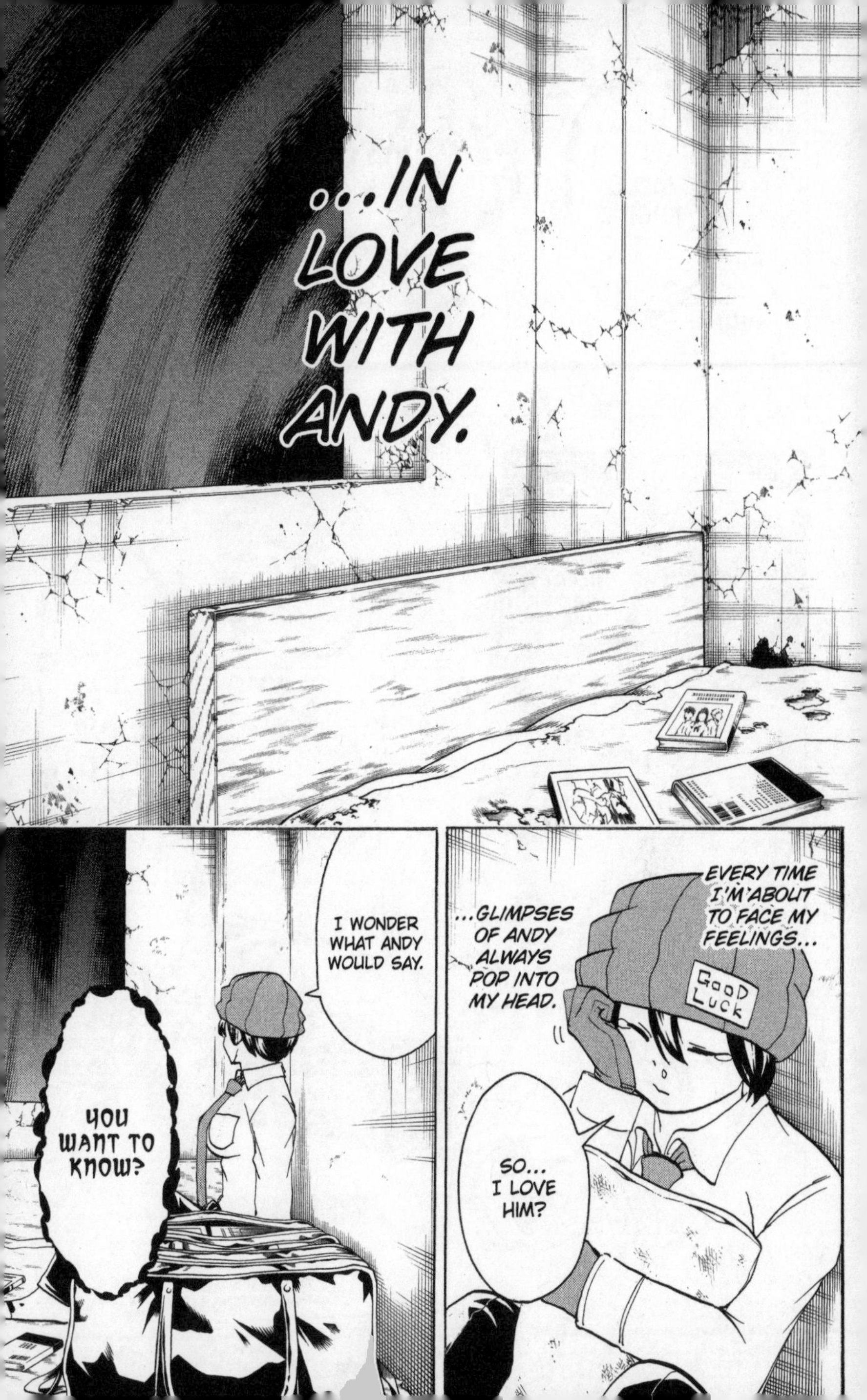
...IN LOVE WITH ANDY.
EVERY TIME I'M ABOUT TO FACE MY FEELINGS...
...GLIMPSES OF ANDY ALWAYS POP INTO MY HEAD.
GOOD LUCK
SO... I LOVE HIM?
I WONDER WHAT ANDY WOULD SAY.
YOU WANT TO KNOW?

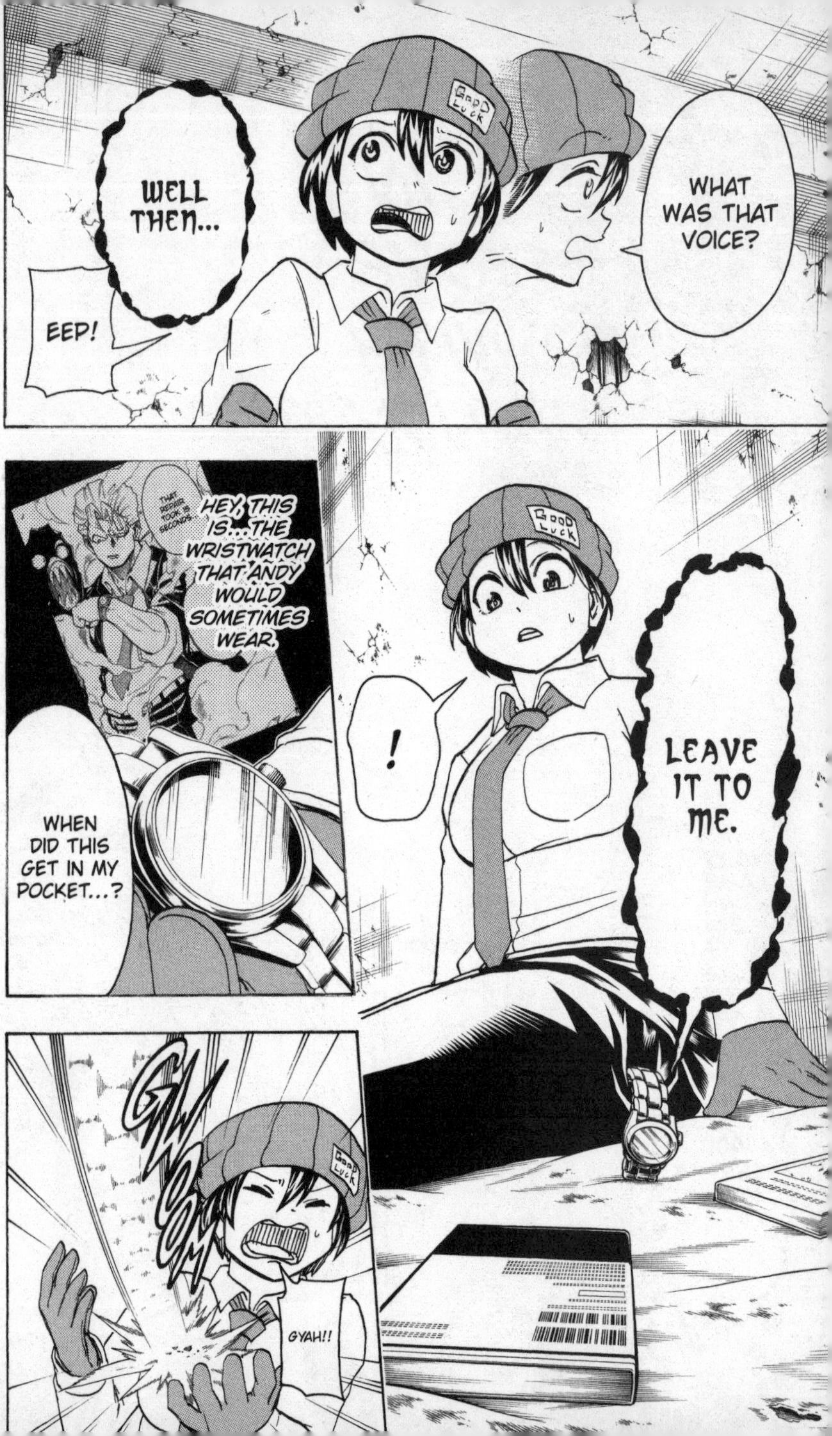
WHAT WAS THAT VOICE?
WELL THEN...
EEP!
LEAVE IT TO ME.
!
THAT REPAIR TOOK 15 SECONDS...
HEY, THIS IS... THE WRISTWATCH THAT ANDY WOULD SOMETIMES WEAR.
WHEN DID THIS GET IN MY POCKET...?
GWOOOM
GYAH!!

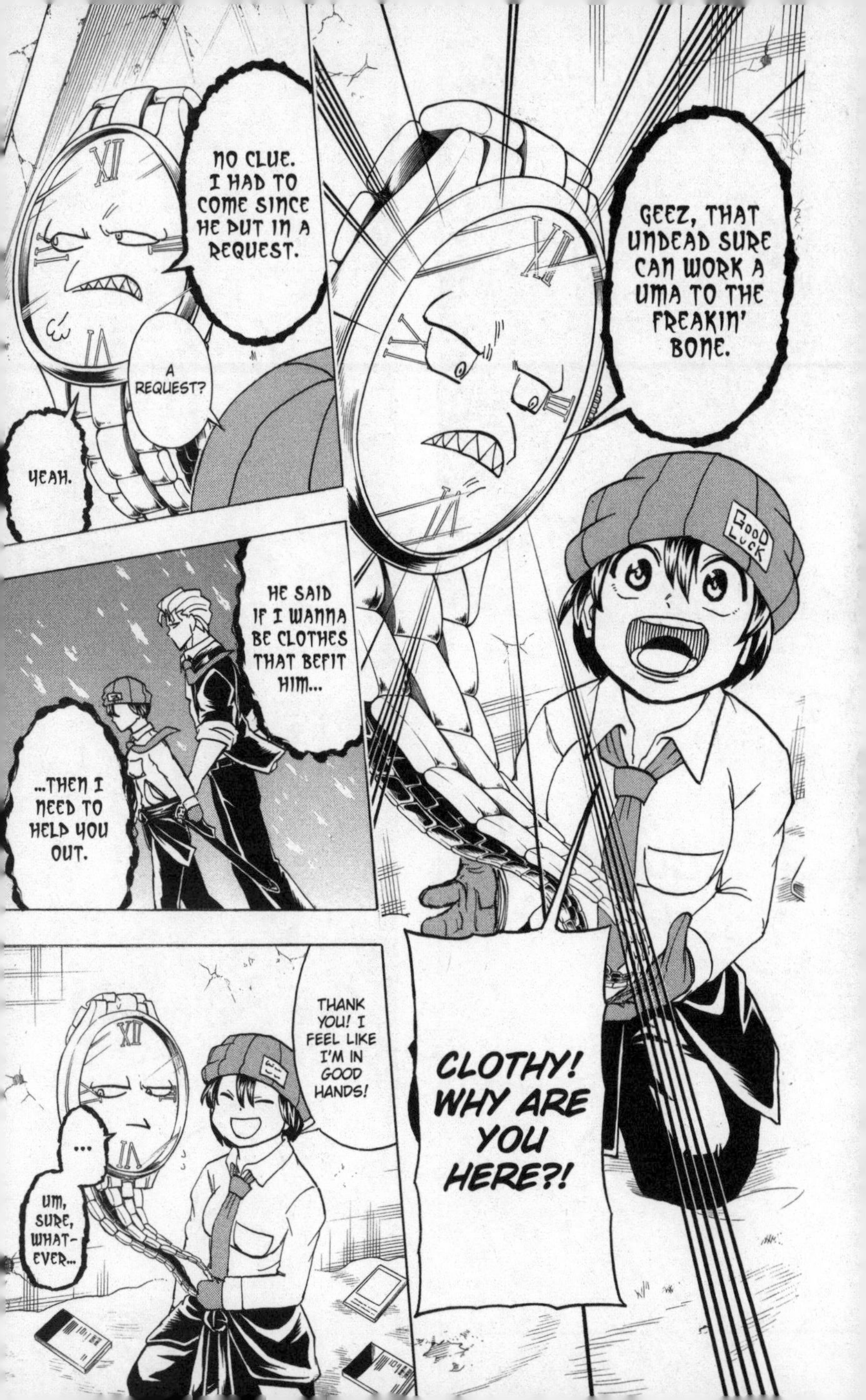
GEEZ, THAT UNDEAD SURE CAN WORK A UMA TO THE FREAKIN' BONE.
CLOTHY! WHY ARE YOU HERE?!
NO CLUE. I HAD TO COME SINCE HE PUT IN A REQUEST.
A REQUEST?
YEAH.
HE SAID IF I WANNA BE CLOTHES THAT BEFIT HIM...
...THEN I NEED TO HELP YOU OUT.
THANK YOU! I FEEL LIKE I'M IN GOOD HANDS!
...
UM, SURE, WHAT-EVER...

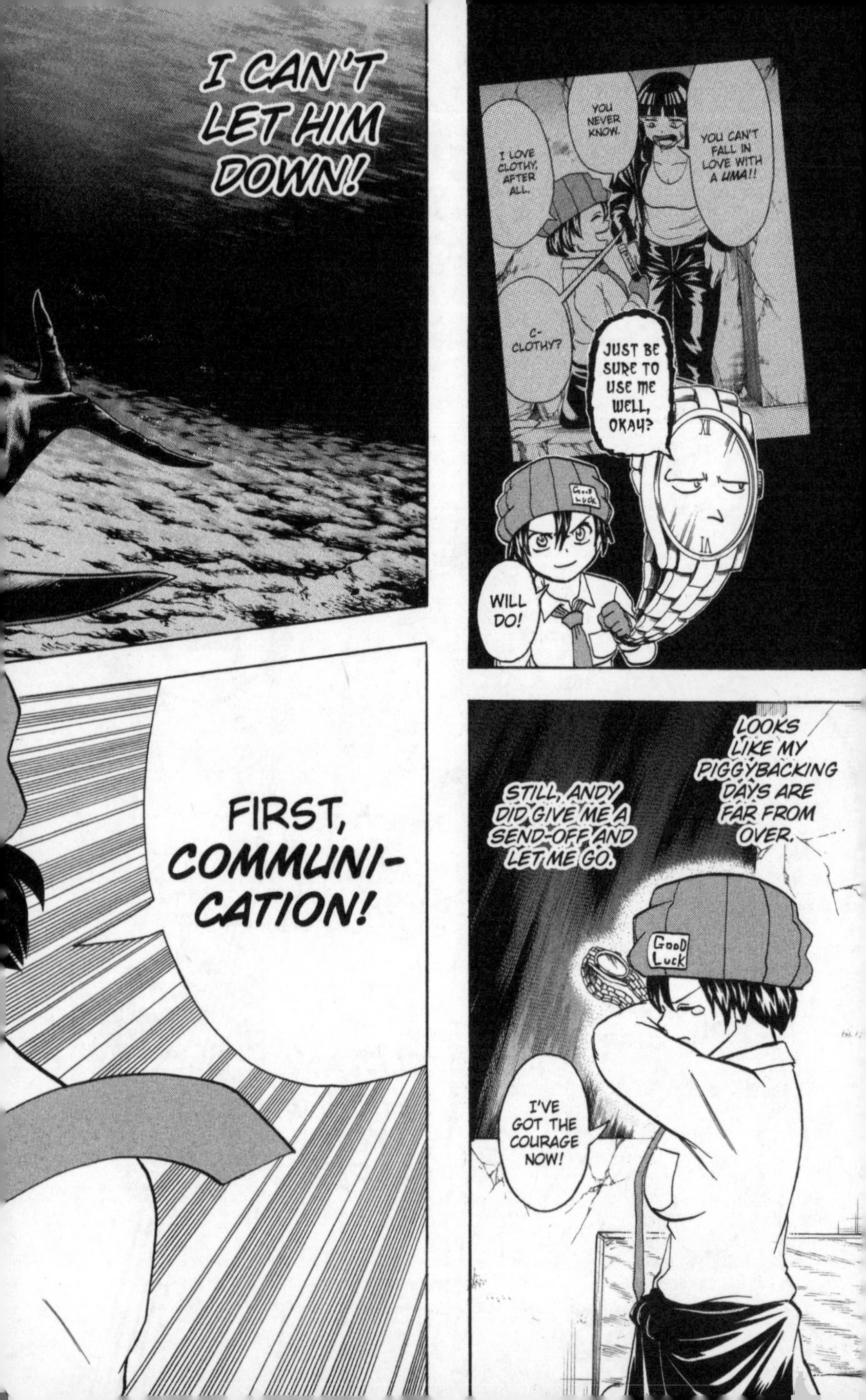
YOU CAN'T FALL IN LOVE WITH A UMA!!
YOU NEVER KNOW.
I LOVE CLOTHY, AFTER ALL.
C-CLOTHY?
JUST BE SURE TO USE ME WELL, OKAY?
WILL DO!
I CAN'T LET HIM DOWN!
LOOKS LIKE MY PIGGYBACKING DAYS ARE FAR FROM OVER.
STILL, ANDY DID GIVE ME A SEND-OFF AND LET ME GO.
I'VE GOT THE COURAGE NOW!
FIRST, COMMUNI-CATION!

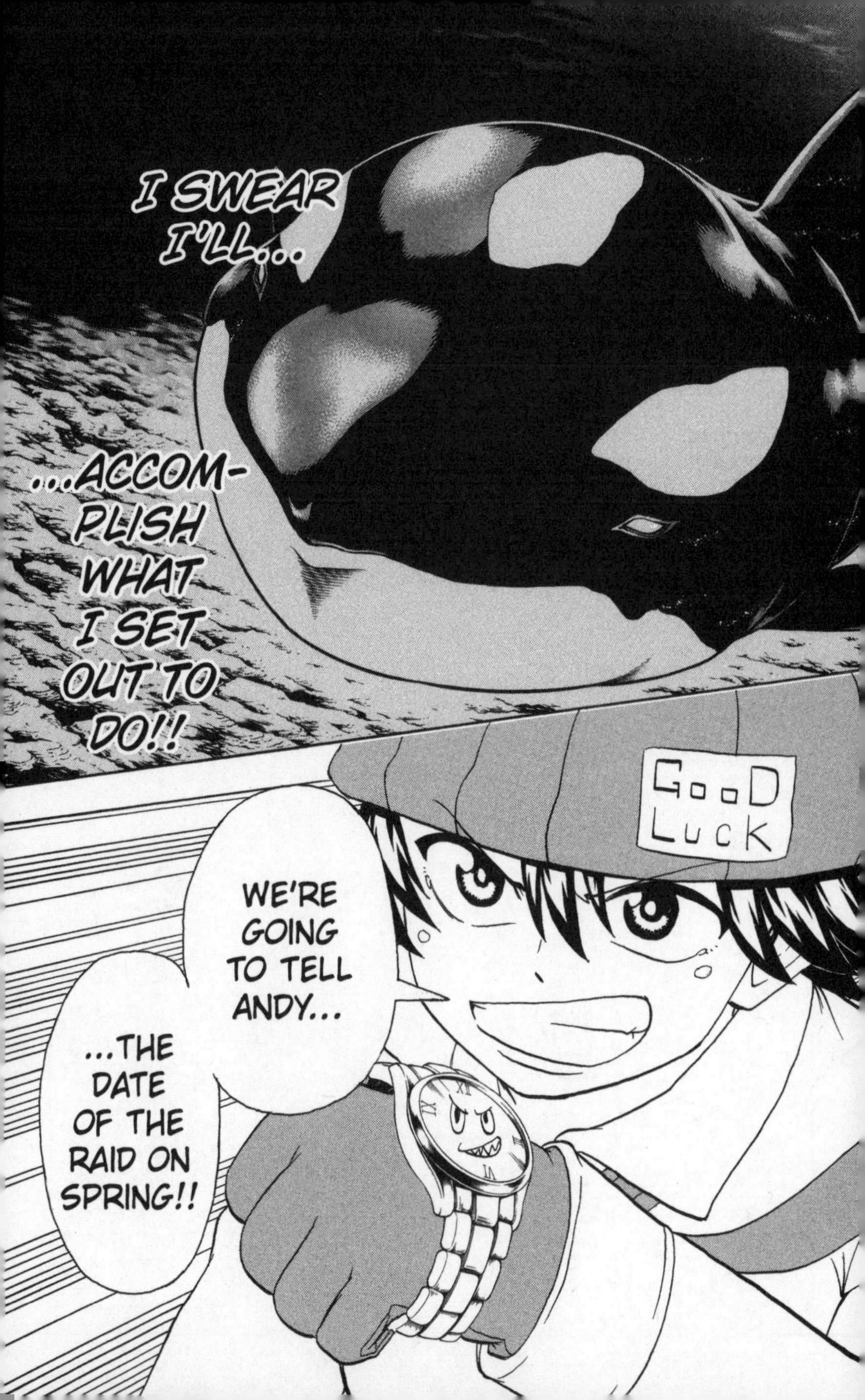
I SWEAR I'LL...
...ACCOM-PLISH WHAT I SET OUT TO DO!!
GOOD LUCK
WE'RE GOING TO TELL ANDY...
...THE DATE OF THE RAID ON SPRING!!

MATCHING OUTFITS

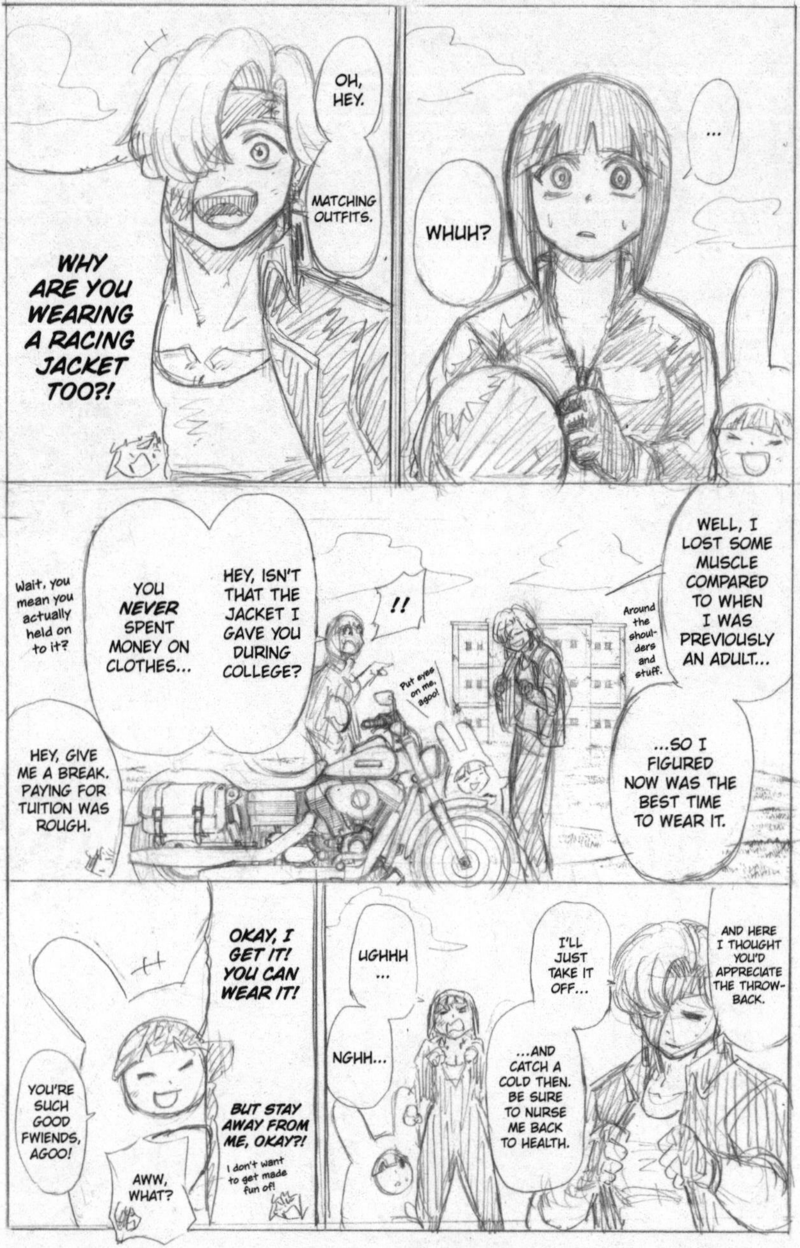
...
WHUH?
OH, HEY.
MATCHING OUTFITS.
WHY ARE YOU WEARING A RACING JACKET TOO?!
WELL, I LOST SOME MUSCLE COMPARED TO WHEN I WAS PREVIOUSLY AN ADULT...
Around the shoulders and stuff.
...SO I FIGURED NOW WAS THE BEST TIME TO WEAR IT.
!!
HEY, ISN'T THAT THE JACKET I GAVE YOU DURING COLLEGE?
Put eyes on me, agoo!
YOU NEVER SPENT MONEY ON CLOTHES...
Wait, you mean you actually held on to it?
HEY, GIVE ME A BREAK. PAYING FOR TUITION WAS ROUGH.
AND HERE I THOUGHT YOU'D APPRECIATE THE THROW-BACK.
I'LL JUST TAKE IT OFF...
...AND CATCH A COLD THEN. BE SURE TO NURSE ME BACK TO HEALTH.
UGHHH...
NGHH...
OKAY, I GET IT! YOU CAN WEAR IT!
BUT STAY AWAY FROM ME, OKAY?!
I don't want to get made fun of!
YOU'RE SUCH GOOD FWIENDS, AGOO!
AWW, WHAT?

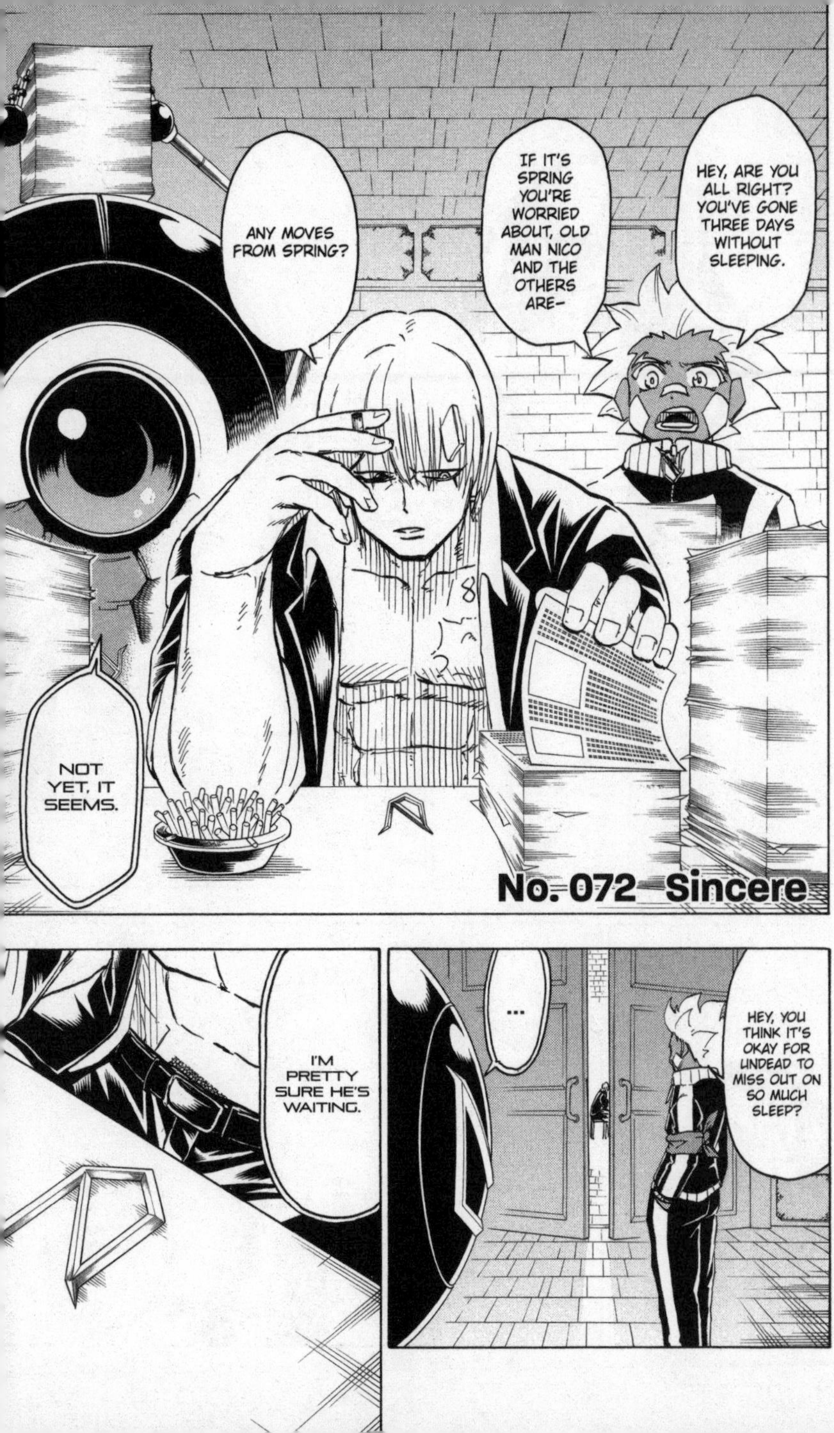
HEY, ARE YOU ALL RIGHT? YOU'VE GONE THREE DAYS WITHOUT SLEEPING.
IF IT'S SPRING YOU'RE WORRIED ABOUT, OLD MAN NICO AND THE OTHERS ARE—
ANY MOVES FROM SPRING?
NOT YET, IT SEEMS.
No. 072 Sincere
HEY, YOU THINK IT'S OKAY FOR UNDEAD TO MISS OUT ON SO MUCH SLEEP?
...
I'M PRETTY SURE HE'S WAITING.

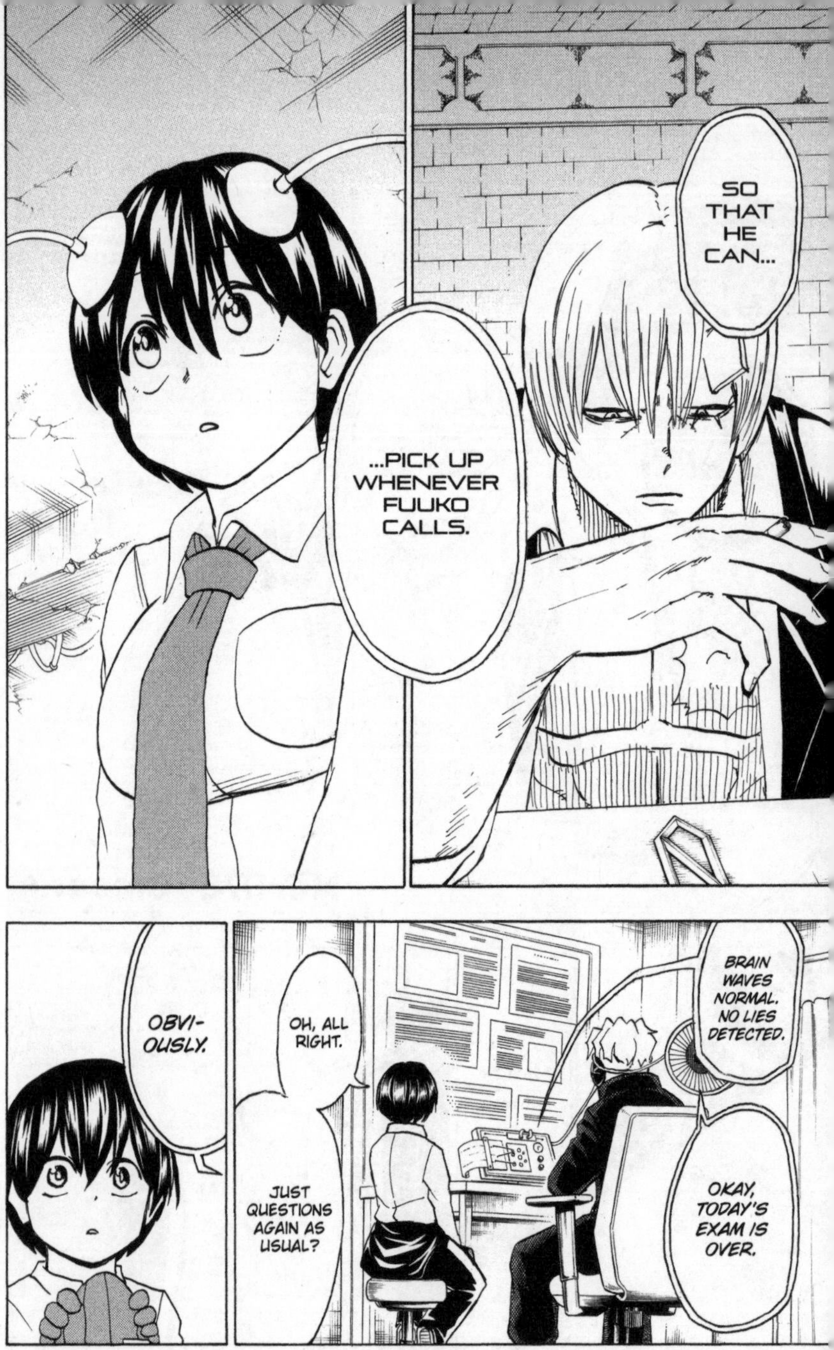
SO THAT HE CAN...
...PICK UP WHENEVER FUUKO CALLS.
BRAIN WAVES NORMAL. NO LIES DETECTED.
OKAY, TODAY'S EXAM IS OVER.
OH, ALL RIGHT.
JUST QUESTIONS AGAIN AS USUAL?
OBVI-OUSLY.

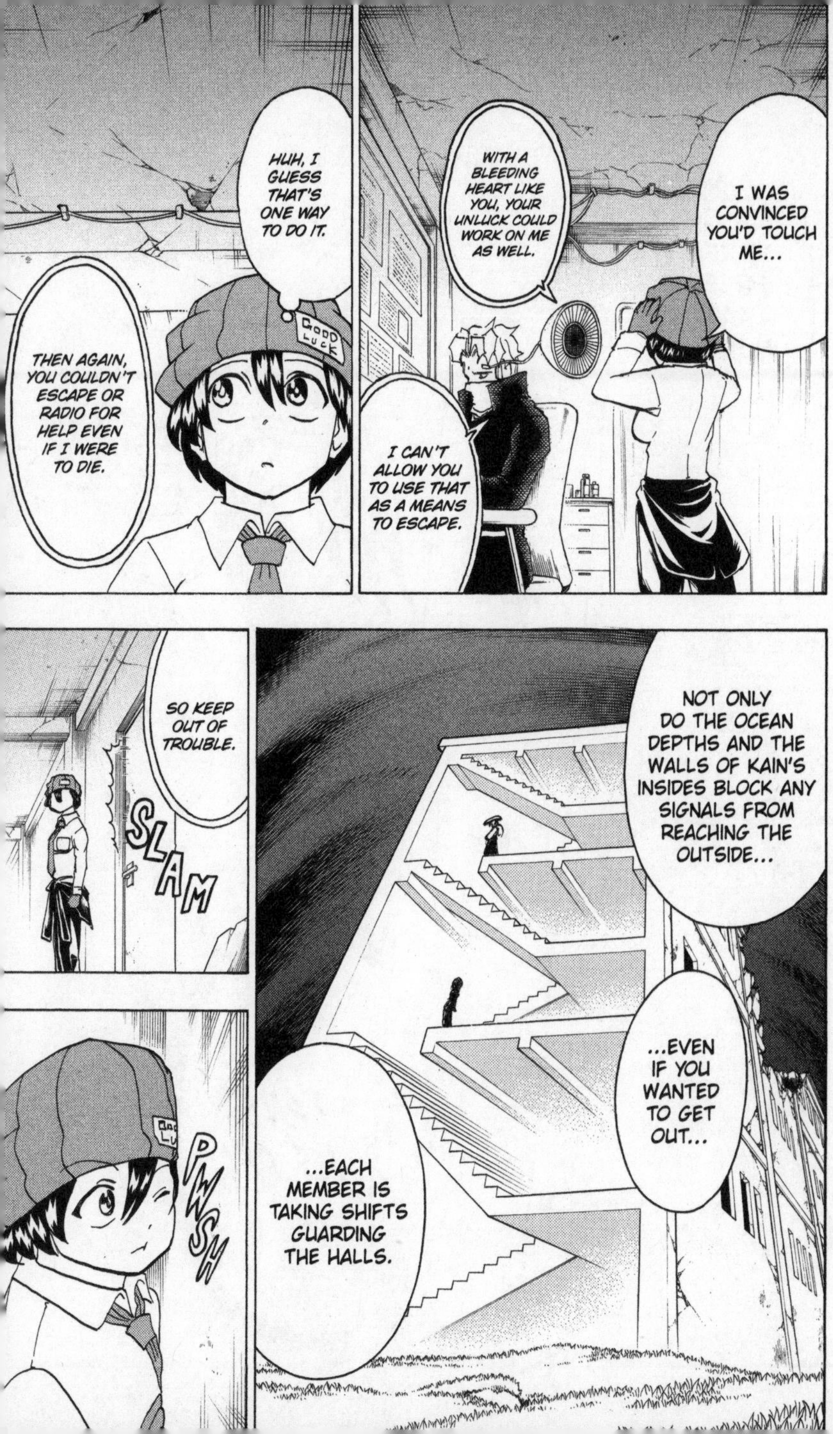
I WAS CONVINCED YOU'D TOUCH ME...
WITH A BLEEDING HEART LIKE YOU, YOUR UNLUCK COULD WORK ON ME AS WELL.
I CAN'T ALLOW YOU TO USE THAT AS A MEANS TO ESCAPE.
HUH, I GUESS THAT'S ONE WAY TO DO IT.
GOOD LUCK
THEN AGAIN, YOU COULDN'T ESCAPE OR RADIO FOR HELP EVEN IF I WERE TO DIE.
NOT ONLY DO THE OCEAN DEPTHS AND THE WALLS OF KAIN'S INSIDES BLOCK ANY SIGNALS FROM REACHING THE OUTSIDE...
...EVEN IF YOU WANTED TO GET OUT...
...EACH MEMBER IS TAKING SHIFTS GUARDING THE HALLS.
SO KEEP OUT OF TROUBLE.
SLAM
PWSH

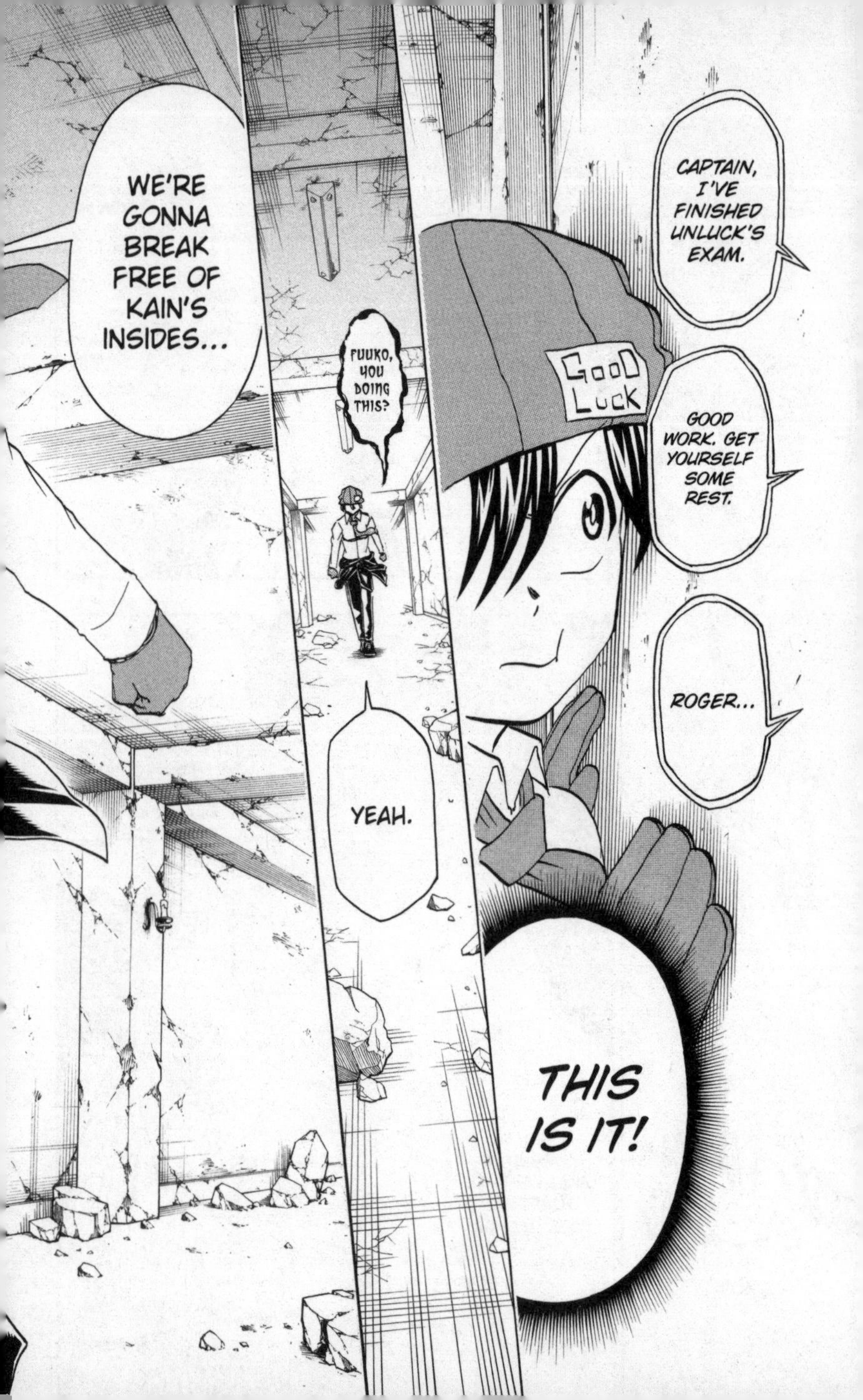
CAPTAIN, I'VE FINISHED UNLUCK'S EXAM.
GOOD LUCK
GOOD WORK. GET YOURSELF SOME REST.
ROGER...
THIS IS IT!
FUUKO, YOU DOING THIS?
YEAH.
WE'RE GONNA BREAK FREE OF KAIN'S INSIDES...

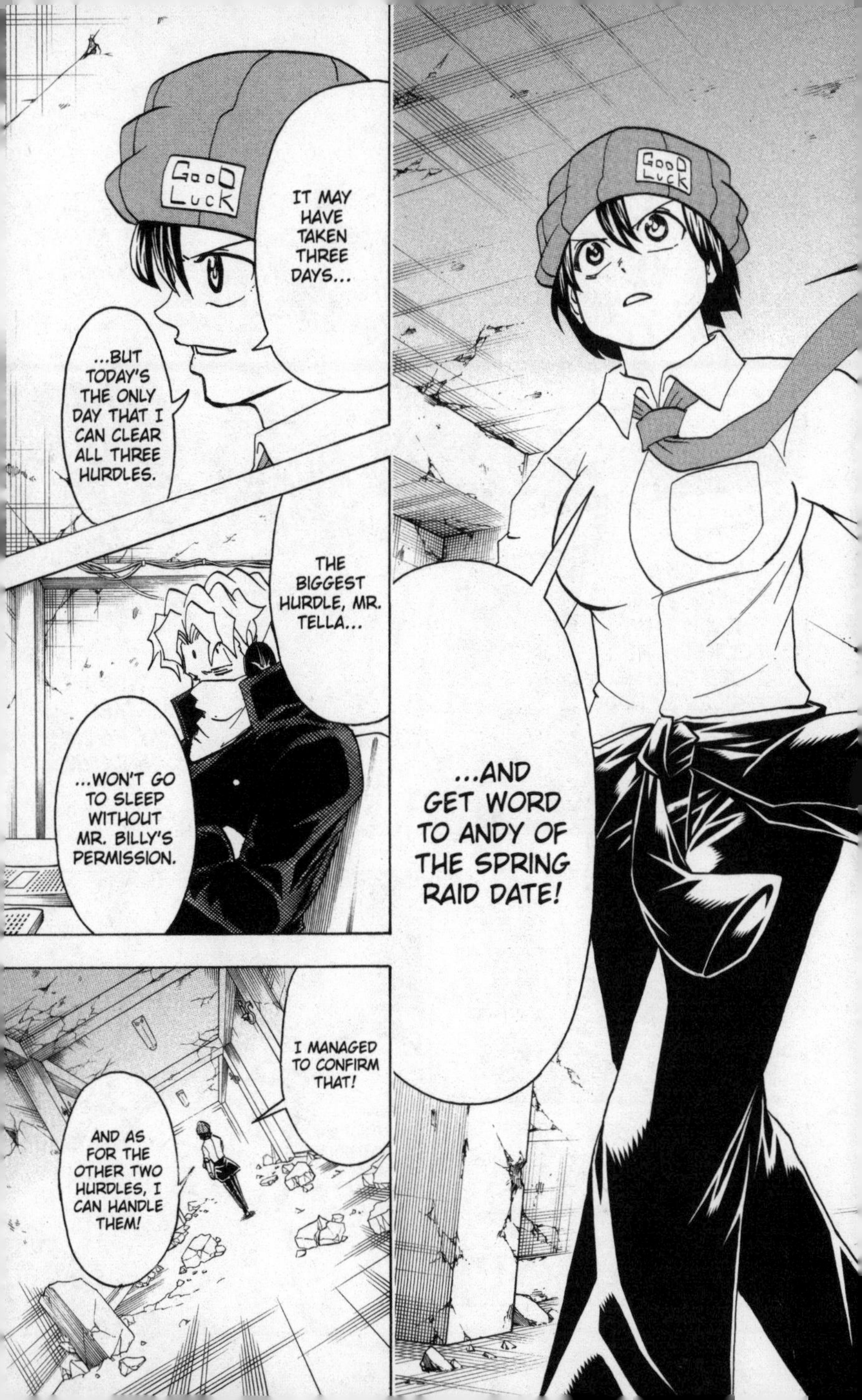
IT MAY HAVE TAKEN THREE DAYS...
...BUT TODAY'S THE ONLY DAY THAT I CAN CLEAR ALL THREE HURDLES.
THE BIGGEST HURDLE, MR. TELLA...
...WON'T GO TO SLEEP WITHOUT MR. BILLY'S PERMISSION.
I MANAGED TO CONFIRM THAT!
AND AS FOR THE OTHER TWO HURDLES, I CAN HANDLE THEM!
...AND GET WORD TO ANDY OF THE SPRING RAID DATE!
GOOD LUCK
GOOD LUCK

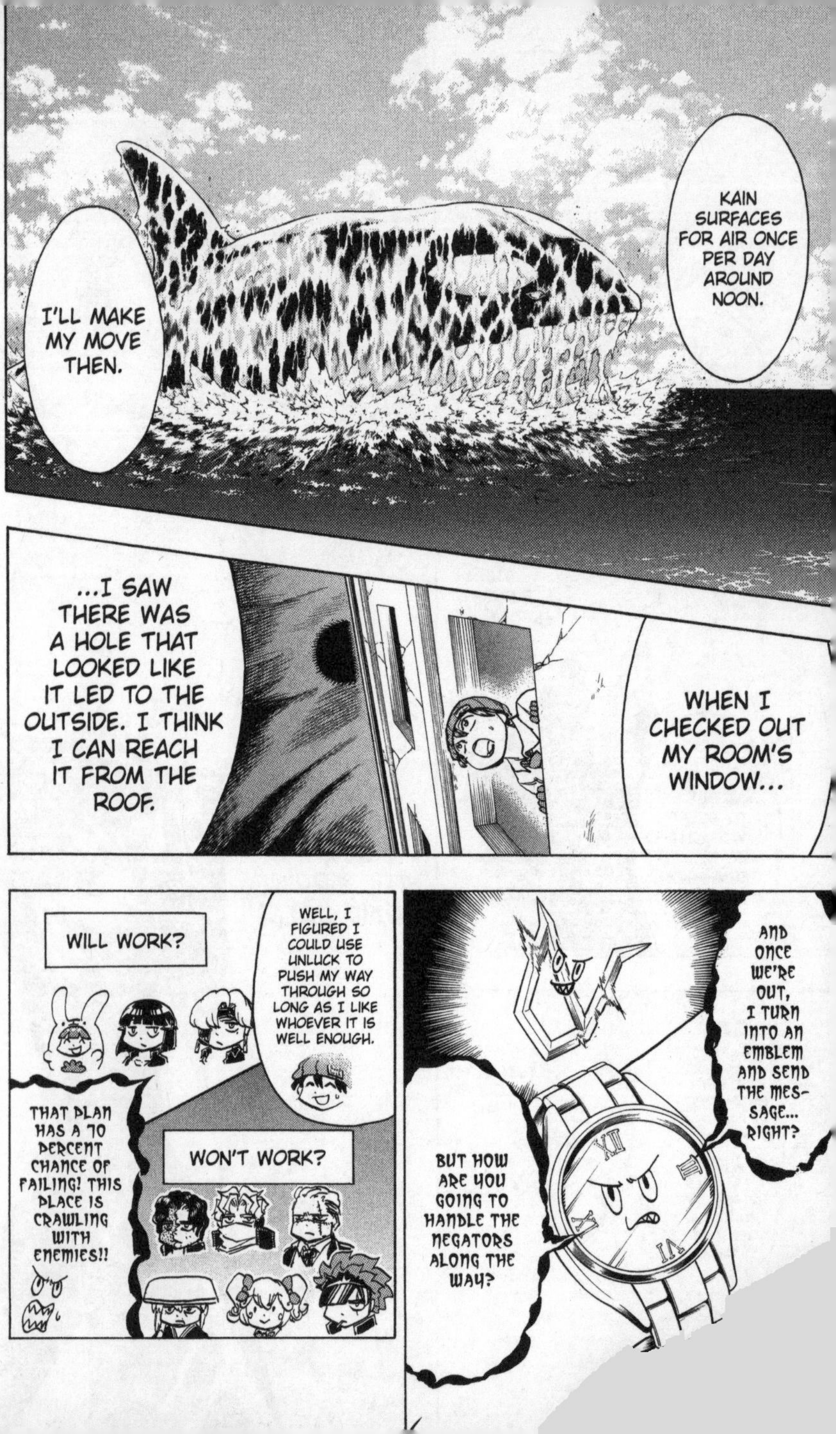
KAIN SURFACES FOR AIR ONCE PER DAY AROUND NOON.
I'LL MAKE MY MOVE THEN.
WHEN I CHECKED OUT MY ROOM'S WINDOW...
...I SAW THERE WAS A HOLE THAT LOOKED LIKE IT LED TO THE OUTSIDE. I THINK I CAN REACH IT FROM THE ROOF.
AND ONCE WE'RE OUT, I TURN INTO AN EMBLEM AND SEND THE MES-SAGE... RIGHT?
BUT HOW ARE YOU GOING TO HANDLE THE NEGATORS ALONG THE WAY?
WELL, I FIGURED I COULD USE UNLUCK TO PUSH MY WAY THROUGH SO LONG AS I LIKE WHOEVER IT IS WELL ENOUGH.
WILL WORK?
WON'T WORK?
THAT PLAN HAS A 70 PERCENT CHANCE OF FAILING! THIS PLACE IS CRAWLING WITH ENEMIES!!

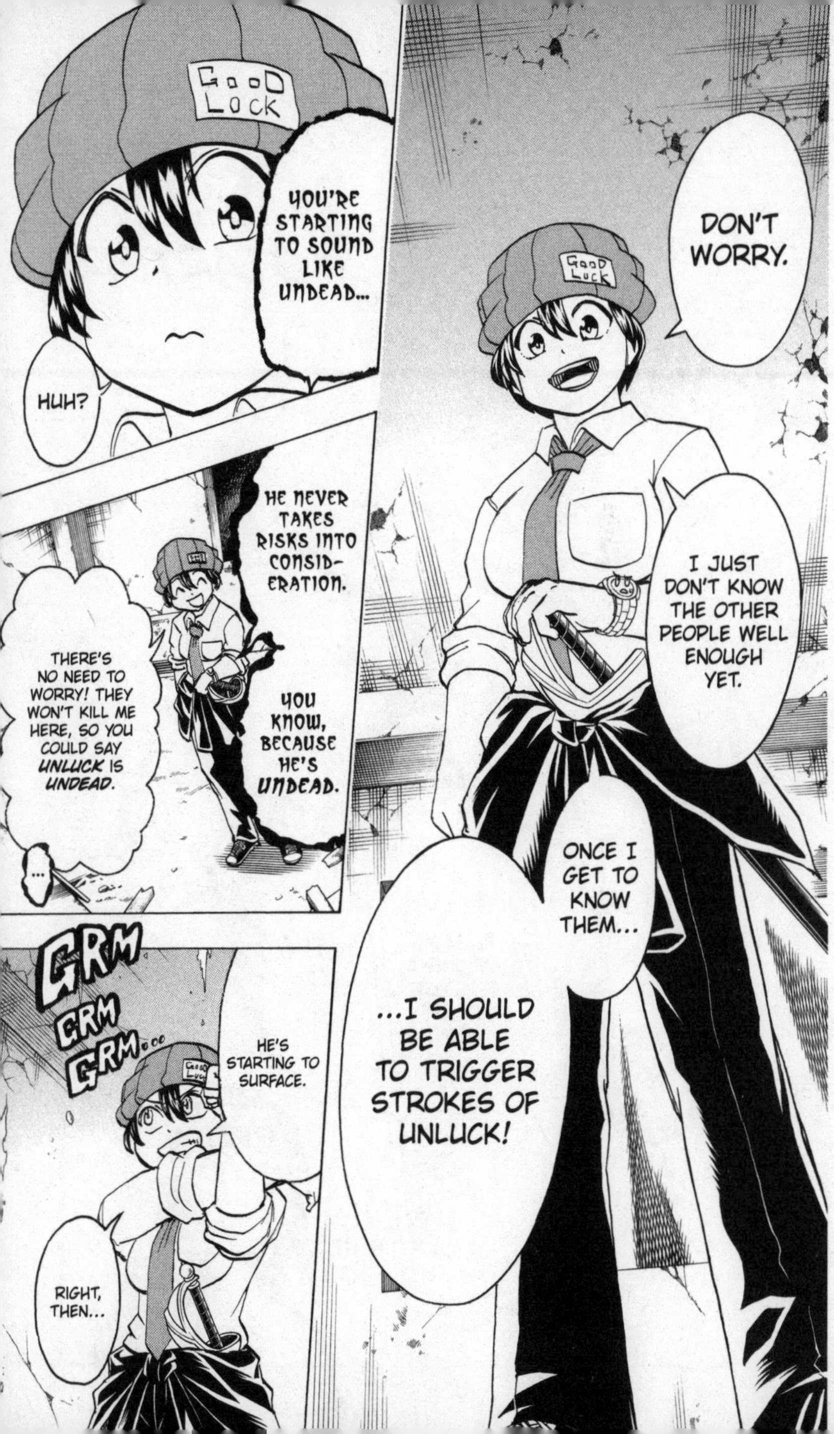
DON'T WORRY.
I JUST DON'T KNOW THE OTHER PEOPLE WELL ENOUGH YET.
ONCE I GET TO KNOW THEM...
...I SHOULD BE ABLE TO TRIGGER STROKES OF UNLUCK!
YOU'RE STARTING TO SOUND LIKE UNDEAD...
HUH?
HE NEVER TAKES RISKS INTO CONSIDERATION.
YOU KNOW, BECAUSE HE'S UNDEAD.
THERE'S NO NEED TO WORRY! THEY WON'T KILL ME HERE, SO YOU COULD SAY UNLUCK IS UNDEAD.
...
GRM GRM GRM...
HE'S STARTING TO SURFACE.
RIGHT, THEN...

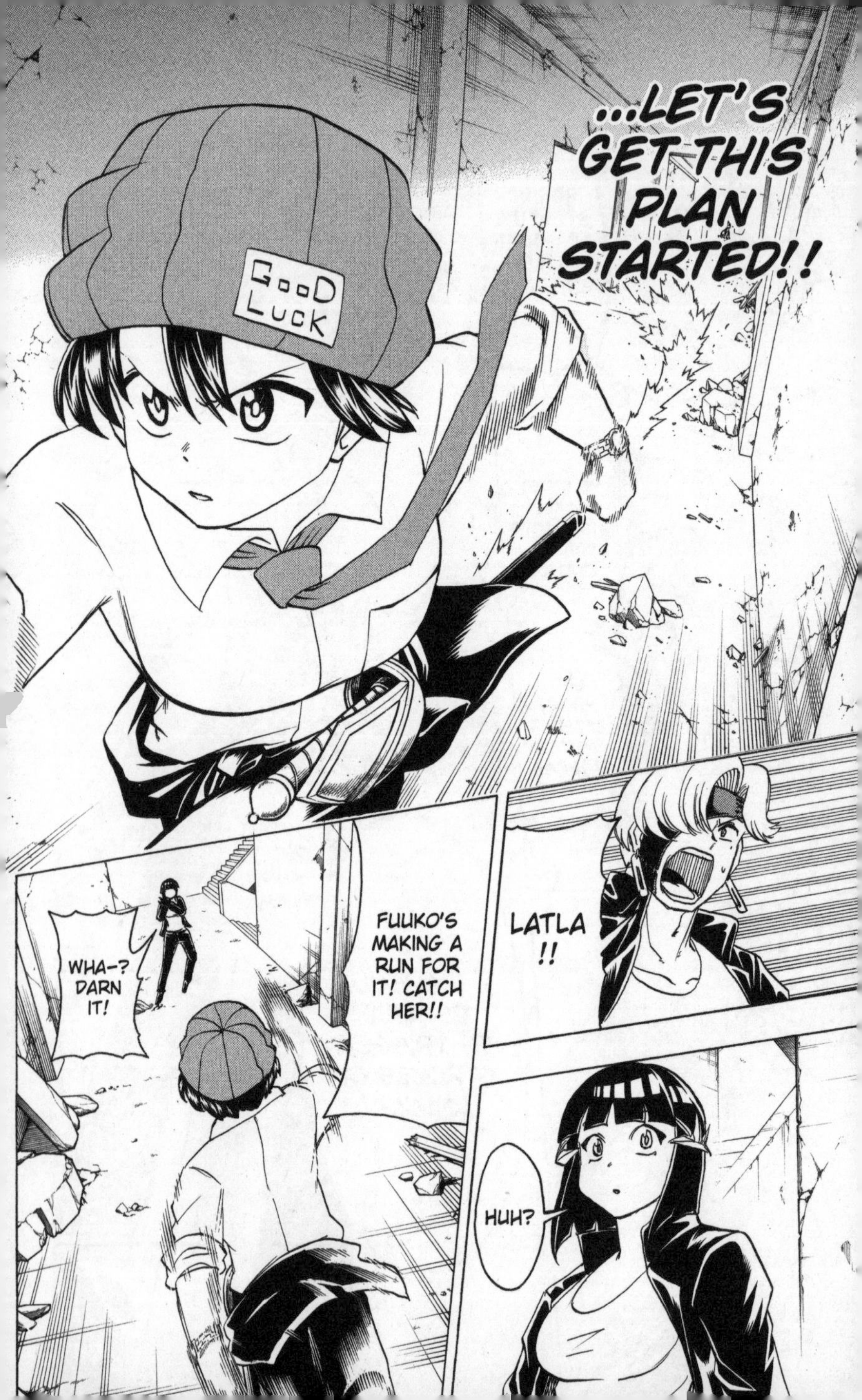
...LET'S GET THIS PLAN STARTED!!
GOOD LUCK
LATLA !!
HUH?
FUUKO'S MAKING A RUN FOR IT! CATCH HER!!
WHA-? DARN IT!

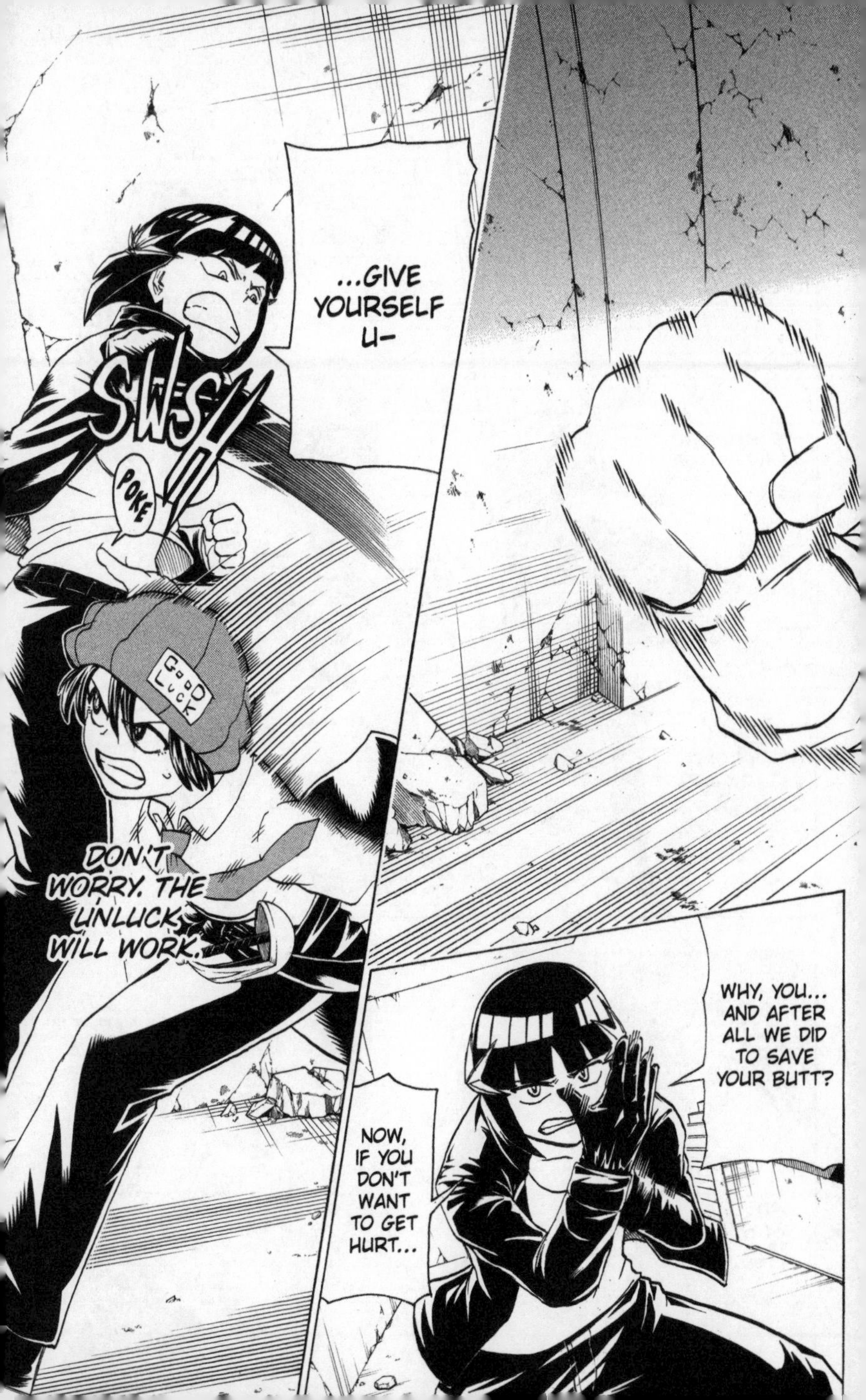
WHY, YOU... AND AFTER ALL WE DID TO SAVE YOUR BUTT?
NOW, IF YOU DON'T WANT TO GET HURT...
...GIVE YOURSELF U-
SWSH
POKE
DON'T WORRY. THE UNLUCK WILL WORK.
GOOD LUCK

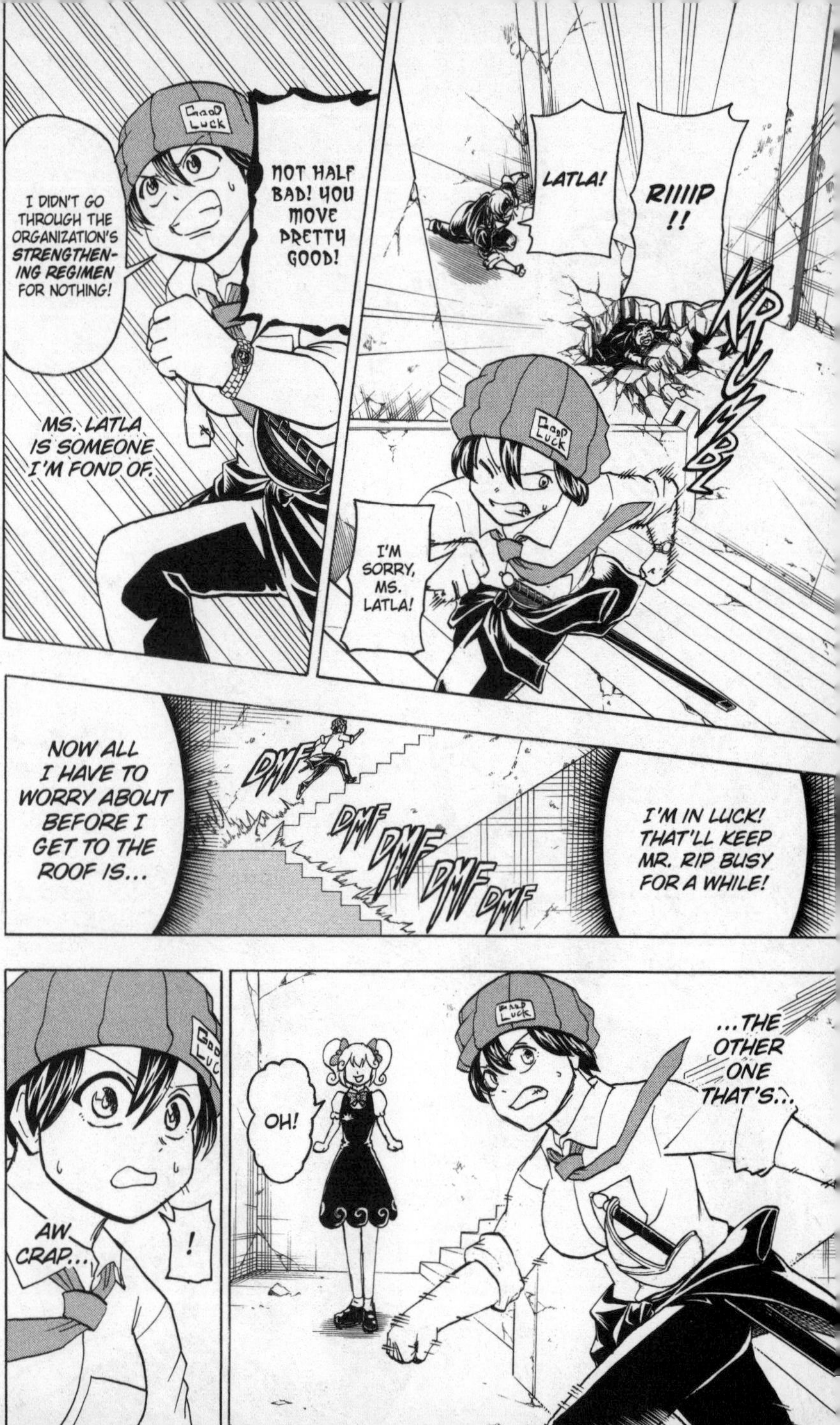
LATLA!
RIIIIP!!
KRUMMBL
I'M SORRY, MS. LATLA!
NOT HALF BAD! YOU MOVE PRETTY GOOD!
I DIDN'T GO THROUGH THE ORGANIZATION'S STRENGTHENING REGIMEN FOR NOTHING!
MS. LATLA IS SOMEONE I'M FOND OF.
I'M IN LUCK! THAT'LL KEEP MR. RIP BUSY FOR A WHILE!
DMF DMF DMF DMF DMF DMF
NOW ALL I HAVE TO WORRY ABOUT BEFORE I GET TO THE ROOF IS...
...THE OTHER ONE THAT'S...
OH!
!
AW CRAP...

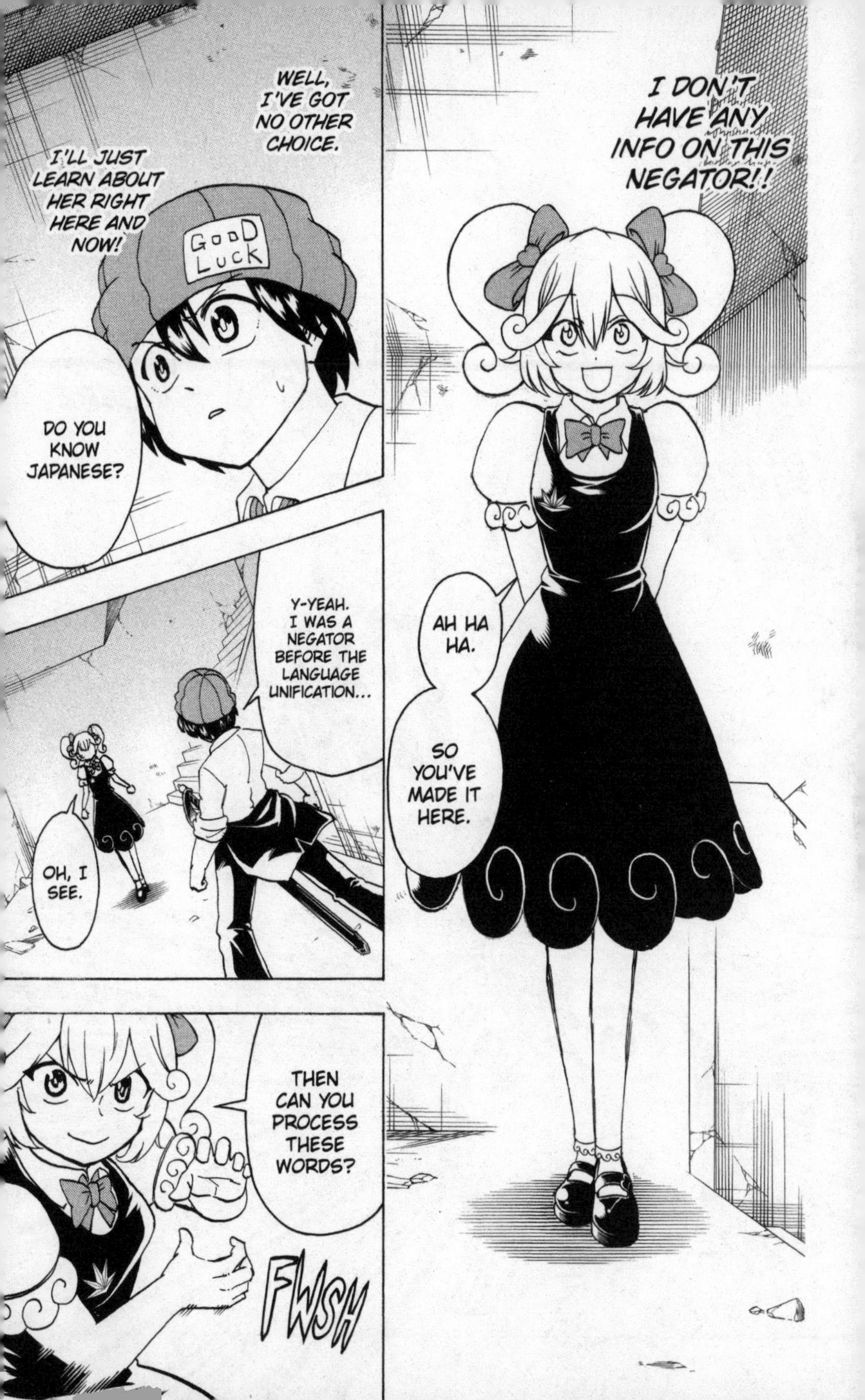
I DON'T HAVE ANY INFO ON THIS NEGATOR!!
AH HA HA.
SO YOU'VE MADE IT HERE.
WELL, I'VE GOT NO OTHER CHOICE.
I'LL JUST LEARN ABOUT HER RIGHT HERE AND NOW!
GOOD LUCK
DO YOU KNOW JAPANESE?
Y-YEAH. I WAS A NEGATOR BEFORE THE LANGUAGE UNIFICATION...
OH, I SEE.
THEN CAN YOU PROCESS THESE WORDS?
FWSH

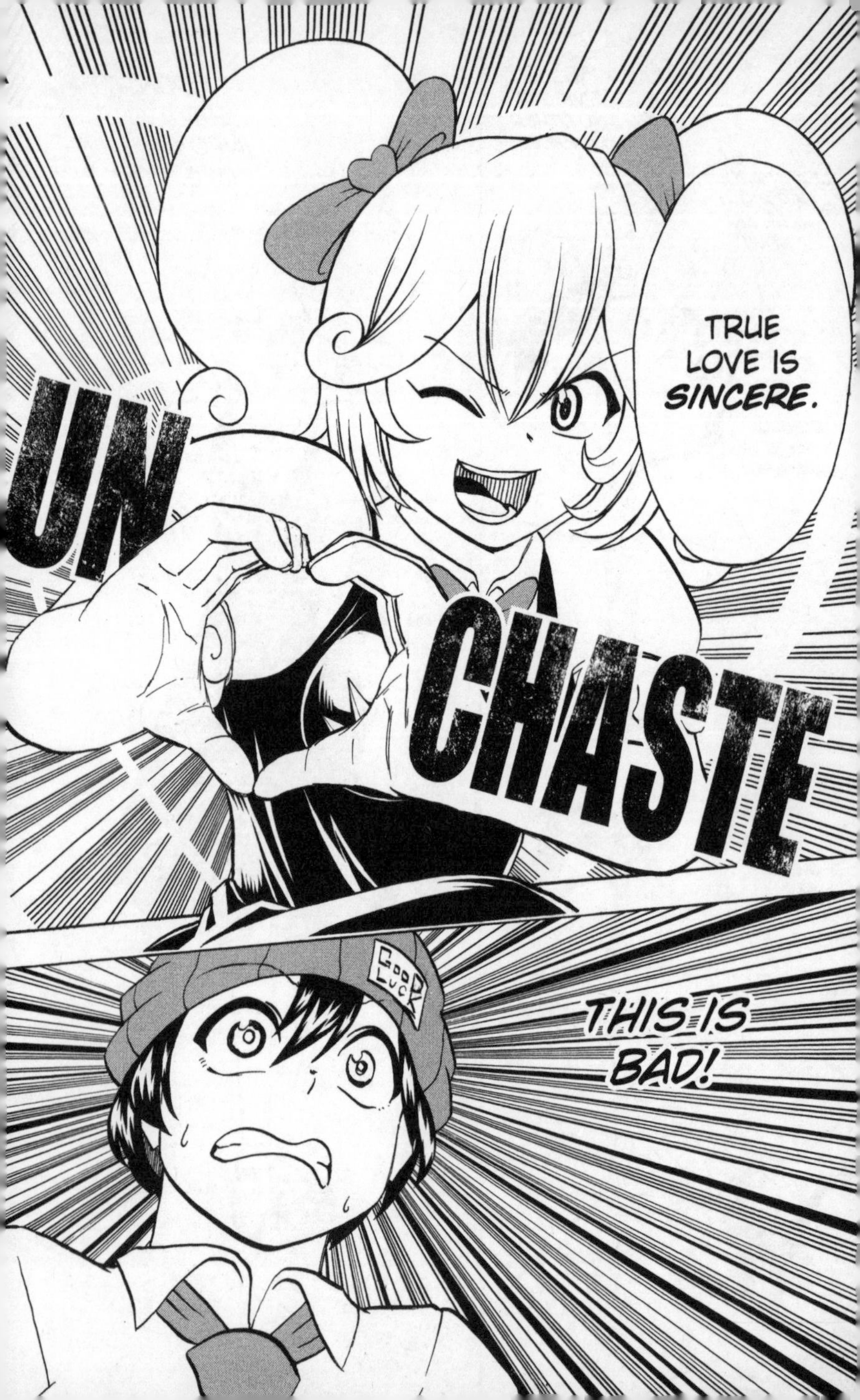
TRUE LOVE IS SINCERE.
UN CHASTE
GOOD LUCK
THIS IS BAD!

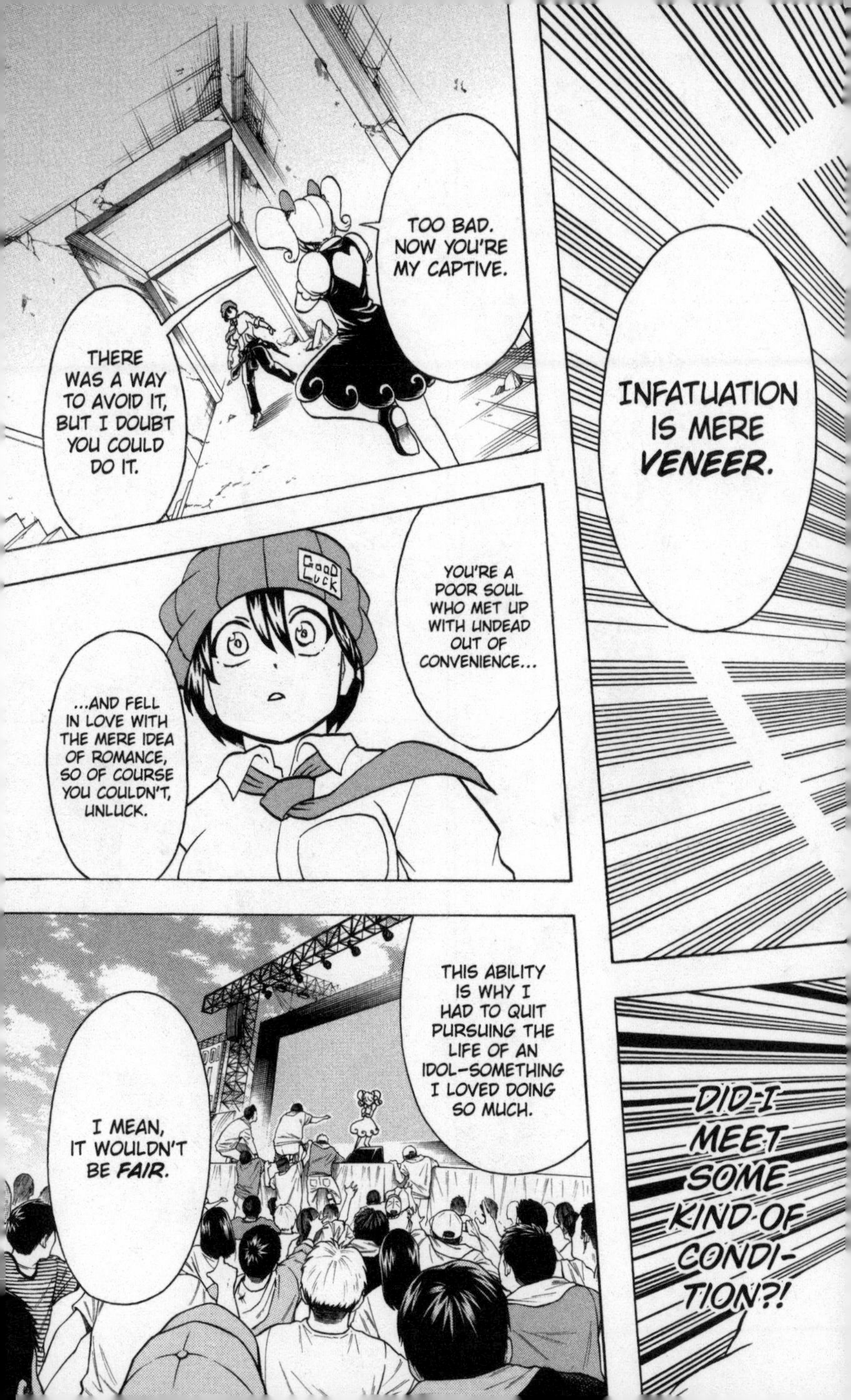
INFATUATION IS MERE VENEER.
DID I MEET SOME KIND OF CONDI-TION?!
TOO BAD. NOW YOU'RE MY CAPTIVE.
THERE WAS A WAY TO AVOID IT, BUT I DOUBT YOU COULD DO IT.
YOU'RE A POOR SOUL WHO MET UP WITH UNDEAD OUT OF CONVENIENCE...
...AND FELL IN LOVE WITH THE MERE IDEA OF ROMANCE, SO OF COURSE YOU COULDN'T, UNLUCK.
GOOD LUCK
THIS ABILITY IS WHY I HAD TO QUIT PURSUING THE LIFE OF AN IDOL—SOMETHING I LOVED DOING SO MUCH.
I MEAN, IT WOULDN'T BE FAIR.

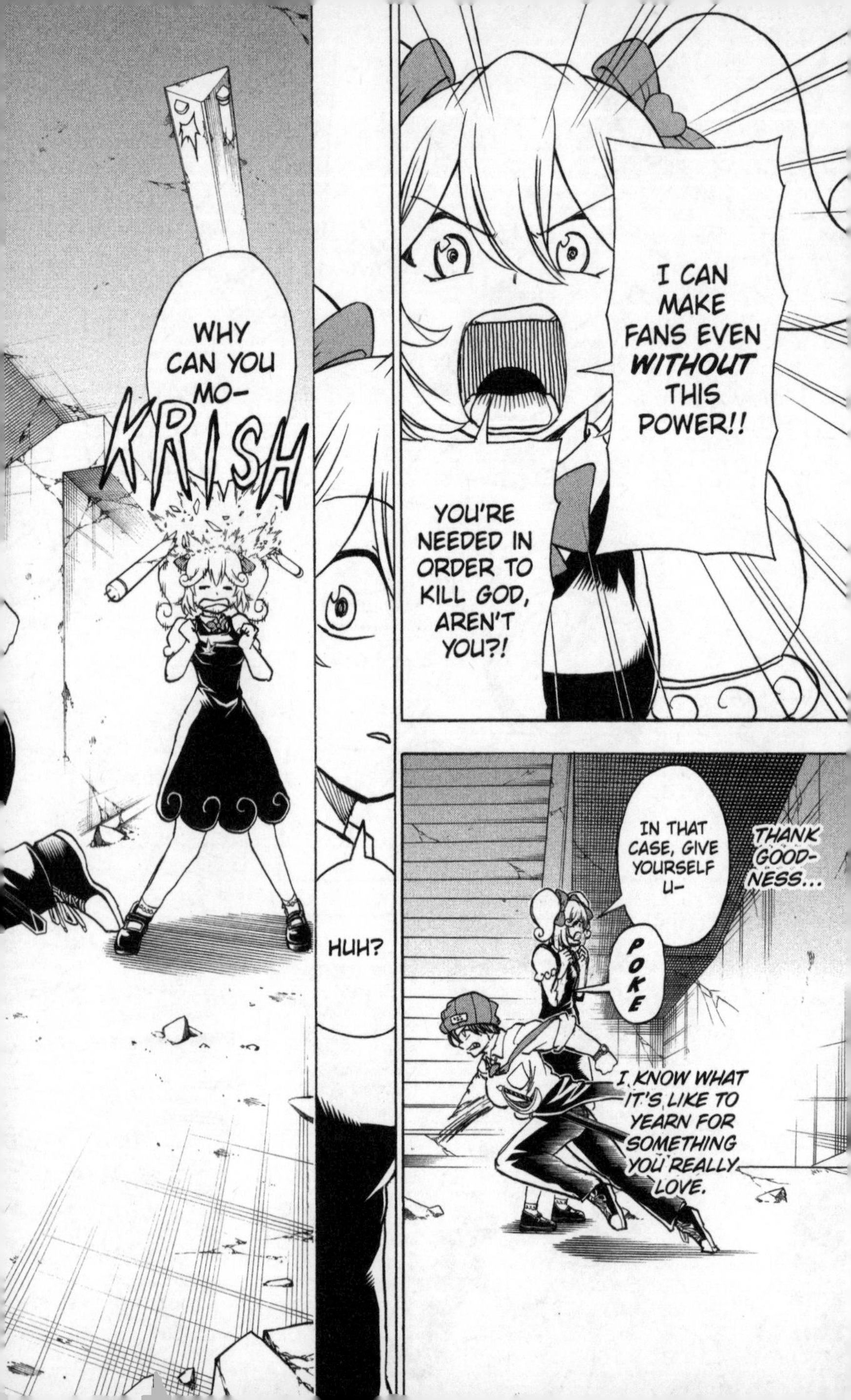
I CAN MAKE FANS EVEN WITHOUT THIS POWER!!
YOU'RE NEEDED IN ORDER TO KILL GOD, AREN'T YOU?!
THANK GOODNESS...
IN THAT CASE, GIVE YOURSELF U-
POKE
I KNOW WHAT IT'S LIKE TO YEARN FOR SOMETHING YOU REALLY LOVE.
HUH?
WHY CAN YOU MO-
KRISH

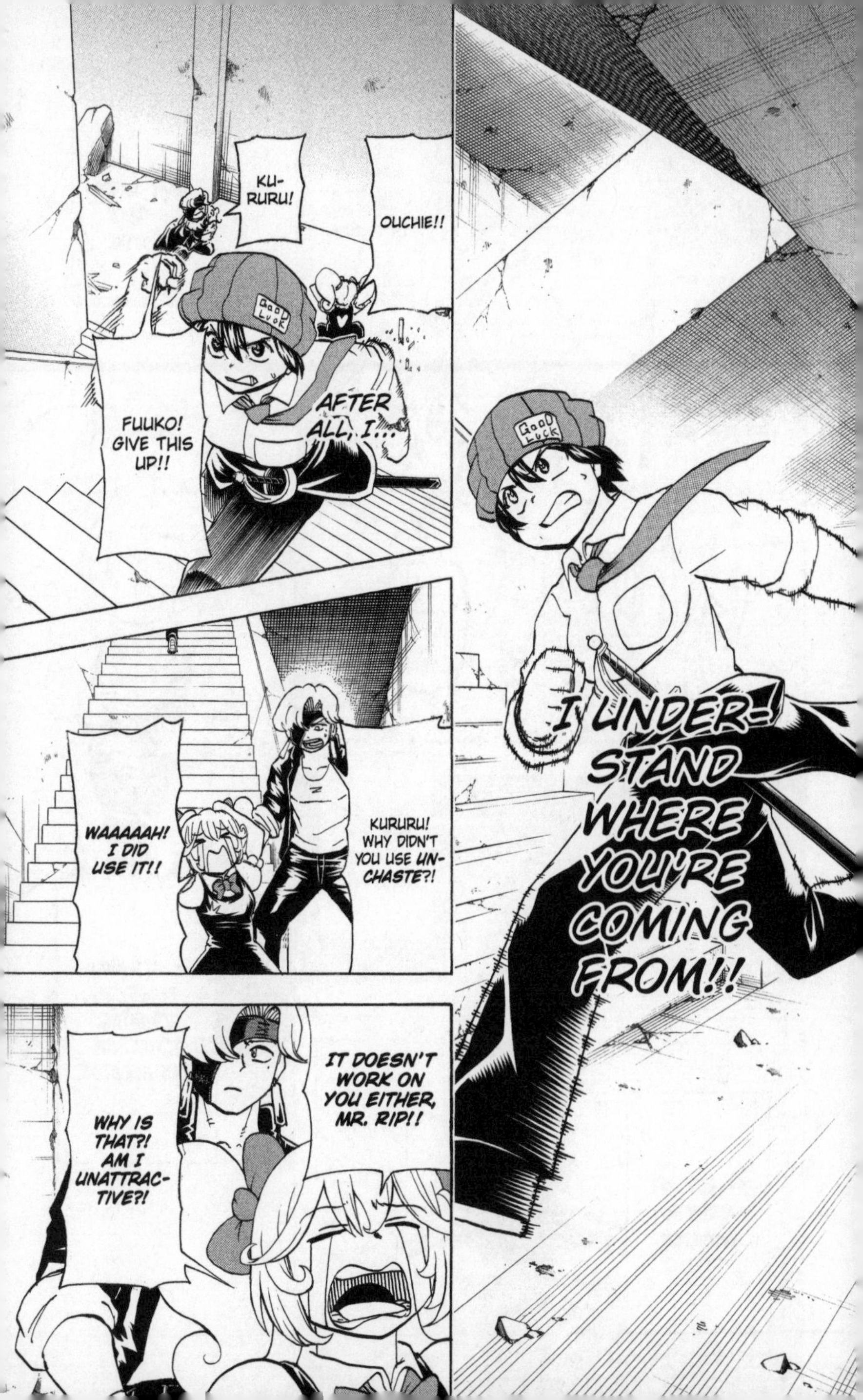
I UNDER-STAND WHERE YOU'RE COMING FROM!!
OUCHIE!!
KU-RURU!
AFTER ALL, I...
FUUKO! GIVE THIS UP!!
KURURU! WHY DIDN'T YOU USE UN-CHASTE?!
WAAAAAH! I DID USE IT!!
IT DOESN'T WORK ON YOU EITHER, MR. RIP!!
WHY IS THAT?! AM I UNATTRAC-TIVE?!

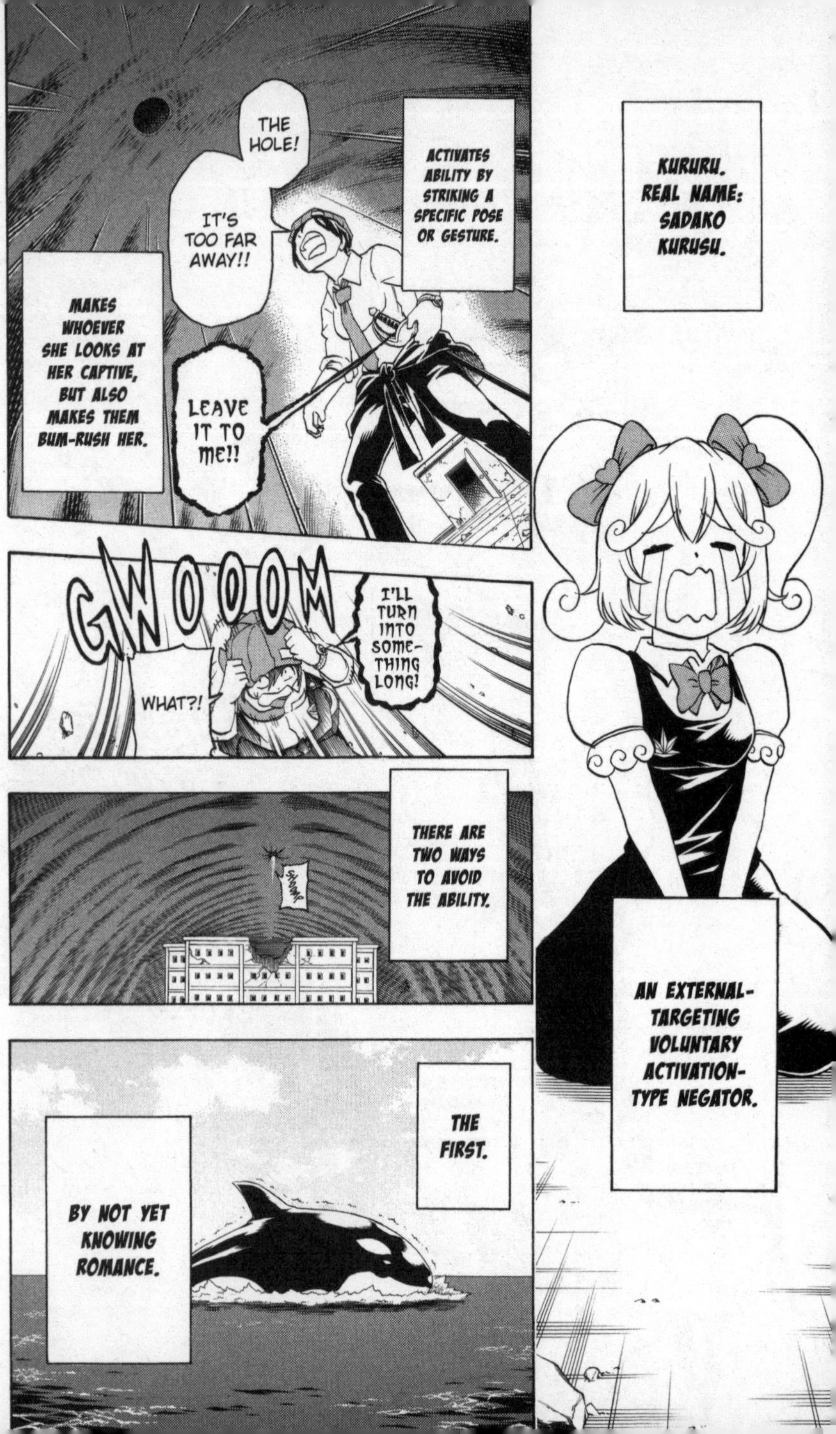
KURURU. REAL NAME: SADAKO KURUSU.
AN EXTERNAL-TARGETING VOLUNTARY ACTIVATION-TYPE NEGATOR.
ACTIVATES ABILITY BY STRIKING A SPECIFIC POSE OR GESTURE.
THE HOLE!
IT'S TOO FAR AWAY!!
LEAVE IT TO ME!!
MAKES WHOEVER SHE LOOKS AT HER CAPTIVE, BUT ALSO MAKES THEM BUM-RUSH HER.
I'LL TURN INTO SOMETHING LONG!
WHAT?!
GWOOOM
THERE ARE TWO WAYS TO AVOID THE ABILITY.
THE FIRST.
BY NOT YET KNOWING ROMANCE.

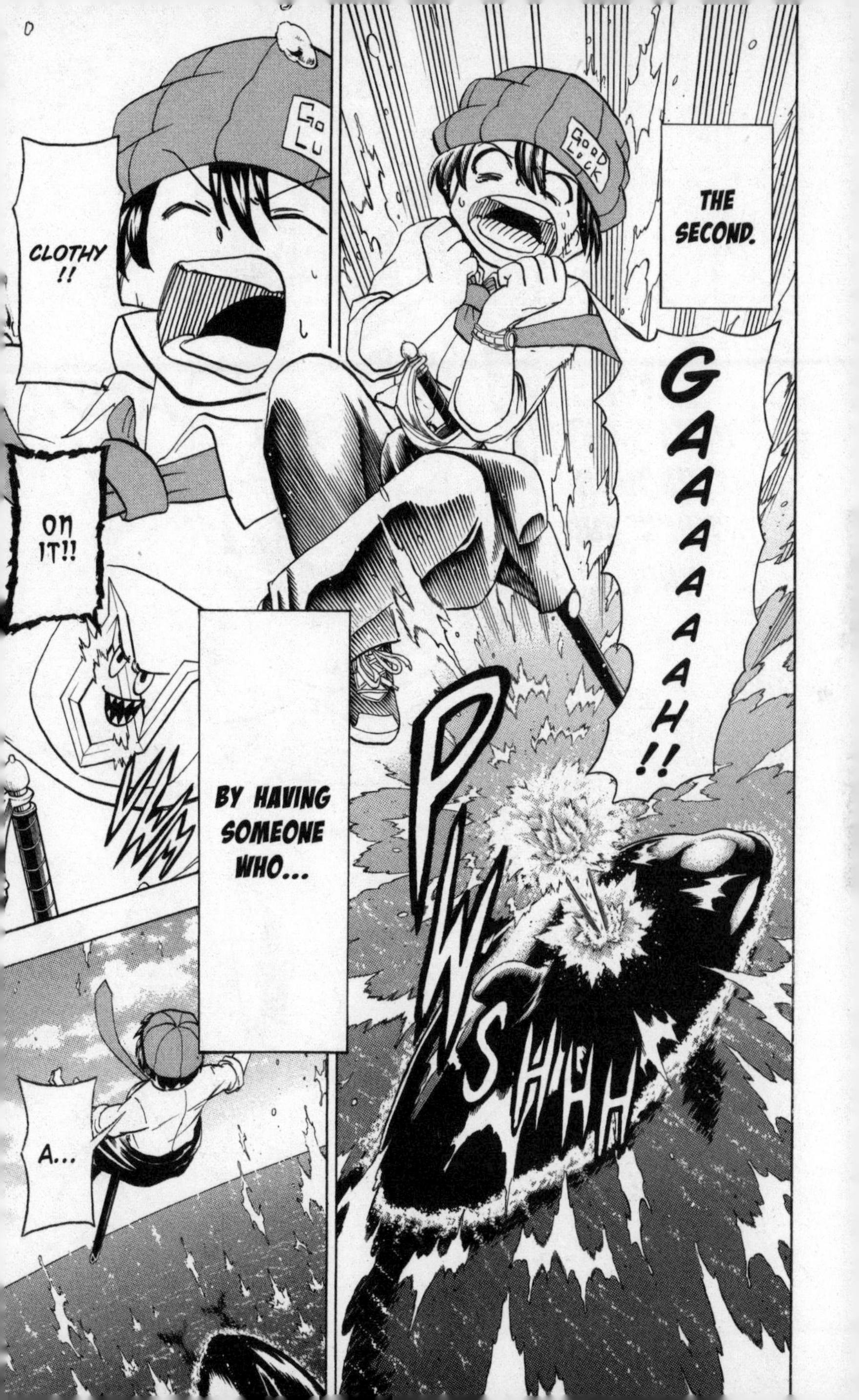
THE SECOND.
GAAAAAAH!!
PWSHHH
CLOTHY!!
ON IT!!
BY HAVING SOMEONE WHO...
A...

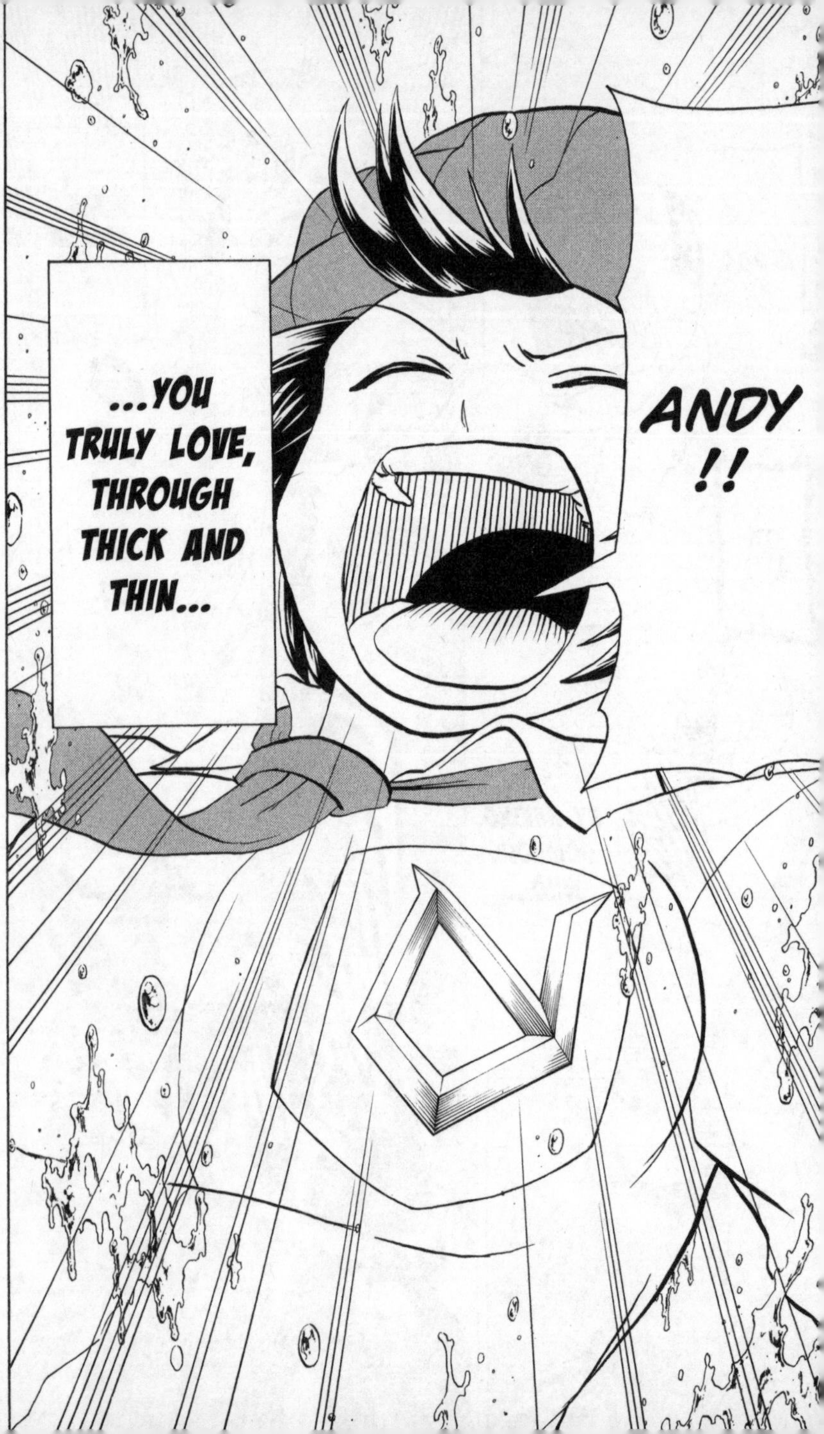
ANDY !!
...YOU TRULY LOVE, THROUGH THICK AND THIN...

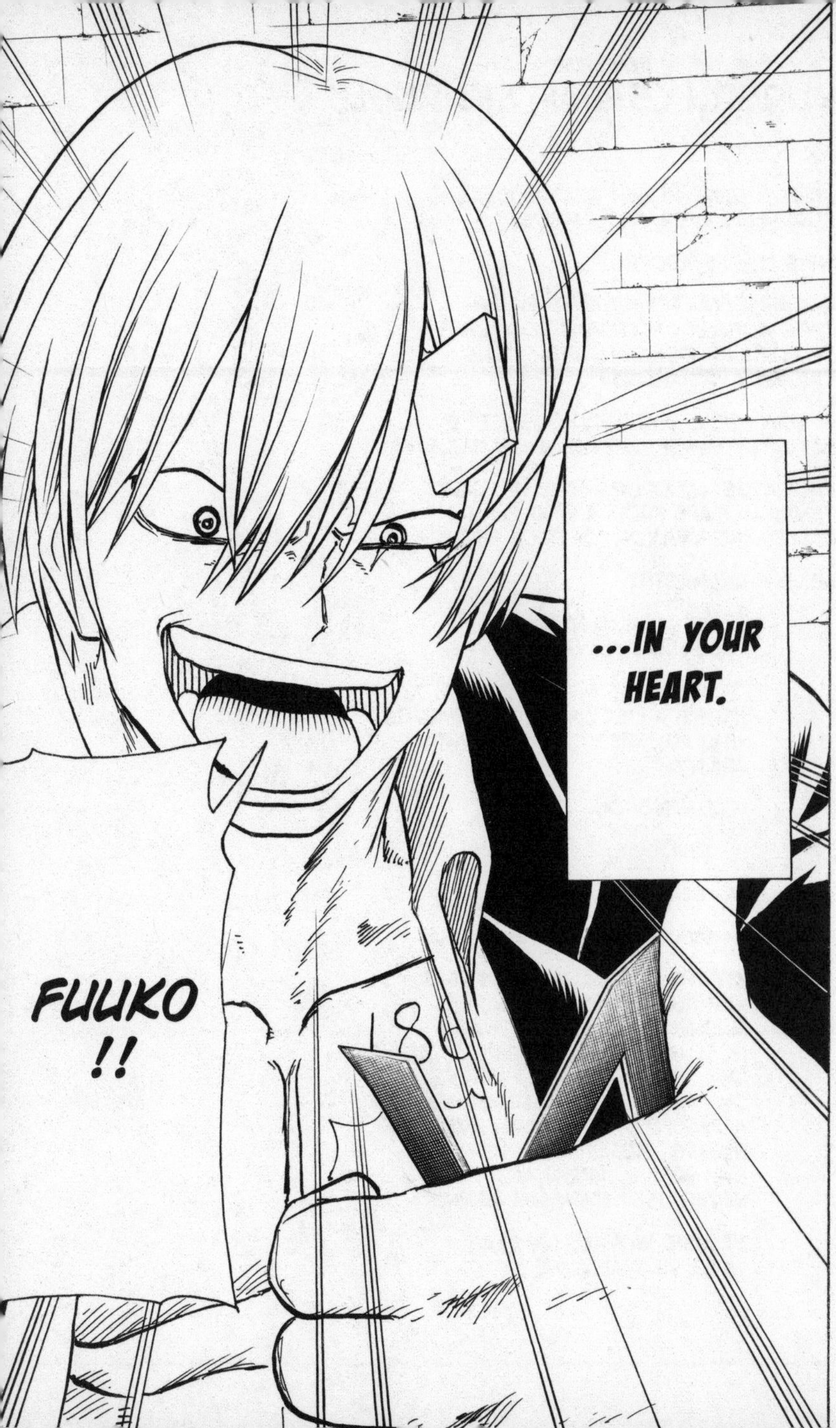
...IN YOUR HEART.
FUUKO !!

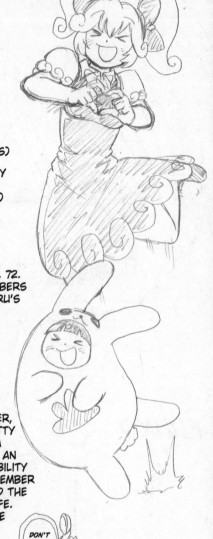

REAL NAME

KURURU (SADAKO KURUSU)

AGE: SECRET

HEIGHT: SAME HEIGHT AS THE IDEAL KURURU IN EVERYONE'S MINDS

WEIGHT: SEE ABOVE

HOBBIES: COLLECTING CUTE THINGS (IT'S ACTUALLY WATCHING FOOTAGE OF POPULAR IDOLS AND PRACTICING SINGING AND DANCING)

SPECIAL SKILLS: KURURU POSE (IT'S ACTUALLY MIMICKING LEGENDARY IDOLS)

FAVORITES: LOLLIPOPS (IT'S ACTUALLY TEMPURA MADE FROM A WILD PLANT CALLED "KOGOMI" OR "OSTRICH FERN")

ABILITY: UNCHASTE

EXTERNAL-TARGETING VOLUNTARY ACTIVATION-TYPE

OPERATES AS DEPICTED IN NO. 72. HERE'S A LIST OF UNDER MEMBERS WHO ARE AFFECTED BY KURURU'S ABILITY...

WILL WORK ON:

TELLA

WON'T WORK ON:

EVERYONE BUT TELLA

BEFORE KURURU JOINED UNDER, HER ABILITY WORKED ON PRETTY MUCH EVERYONE, SO IT WAS A HUGE BLOW TO HER PRIDE AS AN IDOL. AFTER SHE USED HER ABILITY ON TELLA, THE ONLY UNDER MEMBER AFFECTED BY IT, SHE RECEIVED THE BIGGEST SCOLDING OF HER LIFE. SHE WAS SO FRIGHTENED, SHE NEVER USED IT ON HIM AGAIN.

IT ALSO WORKED ON SEAN WHILE HE WAS ALIVE.

DON'T USE THAT AGAIN.

No. 073
Bring It On

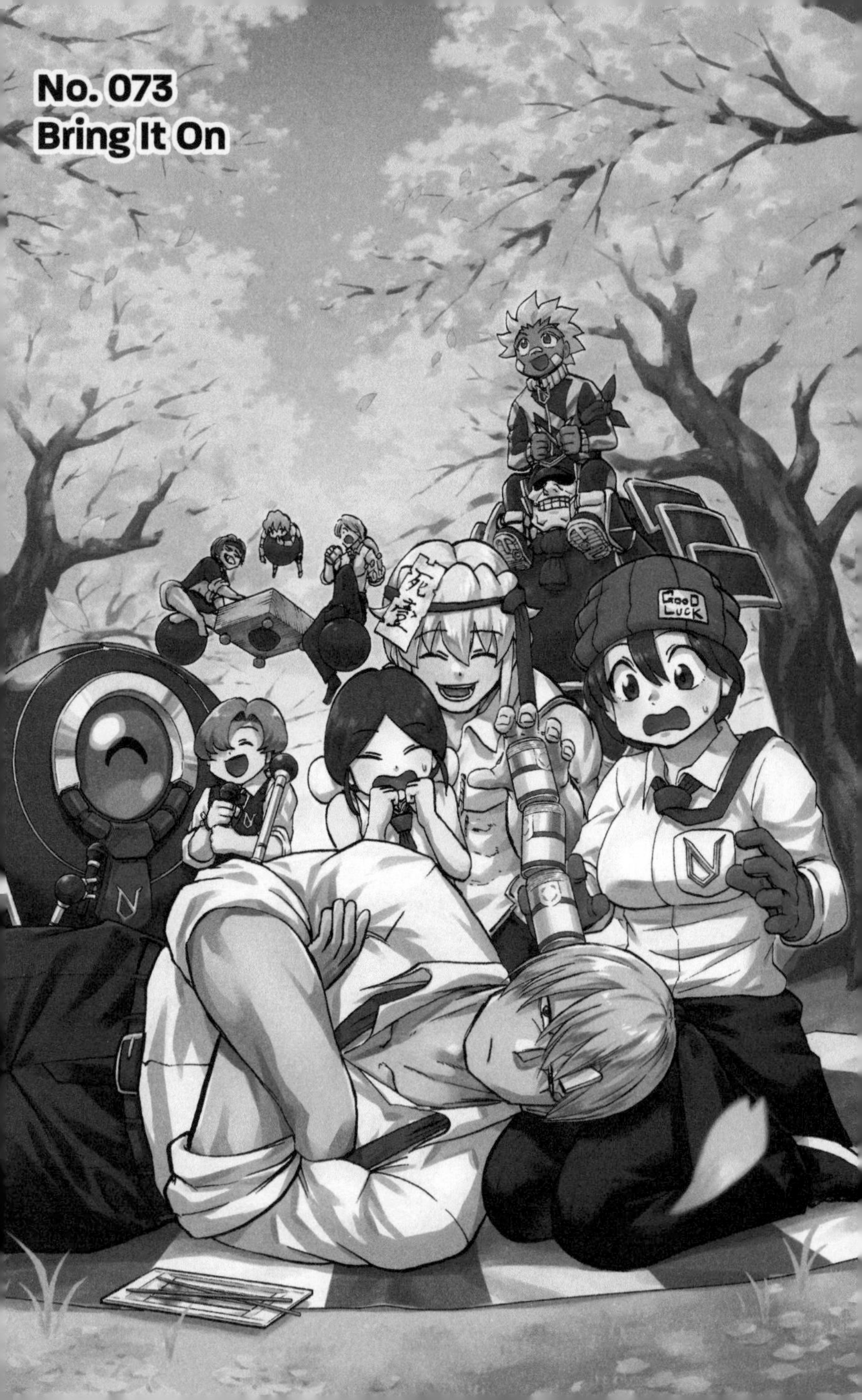
GOOD LUCK

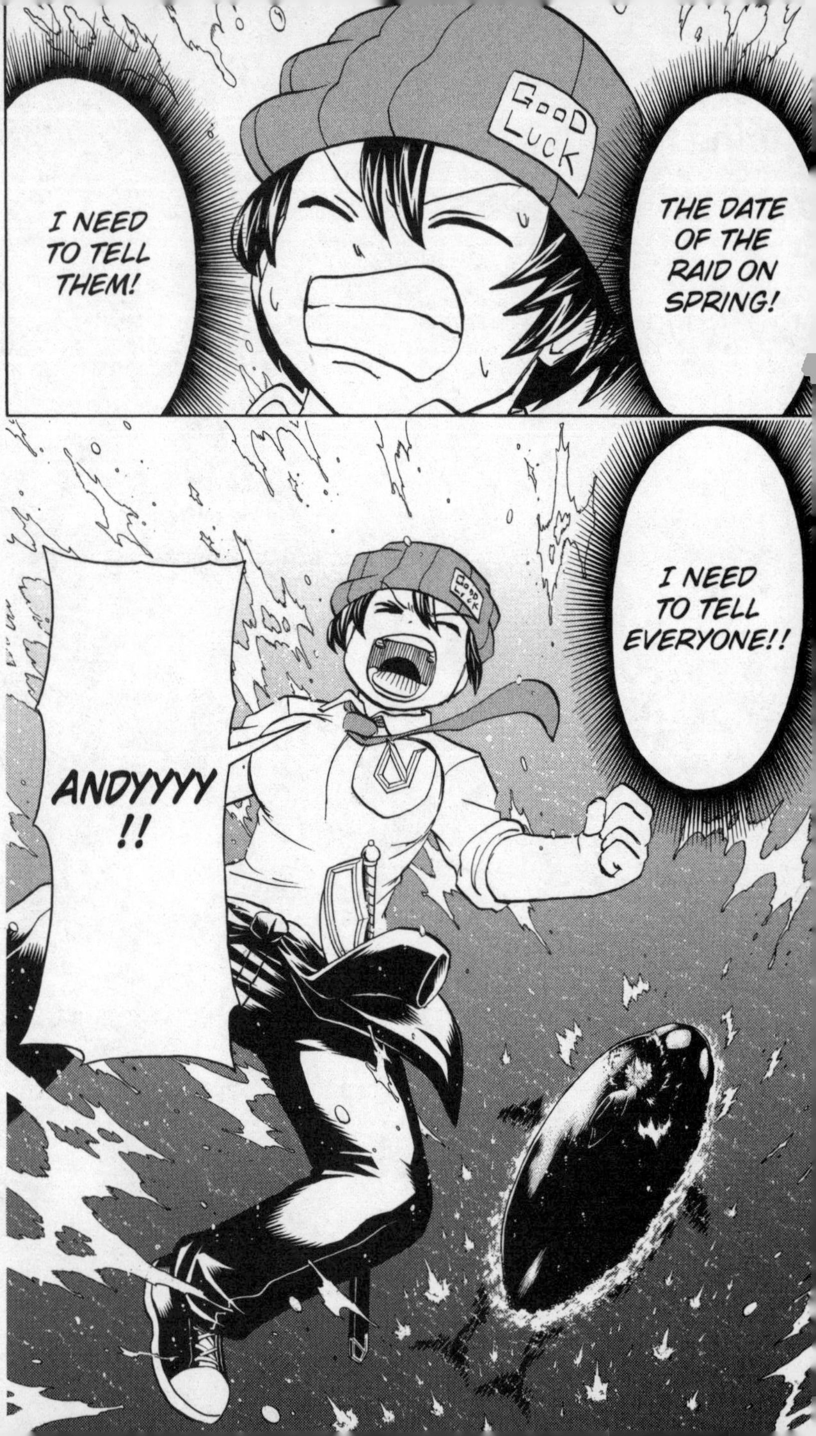
GOOD LUCK
THE DATE OF THE RAID ON SPRING!
I NEED TO TELL THEM!
I NEED TO TELL EVERYONE!!
ANDYYYY!!

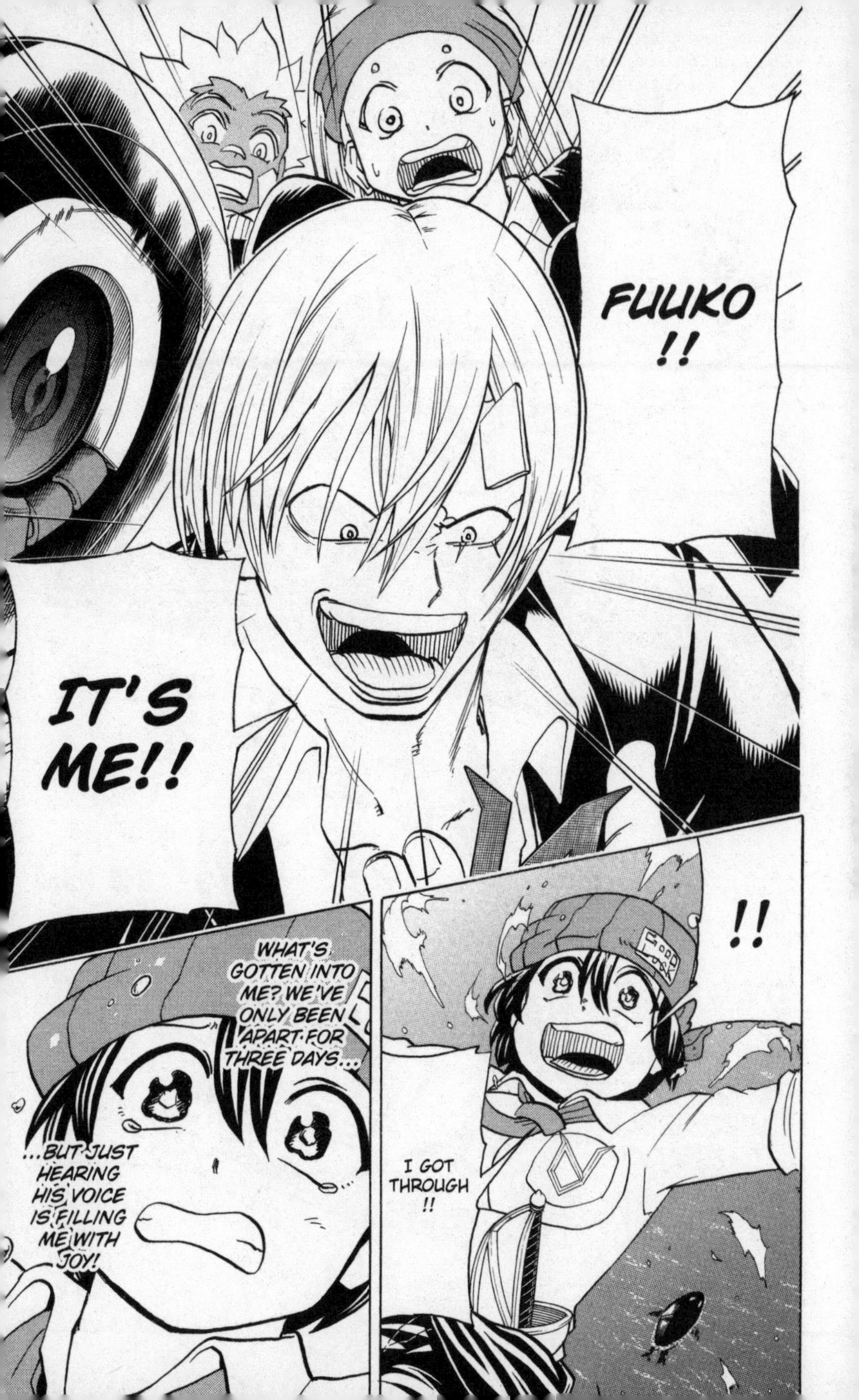
FUUKO !!
IT'S ME!!
!!
I GOT THROUGH !!
WHAT'S GOTTEN INTO ME? WE'VE ONLY BEEN APART FOR THREE DAYS...
...BUT JUST HEARING HIS VOICE IS FILLING ME WITH JOY!

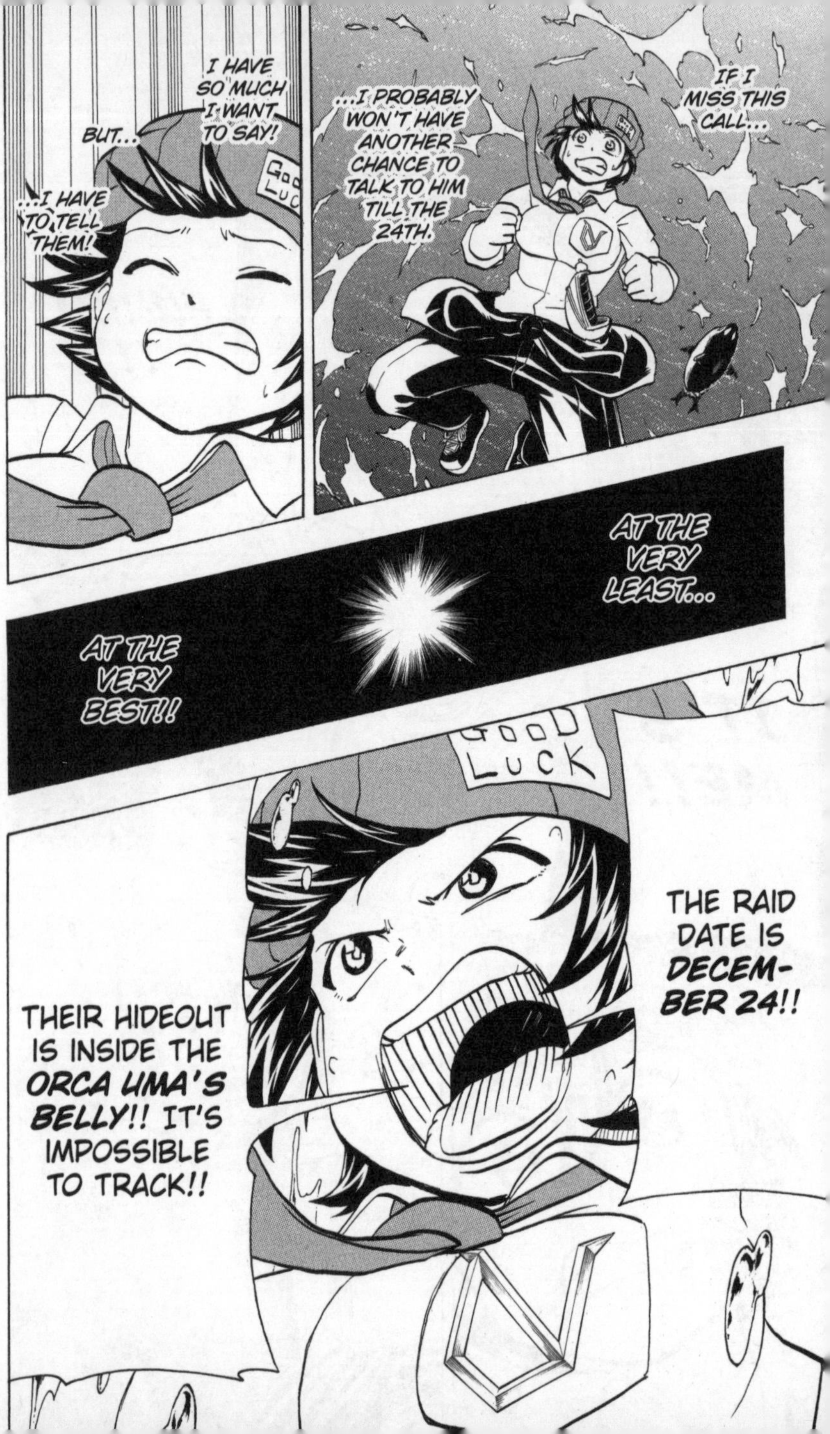

IF I MISS THIS CALL...
...I PROBABLY WON'T HAVE ANOTHER CHANCE TO TALK TO HIM TILL THE 24TH.
I HAVE SO MUCH I WANT TO SAY!
BUT...
...I HAVE TO TELL THEM!
GOOD LUCK
AT THE VERY LEAST...
AT THE VERY BEST!!
GOOD LUCK
THE RAID DATE IS DECEMBER 24!!
THEIR HIDEOUT IS INSIDE THE ORCA UMA'S BELLY!! IT'S IMPOSSIBLE TO TRACK!!

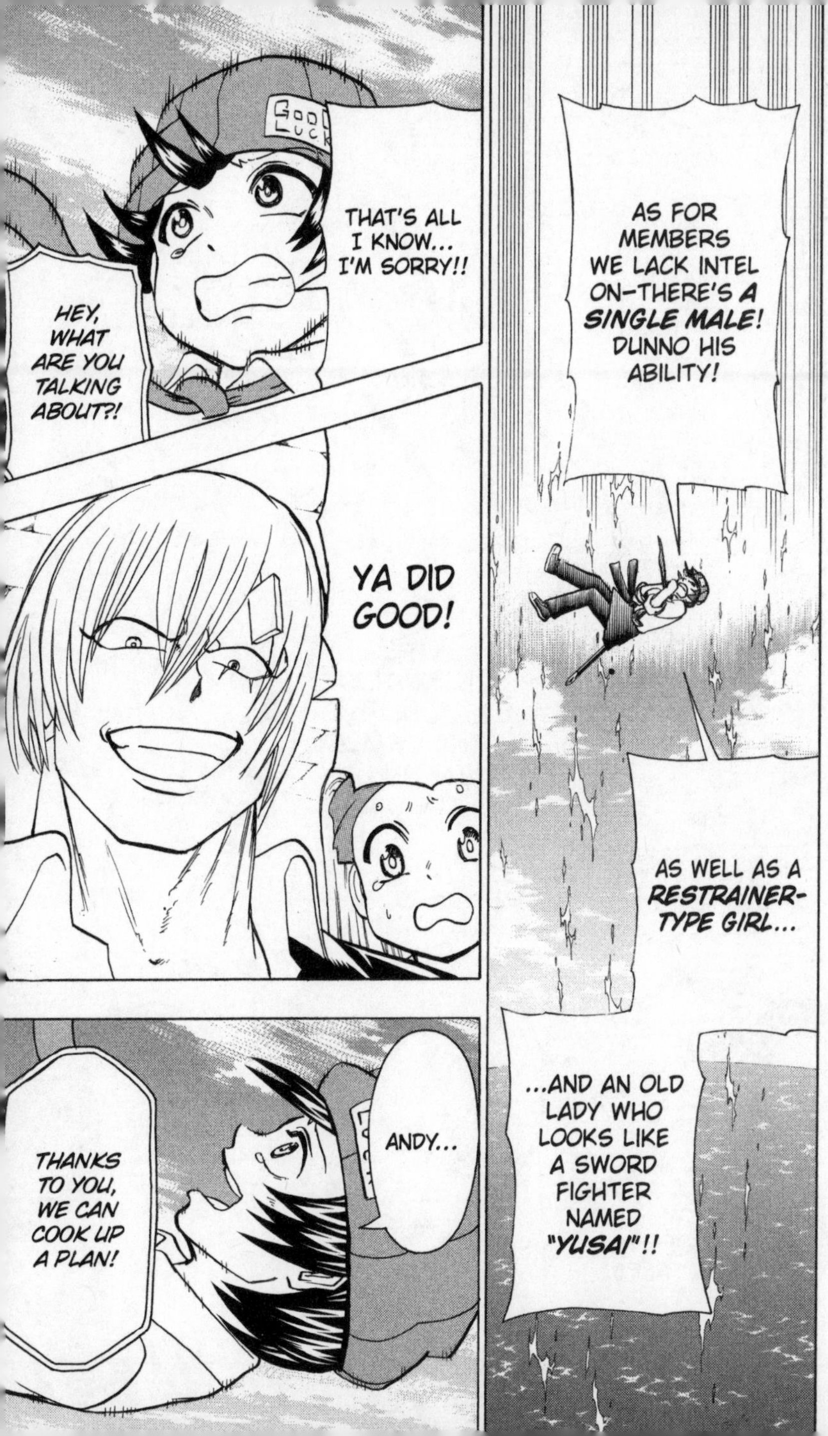
AS FOR MEMBERS WE LACK INTEL ON—THERE'S A SINGLE MALE! DUNNO HIS ABILITY!
AS WELL AS A RESTRAINER-TYPE GIRL...
...AND AN OLD LADY WHO LOOKS LIKE A SWORD FIGHTER NAMED "YUSAI"!!
THAT'S ALL I KNOW... I'M SORRY!!
HEY, WHAT ARE YOU TALKING ABOUT?!
YA DID GOOD!
ANDY...
THANKS TO YOU, WE CAN COOK UP A PLAN!

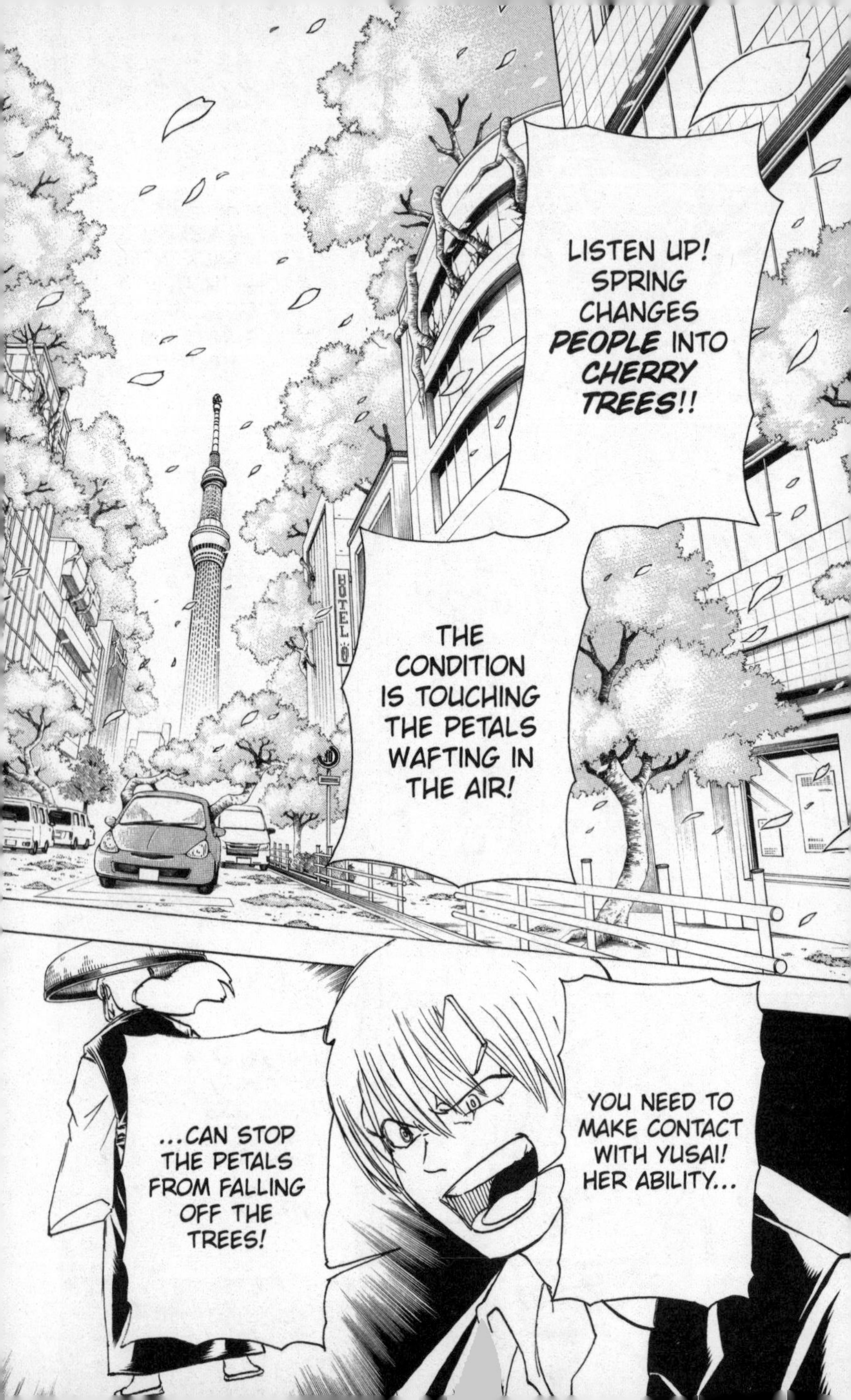
LISTEN UP! SPRING CHANGES PEOPLE INTO CHERRY TREES!!
THE CONDITION IS TOUCHING THE PETALS WAFTING IN THE AIR!
YOU NEED TO MAKE CONTACT WITH YUSAI! HER ABILITY...
...CAN STOP THE PETALS FROM FALLING OFF THE TREES!

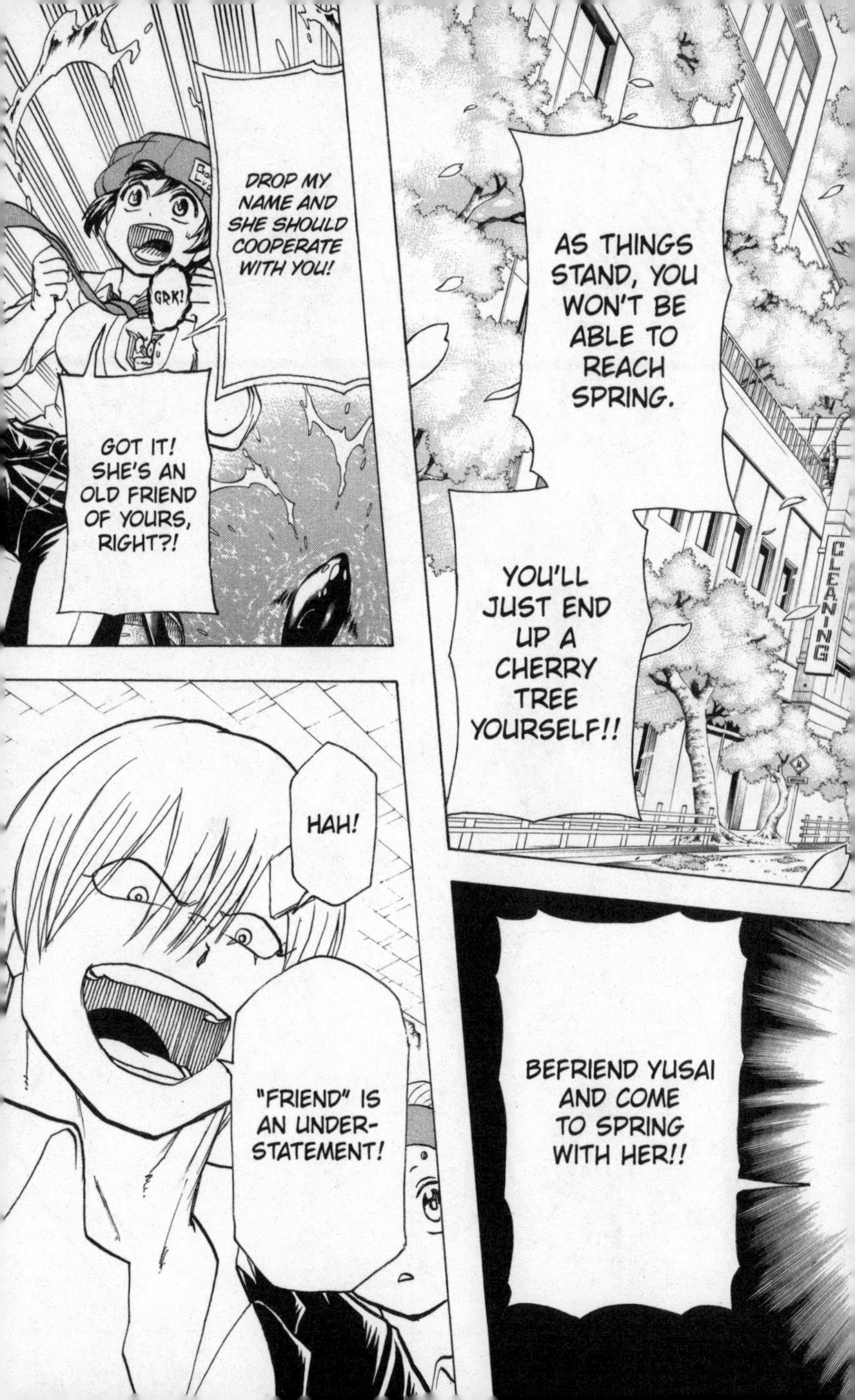

AS THINGS STAND, YOU WON'T BE ABLE TO REACH SPRING.
YOU'LL JUST END UP A CHERRY TREE YOURSELF!!
DROP MY NAME AND SHE SHOULD COOPERATE WITH YOU!
GRK!
GOT IT! SHE'S AN OLD FRIEND OF YOURS, RIGHT?!
HAH!
"FRIEND" IS AN UNDER-STATEMENT!
CLEANING
BEFRIEND YUSAI AND COME TO SPRING WITH HER!!

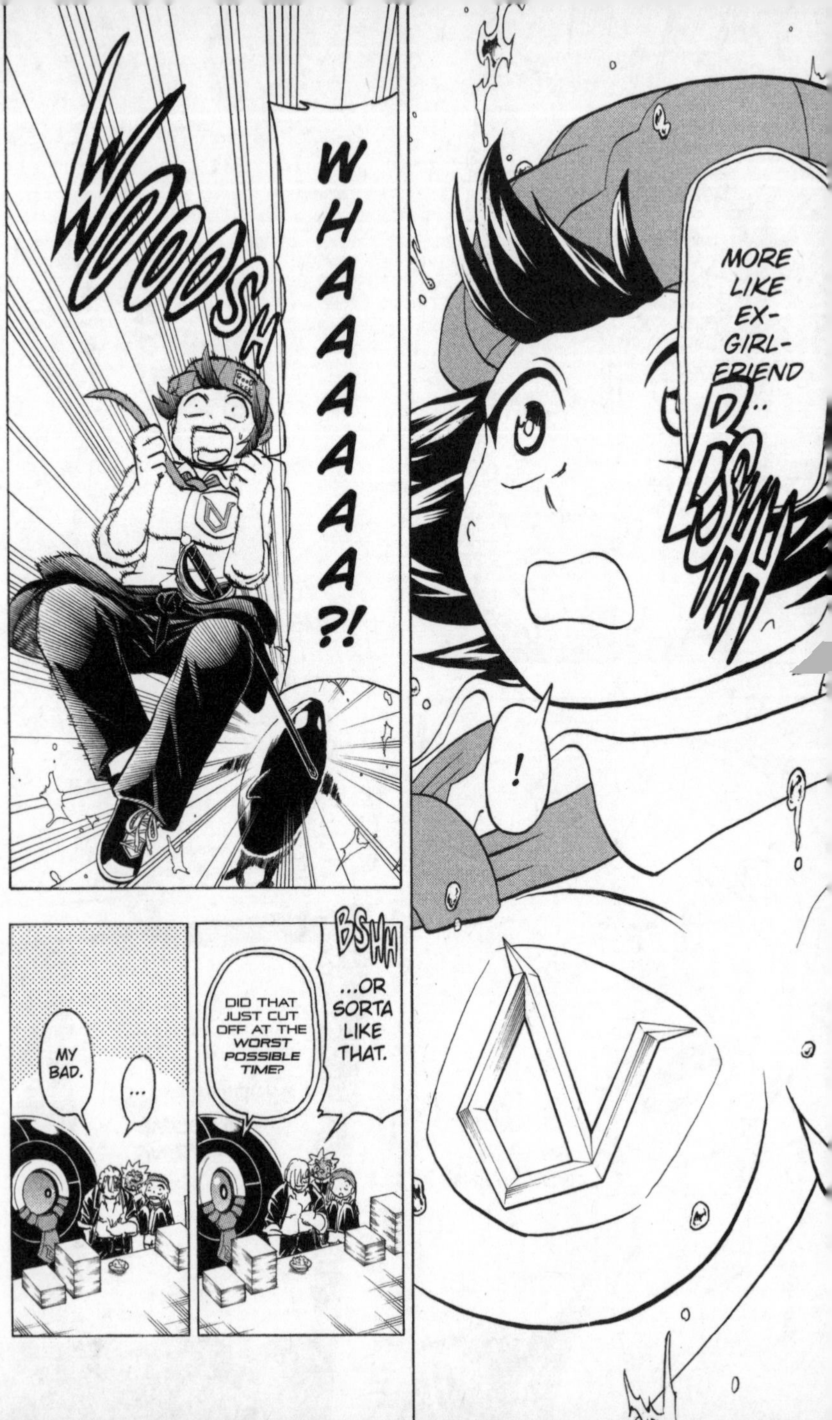
MORE LIKE EX-GIRLFRIEND...
!
WHOOSH
WHAAAAAAAA?!
BSHH
...OR SORTA LIKE THAT.
DID THAT JUST CUT OFF AT THE WORST POSSIBLE TIME?
MY BAD.
...

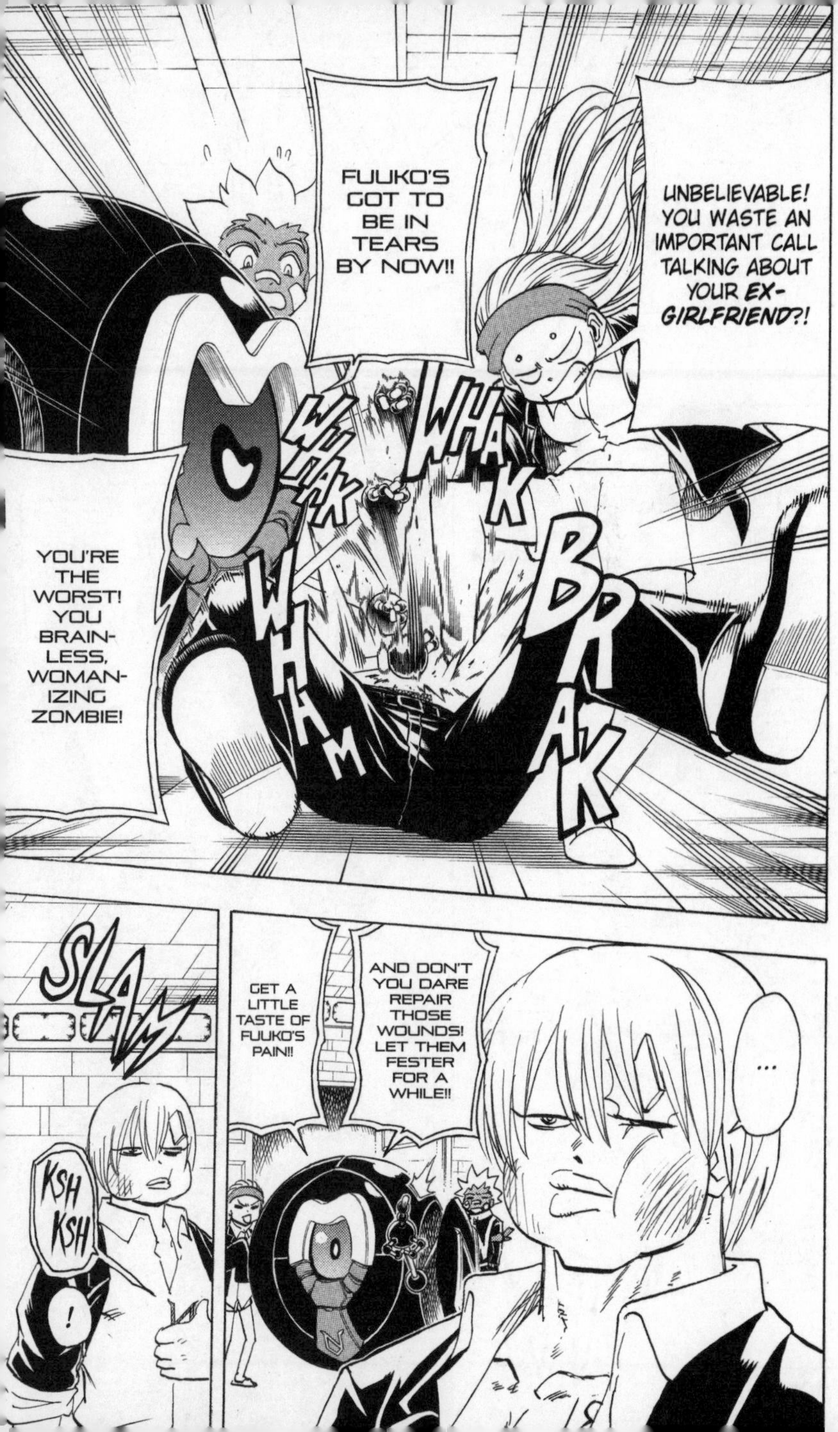
UNBELIEVABLE! YOU WASTE AN IMPORTANT CALL TALKING ABOUT YOUR *EX-GIRLFRIEND*?!
FUUKO'S GOT TO BE IN TEARS BY NOW!!
WHAK
WHAK
BRAK
WHAM
YOU'RE THE WORST! YOU BRAIN-LESS, WOMAN-IZING ZOMBIE!
...
AND DON'T YOU DARE REPAIR THOSE WOUNDS! LET THEM FESTER FOR A WHILE!!
GET A LITTLE TASTE OF FUUKO'S PAIN!!
SLAM
KSH KSH
!

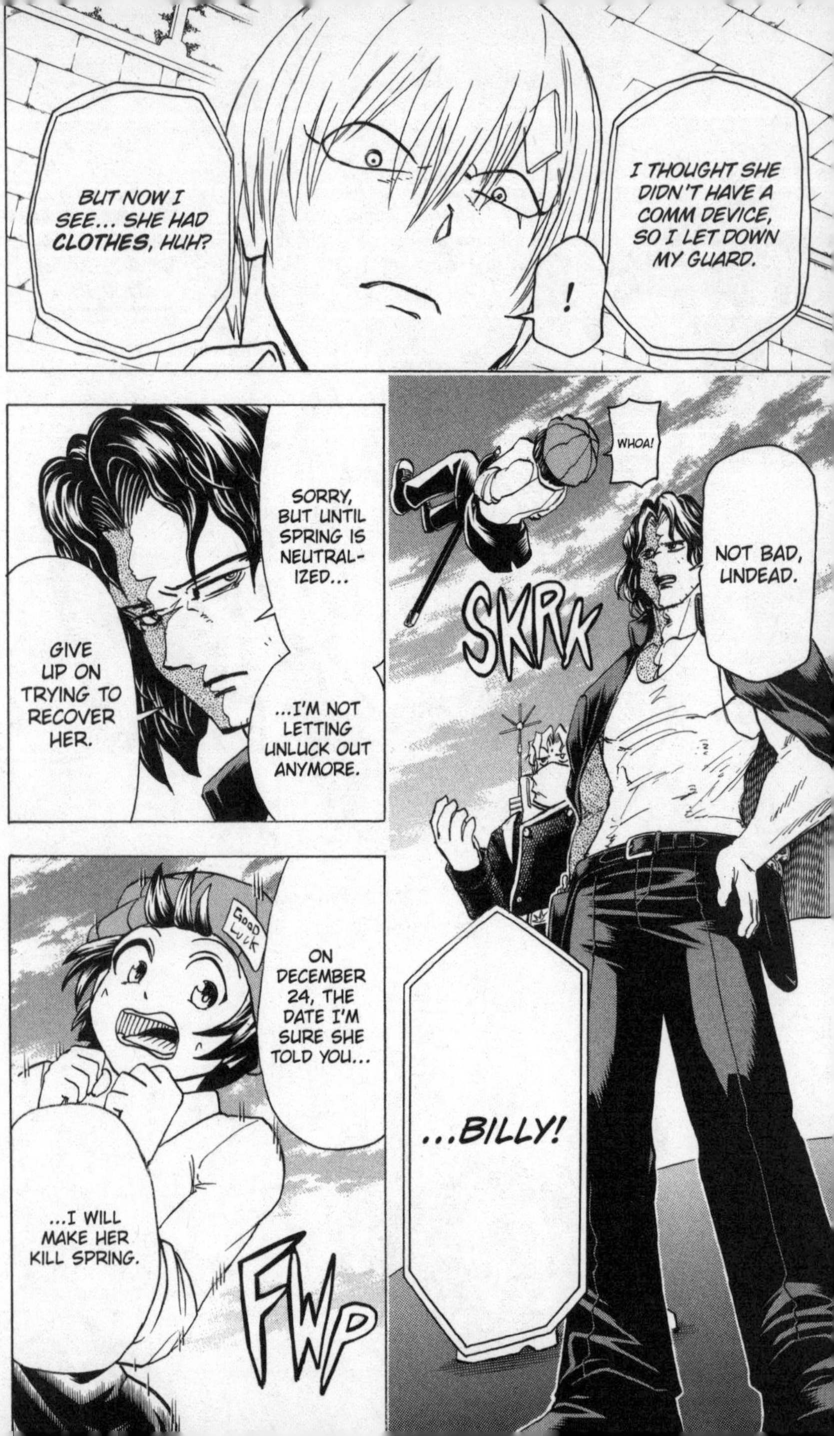
I THOUGHT SHE DIDN'T HAVE A COMM DEVICE, SO I LET DOWN MY GUARD.
!
BUT NOW I SEE... SHE HAD CLOTHES, HUH?
WHOA!
NOT BAD, UNDEAD.
SKRK
...BILLY!
SORRY, BUT UNTIL SPRING IS NEUTRALIZED...
...I'M NOT LETTING UNLUCK OUT ANYMORE.
GIVE UP ON TRYING TO RECOVER HER.
ON DECEMBER 24, THE DATE I'M SURE SHE TOLD YOU...
GOOD LUCK
...I WILL MAKE HER KILL SPRING.
FWP

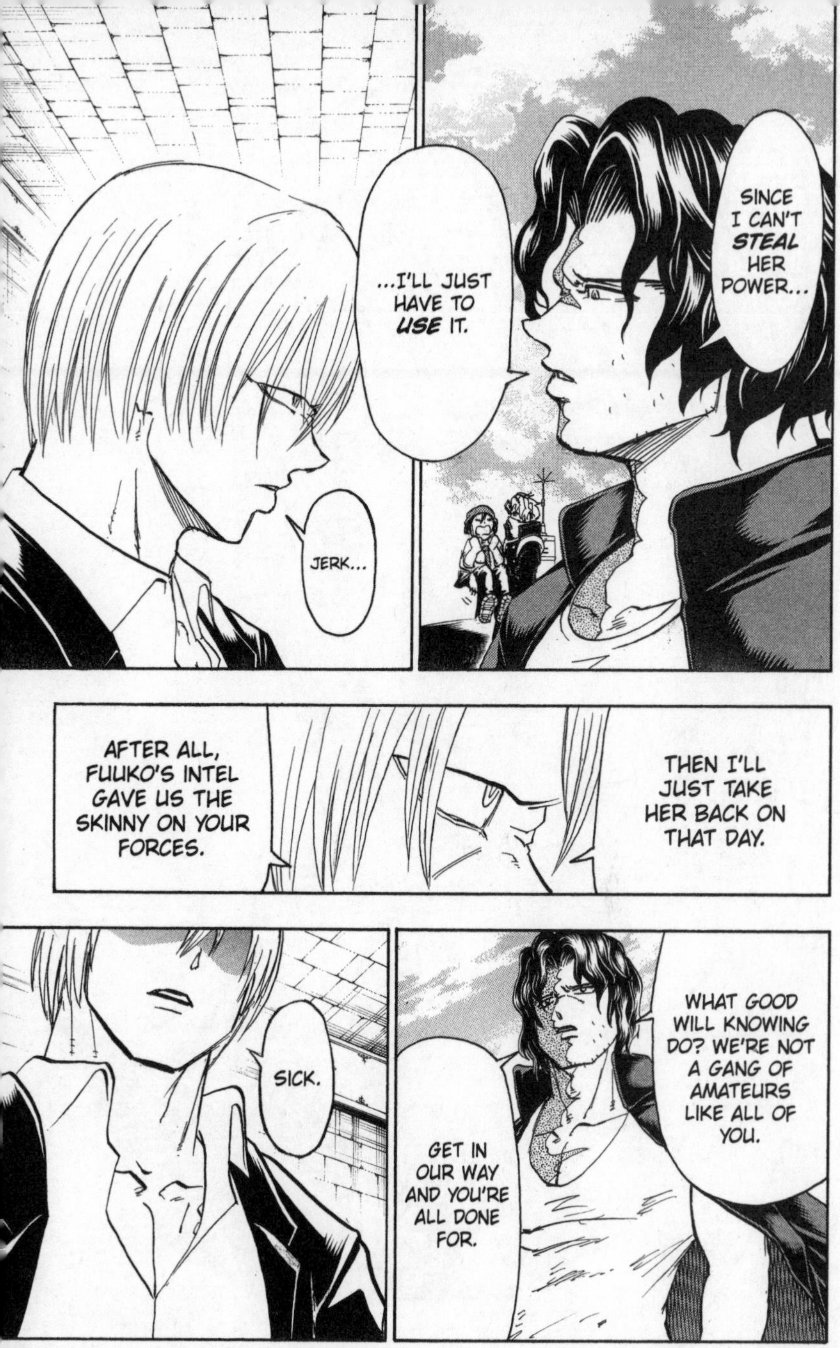
SINCE I CAN'T **STEAL** HER POWER...
...I'LL JUST HAVE TO **USE** IT.
JERK...
THEN I'LL JUST TAKE HER BACK ON THAT DAY.
AFTER ALL, FUUKO'S INTEL GAVE US THE SKINNY ON YOUR FORCES.
WHAT GOOD WILL KNOWING DO? WE'RE NOT A GANG OF AMATEURS LIKE ALL OF YOU.
GET IN OUR WAY AND YOU'RE ALL DONE FOR.
SICK.

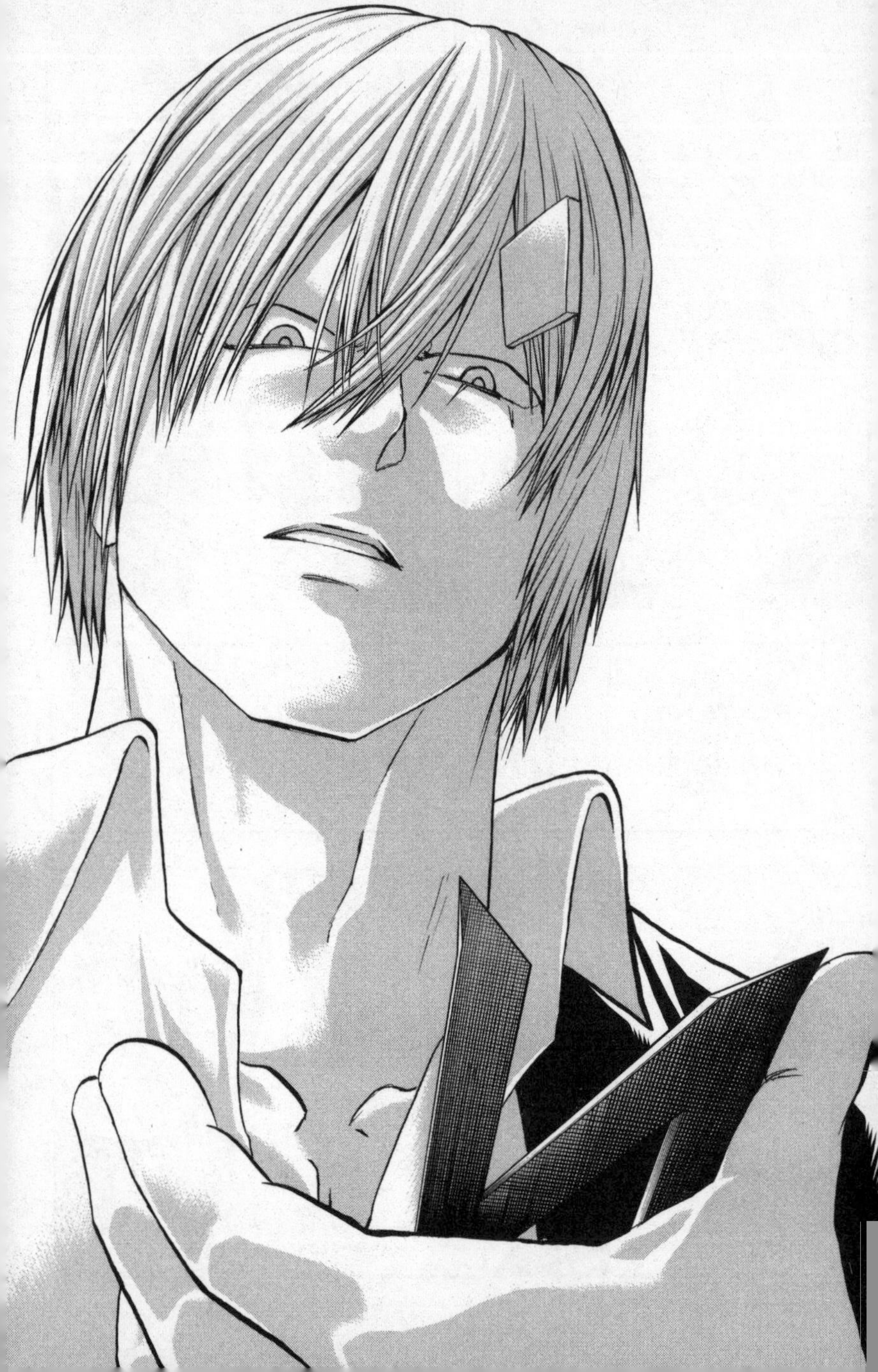

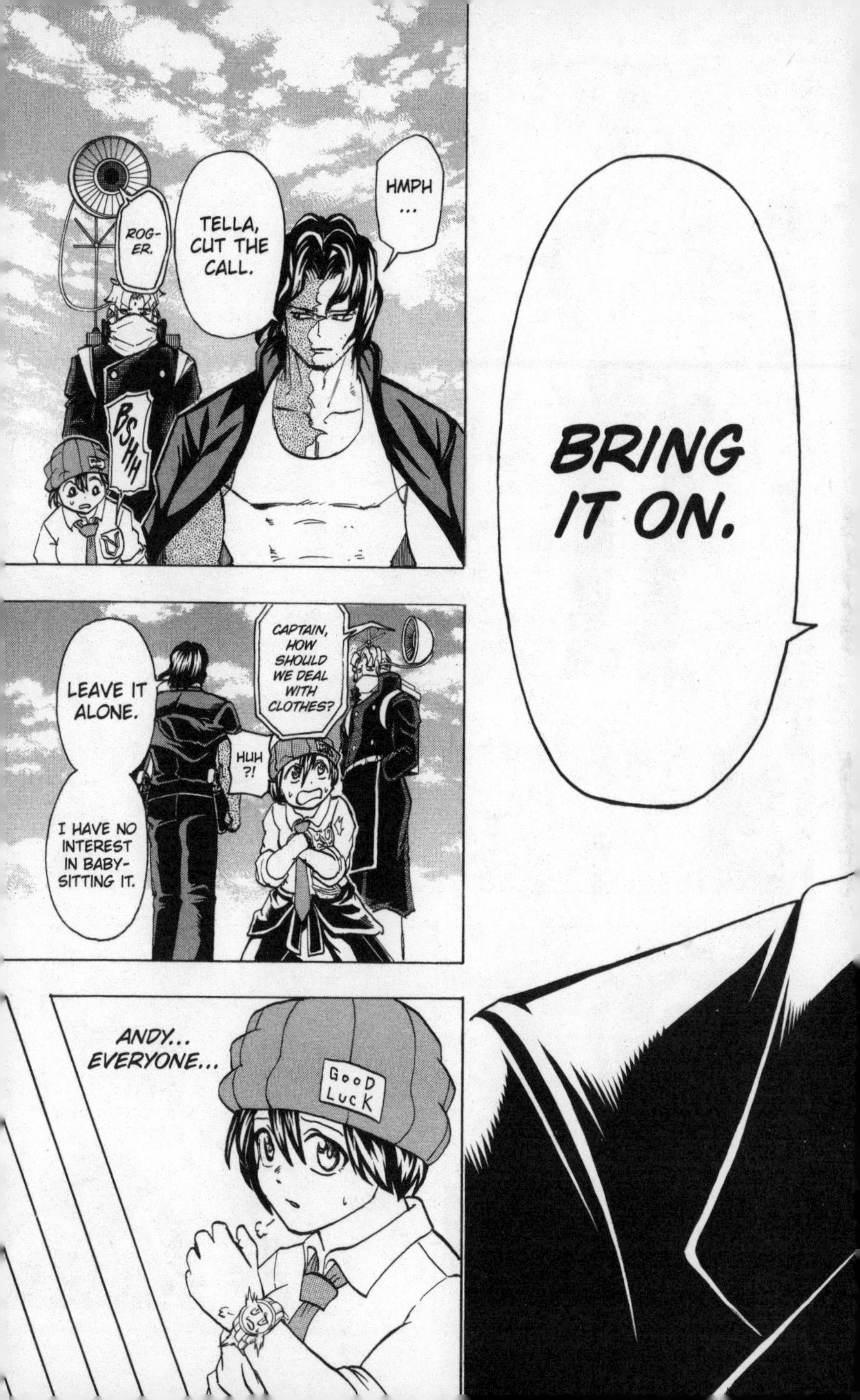
BRING IT ON.
HMPH ...
TELLA, CUT THE CALL.
ROG-ER.
BSHH
CAPTAIN, HOW SHOULD WE DEAL WITH CLOTHES?
HUH ?!
LEAVE IT ALONE.
I HAVE NO INTEREST IN BABY-SITTING IT.
ANDY... EVERYONE...
GOOD LUCK

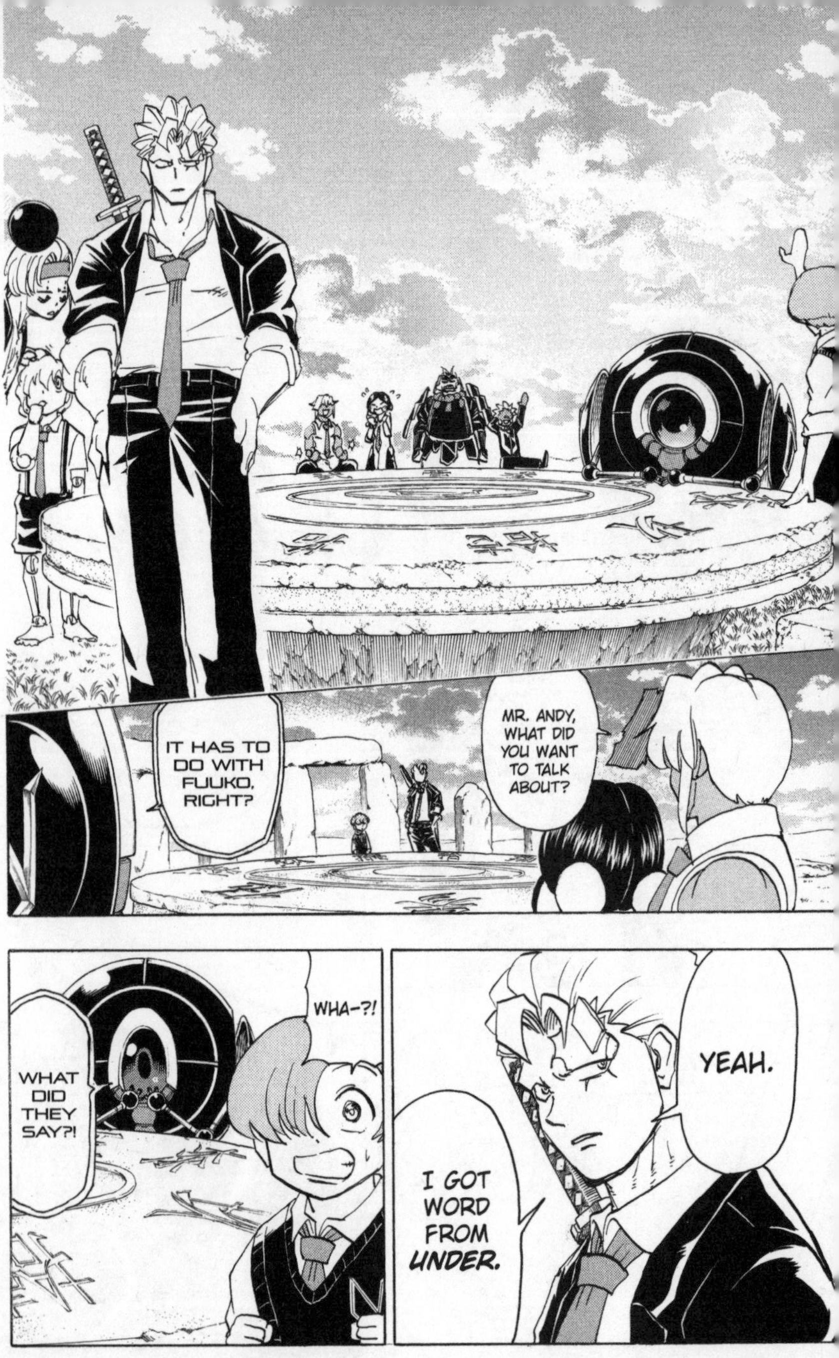
MR. ANDY, WHAT DID YOU WANT TO TALK ABOUT?
IT HAS TO DO WITH FUUKO, RIGHT?
YEAH.
I GOT WORD FROM UNDER.
WHA-?!
WHAT DID THEY SAY?!

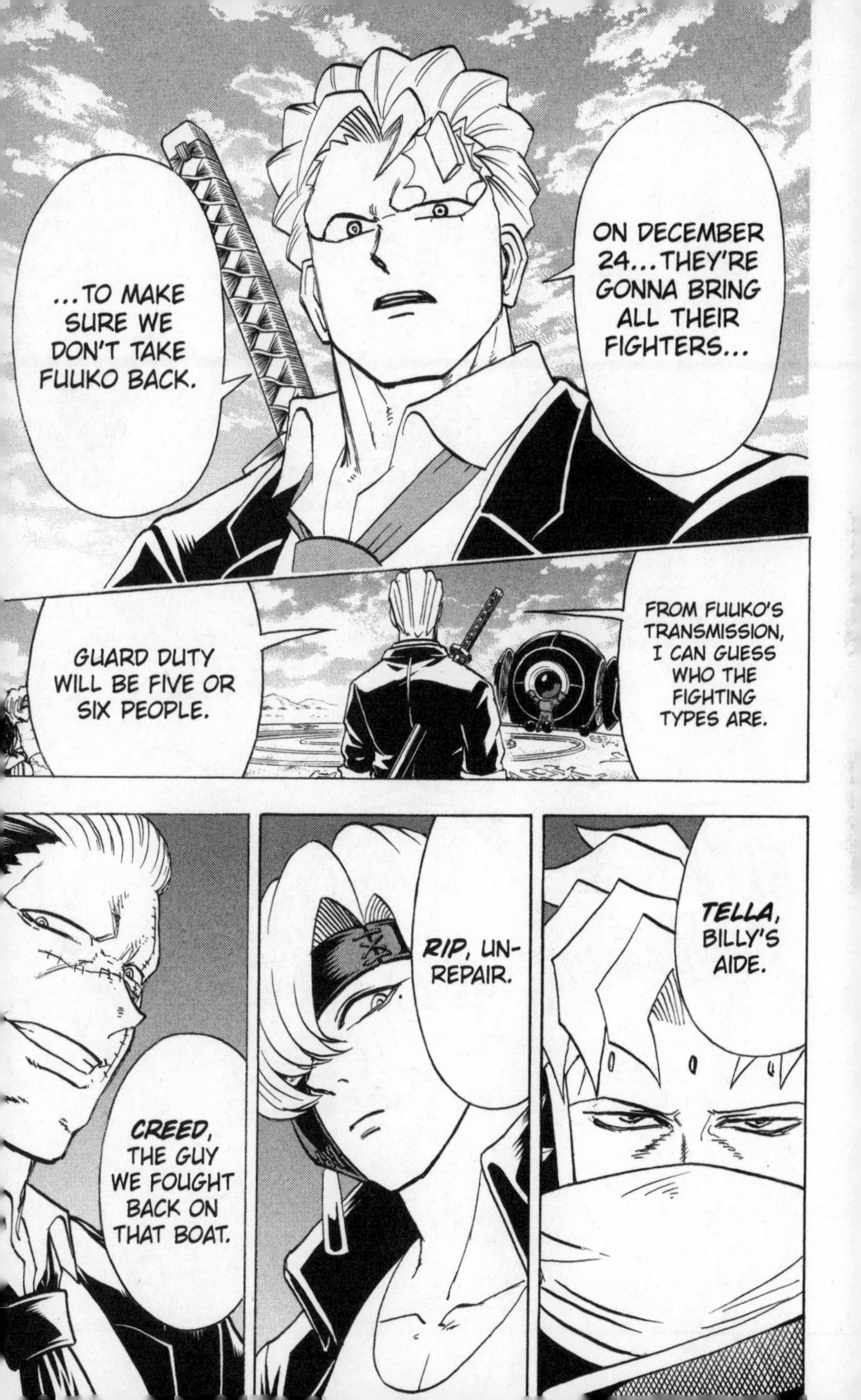
ON DECEMBER 24...THEY'RE GONNA BRING ALL THEIR FIGHTERS...
...TO MAKE SURE WE DON'T TAKE FUUKO BACK.
FROM FUUKO'S TRANSMISSION, I CAN GUESS WHO THE FIGHTING TYPES ARE.
GUARD DUTY WILL BE FIVE OR SIX PEOPLE.
TELLA, BILLY'S AIDE.
RIP, UN-REPAIR.
CREED, THE GUY WE FOUGHT BACK ON THAT BOAT.

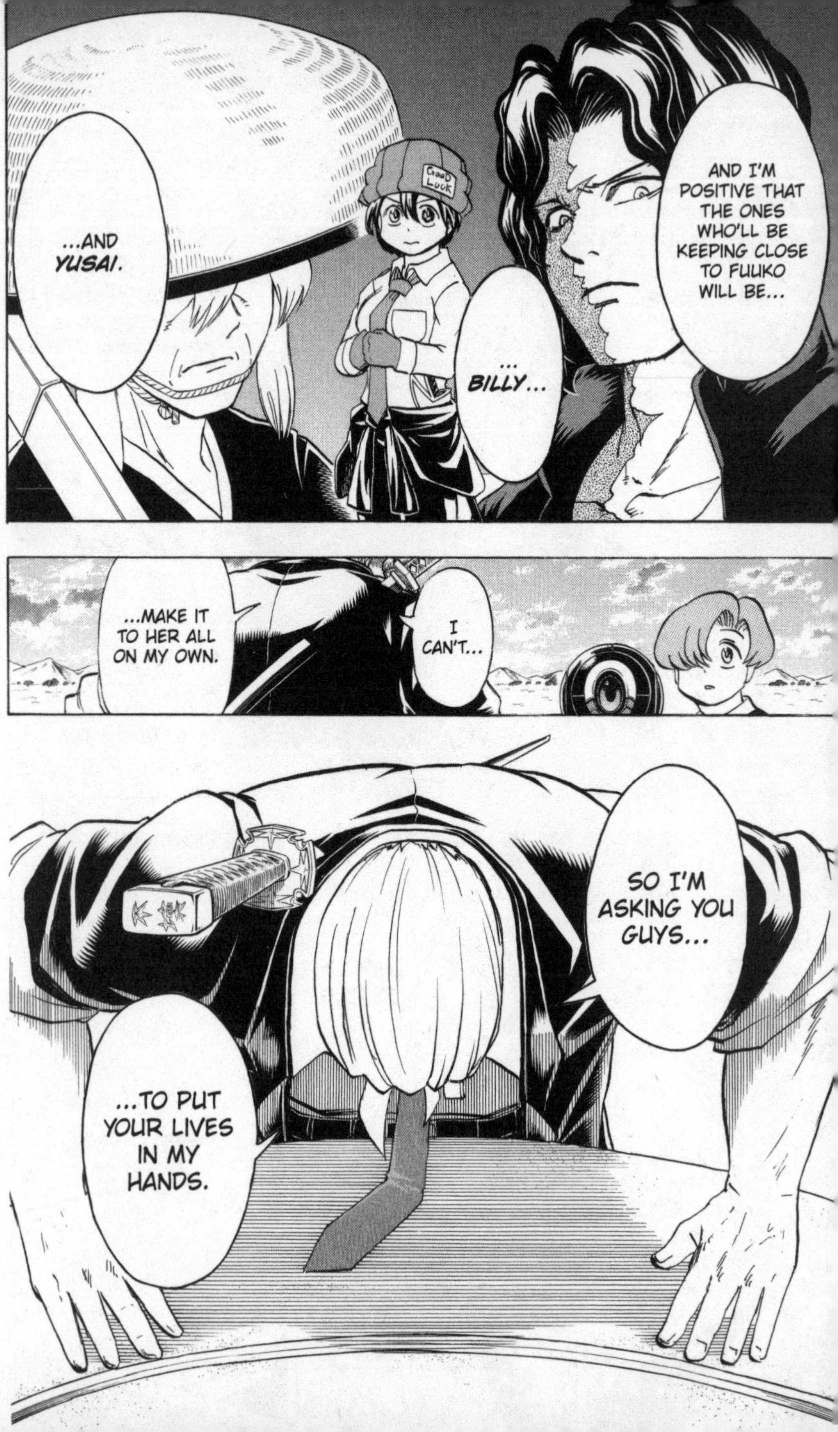
AND I'M POSITIVE THAT THE ONES WHO'LL BE KEEPING CLOSE TO FUUKO WILL BE...
... BILLY...
GOOD LUCK
...AND YUSAI.
I CAN'T...
...MAKE IT TO HER ALL ON MY OWN.
SO I'M ASKING YOU GUYS...
...TO PUT YOUR LIVES IN MY HANDS.

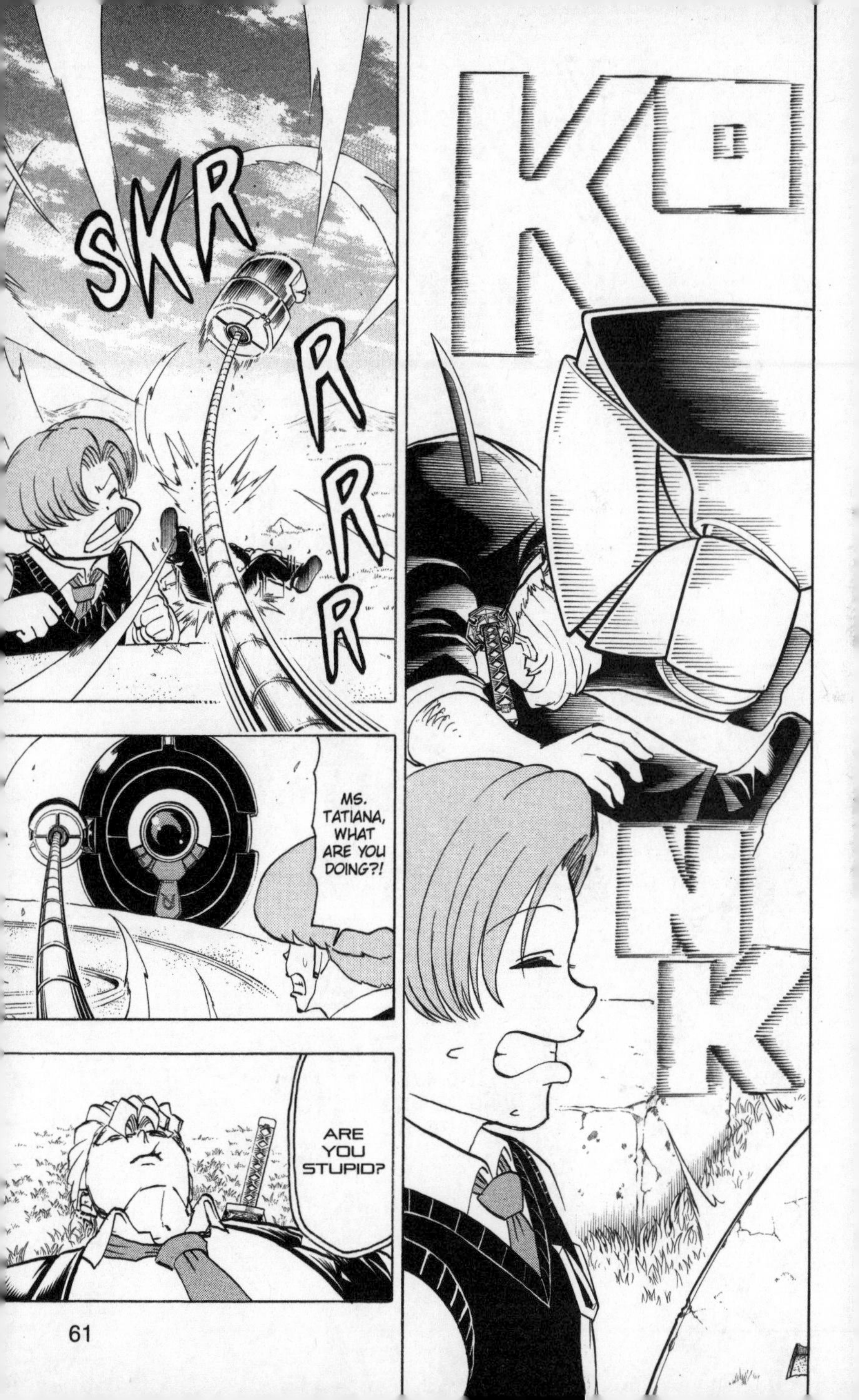

KONK
SKRRRR
MS. TATIANA, WHAT ARE YOU DOING?!
ARE YOU STUPID?

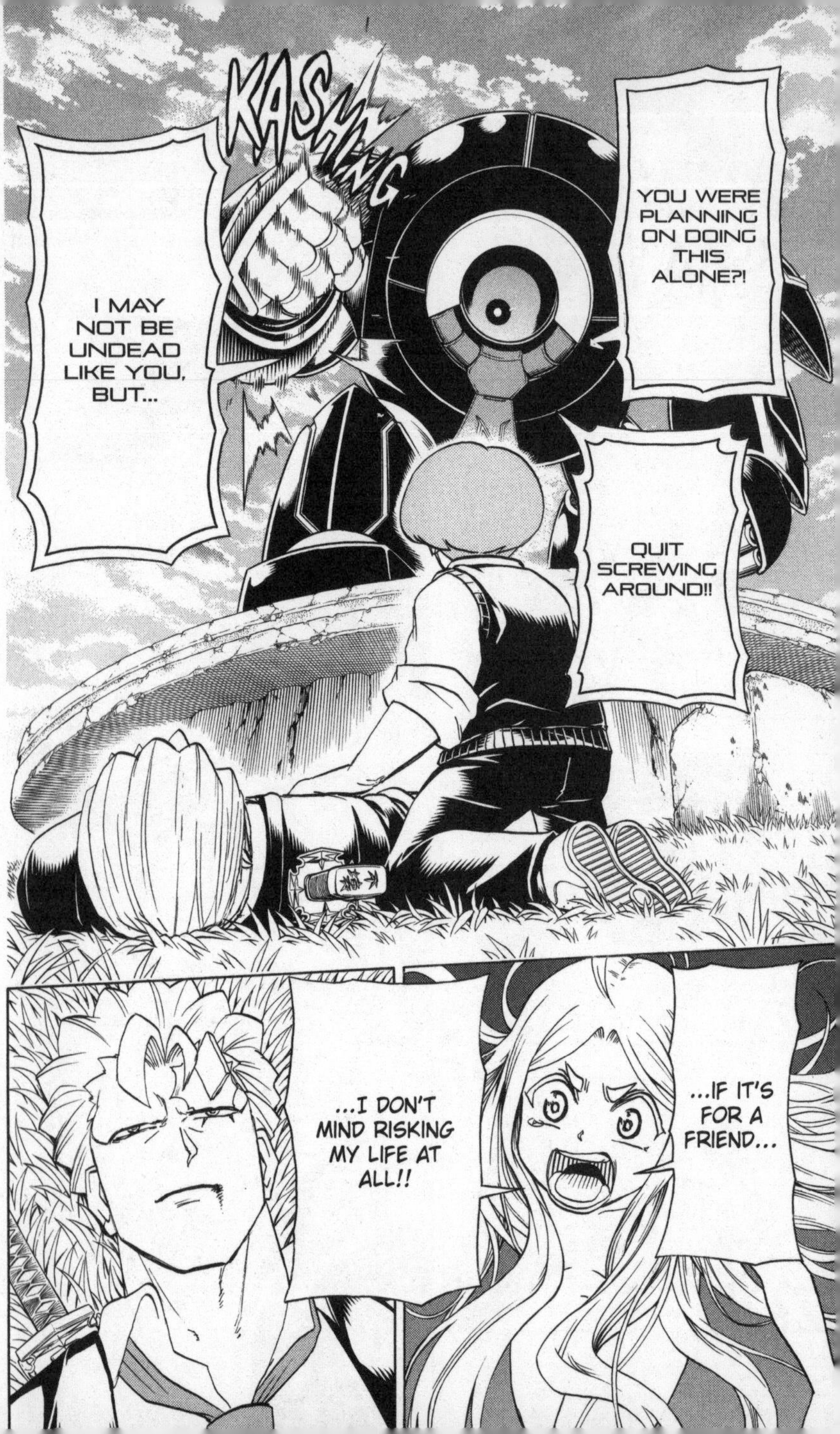
KASHING
YOU WERE PLANNING ON DOING THIS ALONE?!
QUIT SCREWING AROUND!!
I MAY NOT BE UNDEAD LIKE YOU, BUT...
...IF IT'S FOR A FRIEND...
...I DON'T MIND RISKING MY LIFE AT ALL!!

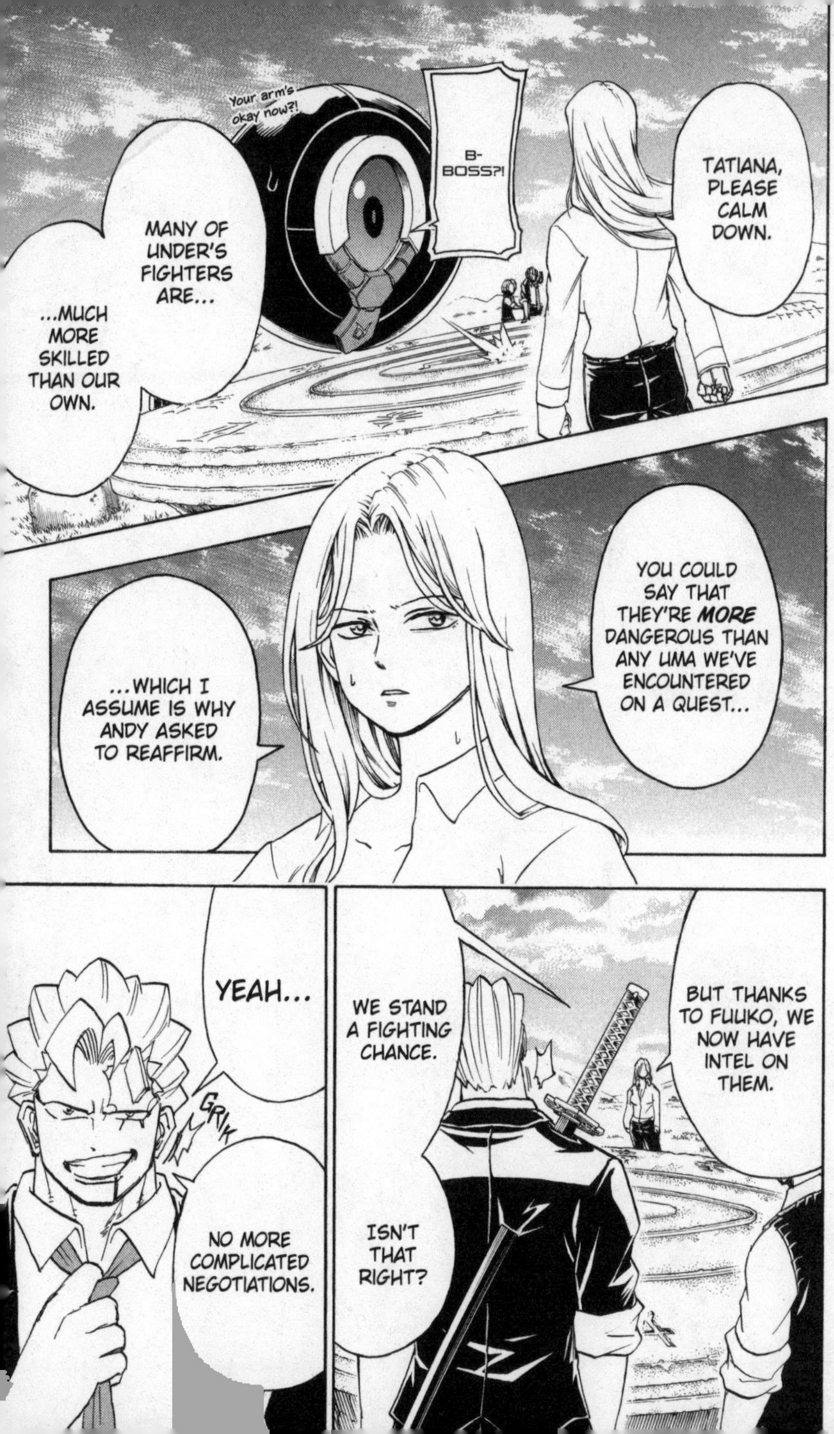
TATIANA, PLEASE CALM DOWN.
B-BOSS?!
Your arm's okay now?!
MANY OF UNDER'S FIGHTERS ARE...
...MUCH MORE SKILLED THAN OUR OWN.
YOU COULD SAY THAT THEY'RE *MORE* DANGEROUS THAN ANY UMA WE'VE ENCOUNTERED ON A QUEST...
...WHICH I ASSUME IS WHY ANDY ASKED TO REAFFIRM.
BUT THANKS TO FUUKO, WE NOW HAVE INTEL ON THEM.
WE STAND A FIGHTING CHANCE.
ISN'T THAT RIGHT?
YEAH...
GRIK
NO MORE COMPLICATED NEGOTIATIONS.

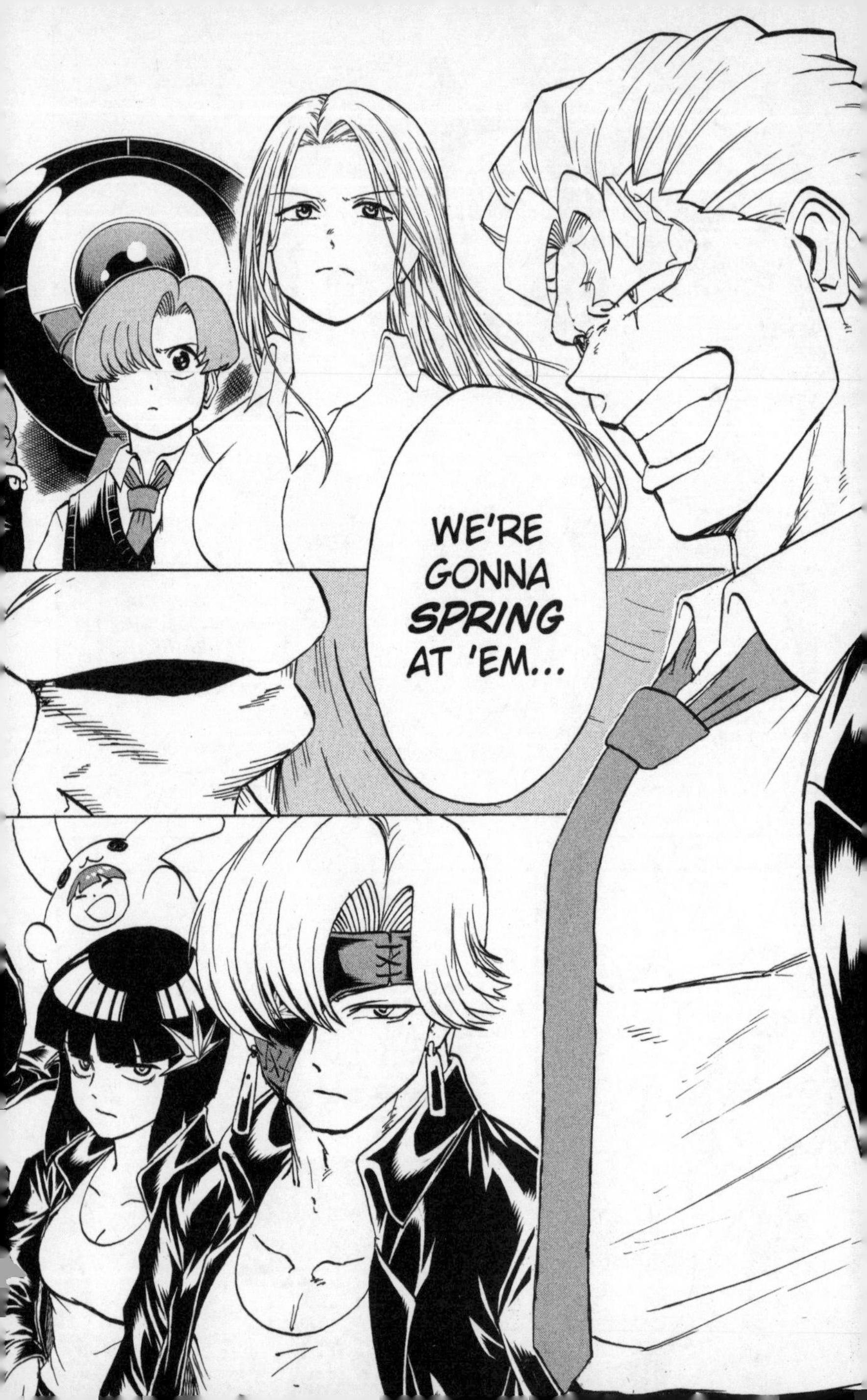
WE'RE GONNA SPRING AT 'EM...

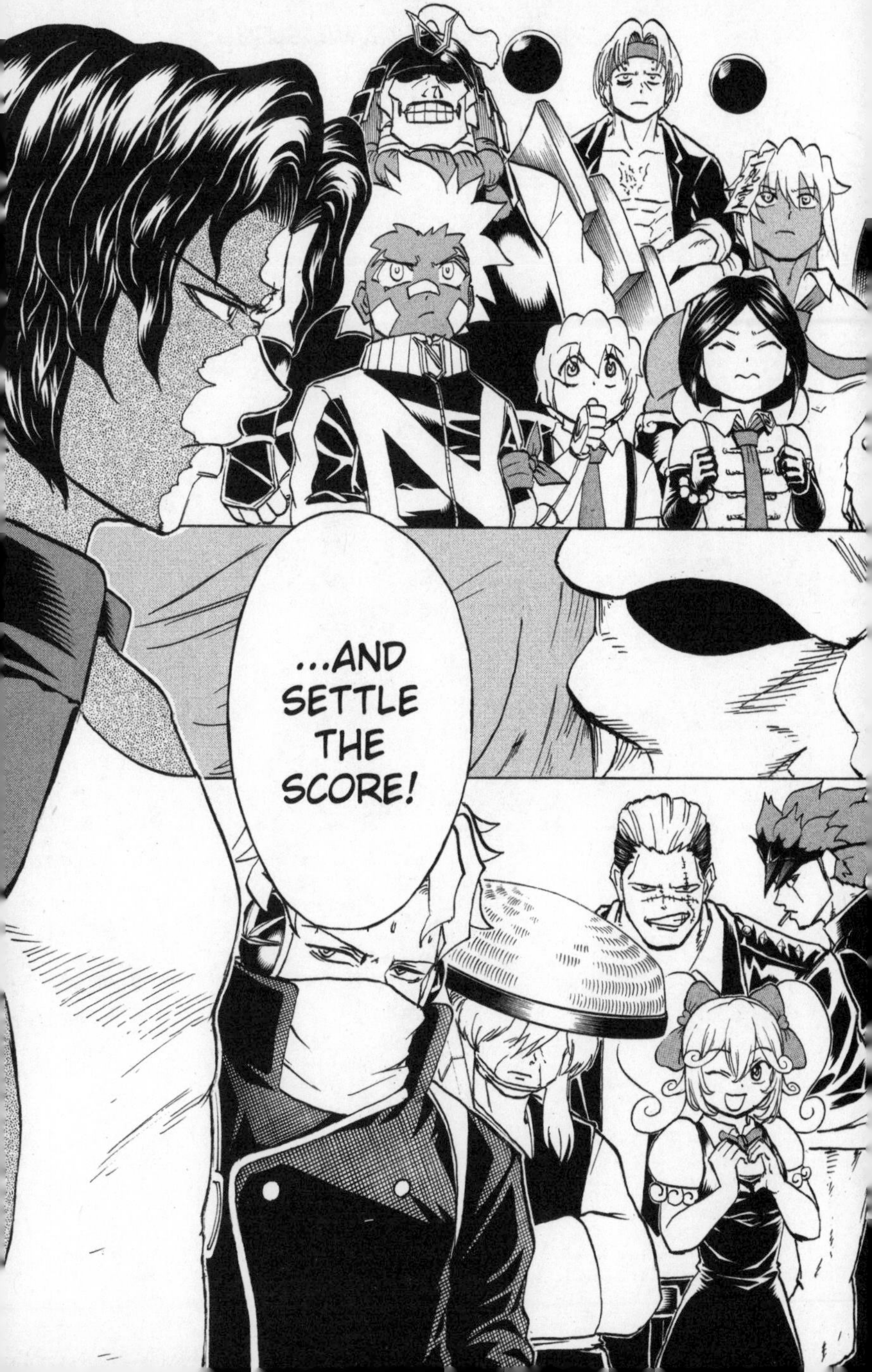
...AND SETTLE THE SCORE!

ANTI-CHERRY BLOSSOM MEASURES

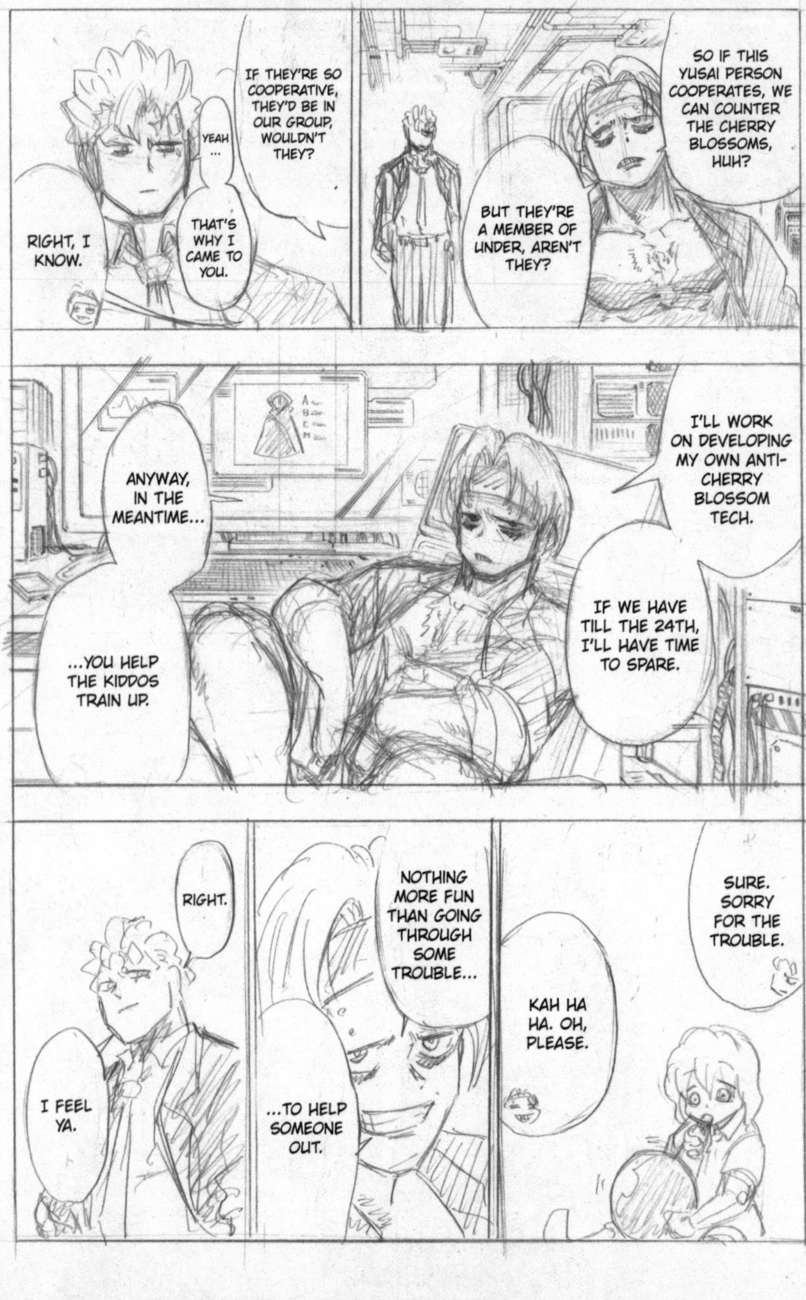
SO IF THIS YUSAI PERSON COOPERATES, WE CAN COUNTER THE CHERRY BLOSSOMS, HUH?
BUT THEY'RE A MEMBER OF UNDER, AREN'T THEY?
IF THEY'RE SO COOPERATIVE, THEY'D BE IN OUR GROUP, WOULDN'T THEY?
YEAH...
THAT'S WHY I CAME TO YOU.
RIGHT, I KNOW.
I'LL WORK ON DEVELOPING MY OWN ANTI-CHERRY BLOSSOM TECH.
IF WE HAVE TILL THE 24TH, I'LL HAVE TIME TO SPARE.
ANYWAY, IN THE MEANTIME...
...YOU HELP THE KIDDOS TRAIN UP.
SURE. SORRY FOR THE TROUBLE.
KAH HA HA. OH, PLEASE.
NOTHING MORE FUN THAN GOING THROUGH SOME TROUBLE...
...TO HELP SOMEONE OUT.
RIGHT.
I FEEL YA.

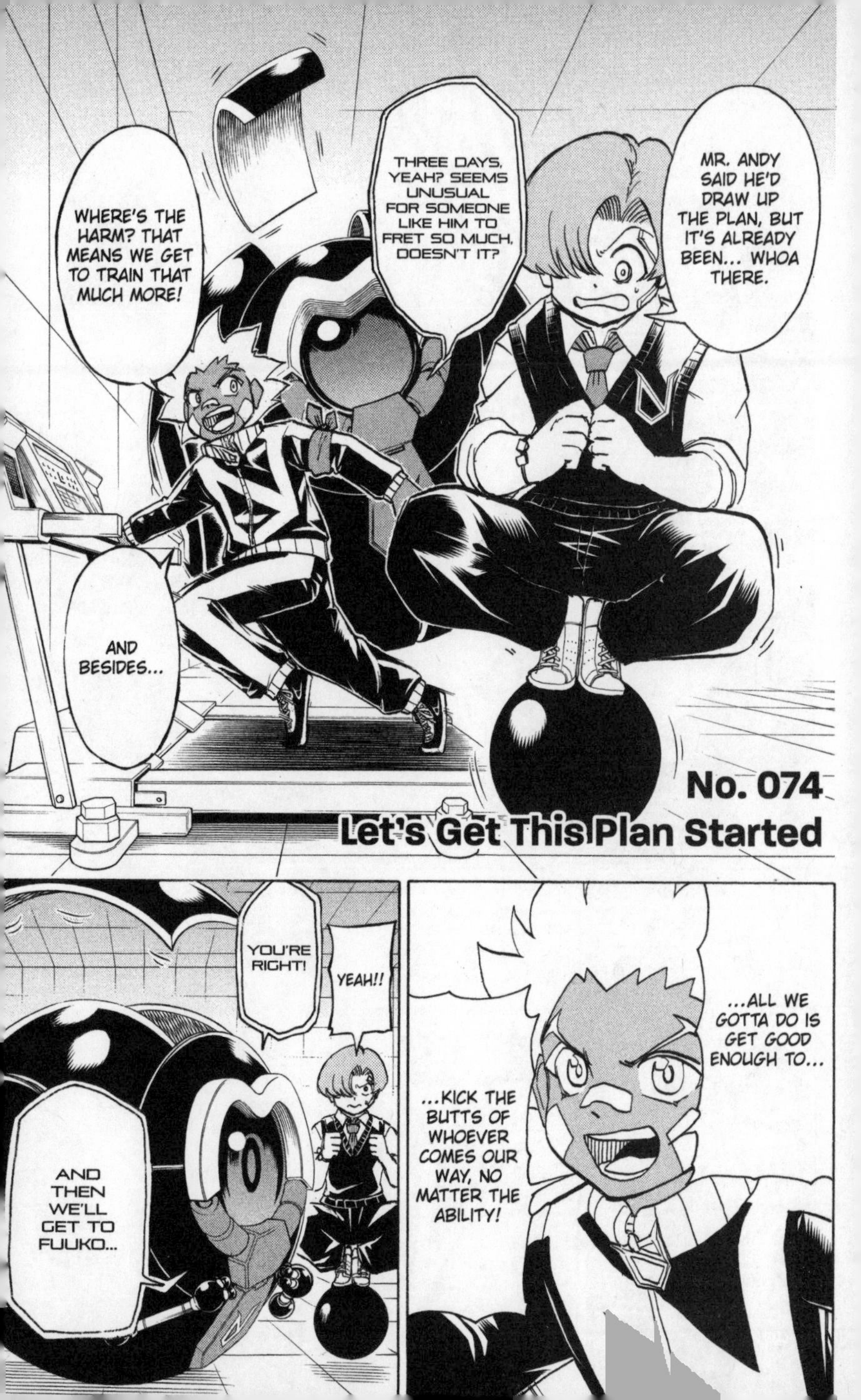
MR. ANDY SAID HE'D DRAW UP THE PLAN, BUT IT'S ALREADY BEEN... WHOA THERE.
THREE DAYS, YEAH? SEEMS UNUSUAL FOR SOMEONE LIKE HIM TO FRET SO MUCH, DOESN'T IT?
WHERE'S THE HARM? THAT MEANS WE GET TO TRAIN THAT MUCH MORE!
AND BESIDES...
No. 074
Let's Get This Plan Started
...ALL WE GOTTA DO IS GET GOOD ENOUGH TO...
...KICK THE BUTTS OF WHOEVER COMES OUR WAY, NO MATTER THE ABILITY!
YOU'RE RIGHT!
YEAH!!
AND THEN WE'LL GET TO FUUKO...

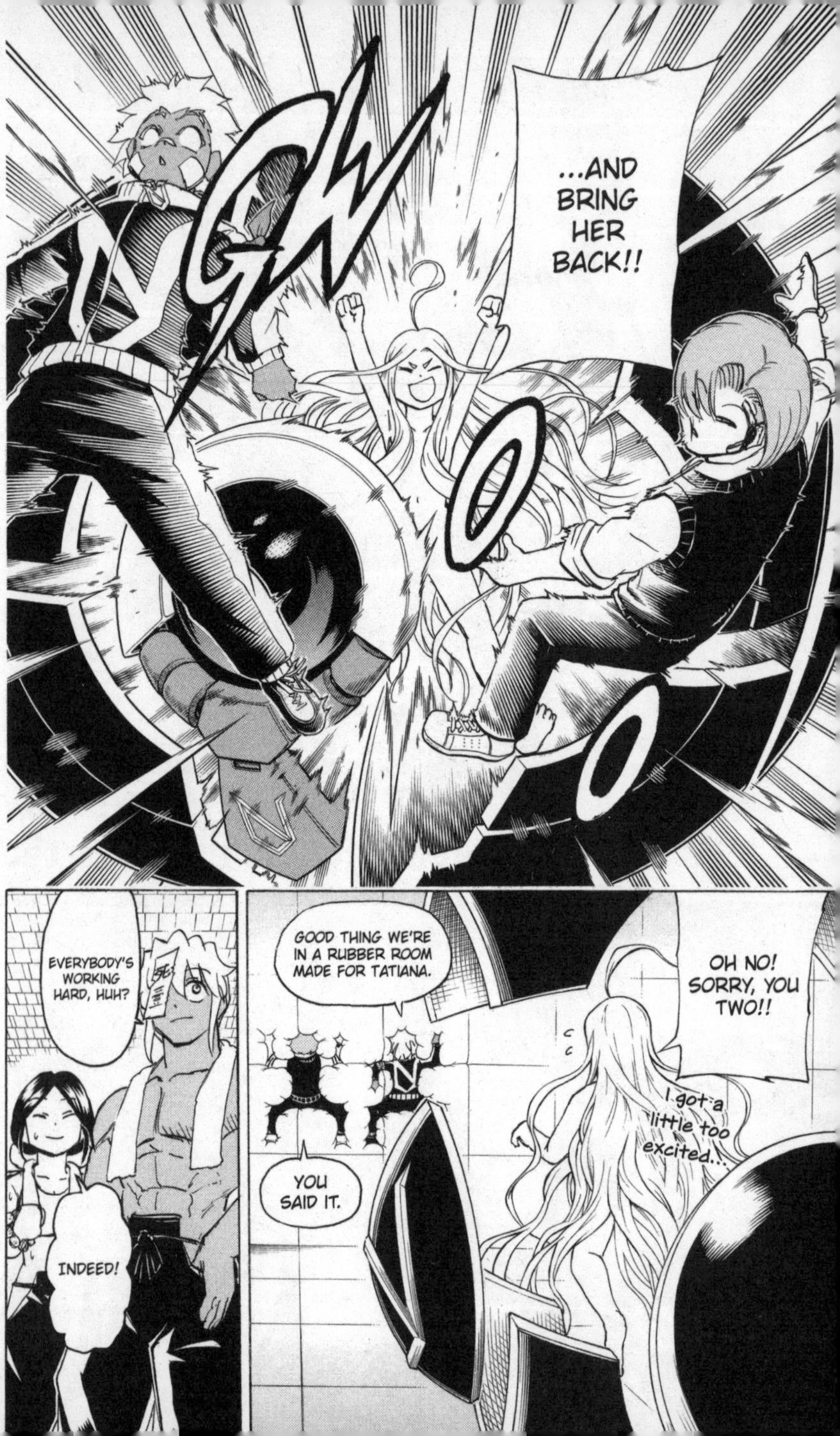
...AND BRING HER BACK!!
OH NO! SORRY, YOU TWO!!
GOOD THING WE'RE IN A RUBBER ROOM MADE FOR TATIANA.
I got a little too excited...
YOU SAID IT.
EVERYBODY'S WORKING HARD, HUH?
INDEED!

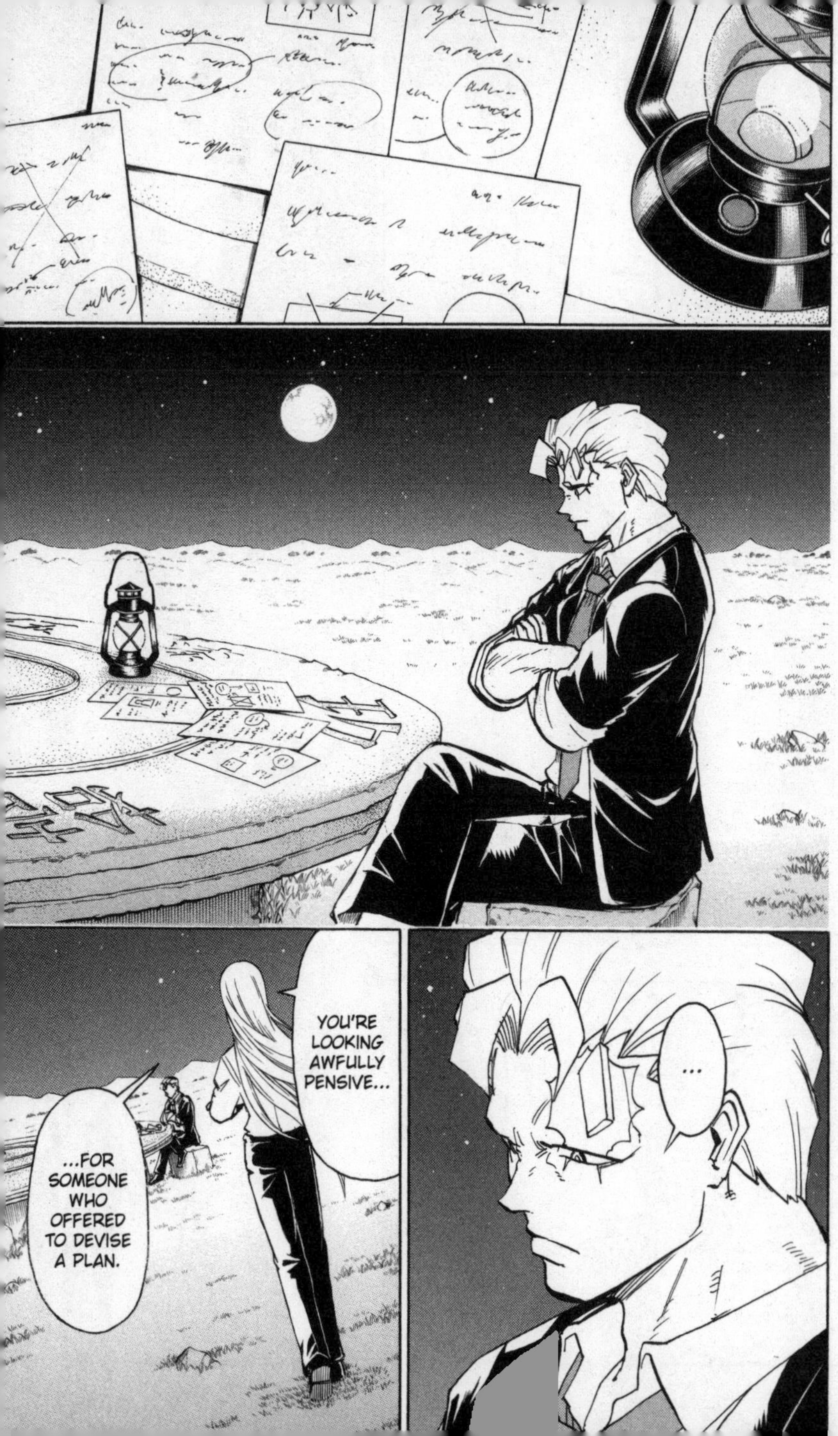
...
YOU'RE LOOKING AWFULLY PENSIVE...
...FOR SOMEONE WHO OFFERED TO DEVISE A PLAN.

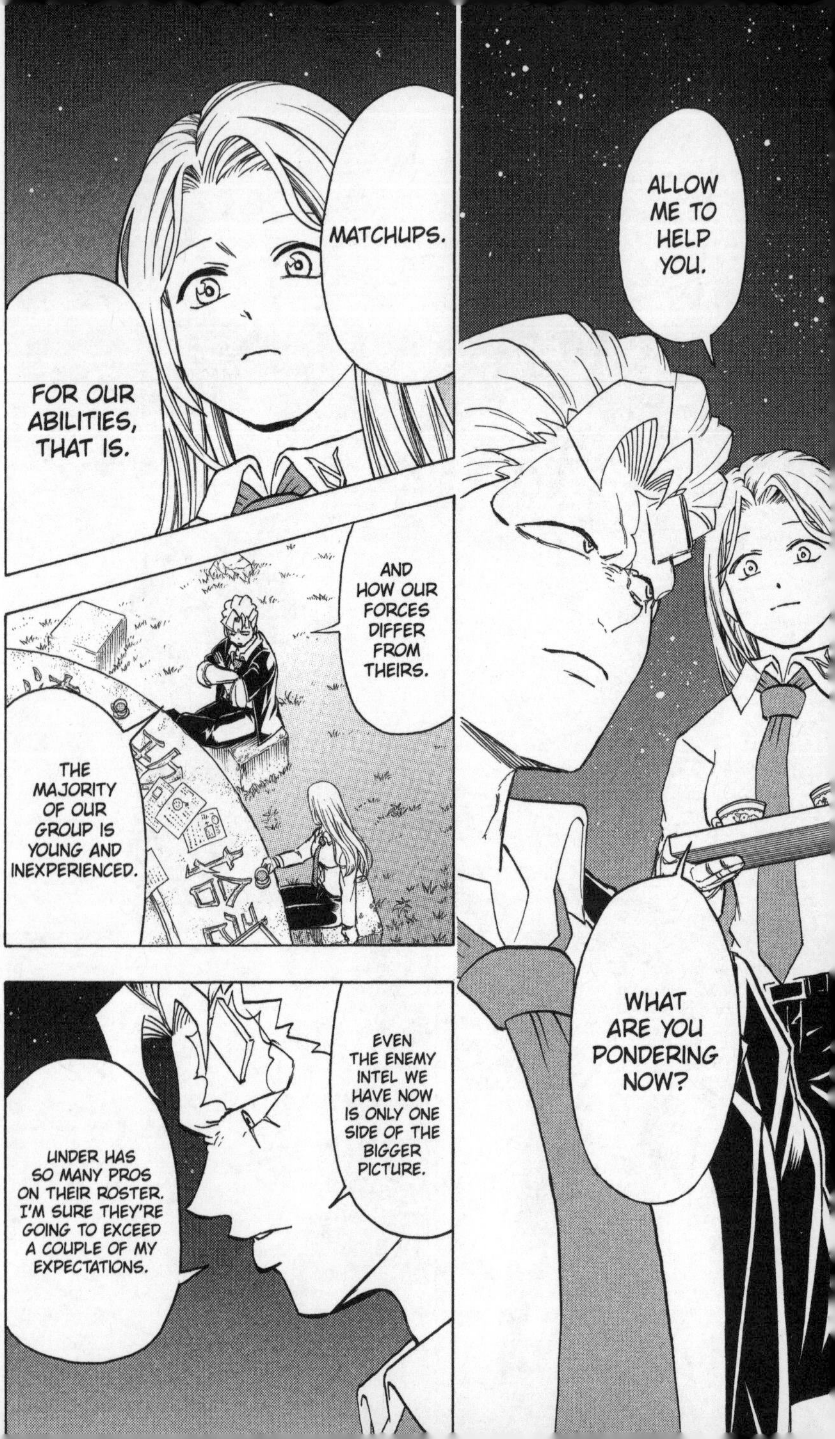
ALLOW ME TO HELP YOU.
WHAT ARE YOU PONDERING NOW?
MATCHUPS.
FOR OUR ABILITIES, THAT IS.
AND HOW OUR FORCES DIFFER FROM THEIRS.
THE MAJORITY OF OUR GROUP IS YOUNG AND INEXPERIENCED.
EVEN THE ENEMY INTEL WE HAVE NOW IS ONLY ONE SIDE OF THE BIGGER PICTURE.
UNDER HAS SO MANY PROS ON THEIR ROSTER. I'M SURE THEY'RE GOING TO EXCEED A COUPLE OF MY EXPECTATIONS.

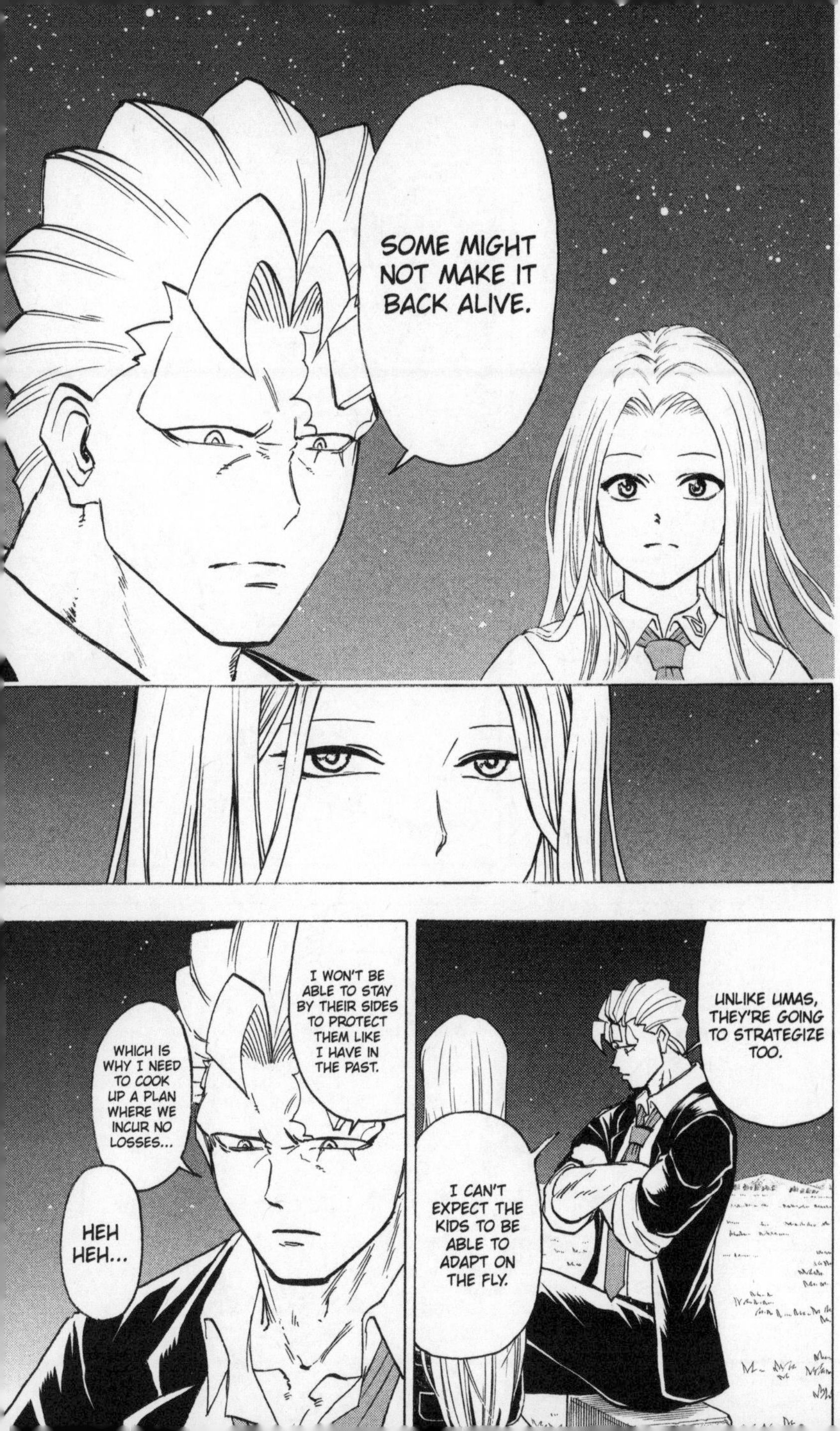
SOME MIGHT NOT MAKE IT BACK ALIVE.
UNLIKE UMAS, THEY'RE GOING TO STRATEGIZE TOO.
I CAN'T EXPECT THE KIDS TO BE ABLE TO ADAPT ON THE FLY.
I WON'T BE ABLE TO STAY BY THEIR SIDES TO PROTECT THEM LIKE I HAVE IN THE PAST.
WHICH IS WHY I NEED TO COOK UP A PLAN WHERE WE INCUR NO LOSSES...
HEH HEH...

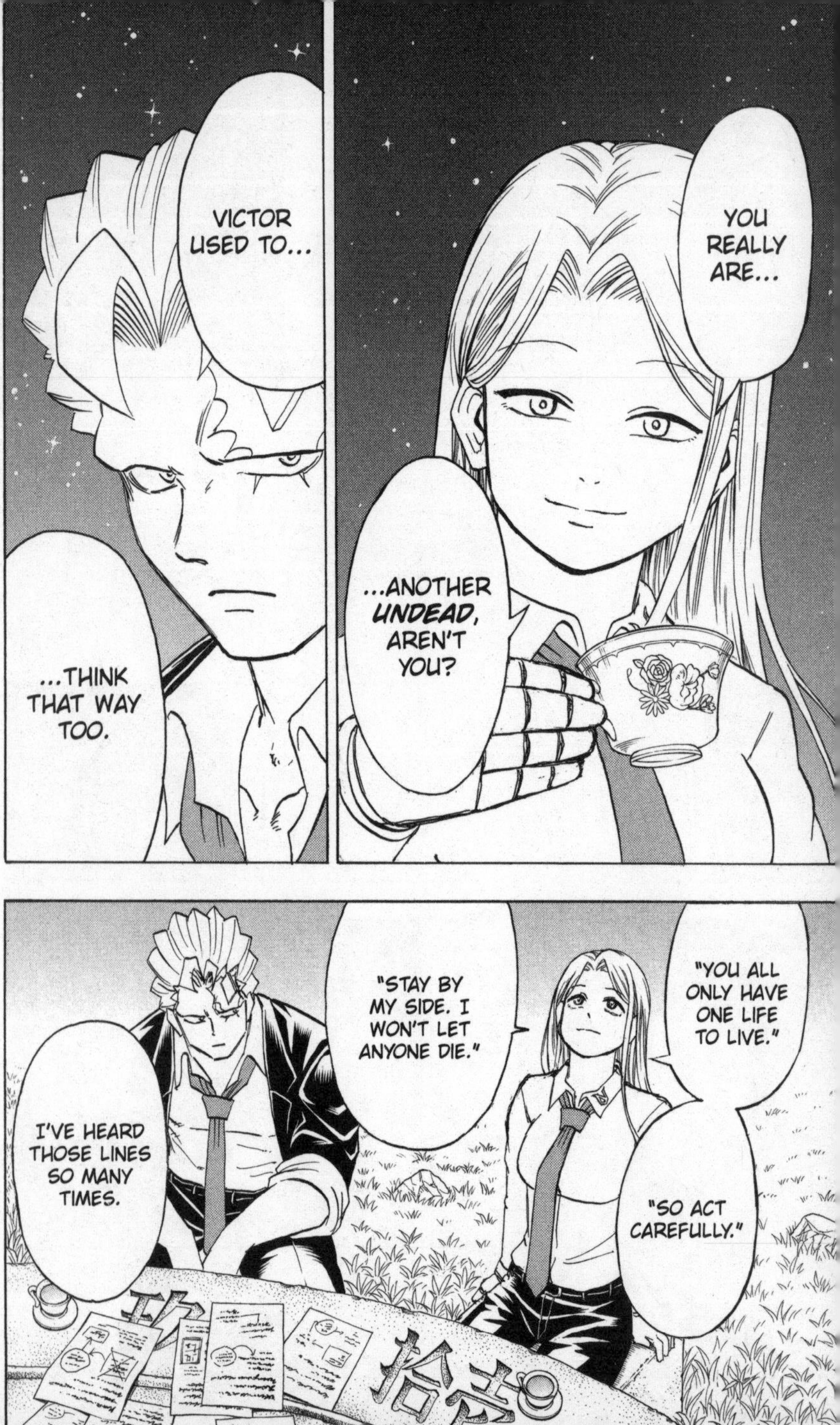
YOU REALLY ARE...
...ANOTHER UNDEAD, AREN'T YOU?
VICTOR USED TO...
...THINK THAT WAY TOO.
"YOU ALL ONLY HAVE ONE LIFE TO LIVE."
"SO ACT CAREFULLY."
"STAY BY MY SIDE. I WON'T LET ANYONE DIE."
I'VE HEARD THOSE LINES SO MANY TIMES.

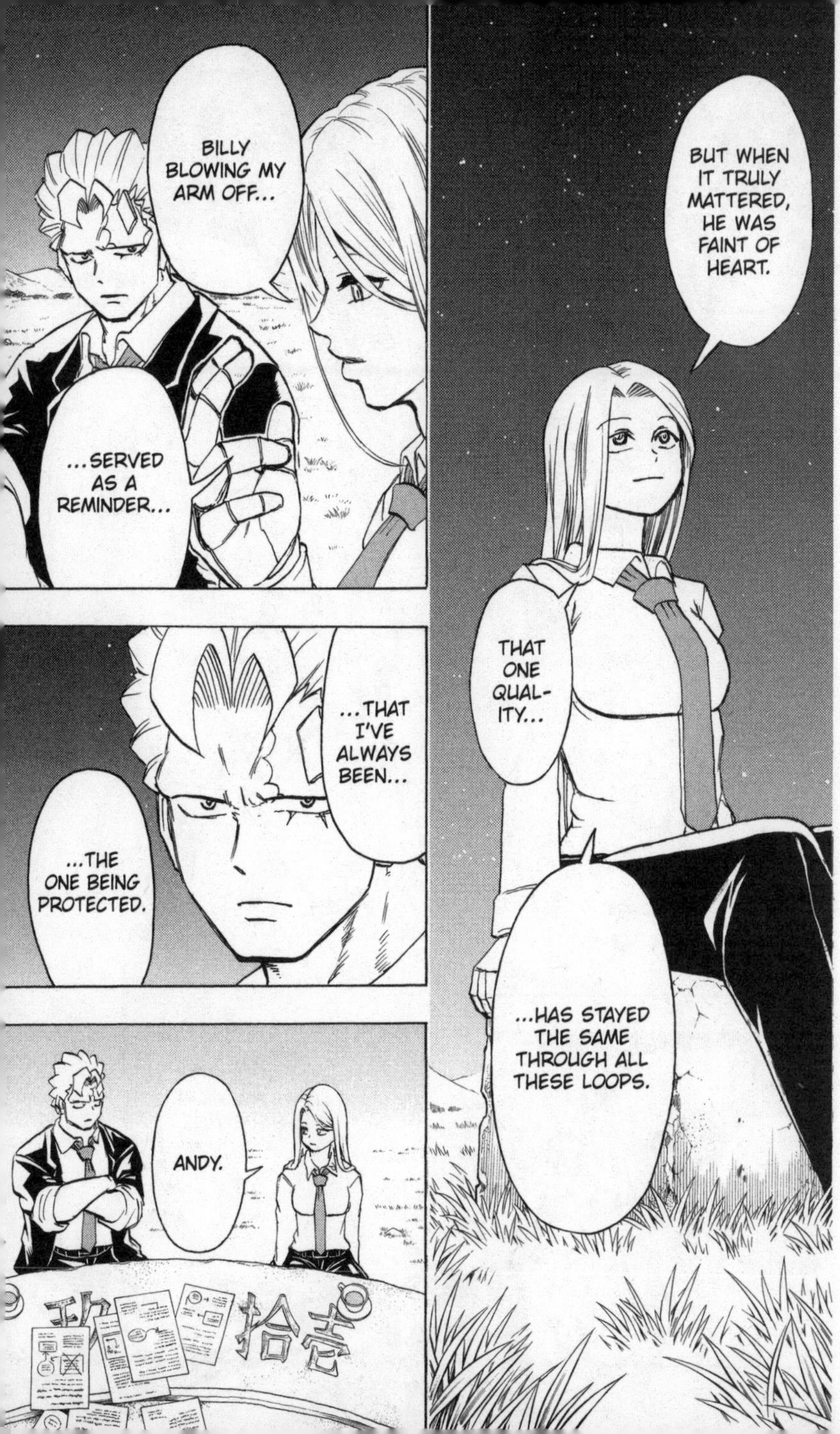

BUT WHEN IT TRULY MATTERED, HE WAS FAINT OF HEART.
THAT ONE QUALITY...
...HAS STAYED THE SAME THROUGH ALL THESE LOOPS.
BILLY BLOWING MY ARM OFF...
...SERVED AS A REMINDER...
...THAT I'VE ALWAYS BEEN...
...THE ONE BEING PROTECTED.
ANDY.
拾壱

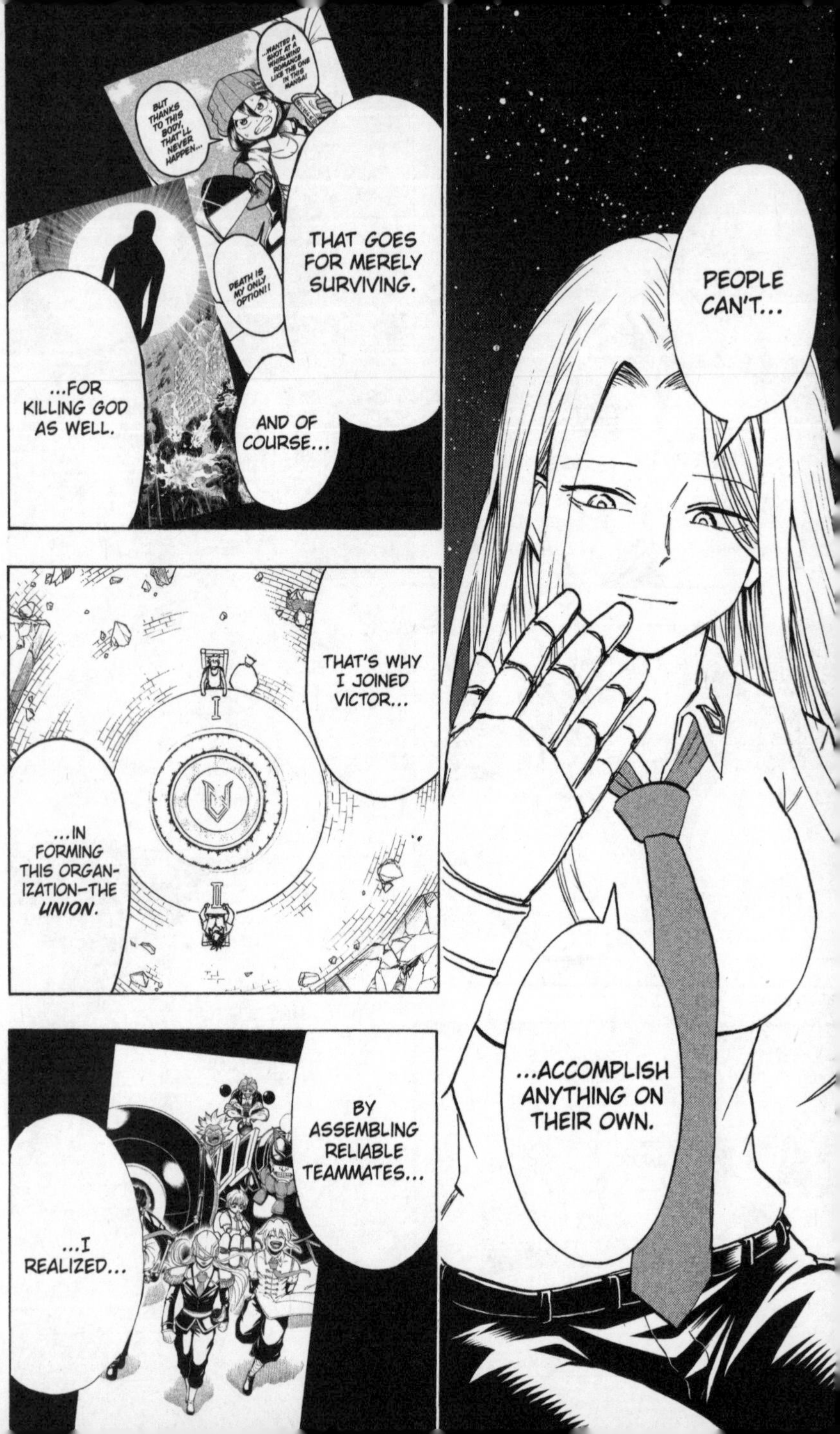
PEOPLE CAN'T...
...ACCOMPLISH ANYTHING ON THEIR OWN.
...WANTED A SHOT AT A WHIRLWIND ROMANCE LIKE THE ONE IN THIS MANGA!
BUT THANKS TO THIS BODY, THAT'LL NEVER HAPPEN...
DEATH IS MY ONLY OPTION!!
THAT GOES FOR MERELY SURVIVING.
AND OF COURSE...
...FOR KILLING GOD AS WELL.
THAT'S WHY I JOINED VICTOR...
...IN FORMING THIS ORGAN-IZATION—THE *UNION*.
BY ASSEMBLING RELIABLE TEAMMATES...
...I REALIZED...

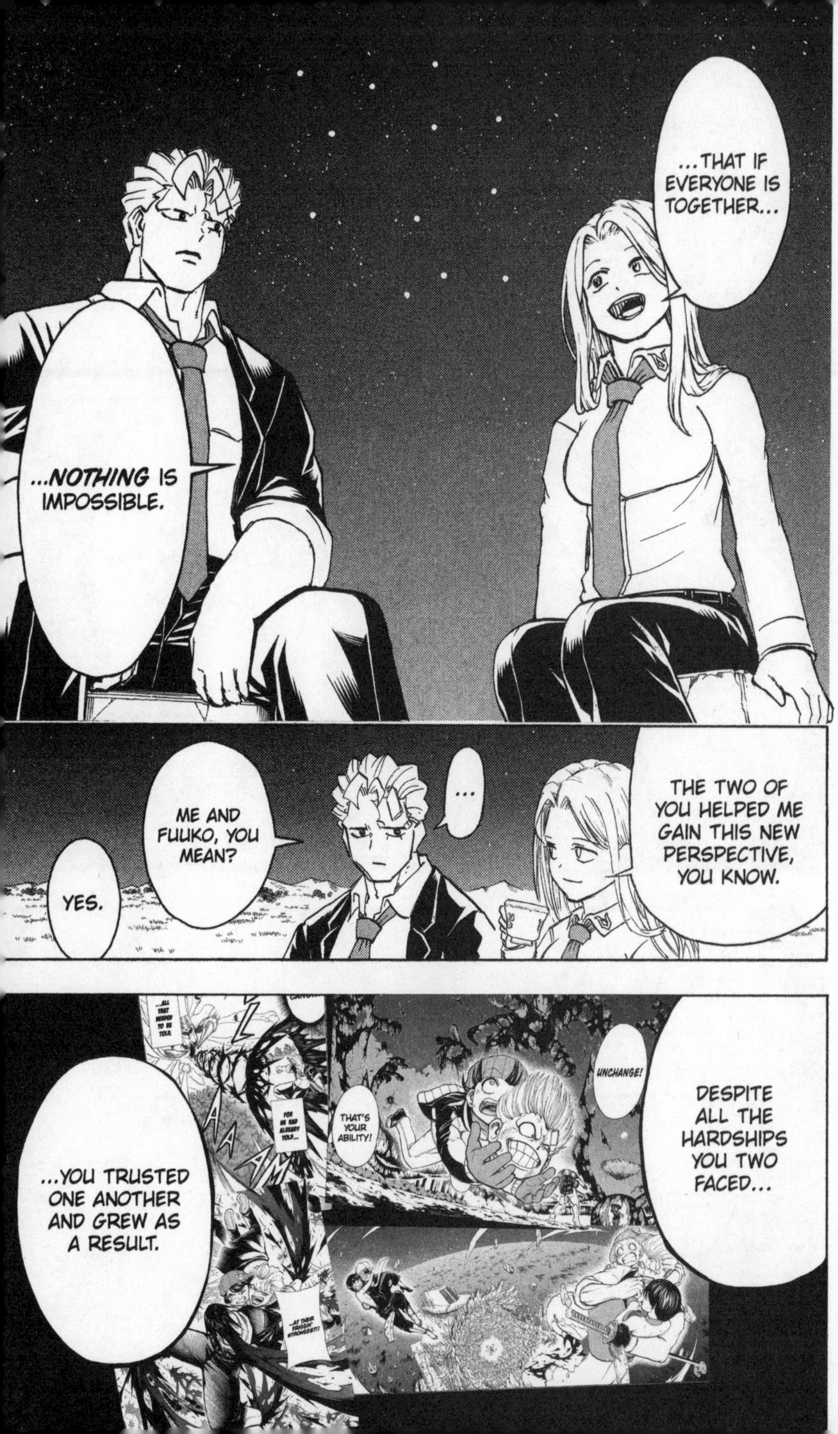
...THAT IF EVERYONE IS TOGETHER...
...*NOTHING* IS IMPOSSIBLE.
THE TWO OF YOU HELPED ME GAIN THIS NEW PERSPECTIVE, YOU KNOW.
...
ME AND FUUKO, YOU MEAN?
YES.
DESPITE ALL THE HARDSHIPS YOU TWO FACED...
UNCHANGE!
THAT'S YOUR ABILITY!
...YOU TRUSTED ONE ANOTHER AND GREW AS A RESULT.

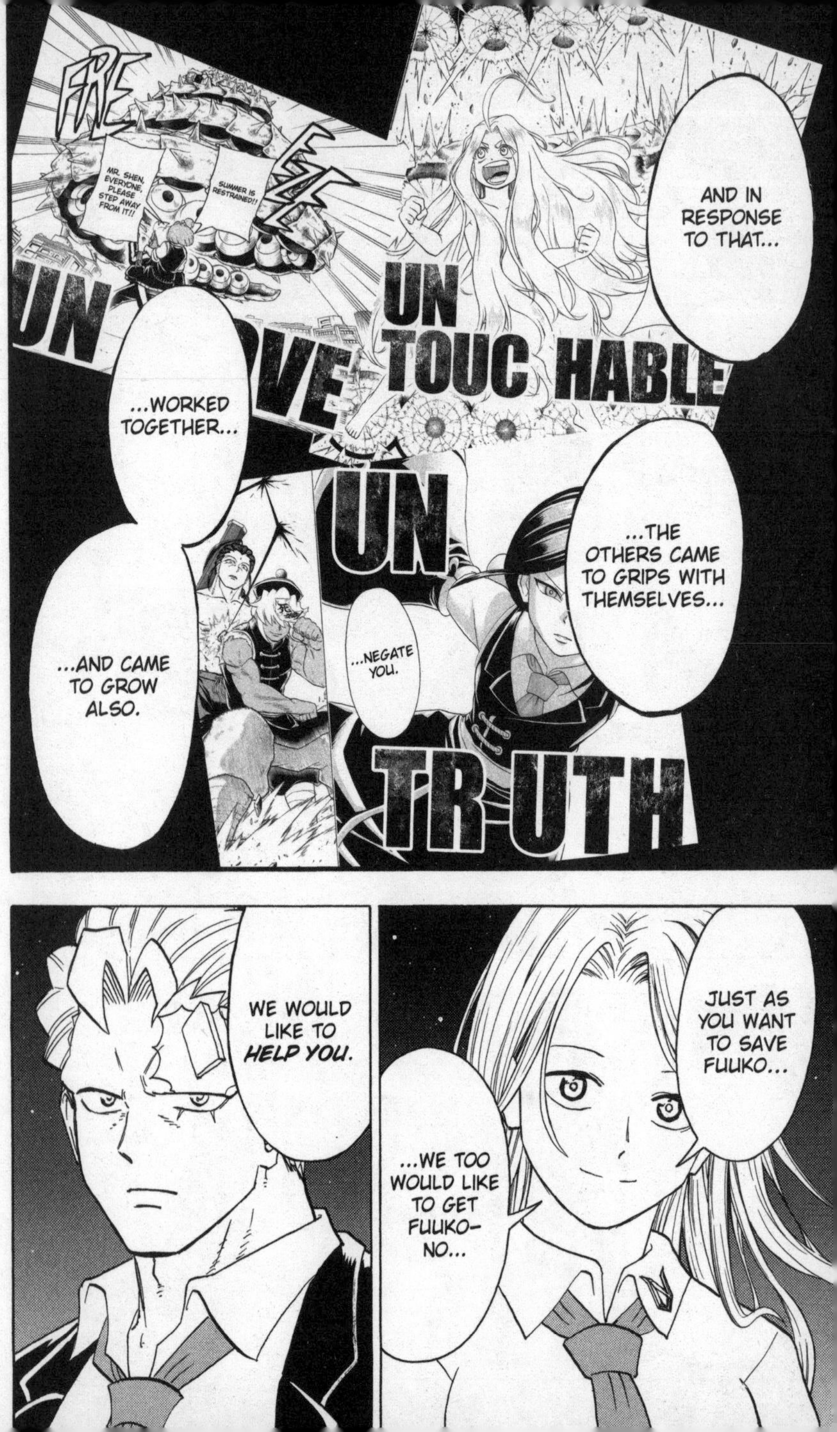
AND IN RESPONSE TO THAT...
UN TOUC HABLE
SUMMER IS RESTRAINED!!
MR. SHEN, EVERYONE, PLEASE STEP AWAY FROM IT!!
FRE EZE
UN VE
...WORKED TOGETHER...
...THE OTHERS CAME TO GRIPS WITH THEMSELVES...
UN
...NEGATE YOU.
TR-UTH
...AND CAME TO GROW ALSO.
JUST AS YOU WANT TO SAVE FUUKO...
...WE TOO WOULD LIKE TO GET FUUKO-NO...
WE WOULD LIKE TO *HELP YOU*.

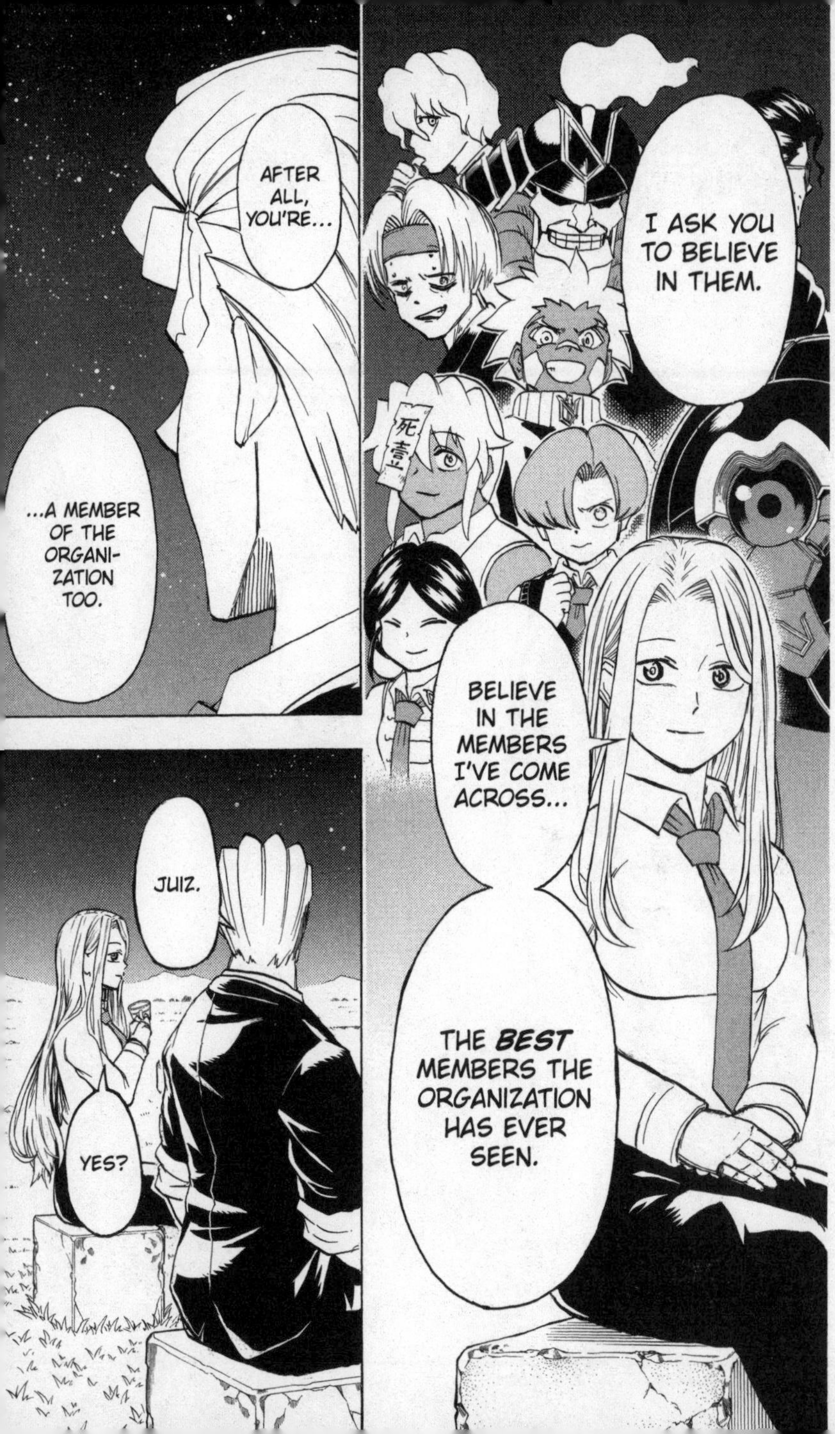
I ASK YOU TO BELIEVE IN THEM.
死壹
BELIEVE IN THE MEMBERS I'VE COME ACROSS...
THE *BEST* MEMBERS THE ORGANIZATION HAS EVER SEEN.
AFTER ALL, YOU'RE...
...A MEMBER OF THE ORGANI-ZATION TOO.
JUIZ.
YES?

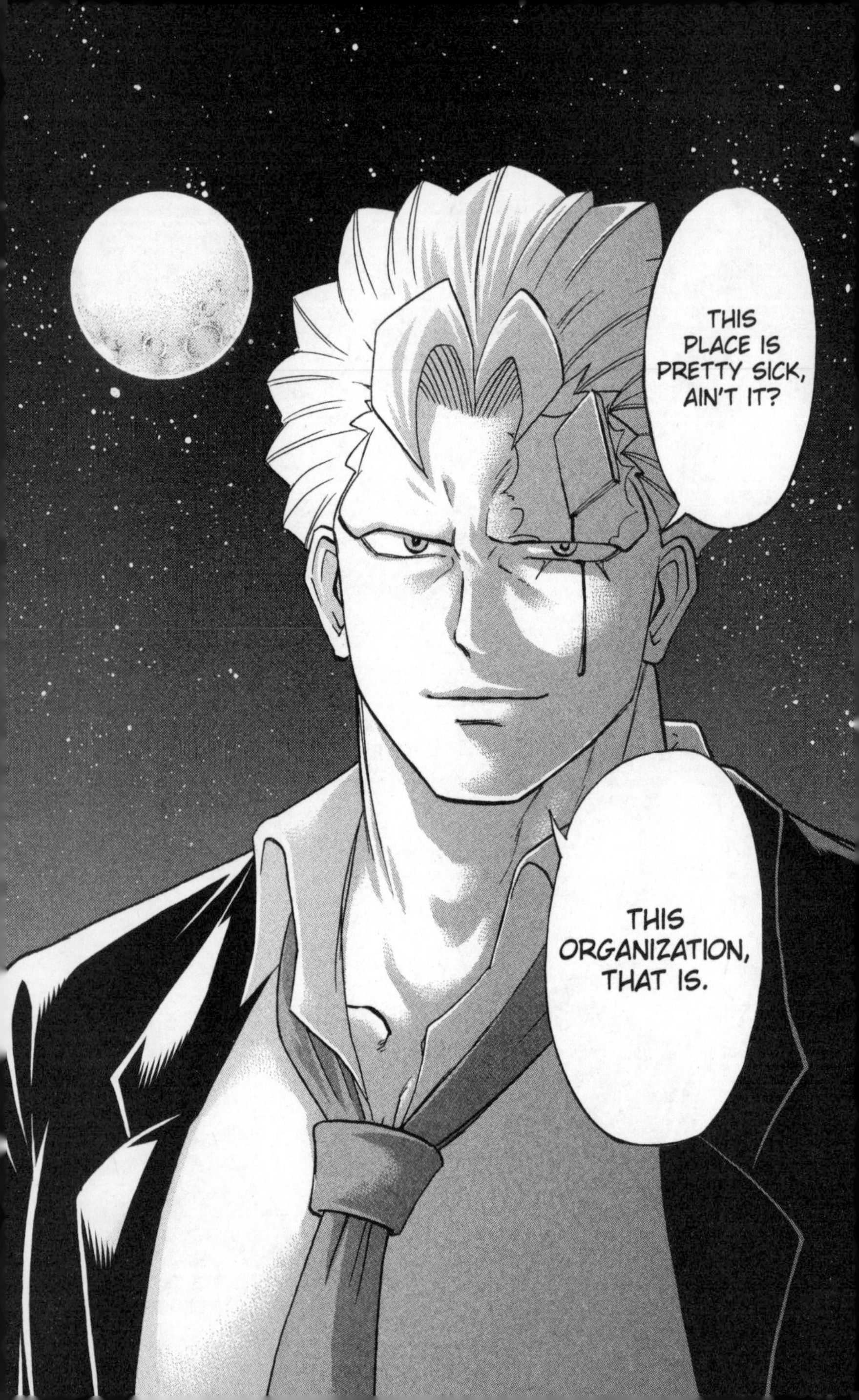
THIS PLACE IS PRETTY SICK, AIN'T IT?
THIS ORGANIZATION, THAT IS.

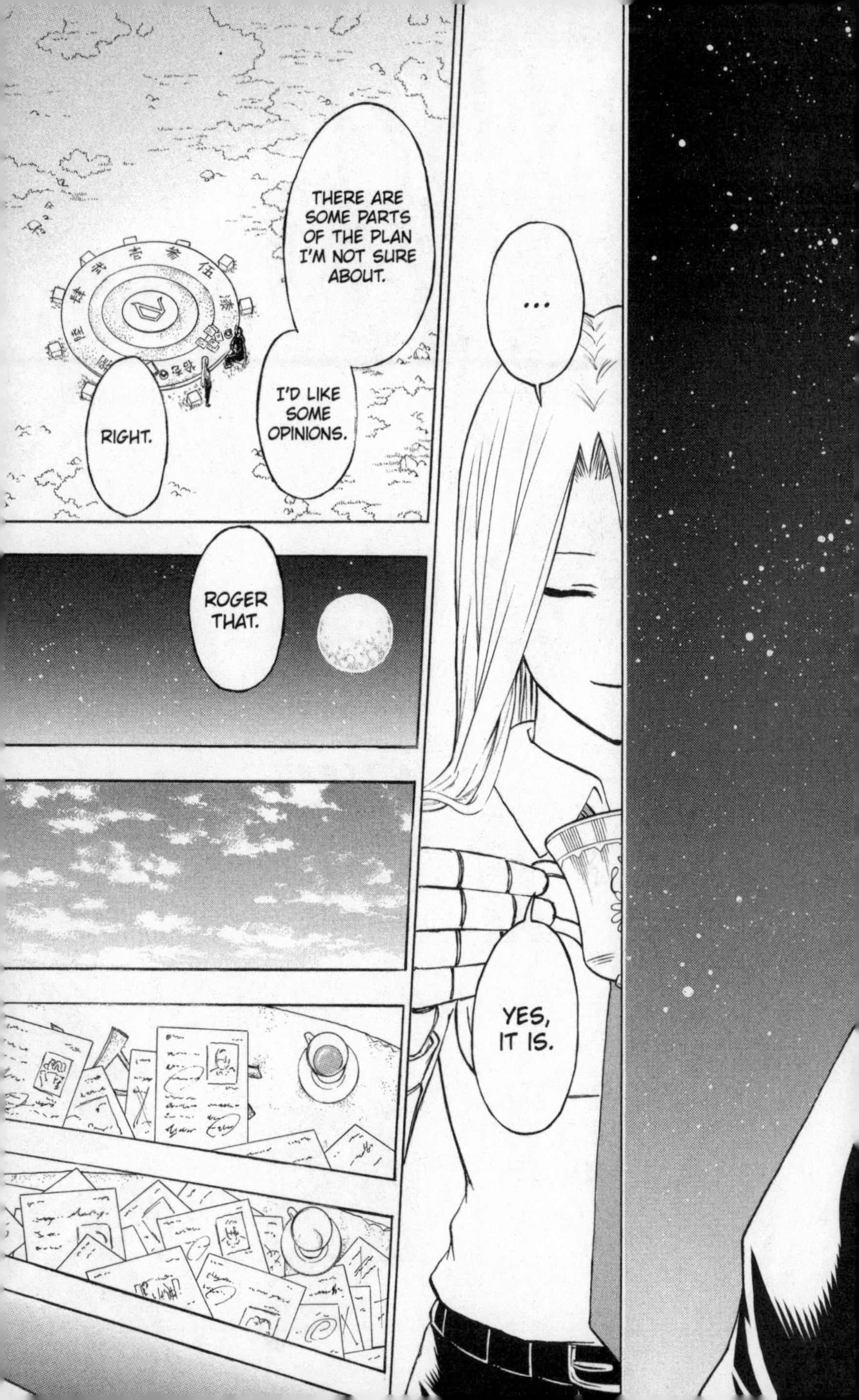
...
YES, IT IS.
THERE ARE SOME PARTS OF THE PLAN I'M NOT SURE ABOUT.
I'D LIKE SOME OPINIONS.
RIGHT.
ROGER THAT.

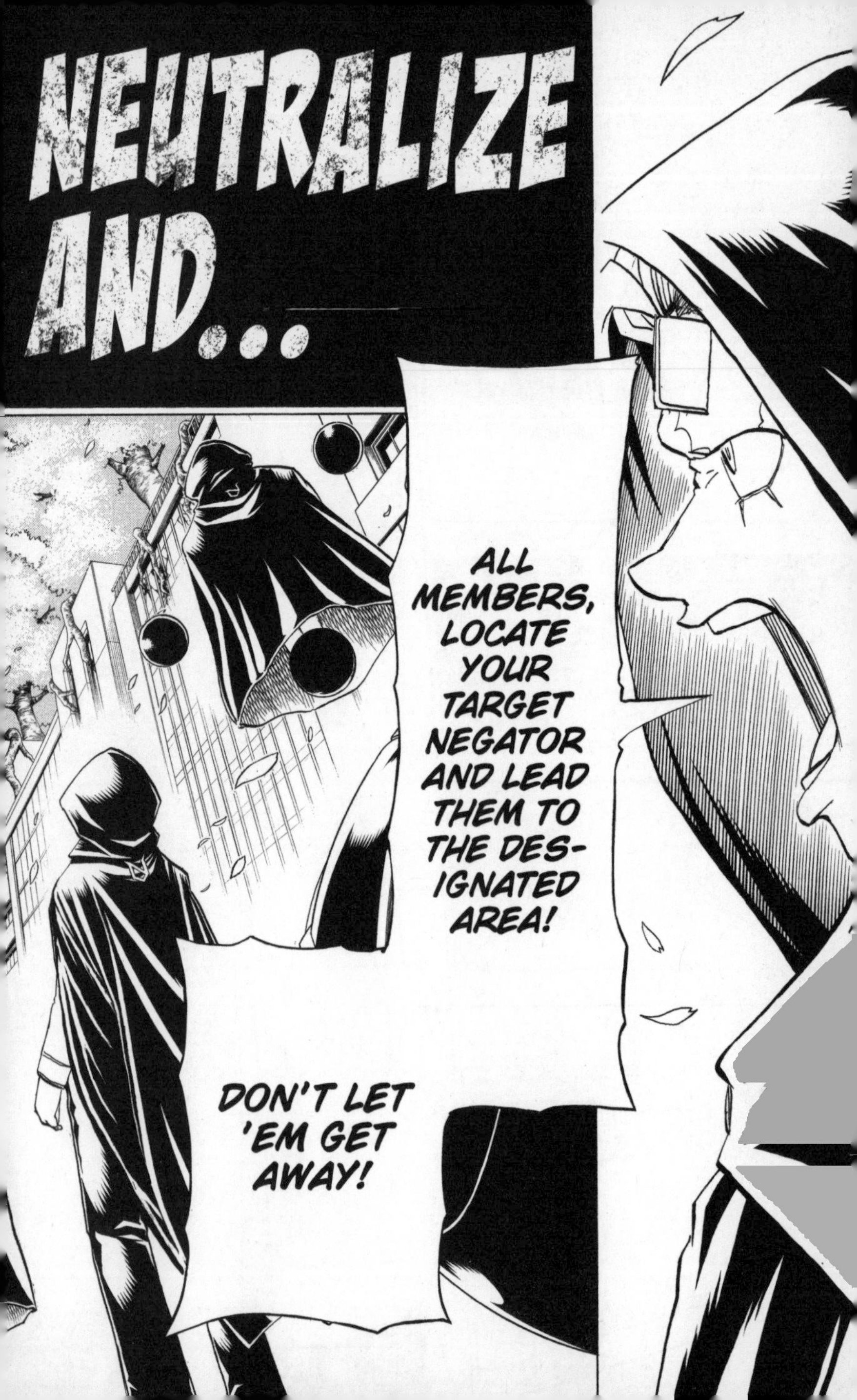
ALL MEMBERS, LOCATE YOUR TARGET NEGATOR AND LEAD THEM TO THE DES-IGNATED AREA!
DON'T LET 'EM GET AWAY!
NEUTRALIZE AND...

OPERATION: UMA SPRING

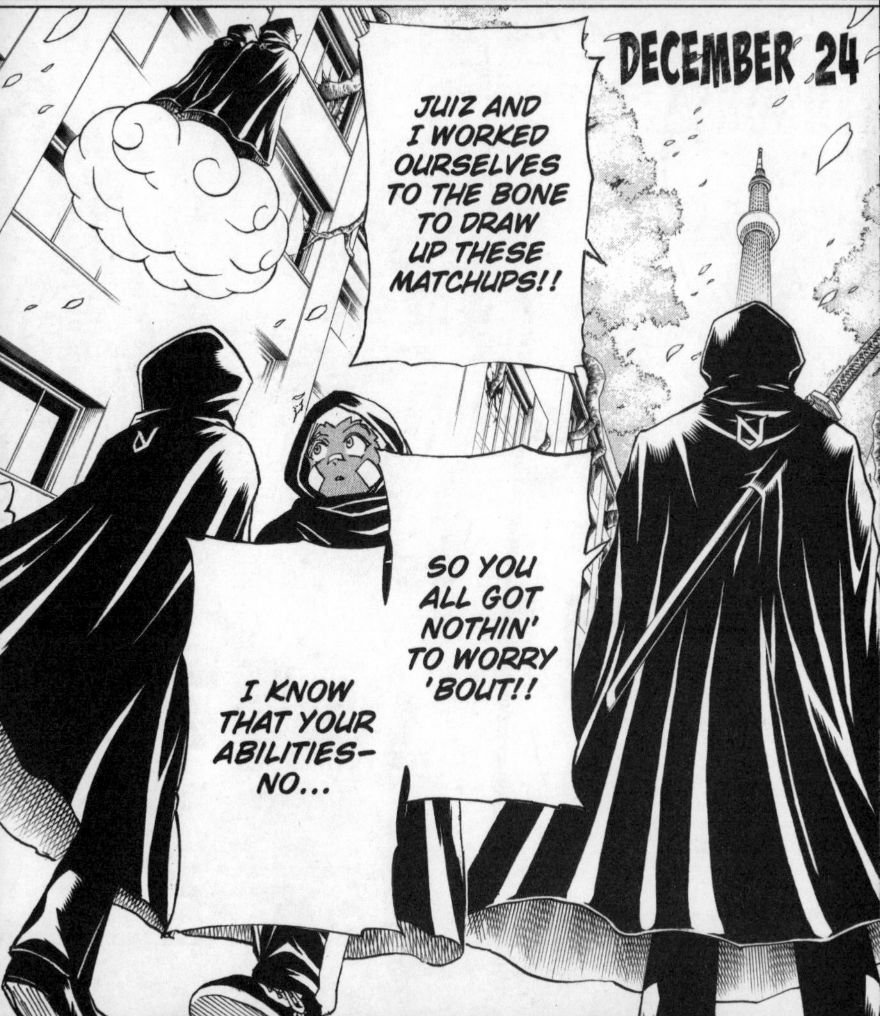
DECEMBER 24
JUIZ AND I WORKED OURSELVES TO THE BONE TO DRAW UP THESE MATCHUPS!!
SO YOU ALL GOT NOTHIN' TO WORRY 'BOUT!!
I KNOW THAT YOUR ABILITIES— NO...

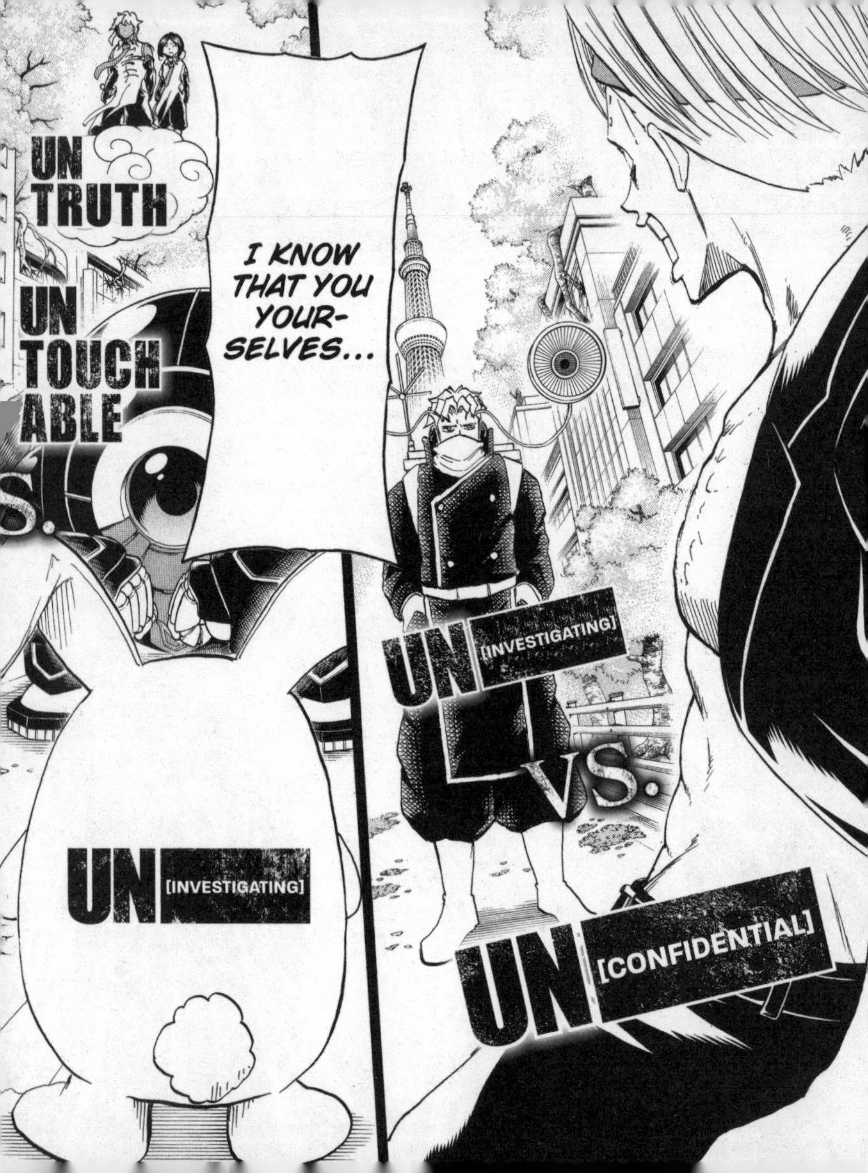
UN [INVESTIGATING]
VS.
UN [CONFIDENTIAL]
I KNOW THAT YOU YOURSELVES...
UN TRUTH
UN TOUCHABLE
UN [INVESTIGATING]

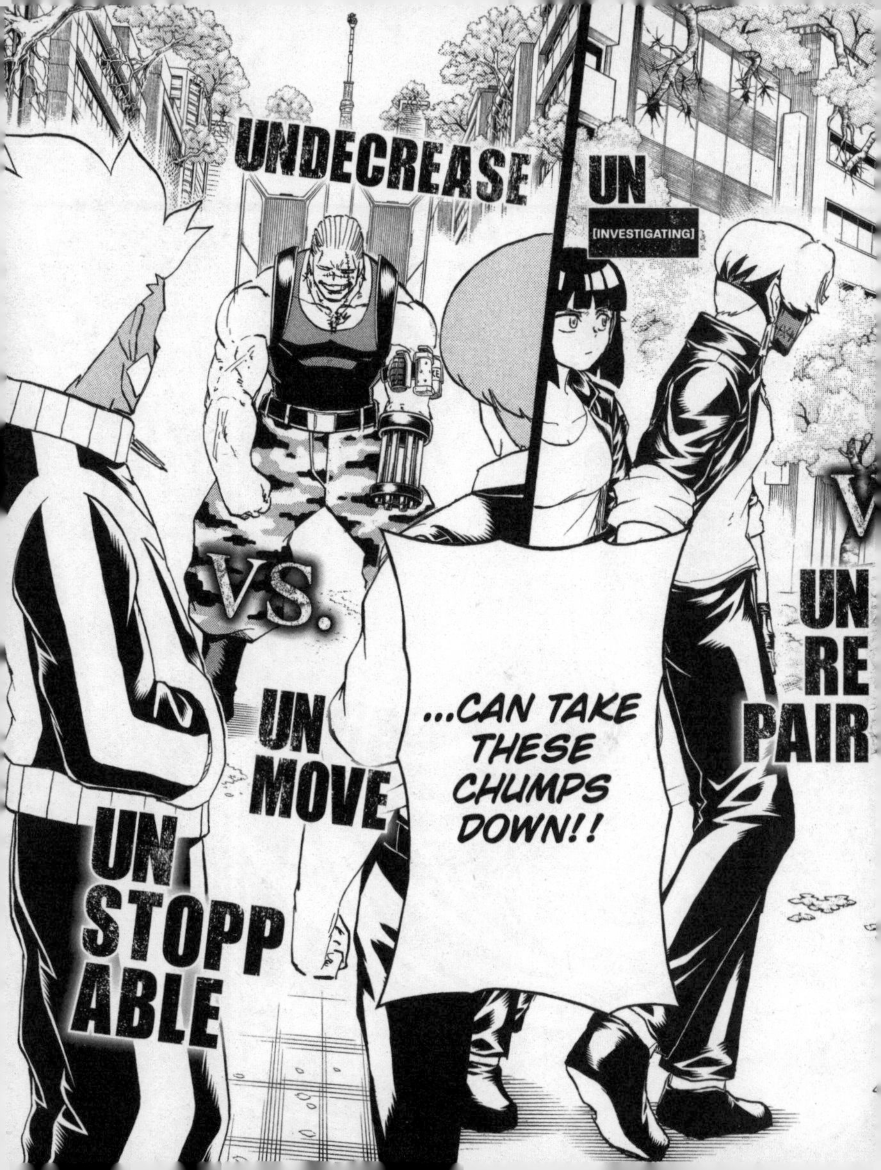
UN
[INVESTIGATING]
UNDECREASE
UN RE PAIR
VS.
...CAN TAKE THESE CHUMPS DOWN!!
UN MOVE
UN STOPP ABLE

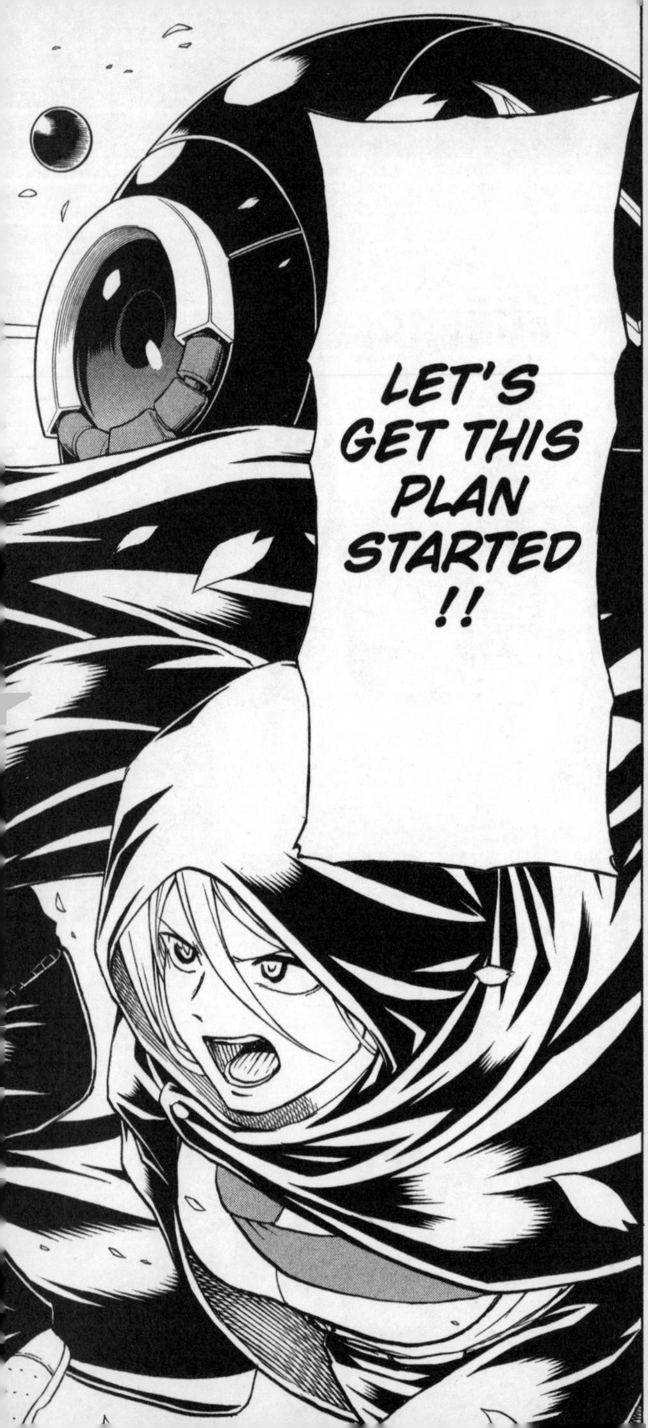
LET'S GET THIS PLAN STARTED !!

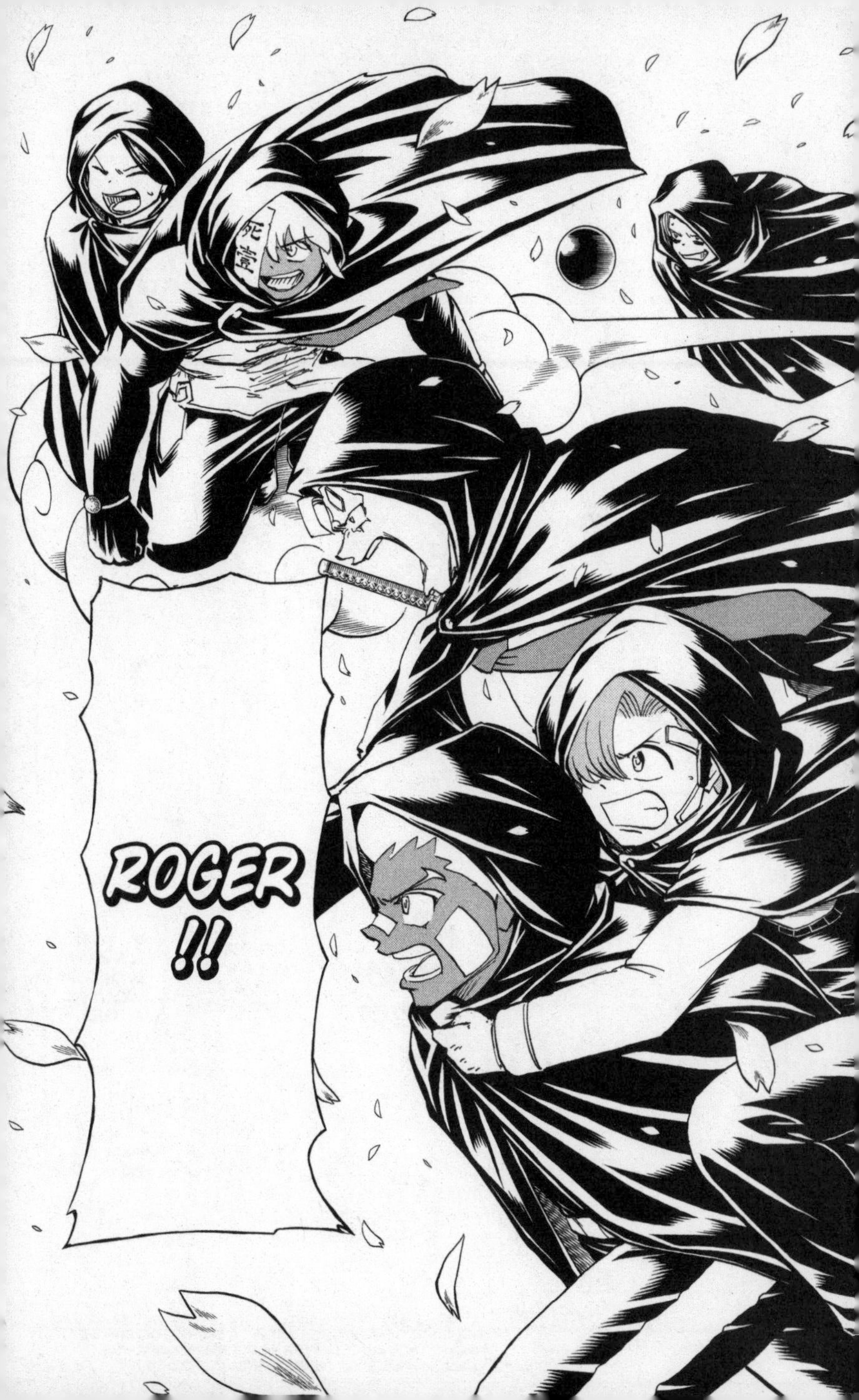
ROGER !!

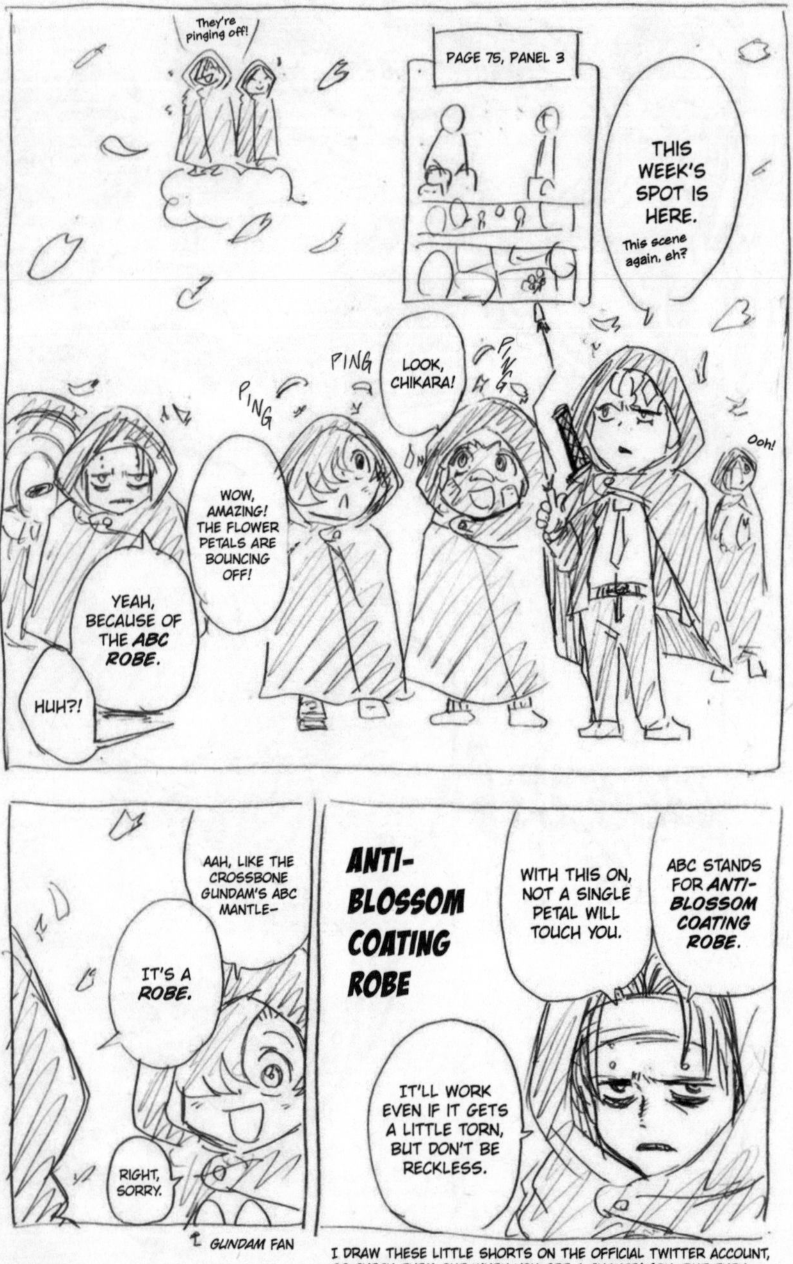
THIS WEEK'S SPOT IS HERE.
This scene again, eh?
PAGE 75, PANEL 3
They're pinging off!
Ooh!
PING
LOOK, CHIKARA!
PING
PING
WOW, AMAZING! THE FLOWER PETALS ARE BOUNCING OFF!
YEAH, BECAUSE OF THE ABC ROBE.
HUH?!
Good thing I don't need one of those things.
ABC STANDS FOR ANTI-BLOSSOM COATING ROBE.
WITH THIS ON, NOT A SINGLE PETAL WILL TOUCH YOU.
ANTI-BLOSSOM COATING ROBE
IT'LL WORK EVEN IF IT GETS A LITTLE TORN, BUT DON'T BE RECKLESS.
AAH, LIKE THE CROSSBONE GUNDAM'S ABC MANTLE–
IT'S A ROBE.
RIGHT, SORRY.
GUNDAM FAN

I DRAW THESE LITTLE SHORTS ON THE OFFICIAL TWITTER ACCOUNT, SO CHECK THEM OUT WHEN YOU GET A CHANCE! (OH, BUT THEY MIGHT CONTAIN SPOILERS FOR PEOPLE KEEPING UP VIA THE GRAPHIC NOVELS, SO TREAD CAREFULLY! –TOZUKA)

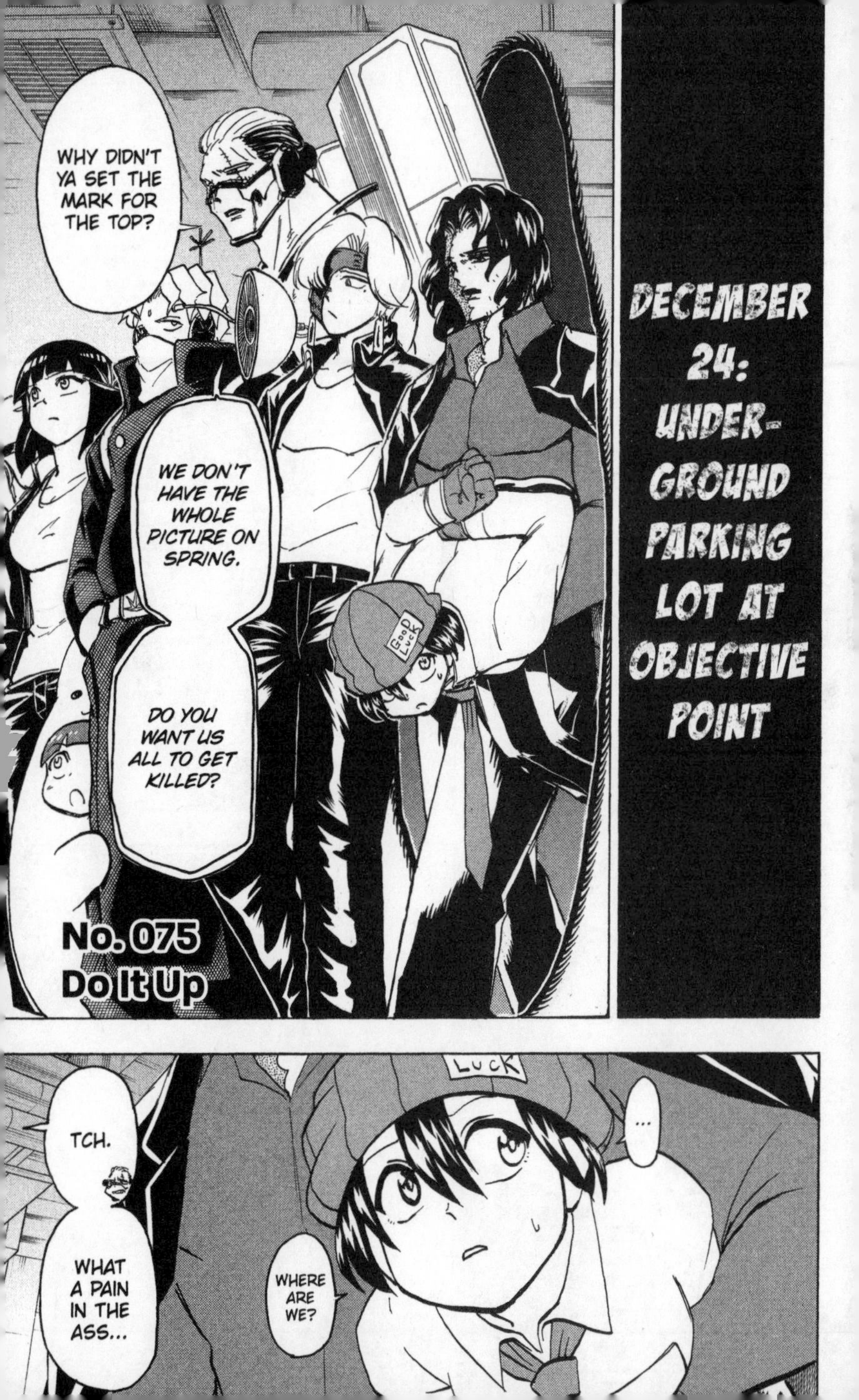
DECEMBER 24: UNDER-GROUND PARKING LOT AT OBJECTIVE POINT
WHY DIDN'T YA SET THE MARK FOR THE TOP?
WE DON'T HAVE THE WHOLE PICTURE ON SPRING.
DO YOU WANT US ALL TO GET KILLED?
GOOD LUCK
No. 075
Do It Up
LUCK
...
WHERE ARE WE?
TCH.
WHAT A PAIN IN THE ASS...

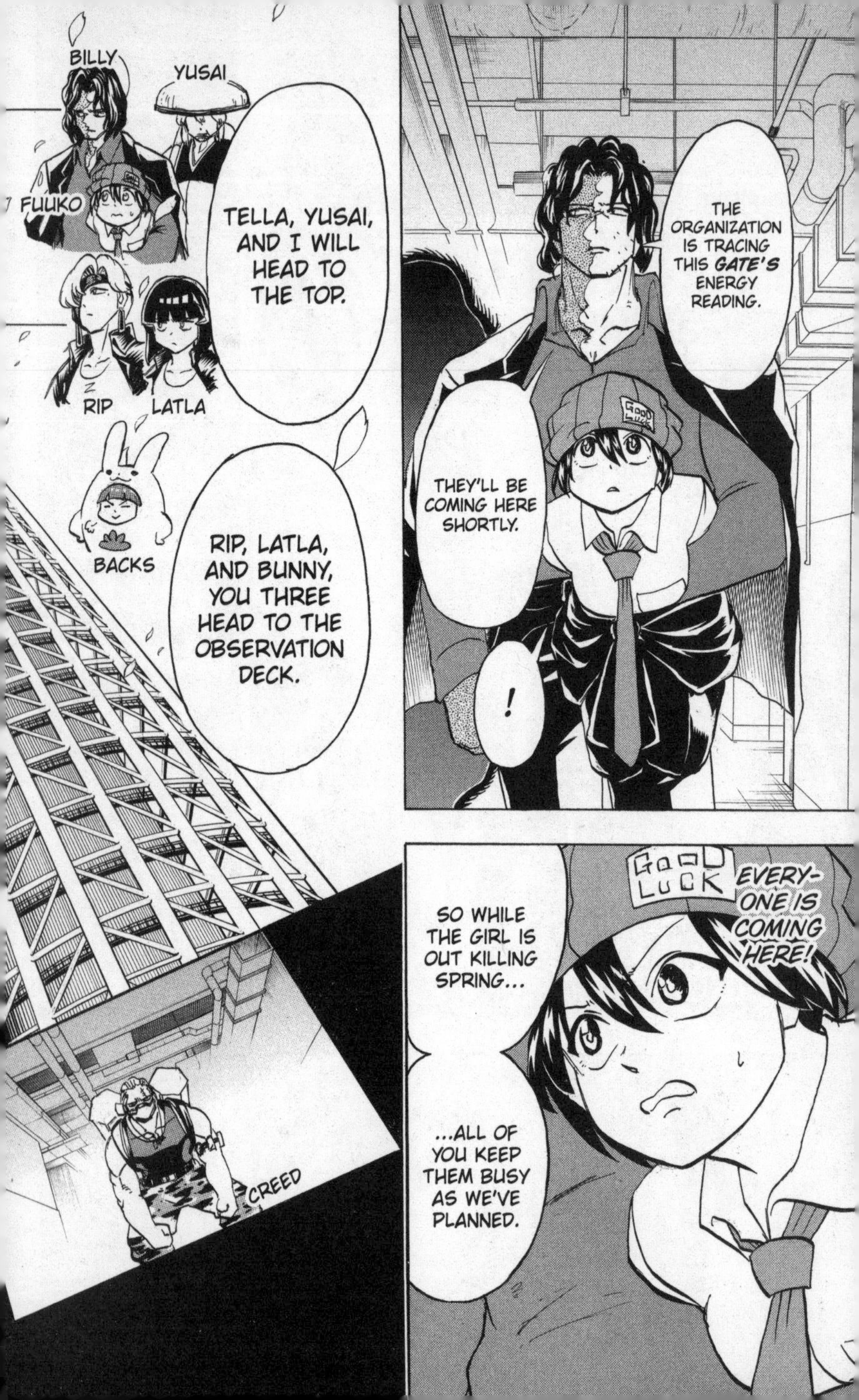

THE ORGANIZATION IS TRACING THIS *GATE'S* ENERGY READING.
THEY'LL BE COMING HERE SHORTLY.
!
GOOD LUCK
SO WHILE THE GIRL IS OUT KILLING SPRING...
...ALL OF YOU KEEP THEM BUSY AS WE'VE PLANNED.
EVERY-ONE IS COMING HERE!
BILLY
YUSAI
FUUKO
TELLA, YUSAI, AND I WILL HEAD TO THE TOP.
RIP
LATLA
BACKS
RIP, LATLA, AND BUNNY, YOU THREE HEAD TO THE OBSERVATION DECK.
CREED

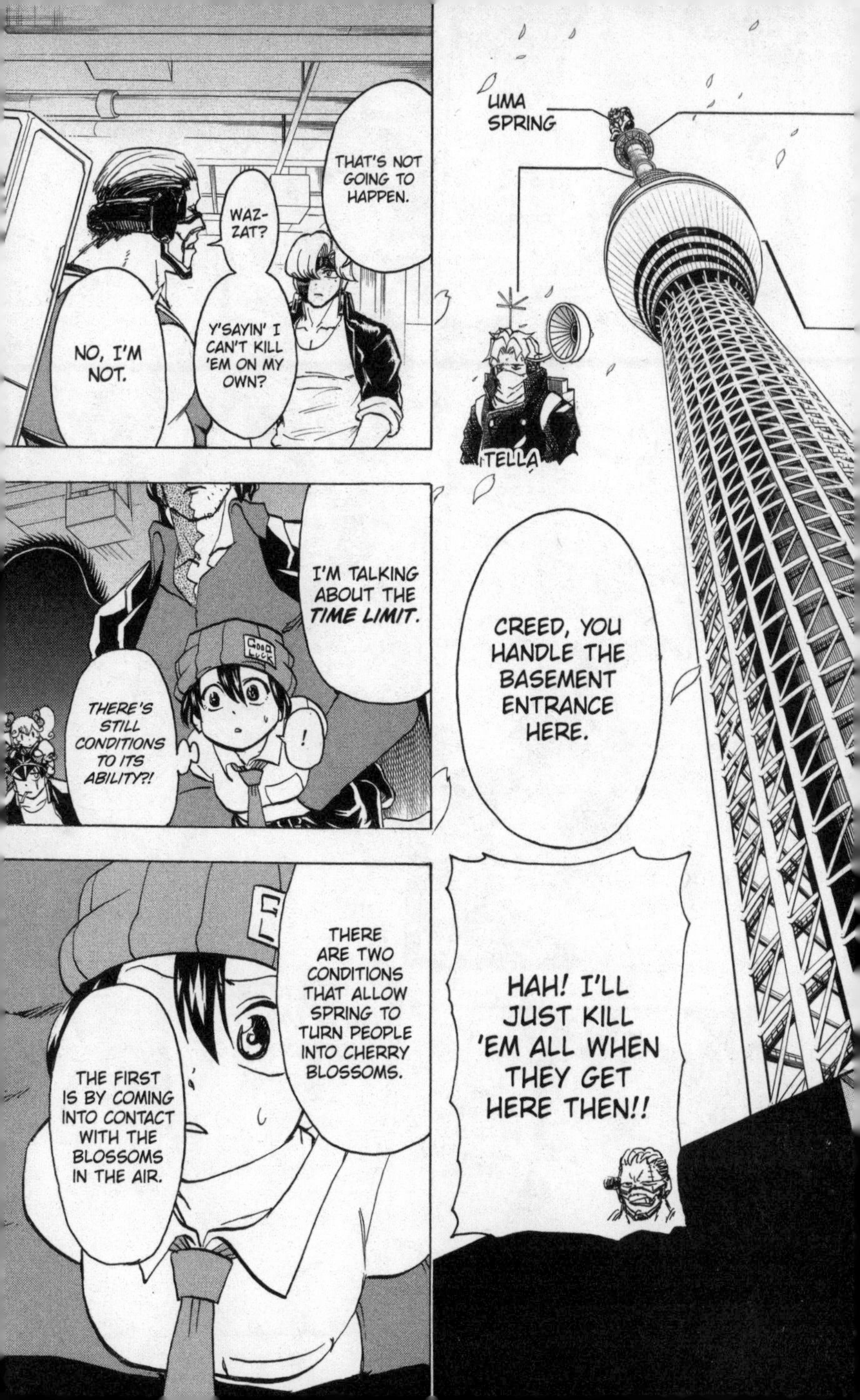
UMA SPRING
TELLA
CREED, YOU HANDLE THE BASEMENT ENTRANCE HERE.
HAH! I'LL JUST KILL 'EM ALL WHEN THEY GET HERE THEN!!
THAT'S NOT GOING TO HAPPEN.
WAZ-ZAT?
Y'SAYIN' I CAN'T KILL 'EM ON MY OWN?
NO, I'M NOT.
I'M TALKING ABOUT THE *TIME LIMIT*.
!
THERE'S STILL CONDITIONS TO ITS ABILITY?!
THERE ARE TWO CONDITIONS THAT ALLOW SPRING TO TURN PEOPLE INTO CHERRY BLOSSOMS.
THE FIRST IS BY COMING INTO CONTACT WITH THE BLOSSOMS IN THE AIR.

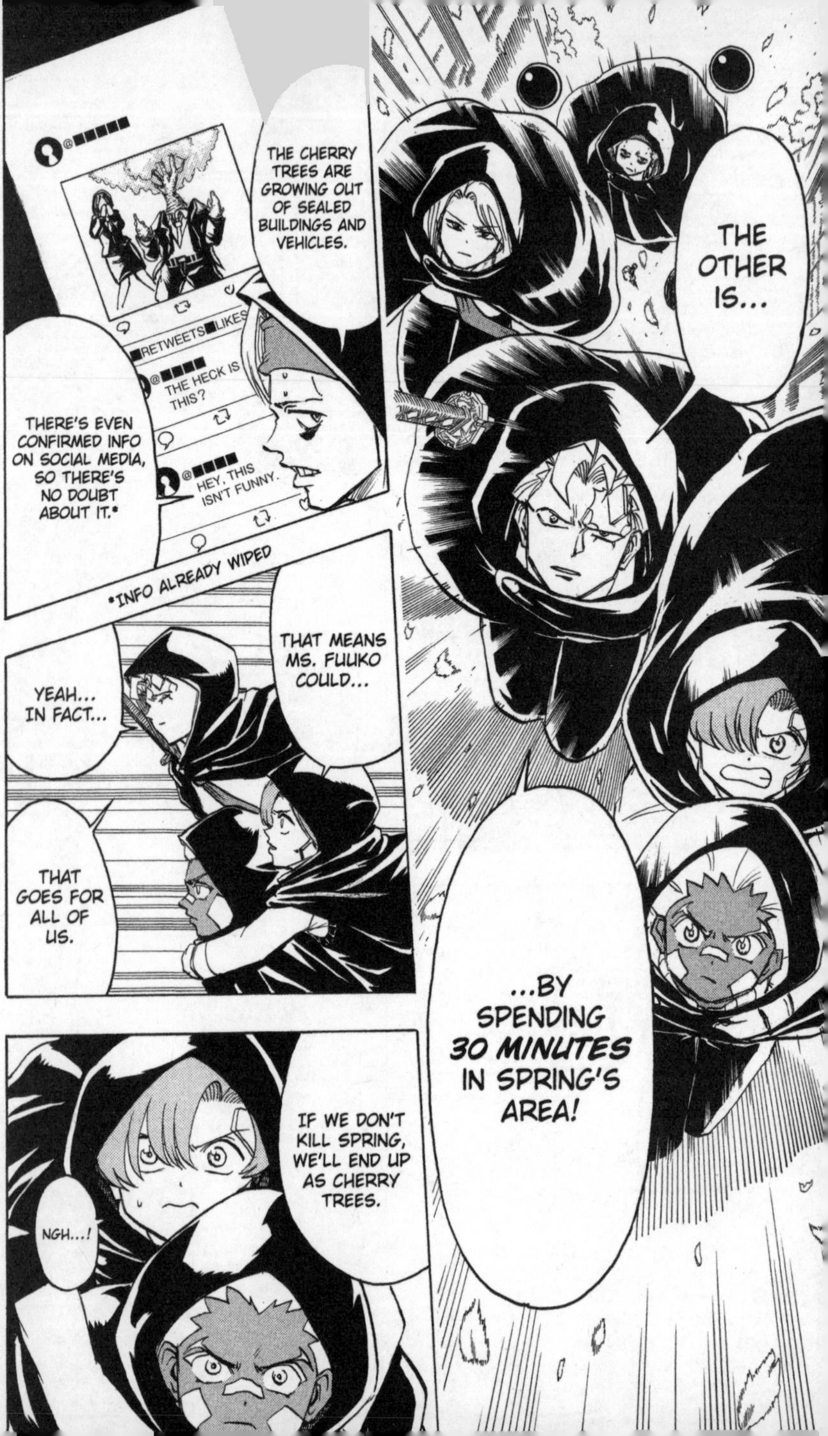
THE OTHER IS...
...BY SPENDING 30 MINUTES IN SPRING'S AREA!
THE CHERRY TREES ARE GROWING OUT OF SEALED BUILDINGS AND VEHICLES.
@[redacted]
[redacted] RETWEETS [redacted] LIKES
@[redacted] THE HECK IS THIS?
@[redacted] HEY, THIS ISN'T FUNNY.
THERE'S EVEN CONFIRMED INFO ON SOCIAL MEDIA, SO THERE'S NO DOUBT ABOUT IT.*
*INFO ALREADY WIPED
THAT MEANS MS. FUUKO COULD...
YEAH... IN FACT...
THAT GOES FOR ALL OF US.
IF WE DON'T KILL SPRING, WE'LL END UP AS CHERRY TREES.
NGH...!

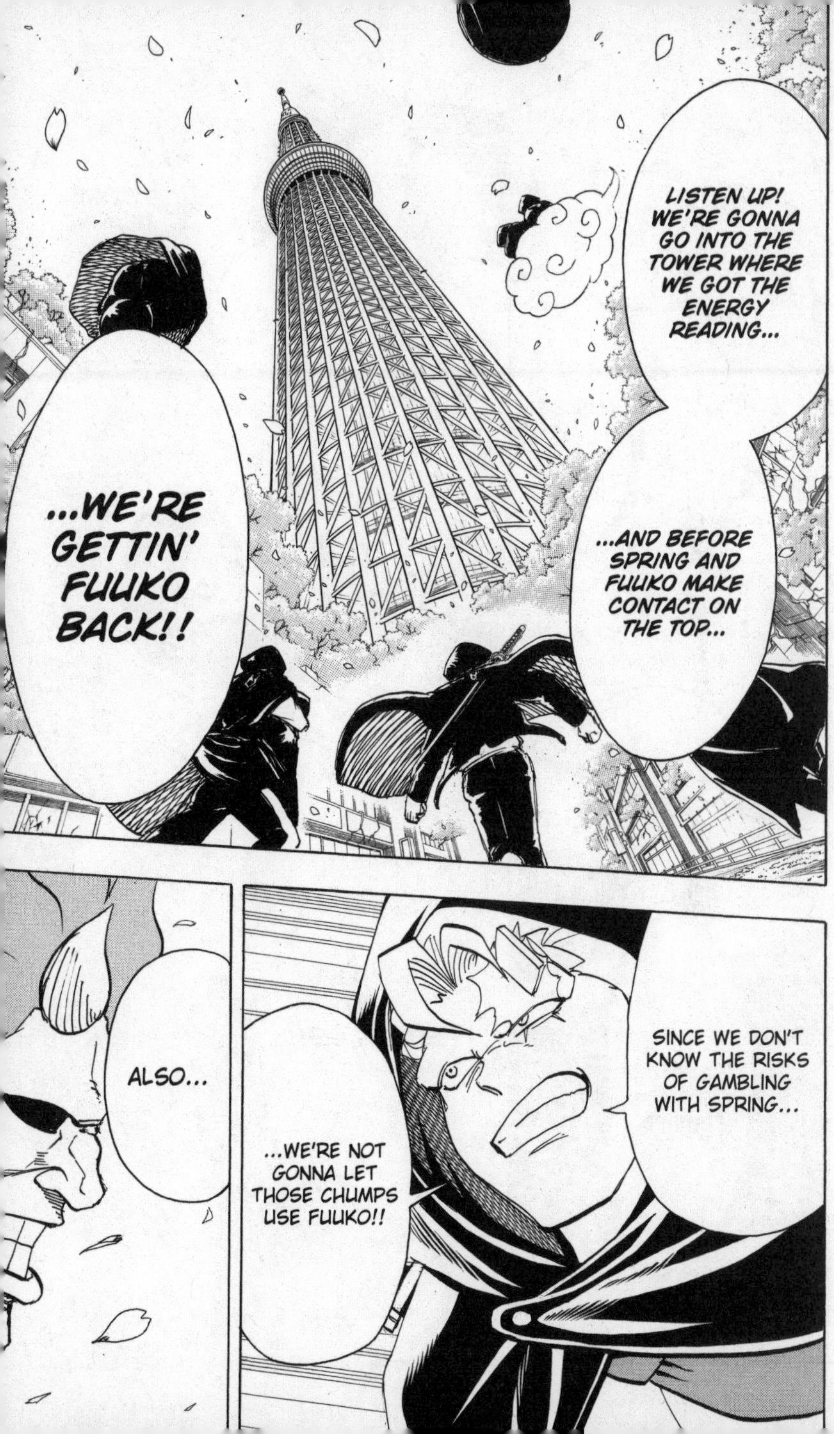
LISTEN UP! WE'RE GONNA GO INTO THE TOWER WHERE WE GOT THE ENERGY READING...
...AND BEFORE SPRING AND FUUKO MAKE CONTACT ON THE TOP...
...WE'RE GETTIN' FUUKO BACK!!
SINCE WE DON'T KNOW THE RISKS OF GAMBLING WITH SPRING...
...WE'RE NOT GONNA LET THOSE CHUMPS USE FUUKO!!
ALSO...

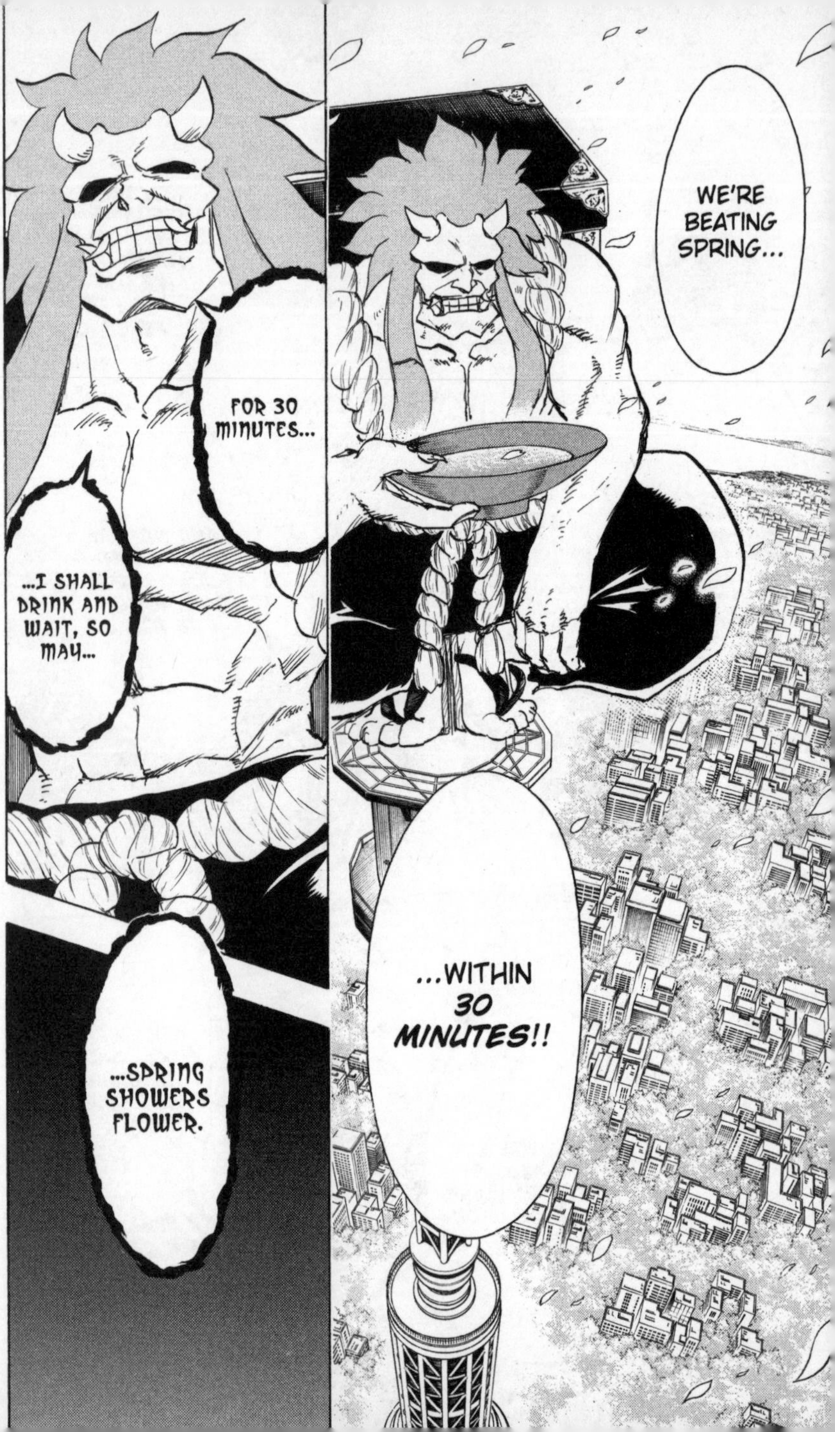
WE'RE BEATING SPRING...
...WITHIN 30 MINUTES!!
FOR 30 MINUTES...
...I SHALL DRINK AND WAIT, SO MAY...
...SPRING SHOWERS FLOWER.

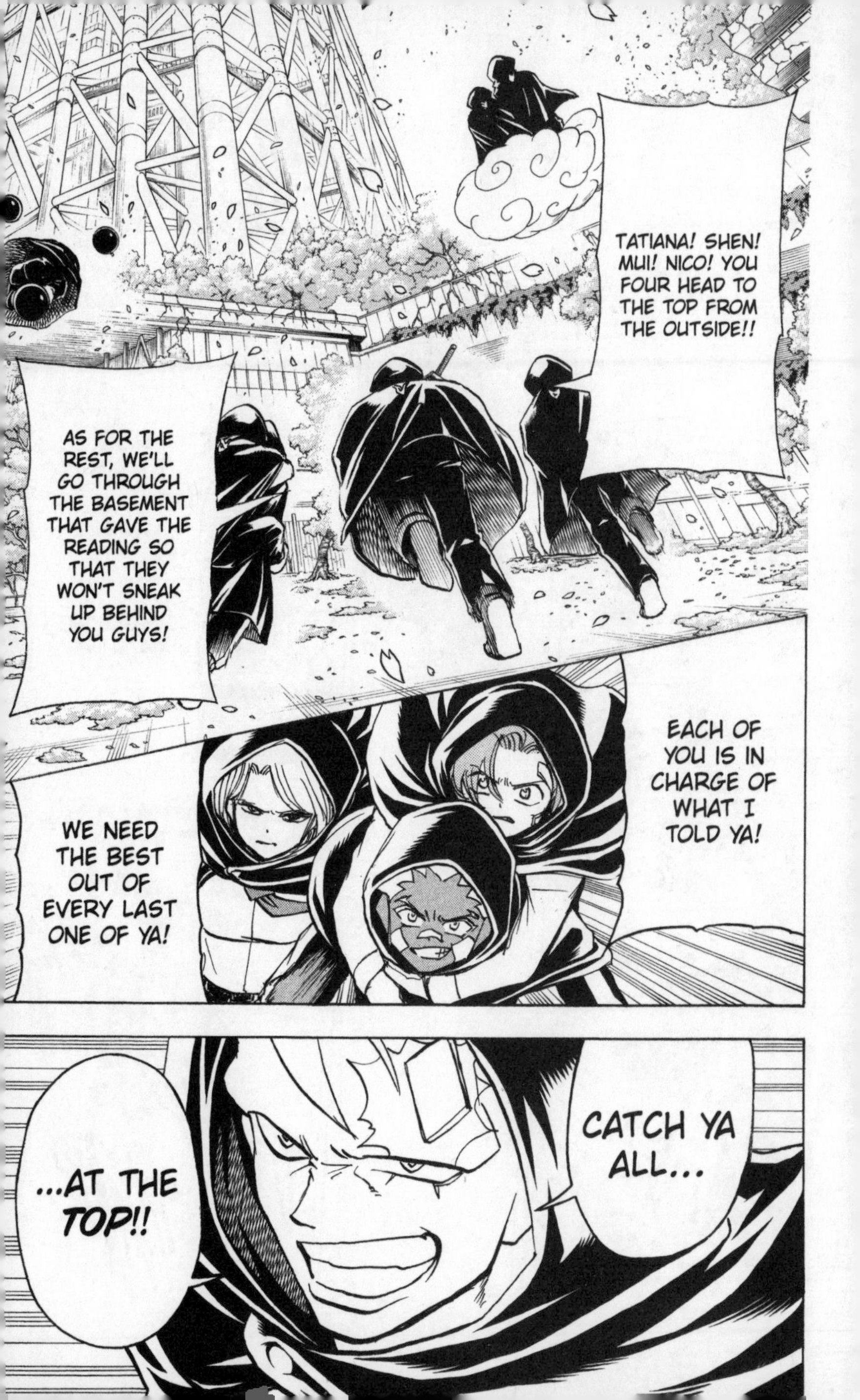
TATIANA! SHEN! MUI! NICO! YOU FOUR HEAD TO THE TOP FROM THE OUTSIDE!!
AS FOR THE REST, WE'LL GO THROUGH THE BASEMENT THAT GAVE THE READING SO THAT THEY WON'T SNEAK UP BEHIND YOU GUYS!
EACH OF YOU IS IN CHARGE OF WHAT I TOLD YA!
WE NEED THE BEST OUT OF EVERY LAST ONE OF YA!
CATCH YA ALL...
...AT THE *TOP*!!

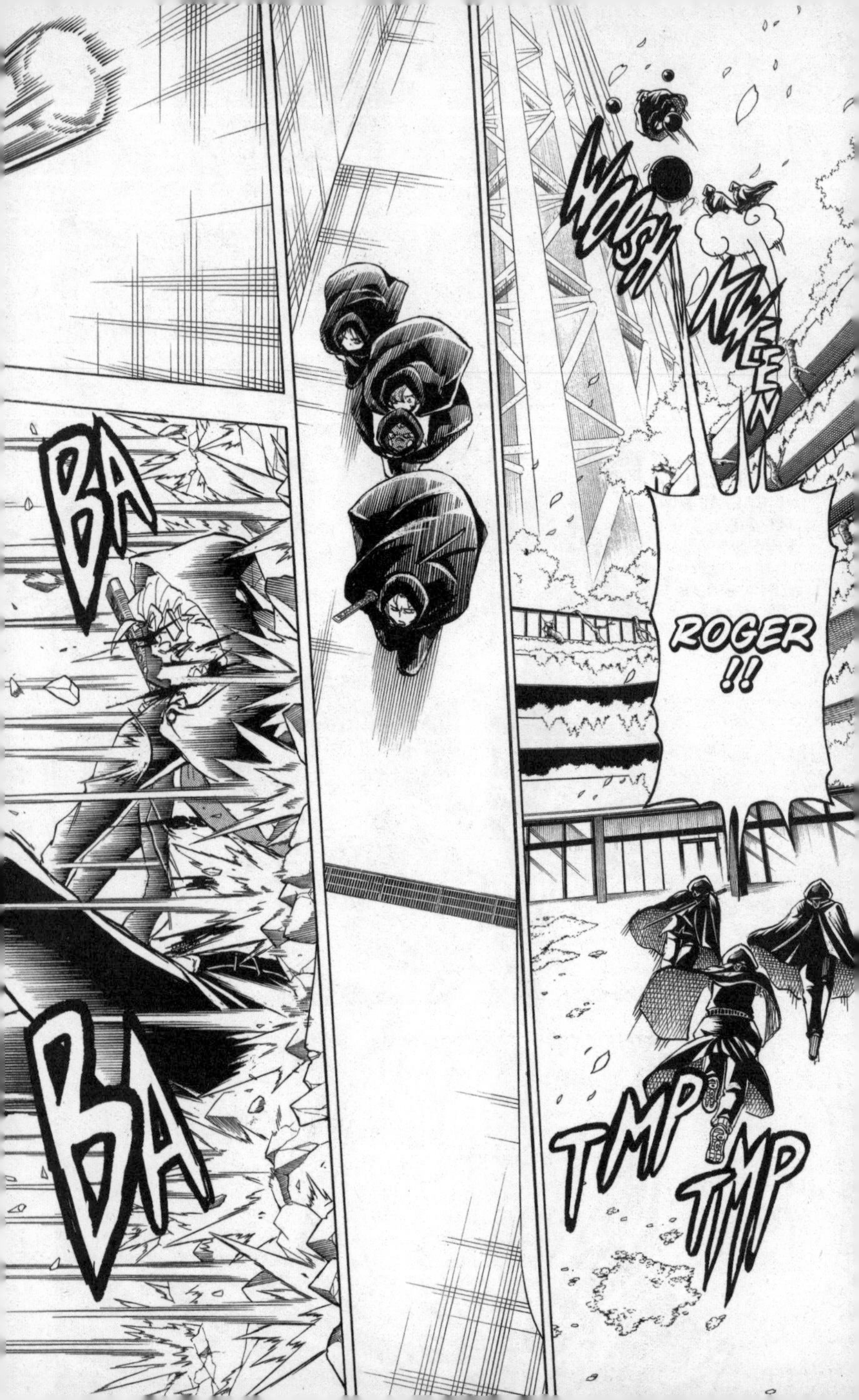
WOOSH
KWEEN
ROGER!!
TMP TMP
BA
BA

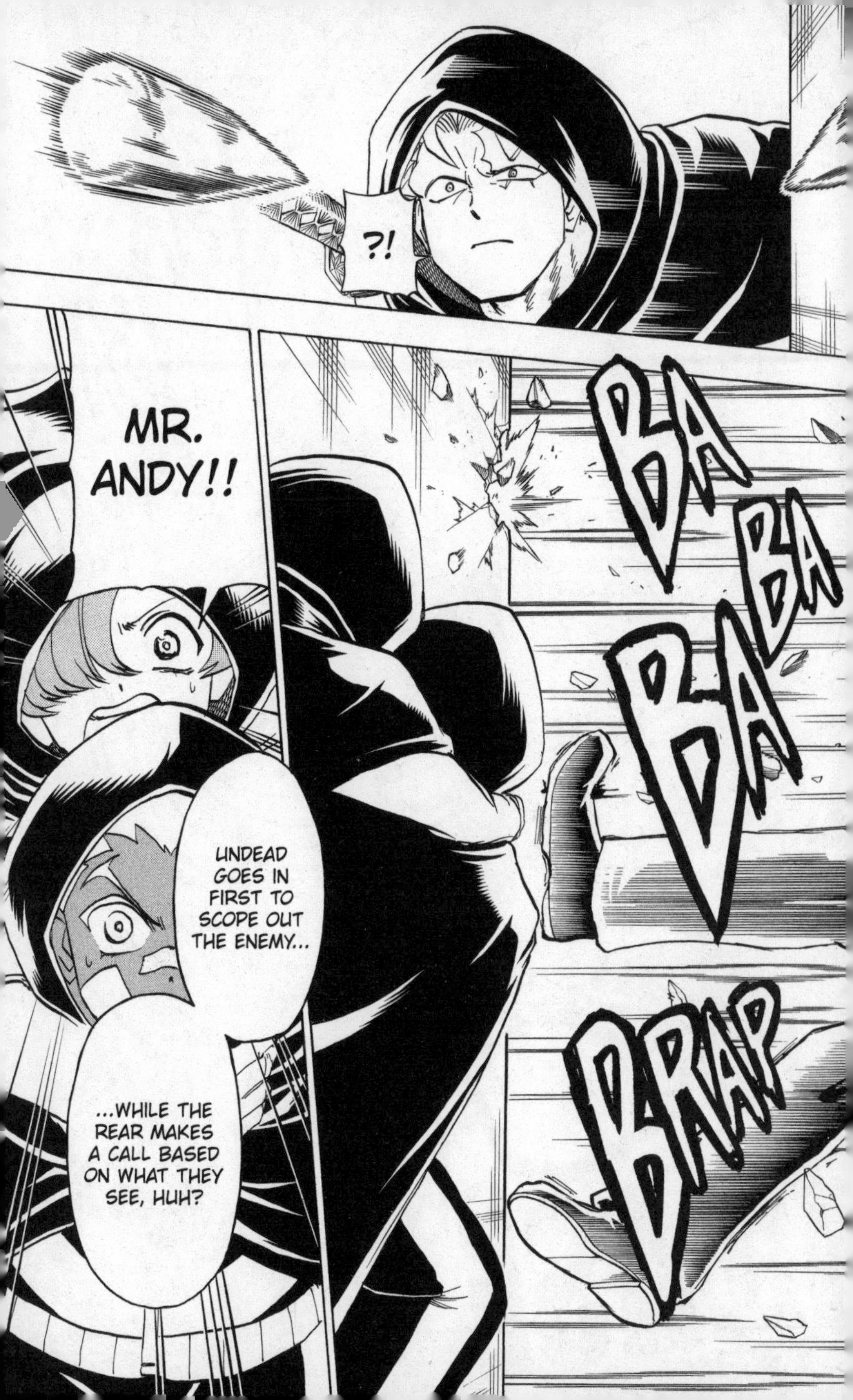
?!
BA BA BA
BRAP
MR. ANDY!!
UNDEAD GOES IN FIRST TO SCOPE OUT THE ENEMY...
...WHILE THE REAR MAKES A CALL BASED ON WHAT THEY SEE, HUH?

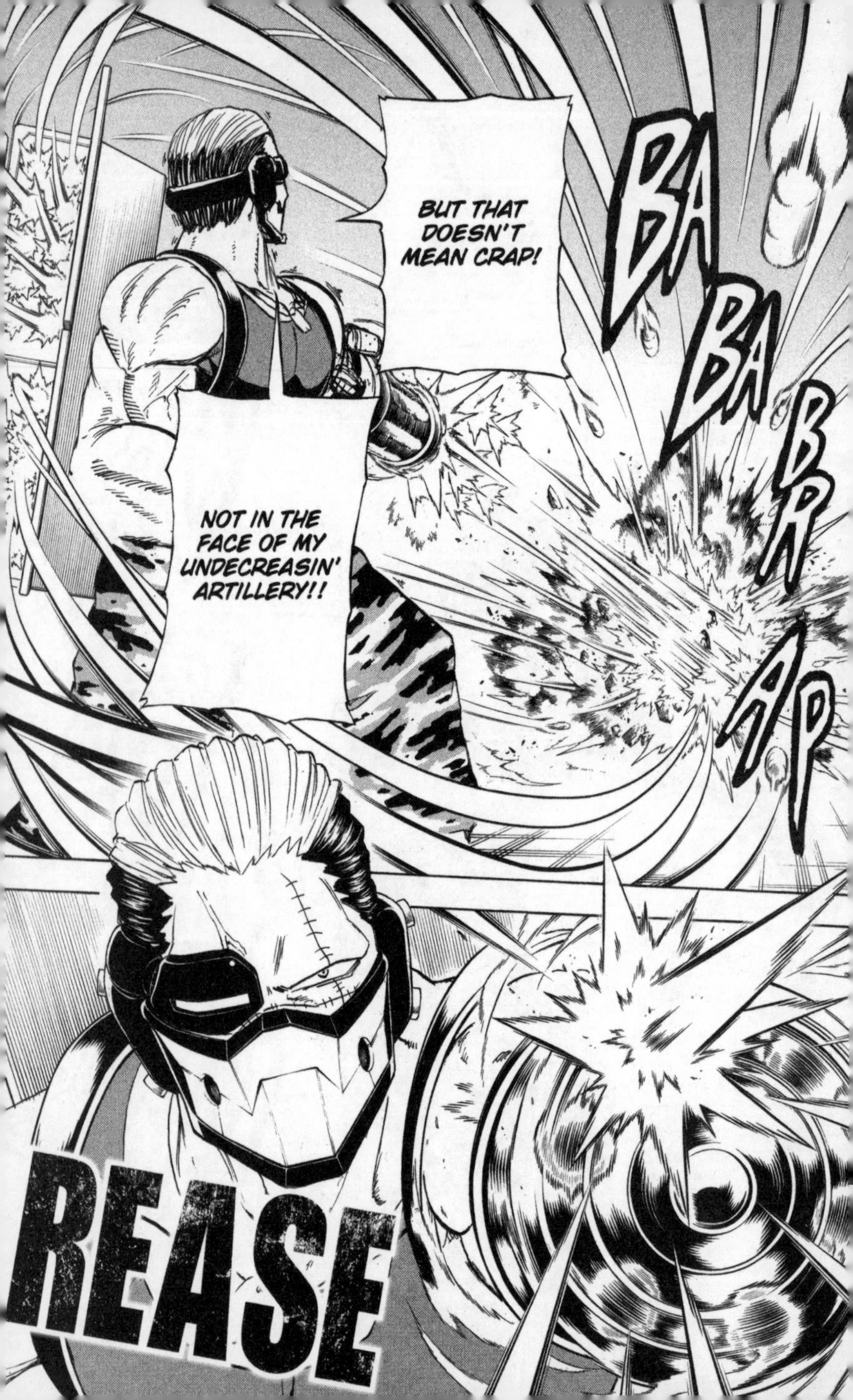
BUT THAT DOESN'T MEAN CRAP!
BABABRRAP
NOT IN THE FACE OF MY UNDECREASIN' ARTILLERY!!
REASE

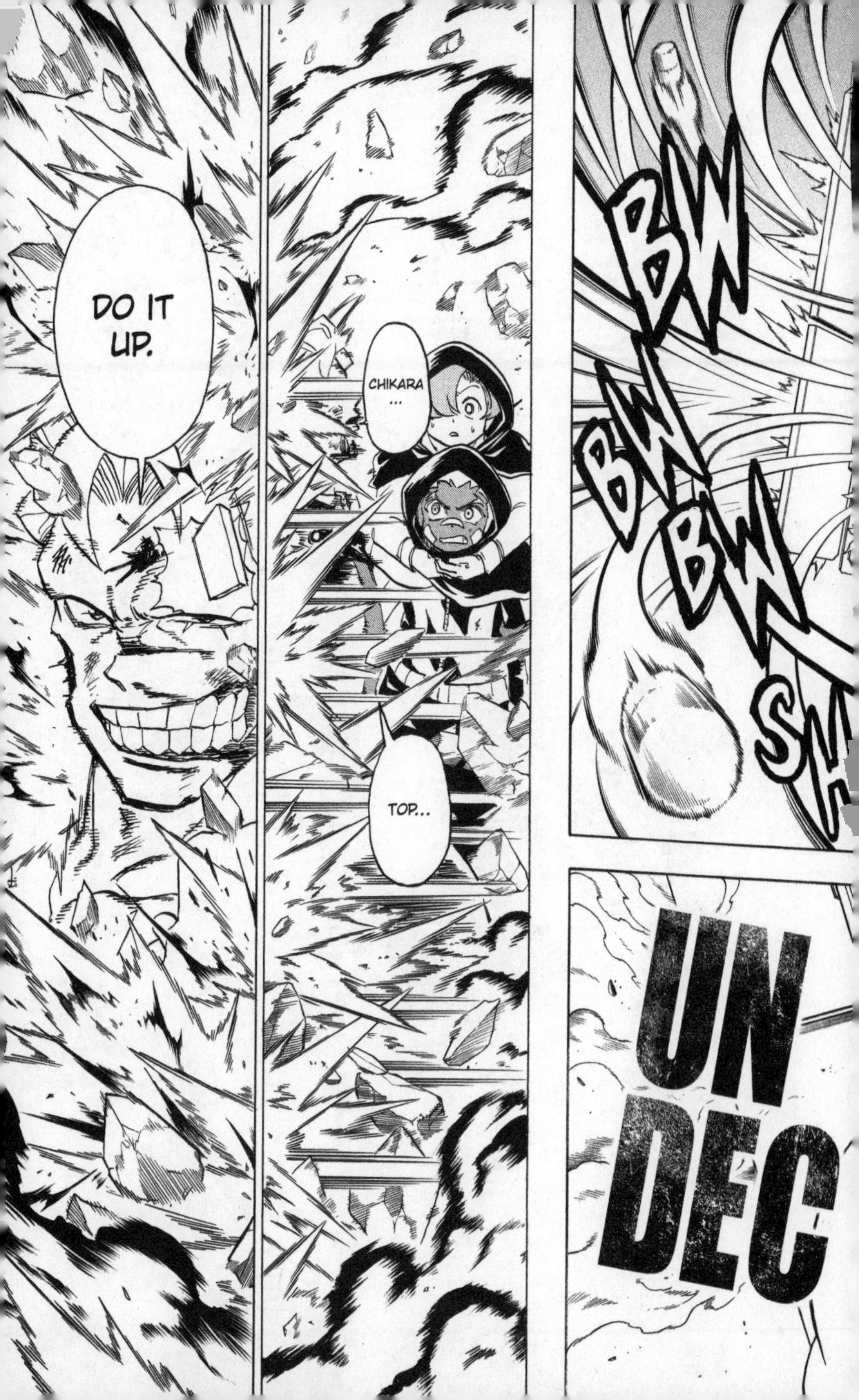
BW
BW
BW
SH
UN
DEC
CHIKARA ...
TOP...
DO IT UP.

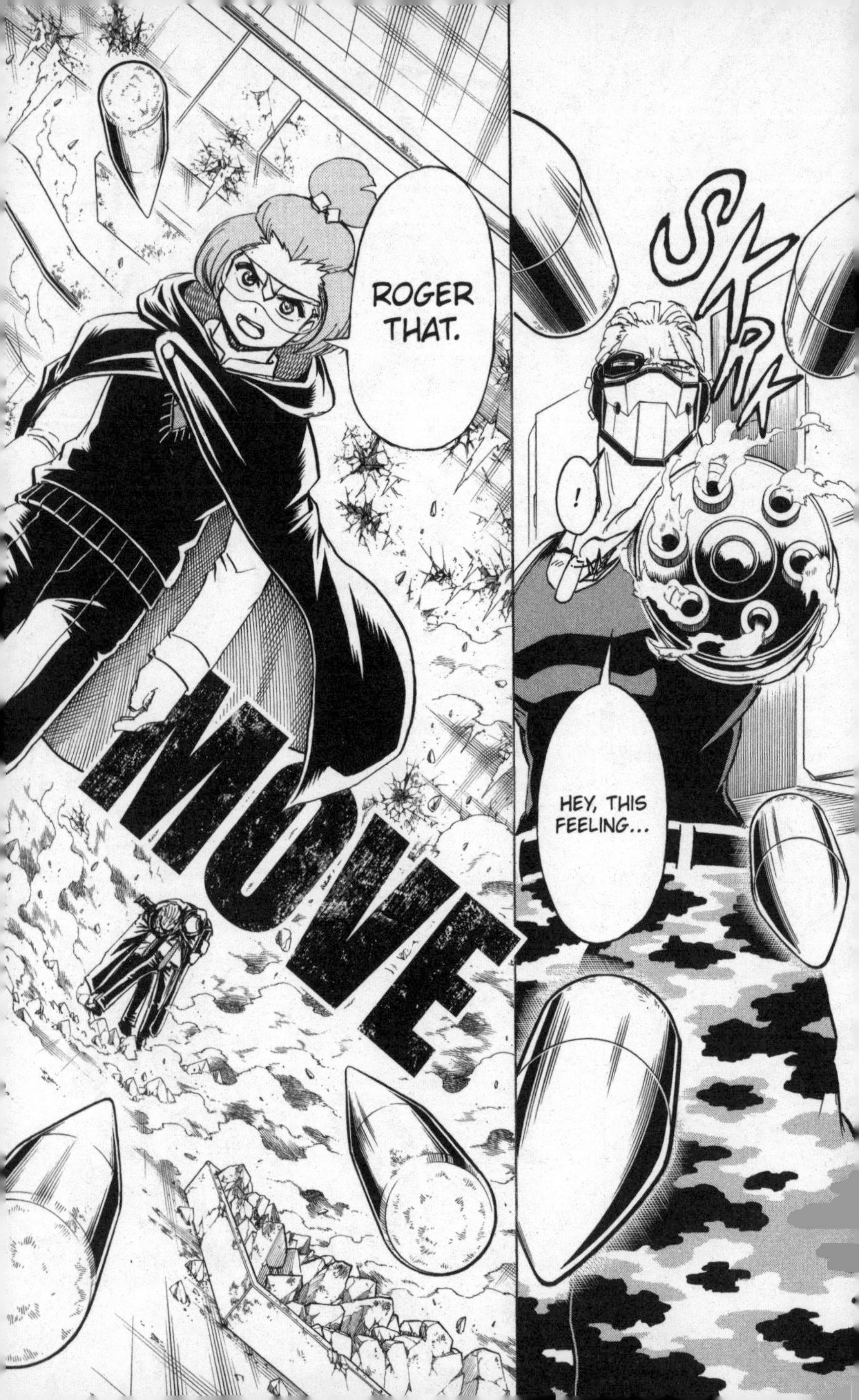
SKRK
!
HEY, THIS FEELING...
ROGER THAT.
MOVE

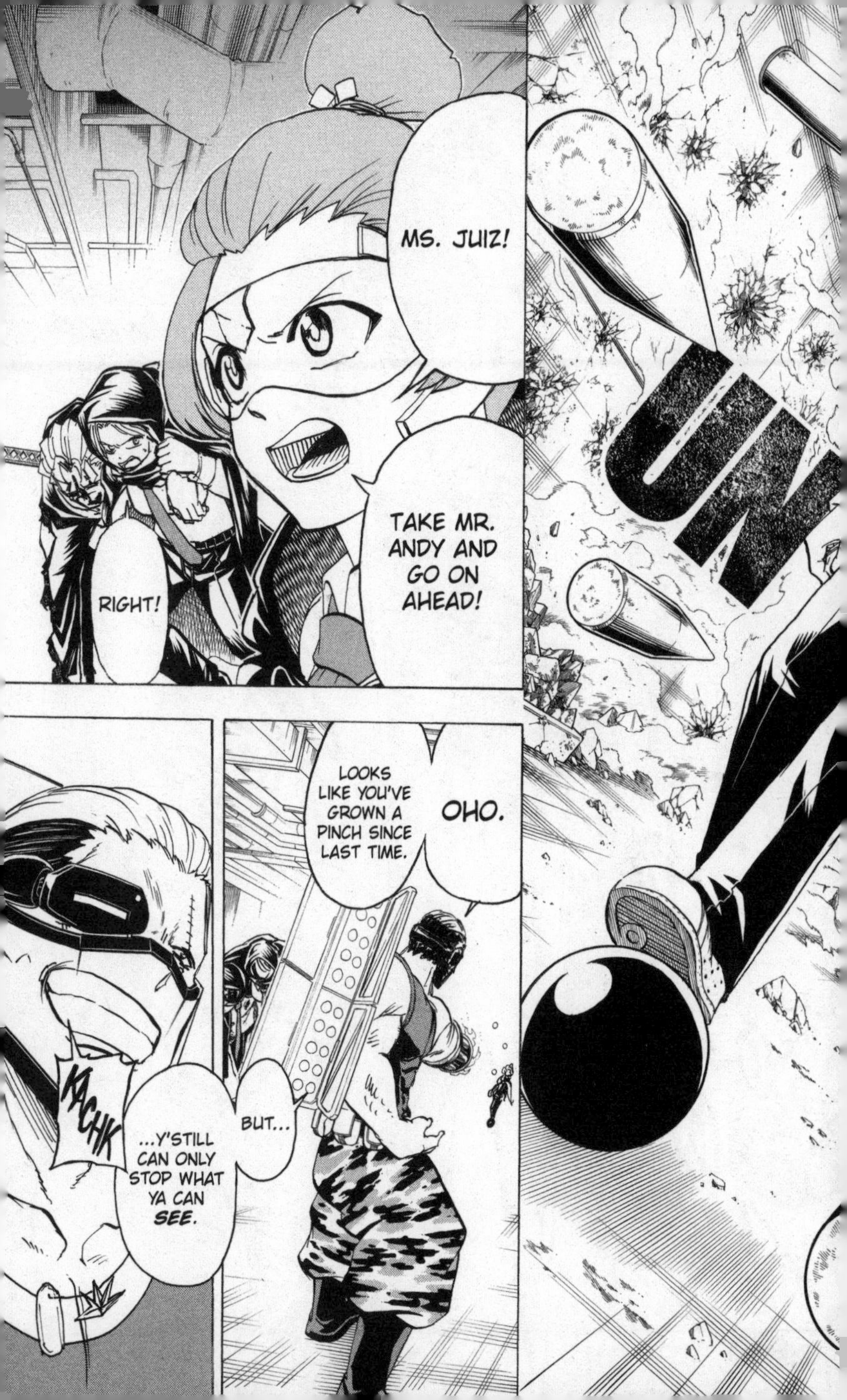
UN
MS. JUIZ!
TAKE MR. ANDY AND GO ON AHEAD!
RIGHT!
OHO.
LOOKS LIKE YOU'VE GROWN A PINCH SINCE LAST TIME.
BUT...
KACHK
...Y'STILL CAN ONLY STOP WHAT YA CAN SEE.

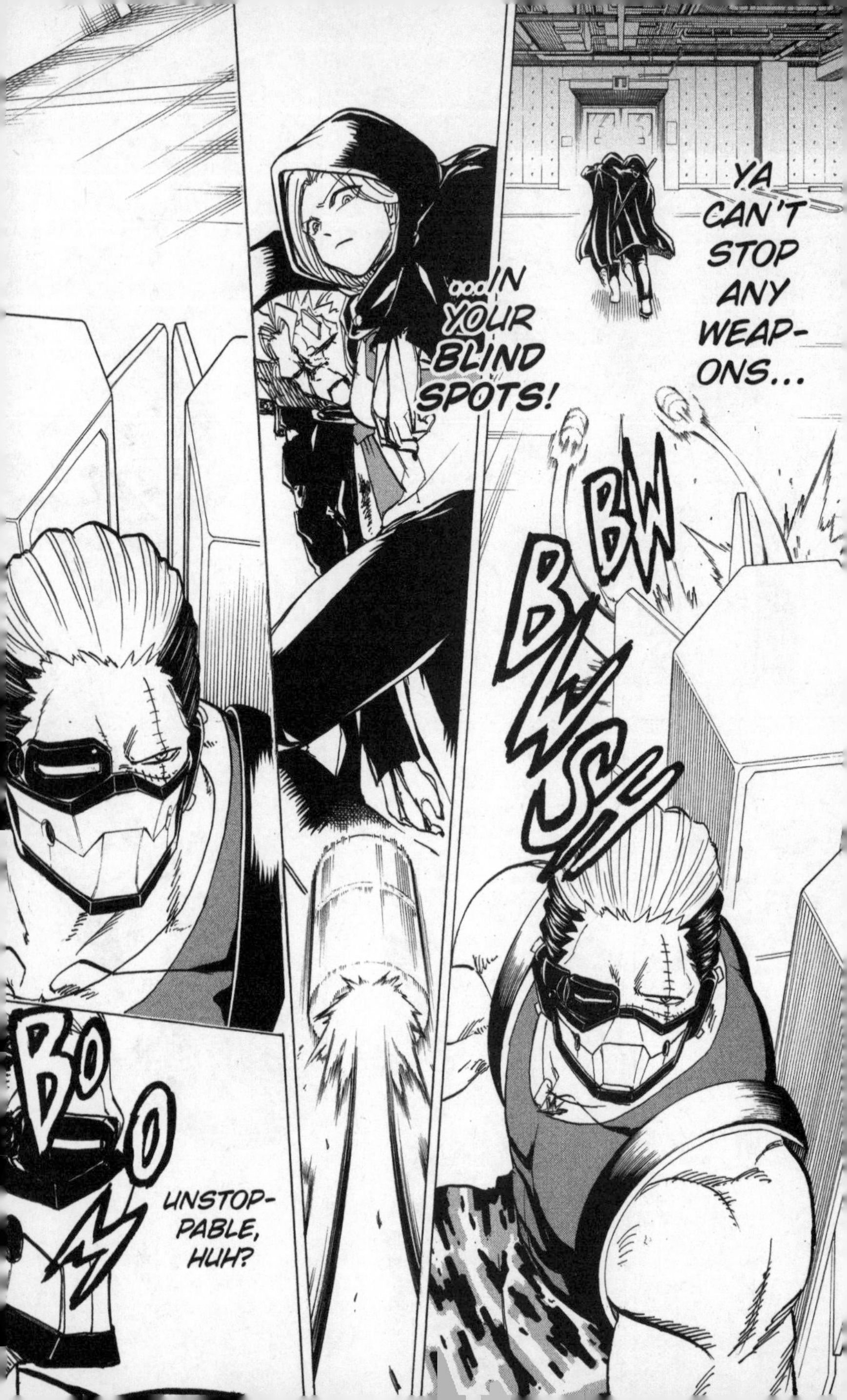
YA CAN'T STOP ANY WEAP-ONS...
BW
BWSH
...IN YOUR BLIND SPOTS!
BOOM
UNSTOP-PABLE, HUH?

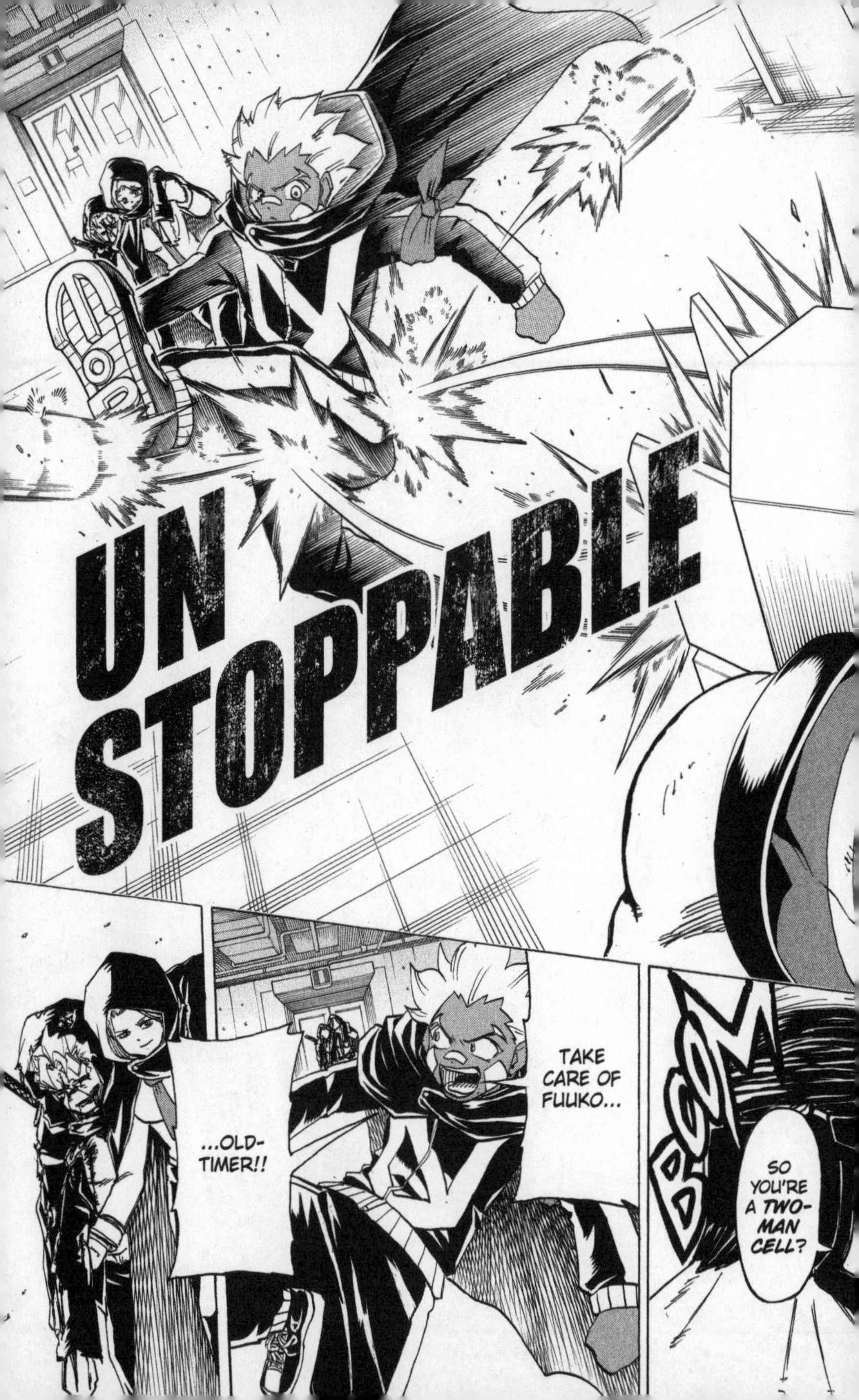
UNSTOPPABLE
BOOM
SO YOU'RE A TWO-MAN CELL?
TAKE CARE OF FUUKO...
...OLD-TIMER!!

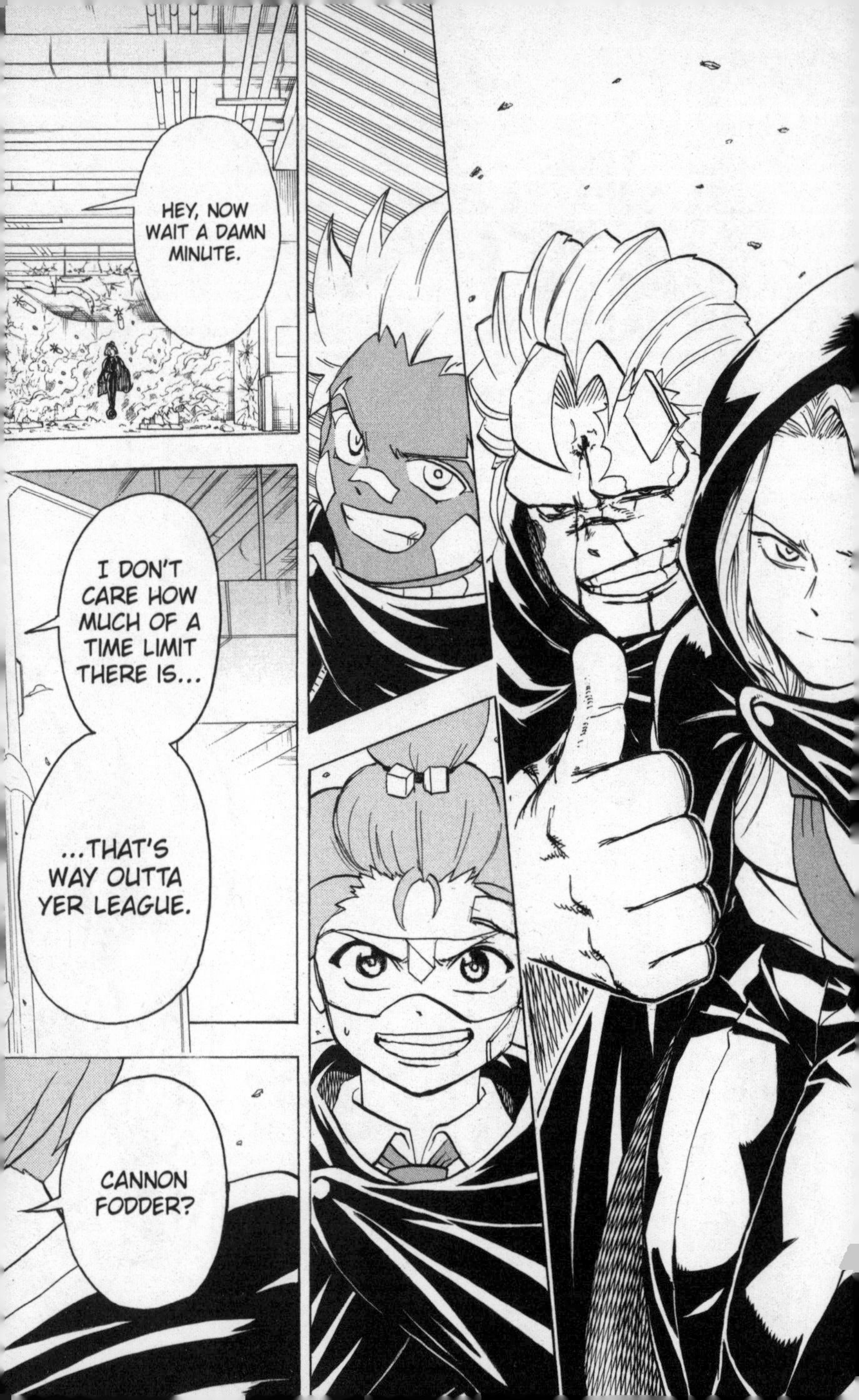
HEY, NOW WAIT A DAMN MINUTE.
I DON'T CARE HOW MUCH OF A TIME LIMIT THERE IS...
...THAT'S WAY OUTTA YER LEAGUE.
CANNON FODDER?

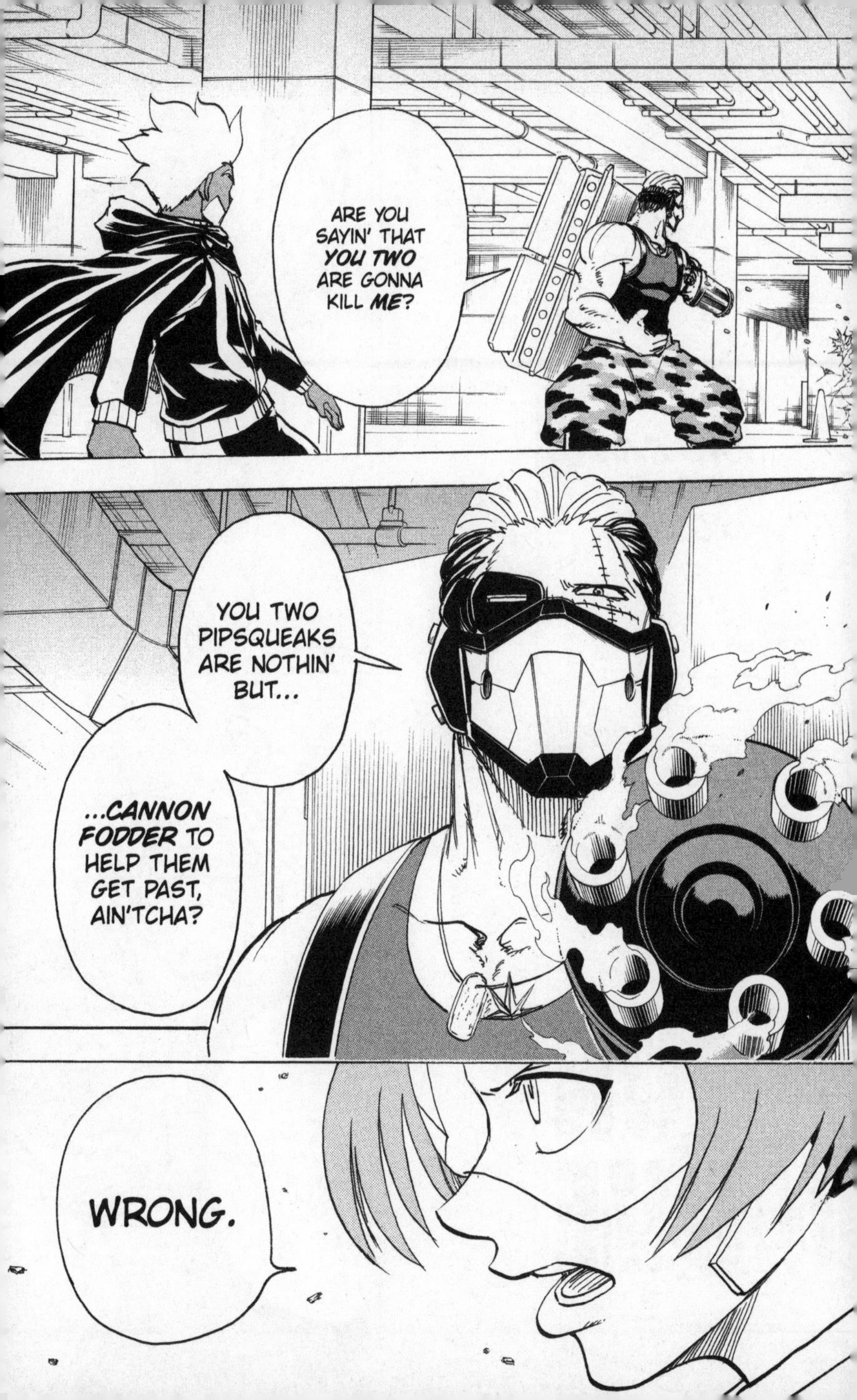
ARE YOU SAYIN' THAT *YOU TWO* ARE GONNA KILL *ME*?
YOU TWO PIPSQUEAKS ARE NOTHIN' BUT...
...*CANNON FODDER* TO HELP THEM GET PAST, AIN'TCHA?
WRONG.

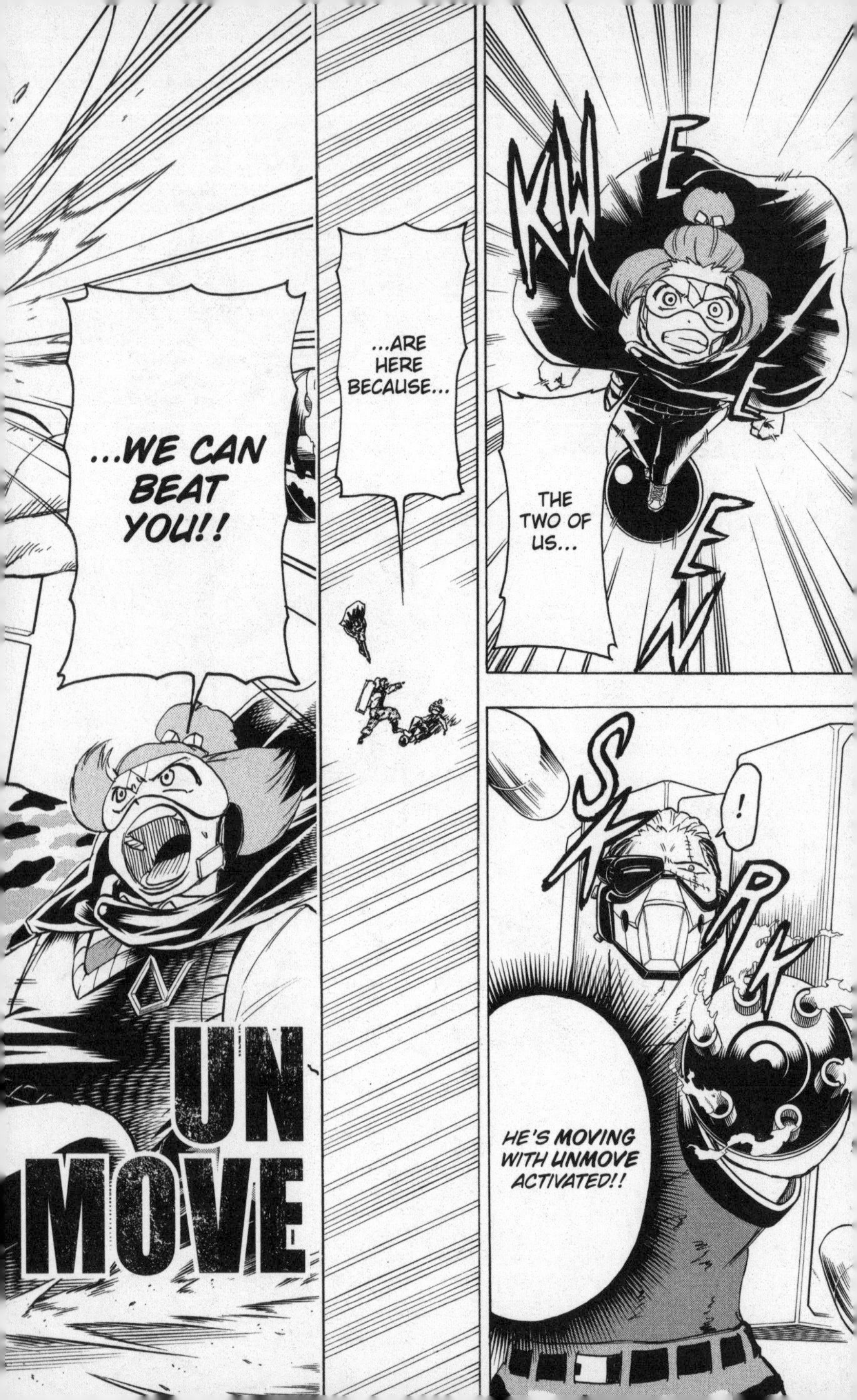
KWEEEN
THE TWO OF US...
SKRRK
!
HE'S MOVING WITH UNMOVE ACTIVATED!!
...ARE HERE BECAUSE...
...WE CAN BEAT YOU!!
UNMOVE

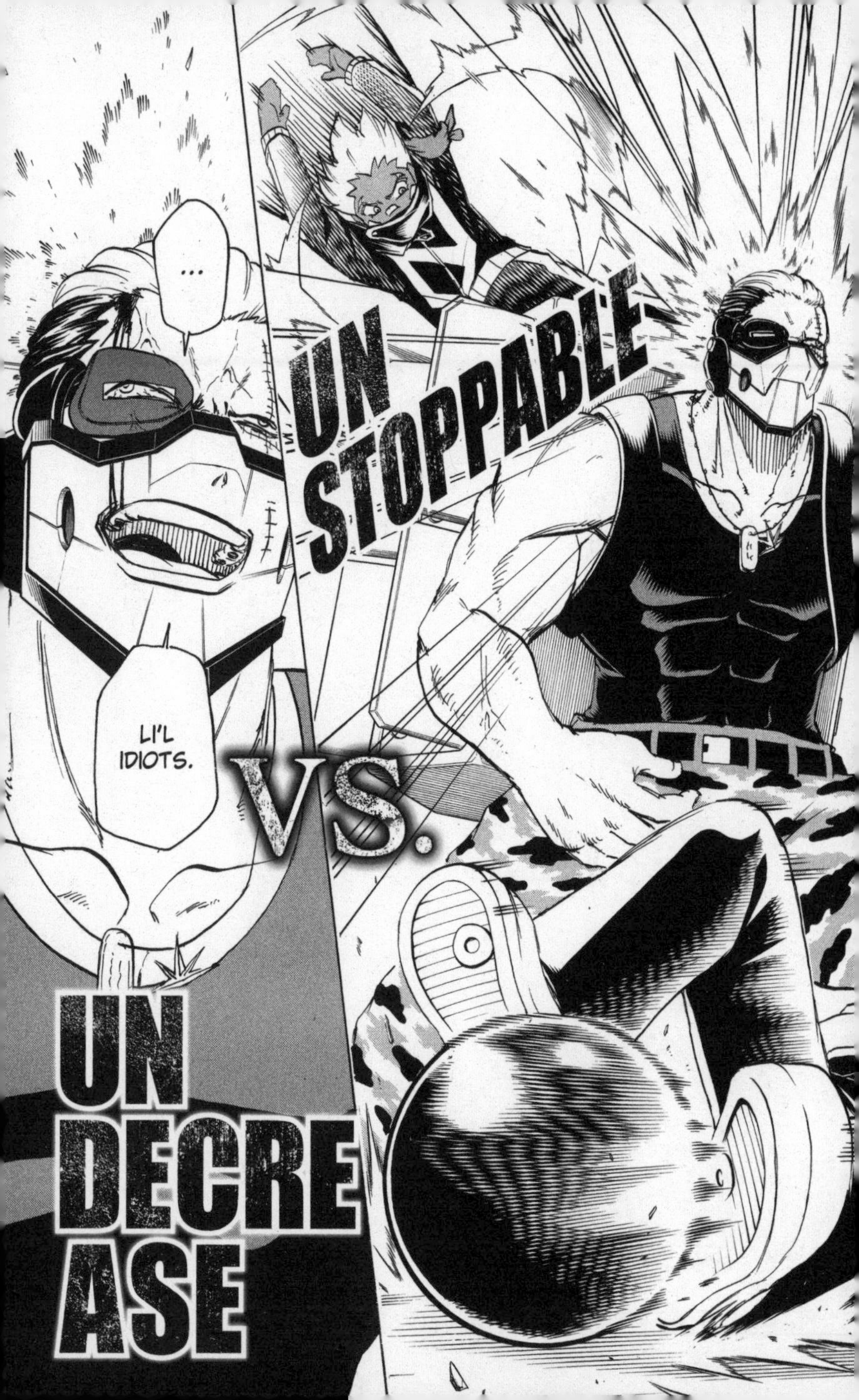
UN STOPPABLE
...
LI'L IDIOTS.
VS.
UN DECRE ASE

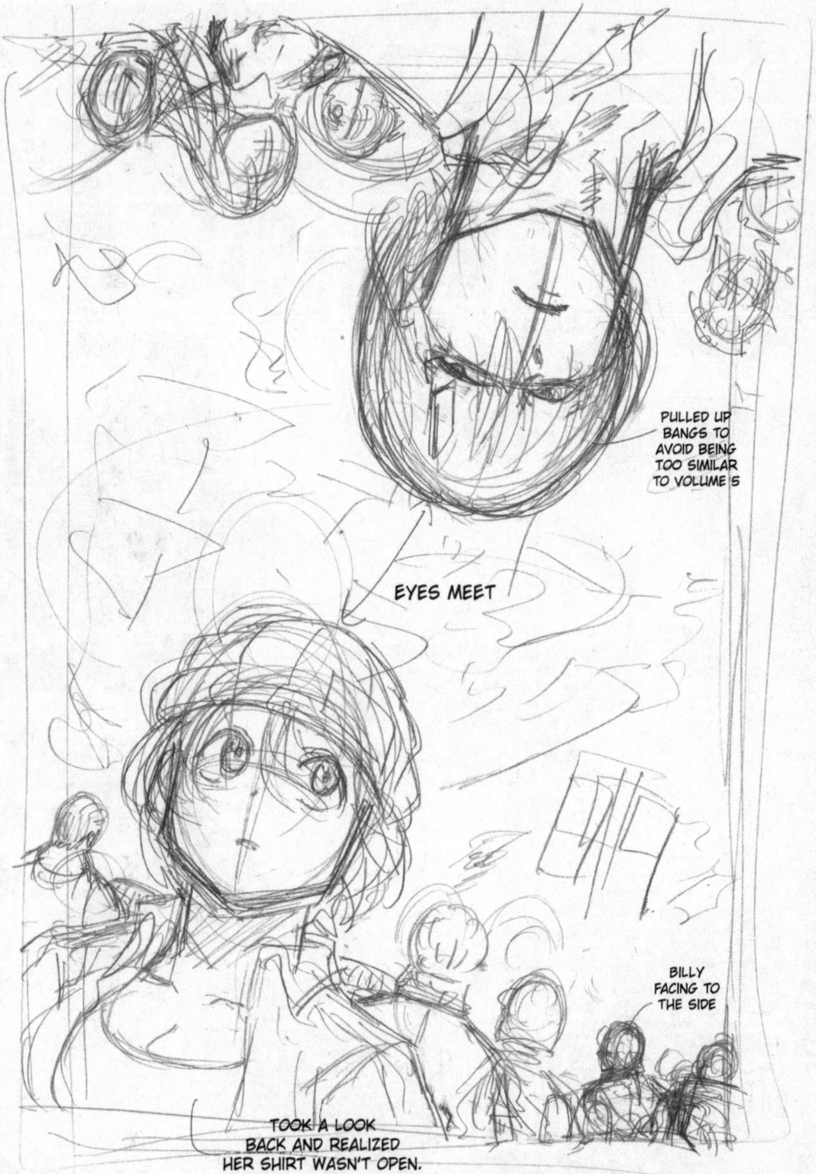
PULLED UP
BANGS TO
AVOID BEING
TOO SIMILAR
TO VOLUME 5
EYES MEET
BILLY
FACING TO
THE SIDE
TOOK A LOOK
BACK AND REALIZED
HER SHIRT WASN'T OPEN.

ROUGH FOR VOLUME 9'S COVER ILLUSTRATION

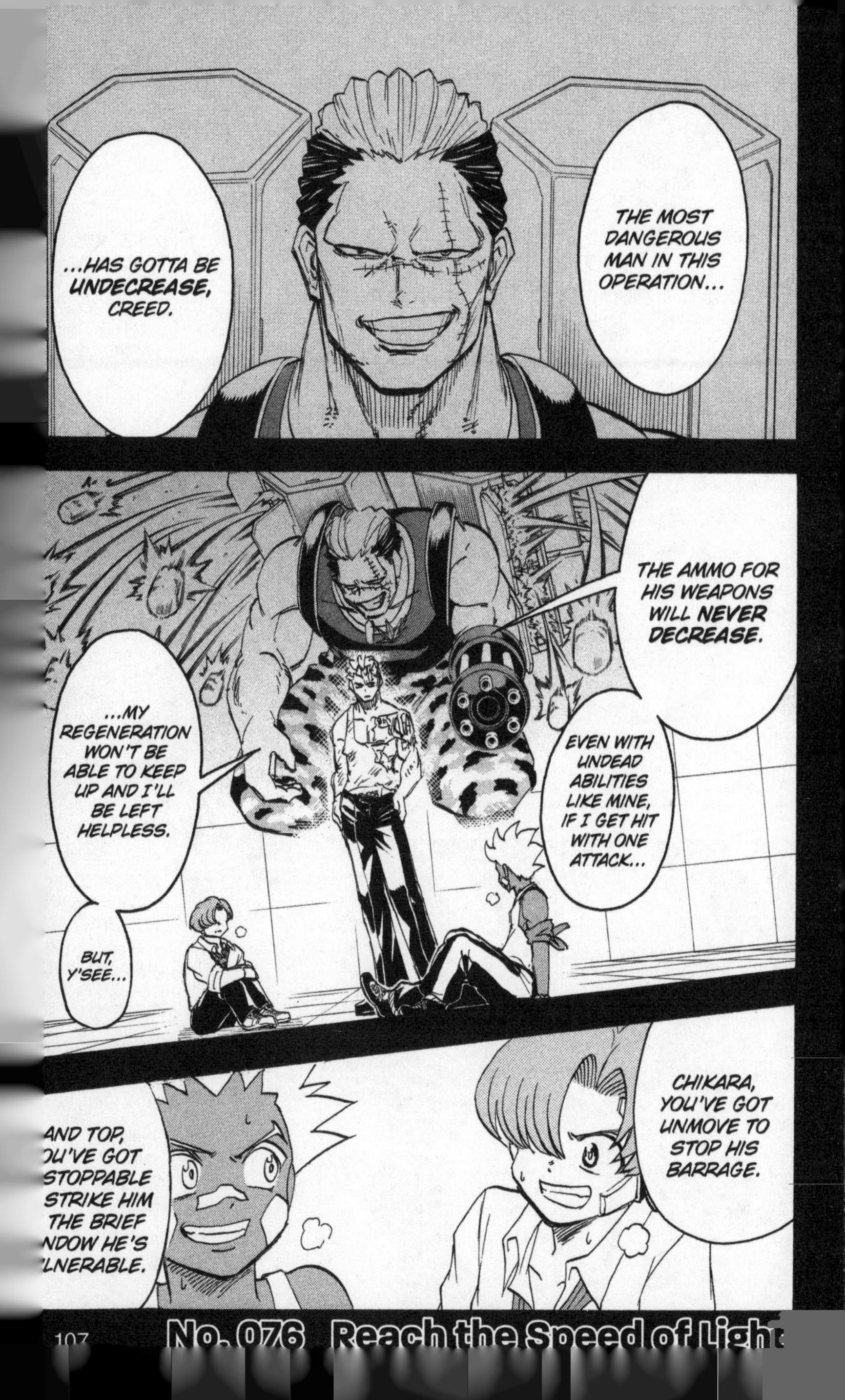
THE MOST DANGEROUS MAN IN THIS OPERATION...
...HAS GOTTA BE UNDECREASE, CREED.
THE AMMO FOR HIS WEAPONS WILL NEVER DECREASE.
EVEN WITH UNDEAD ABILITIES LIKE MINE, IF I GET HIT WITH ONE ATTACK...
...MY REGENERATION WON'T BE ABLE TO KEEP UP AND I'LL BE LEFT HELPLESS.
BUT, Y'SEE...
CHIKARA, YOU'VE GOT UNMOVE TO STOP HIS BARRAGE.
AND TOP, OU'VE GOT STOPPABLE STRIKE HIM THE BRIEF NDOW HE'S LNERABLE.

No. 076 Reach the Speed of Light

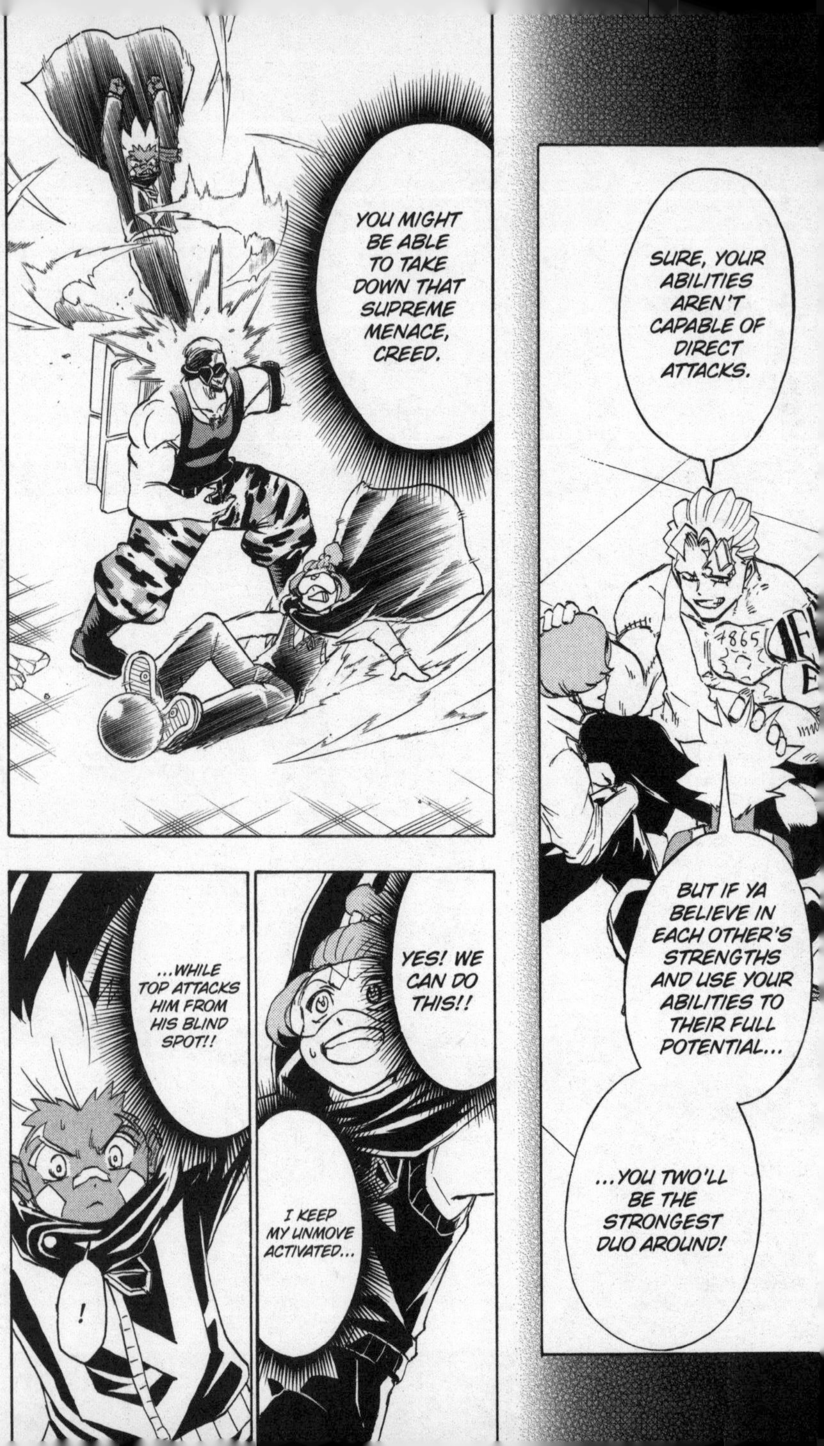
SURE, YOUR ABILITIES AREN'T CAPABLE OF DIRECT ATTACKS.
BUT IF YA BELIEVE IN EACH OTHER'S STRENGTHS AND USE YOUR ABILITIES TO THEIR FULL POTENTIAL...
...YOU TWO'LL BE THE STRONGEST DUO AROUND!
YOU MIGHT BE ABLE TO TAKE DOWN THAT SUPREME MENACE, CREED.
YES! WE CAN DO THIS!!
I KEEP MY UNMOVE ACTIVATED...
...WHILE TOP ATTACKS HIM FROM HIS BLIND SPOT!!
!

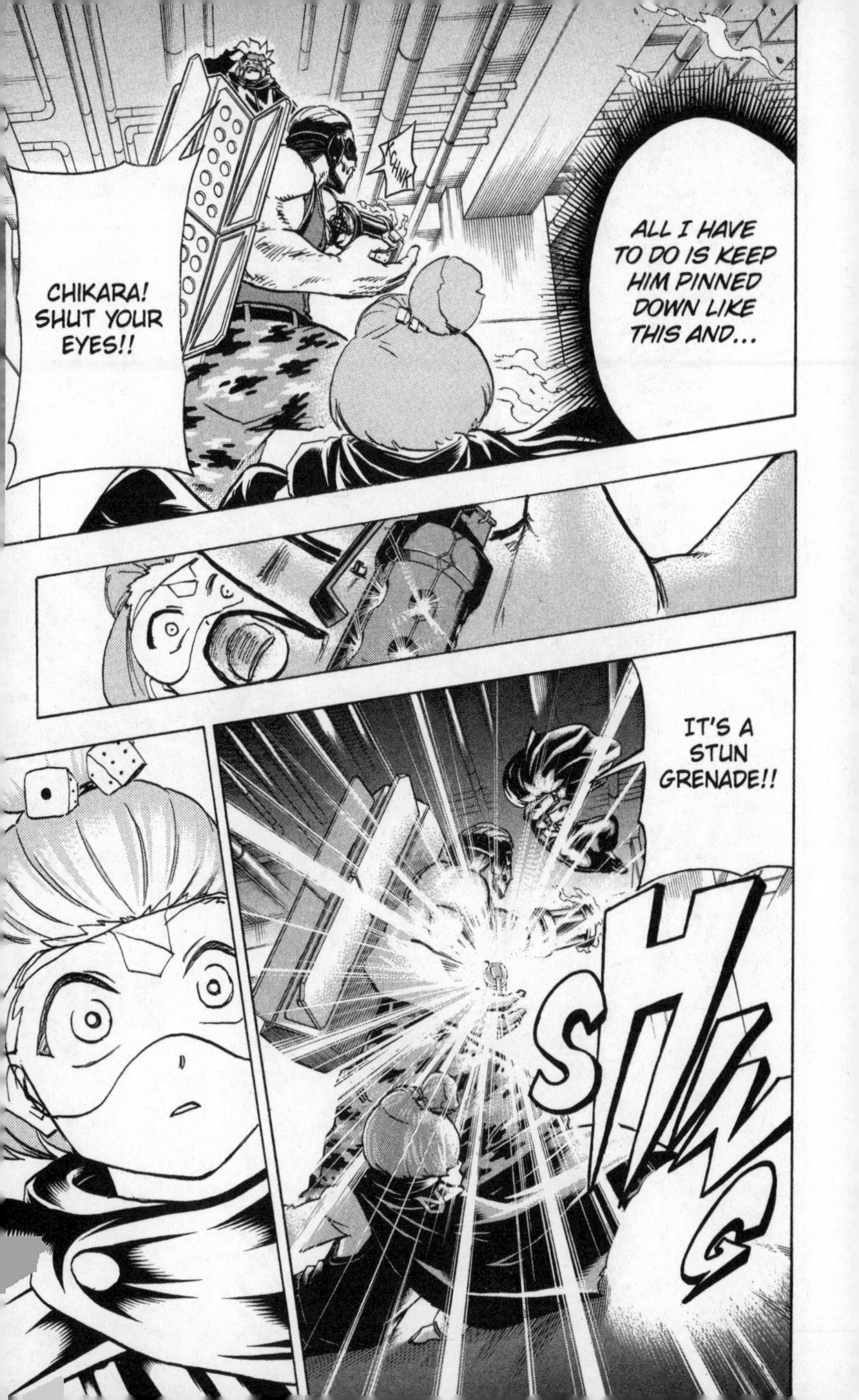
ALL I HAVE TO DO IS KEEP HIM PINNED DOWN LIKE THIS AND...
KCHINK
CHIKARA! SHUT YOUR EYES!!
IT'S A STUN GRENADE!!
SHING

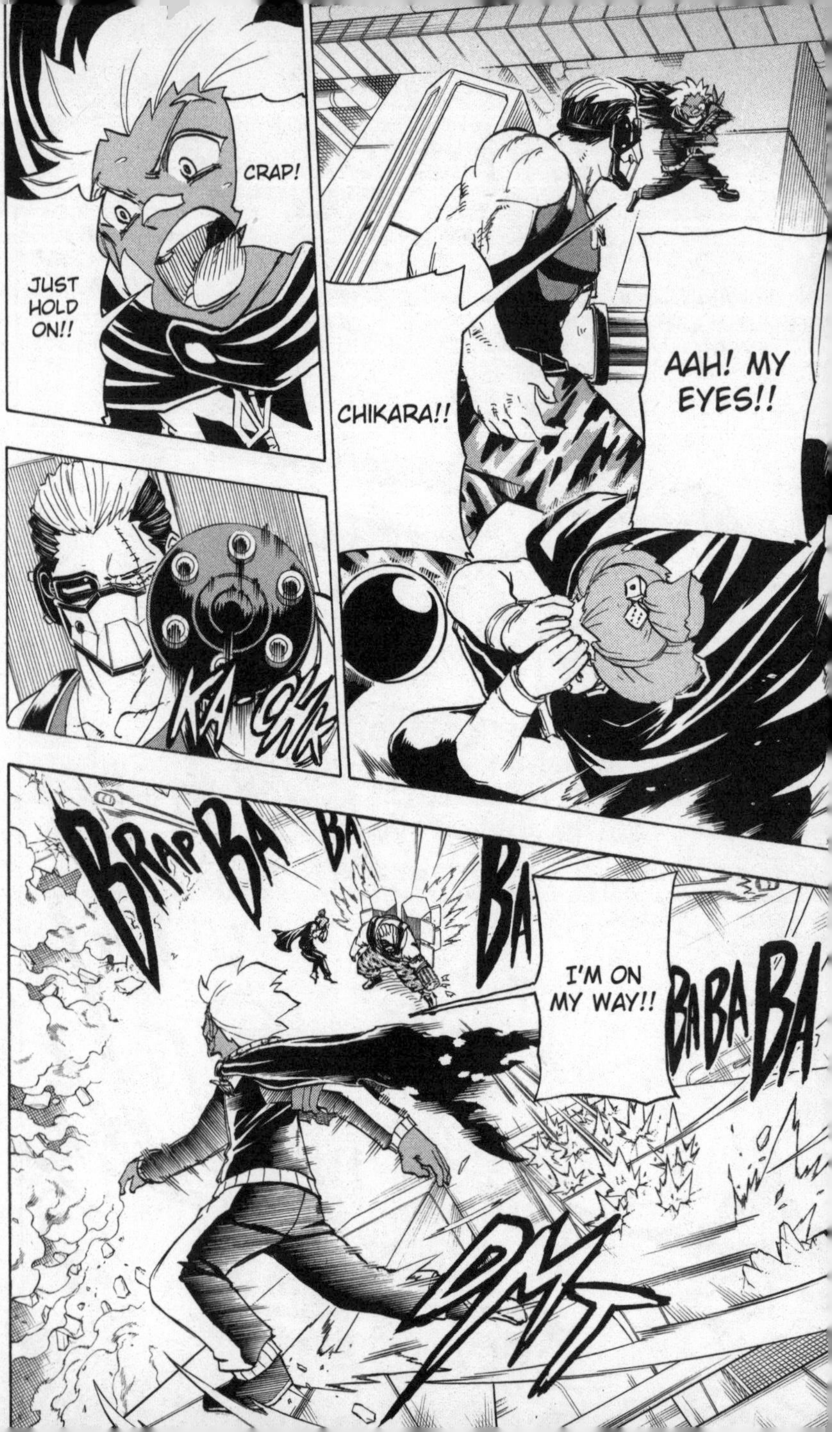
AAH! MY EYES!!
CHIKARA!!
CRAP!
JUST HOLD ON!!
KA-CHK
BABABA
I'M ON MY WAY!!
BA
BA
BRAP BA

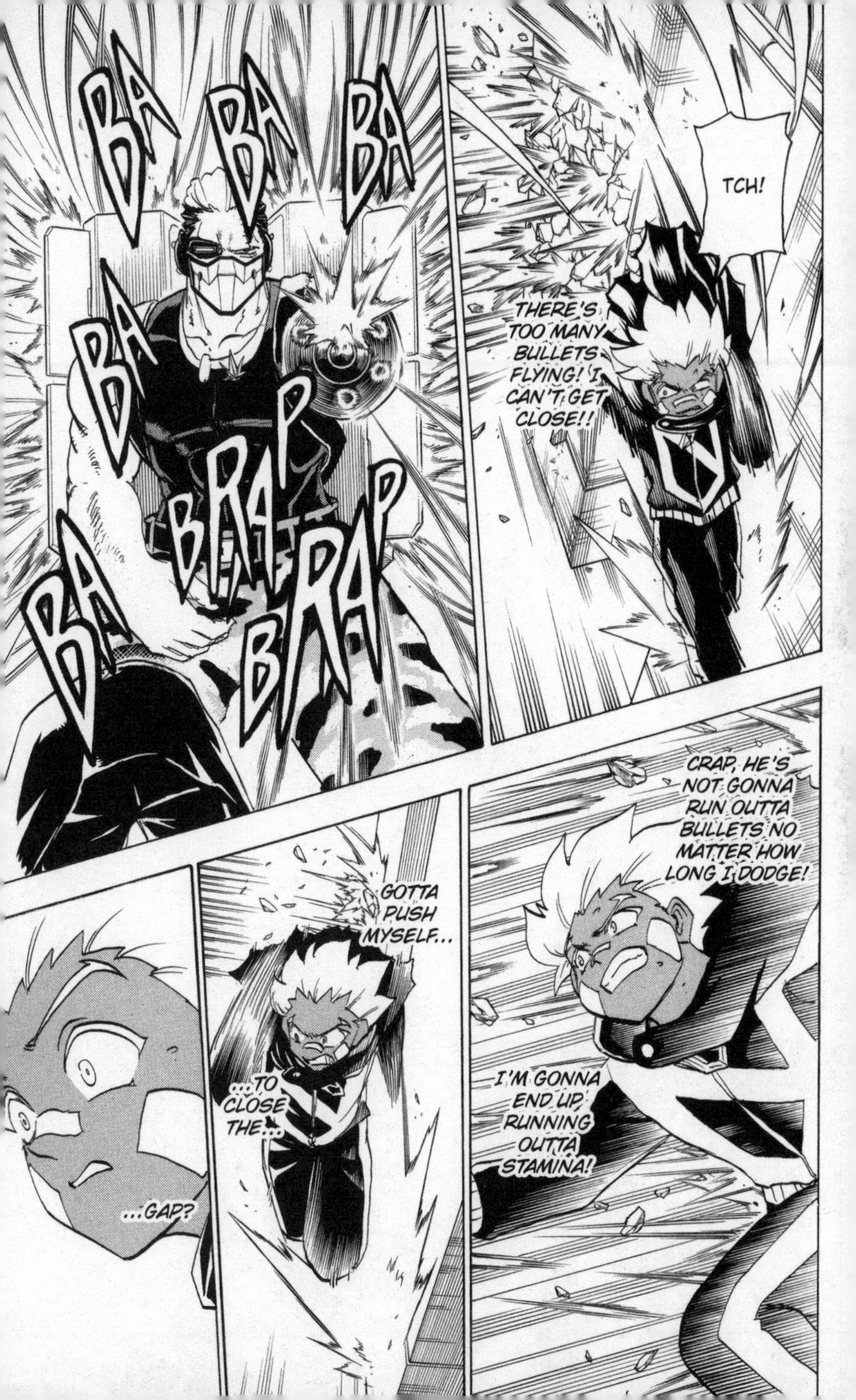
TCH!
THERE'S TOO MANY BULLETS FLYING! I CAN'T GET CLOSE!!
BA BA BA
BA
BRAP
BRAP
BA
BRAP
CRAP, HE'S NOT GONNA RUN OUTTA BULLETS NO MATTER HOW LONG I DODGE!
I'M GONNA END UP RUNNING OUTTA STAMINA!
GOTTA PUSH MYSELF...
...TO CLOSE THE...
...GAP?

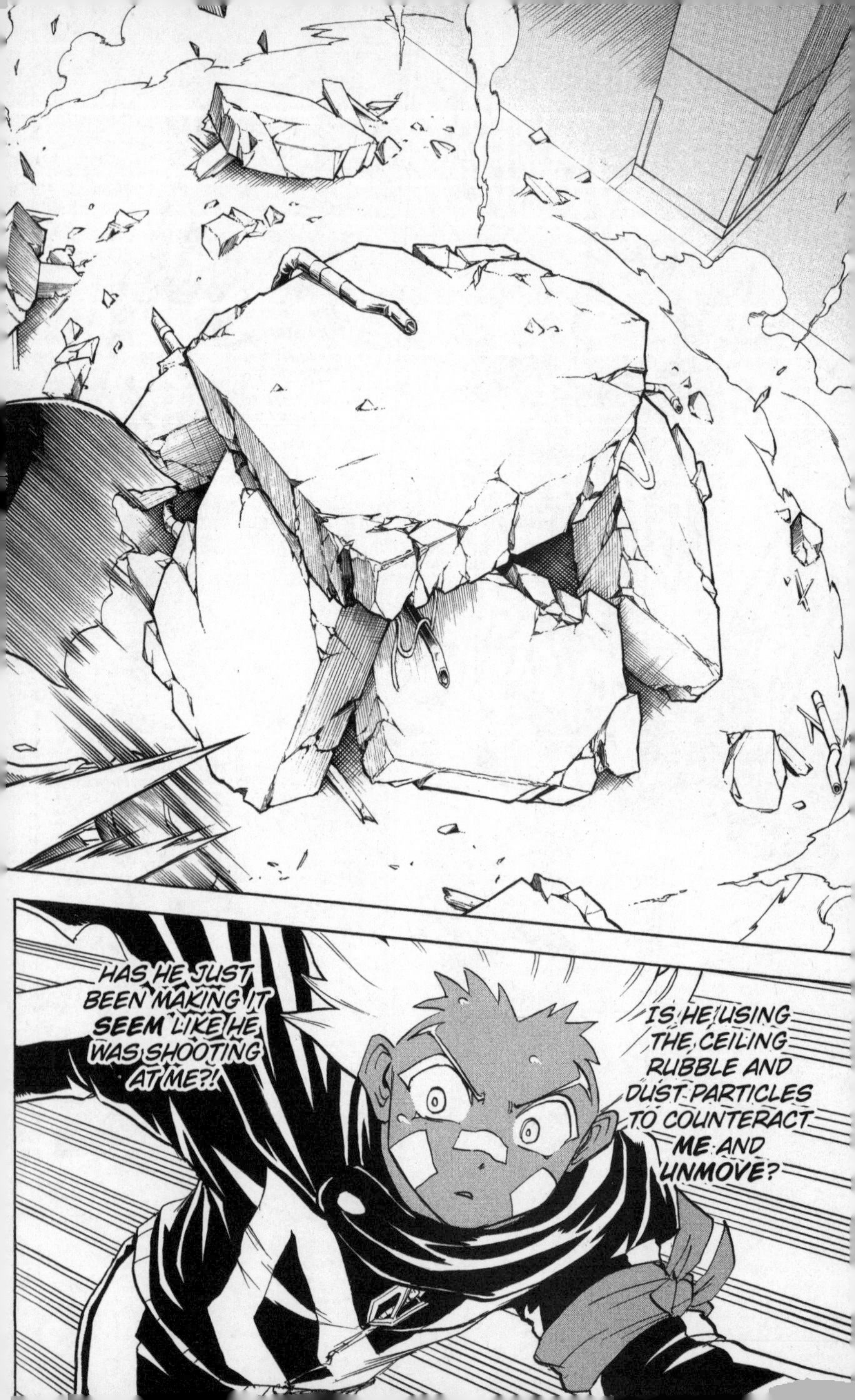
IS HE USING THE CEILING RUBBLE AND DUST PARTICLES TO COUNTERACT ME AND UNMOVE?
HAS HE JUST BEEN MAKING IT SEEM LIKE HE WAS SHOOTING AT ME?!

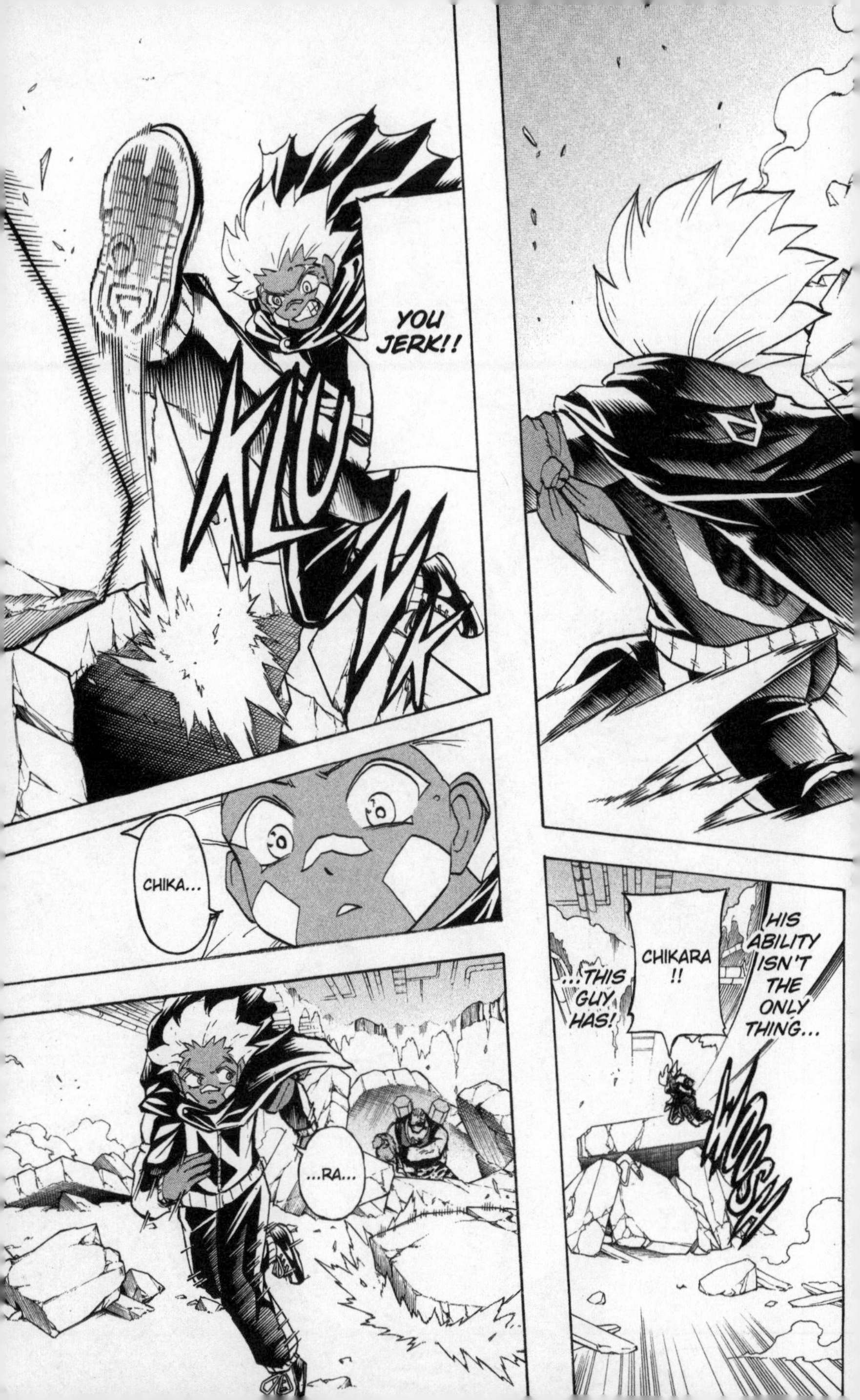
YOU JERK!!
KLUNK
CHIKA...
HIS ABILITY ISN'T THE ONLY THING...
CHIKARA !!
...THIS GUY HAS!
WHOOSH
...RA...

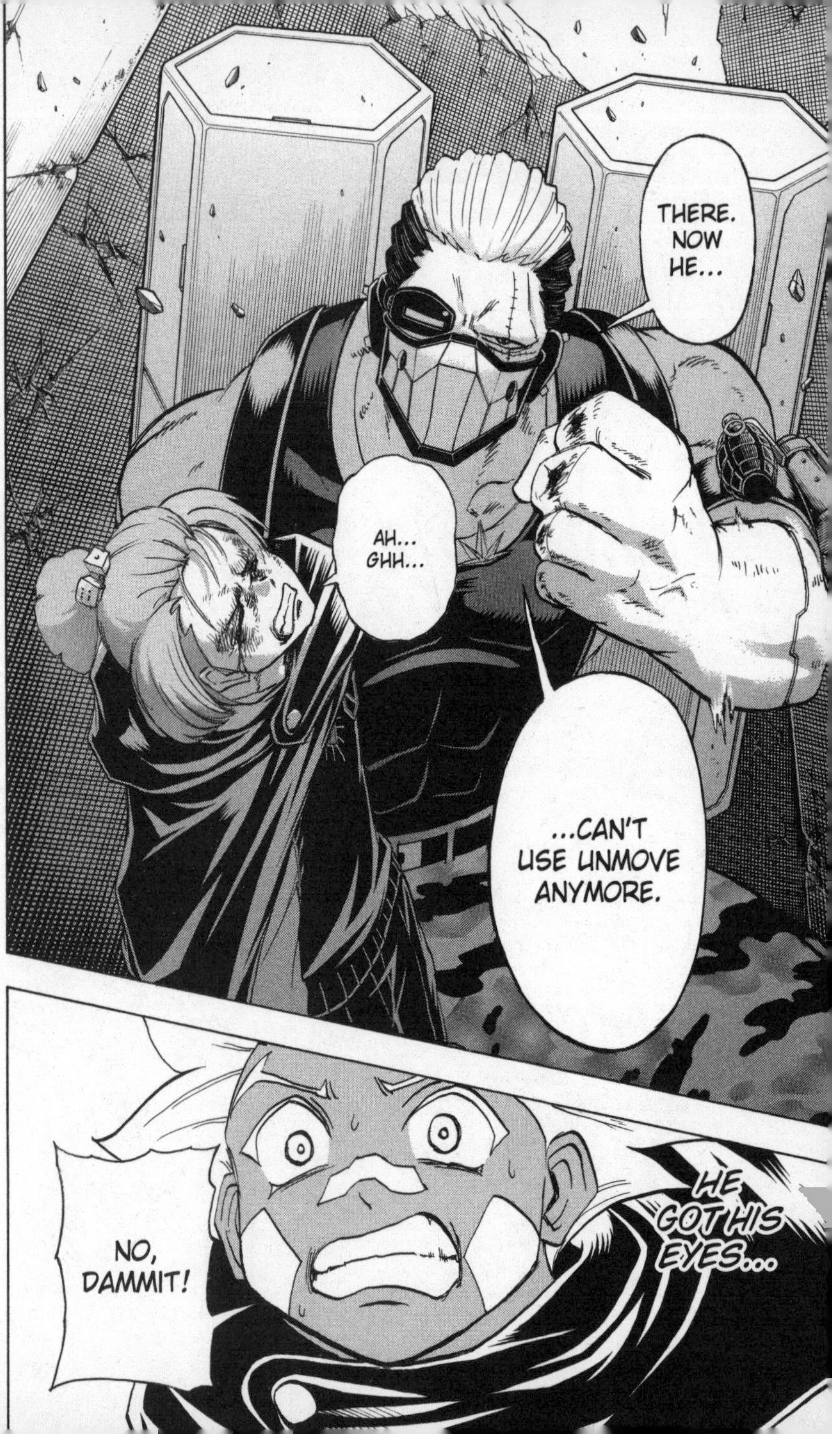
THERE. NOW HE...
AH... GHH...
...CAN'T USE UNMOVE ANYMORE.
HE GOT HIS EYES...
NO, DAMMIT!

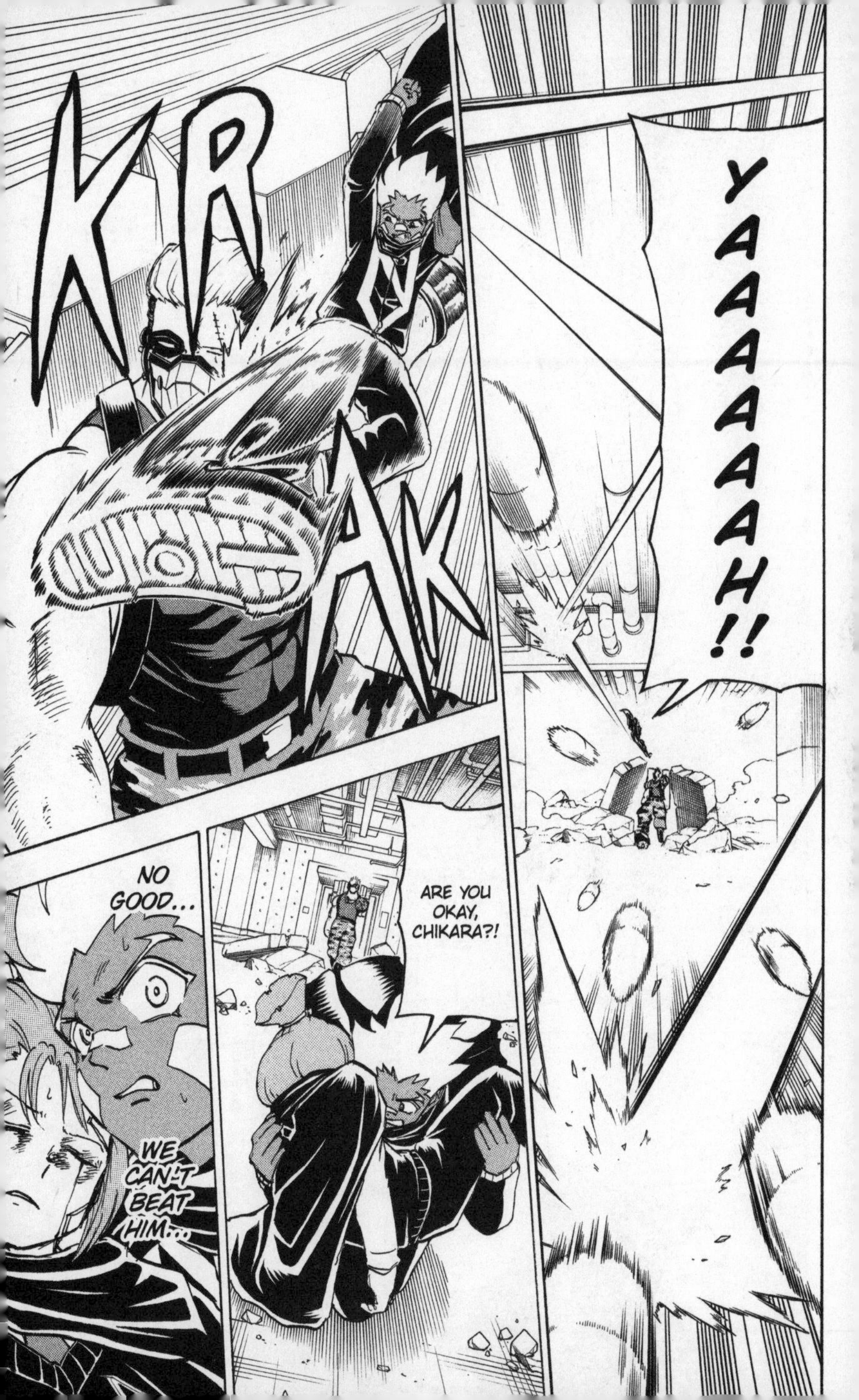
YAAAAAAAH!!
KRAK
ARE YOU OKAY, CHIKARA?!
NO GOOD...
WE CAN'T BEAT HIM...

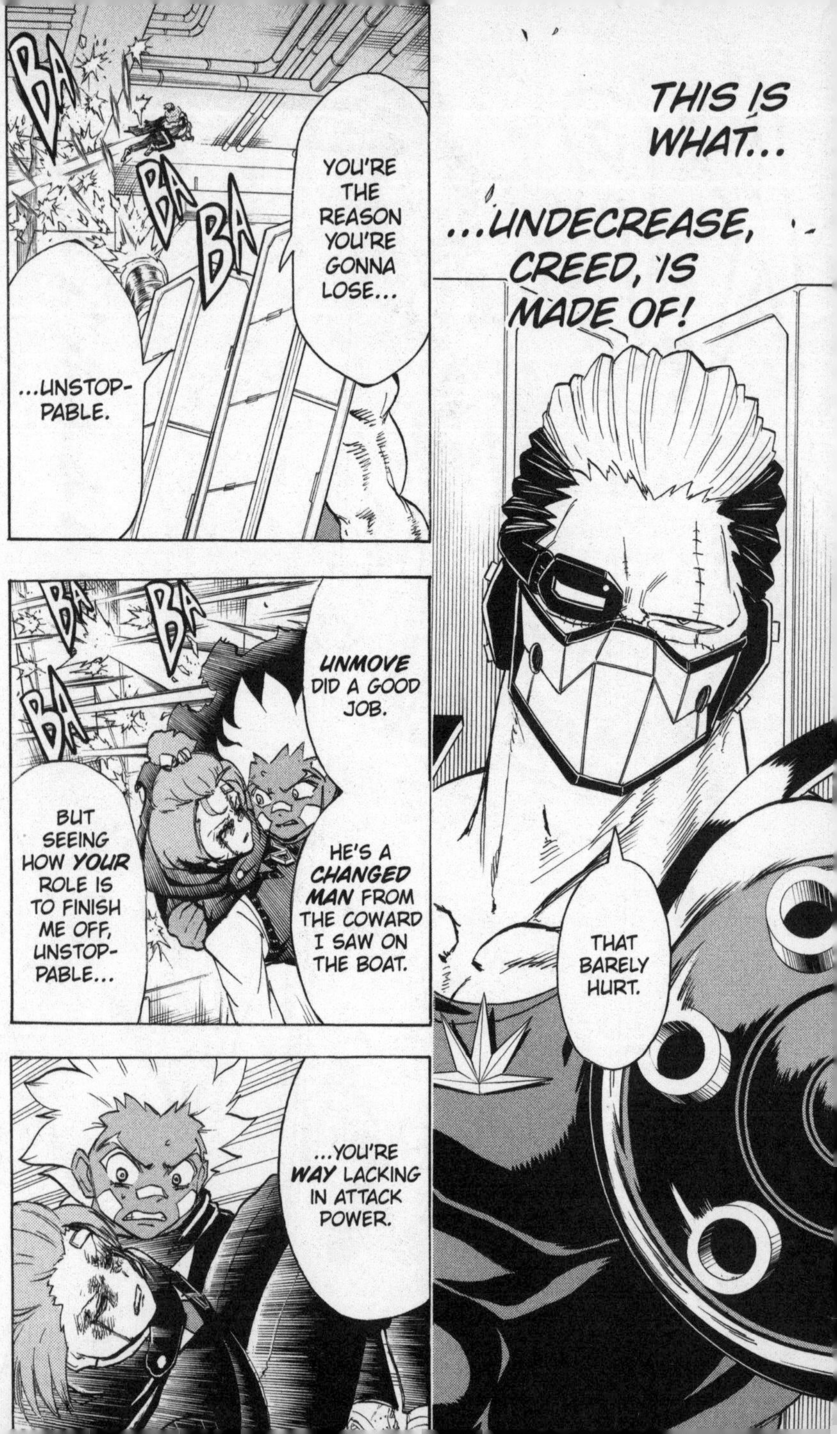
THIS IS WHAT...
...UNDECREASE, CREED, IS MADE OF!
THAT BARELY HURT.
BA
BA
BA
YOU'RE THE REASON YOU'RE GONNA LOSE...
...UNSTOP-PABLE.
BA
BA
BA
UNMOVE DID A GOOD JOB.
HE'S A CHANGED MAN FROM THE COWARD I SAW ON THE BOAT.
BUT SEEING HOW YOUR ROLE IS TO FINISH ME OFF, UNSTOP-PABLE...
...YOU'RE WAY LACKING IN ATTACK POWER.

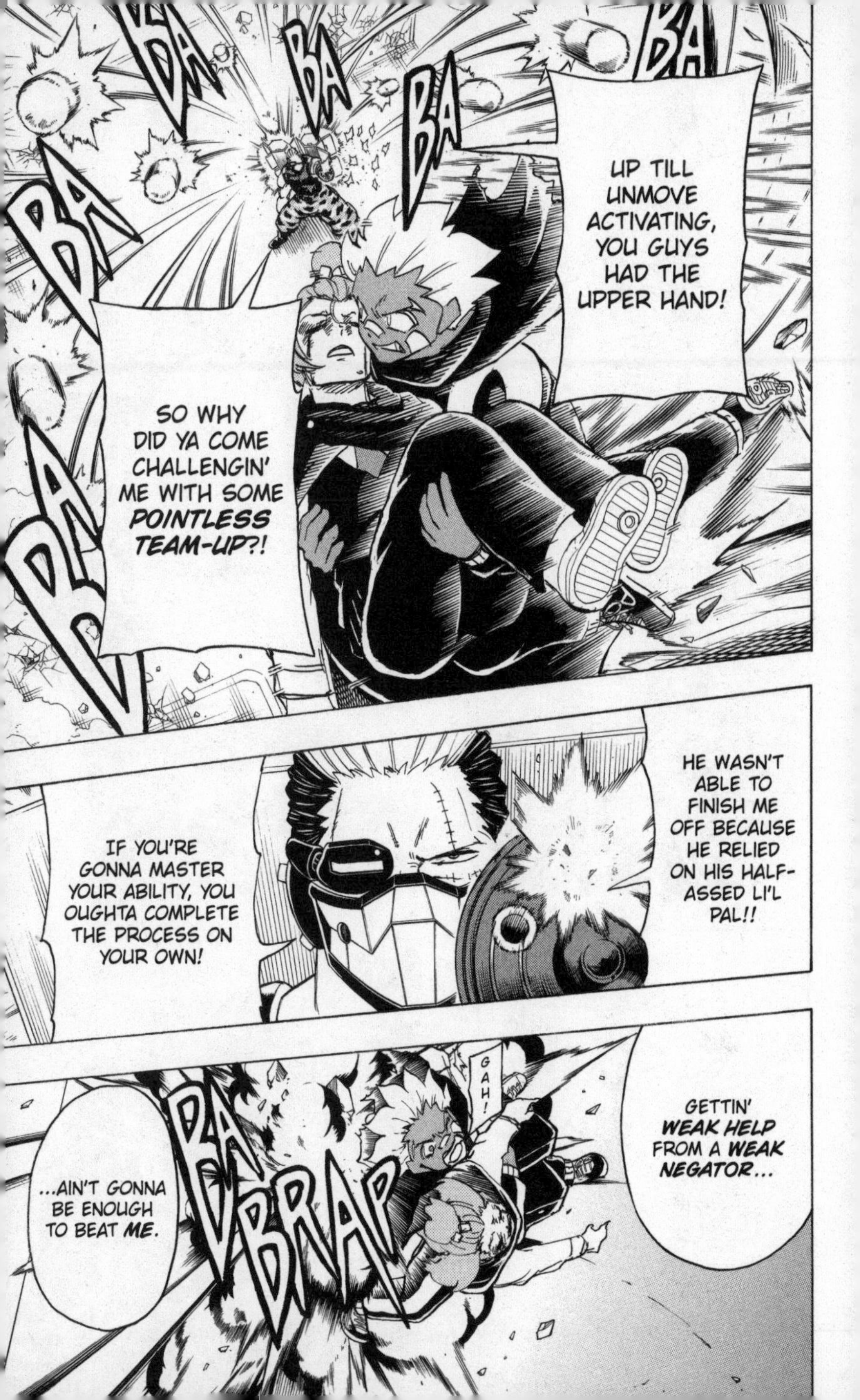
BA
BA
UP TILL UNMOVE ACTIVATING, YOU GUYS HAD THE UPPER HAND!
BA
BA
DA
BA
SO WHY DID YA COME CHALLENGIN' ME WITH SOME POINTLESS TEAM-UP?!
DA
BA
HE WASN'T ABLE TO FINISH ME OFF BECAUSE HE RELIED ON HIS HALF-ASSED LI'L PAL!!
IF YOU'RE GONNA MASTER YOUR ABILITY, YOU OUGHTA COMPLETE THE PROCESS ON YOUR OWN!
GETTIN' WEAK HELP FROM A WEAK NEGATOR...
GAH!
DA
BRAP
...AIN'T GONNA BE ENOUGH TO BEAT ME.

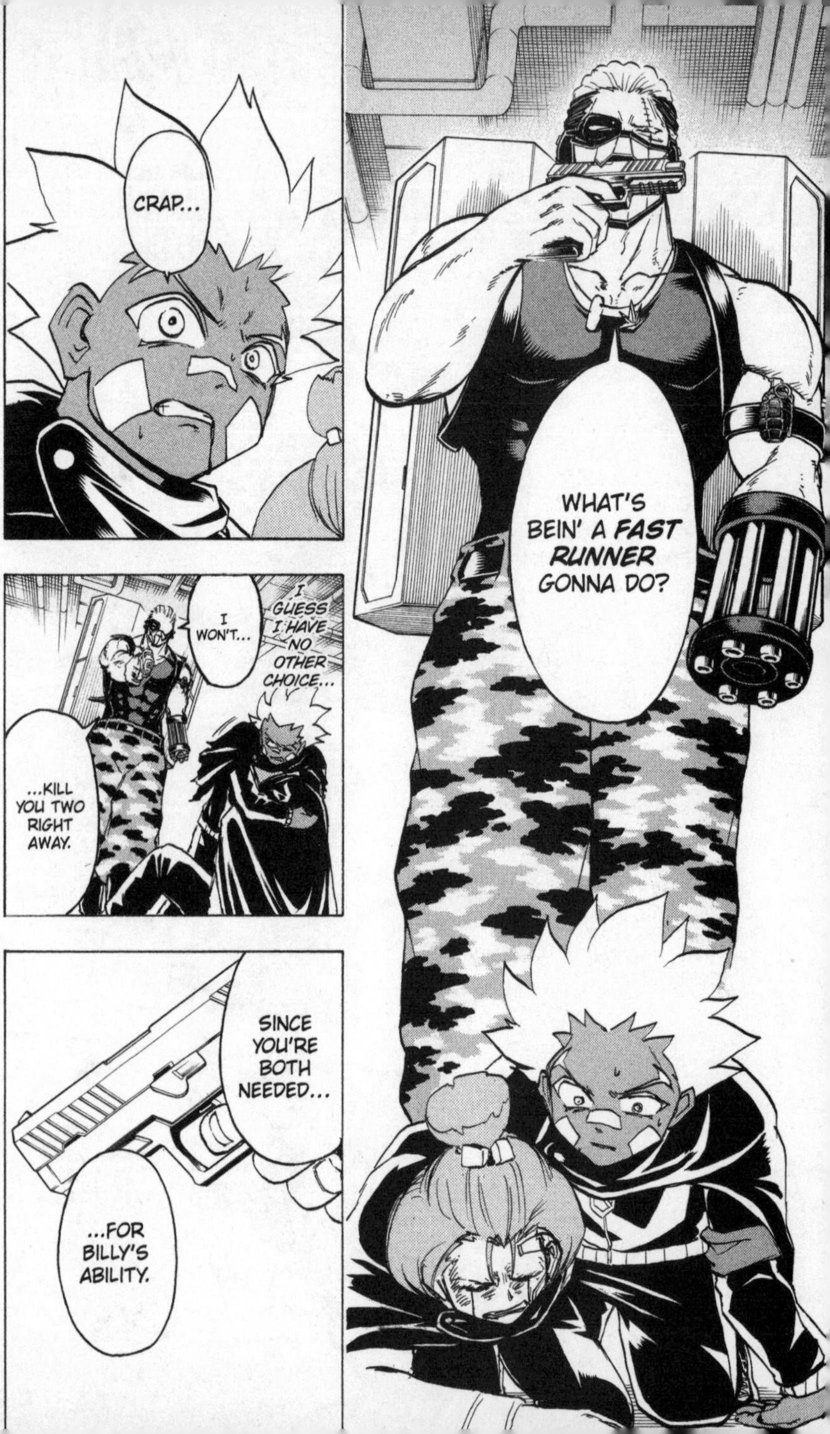
WHAT'S BEIN' A *FAST RUNNER* GONNA DO?
CRAP...
I GUESS I HAVE NO OTHER CHOICE...
I WON'T...
...KILL YOU TWO RIGHT AWAY.
SINCE YOU'RE BOTH NEEDED...
...FOR BILLY'S ABILITY.

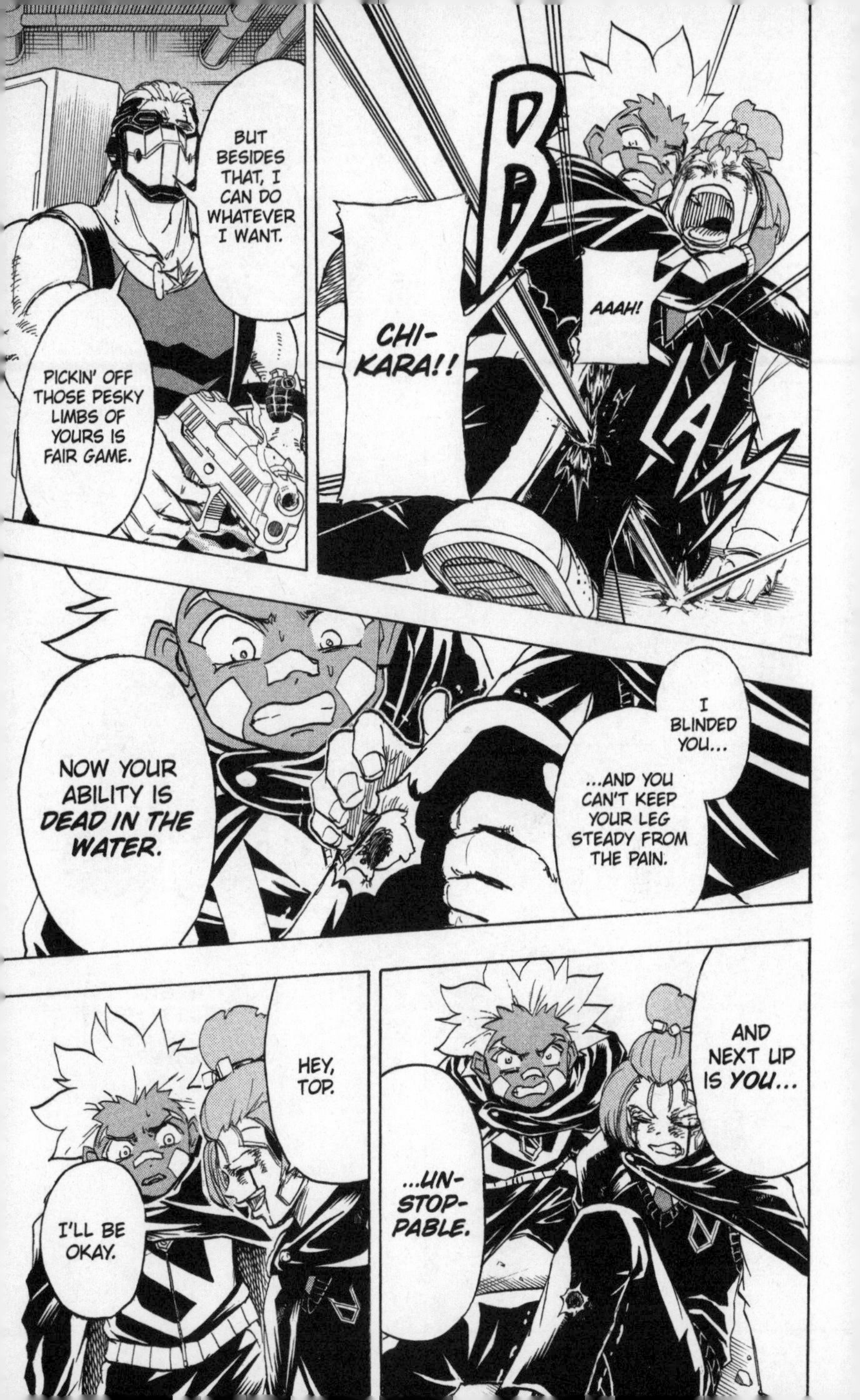
AAAH!
CHI-KARA!!
BLAM
BUT BESIDES THAT, I CAN DO WHATEVER I WANT.
PICKIN' OFF THOSE PESKY LIMBS OF YOURS IS FAIR GAME.
I BLINDED YOU...
...AND YOU CAN'T KEEP YOUR LEG STEADY FROM THE PAIN.
NOW YOUR ABILITY IS DEAD IN THE WATER.
AND NEXT UP IS YOU...
...UN-STOP-PABLE.
HEY, TOP.
I'LL BE OKAY.

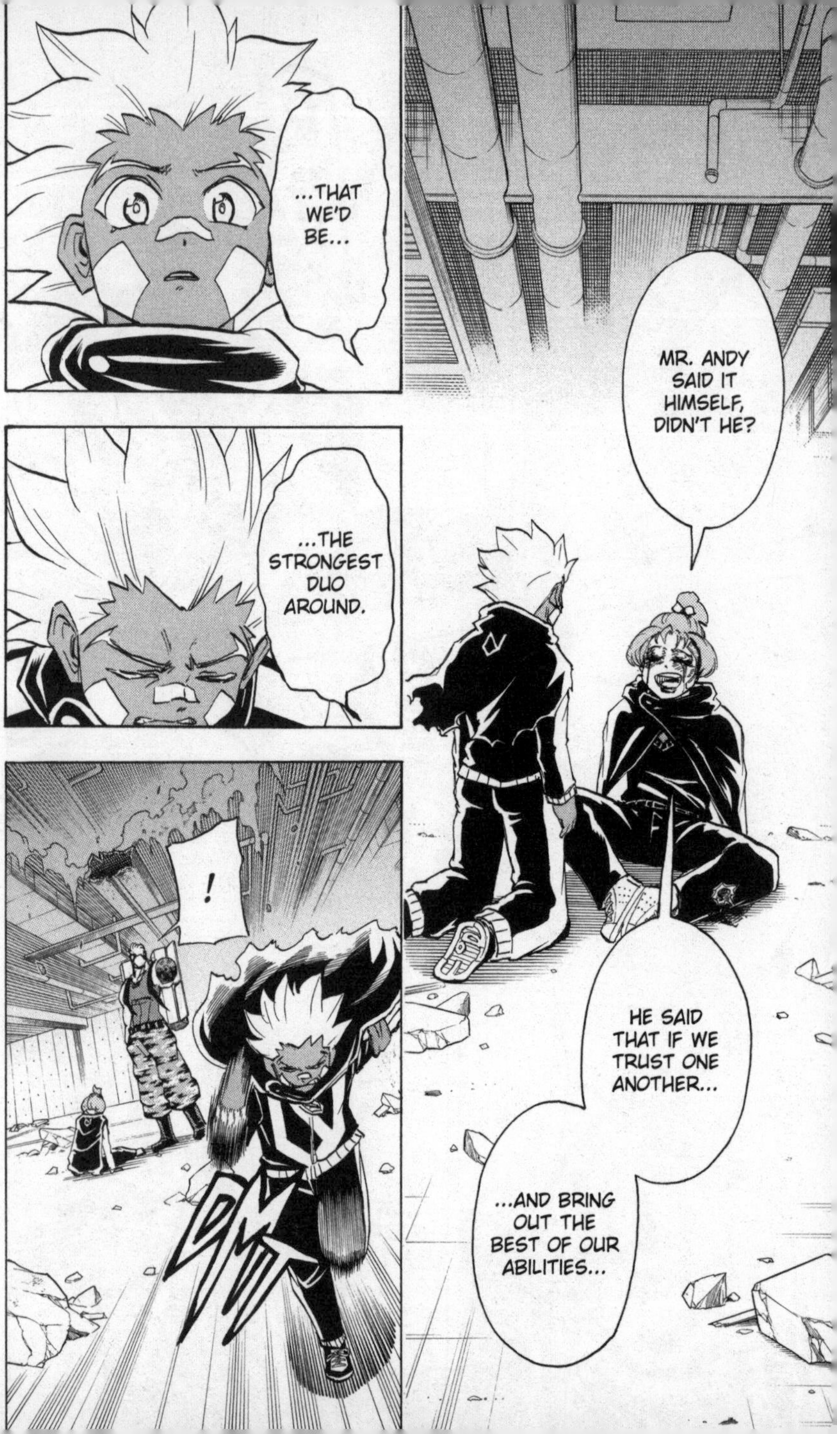
MR. ANDY SAID IT HIMSELF, DIDN'T HE?
HE SAID THAT IF WE TRUST ONE ANOTHER...
...AND BRING OUT THE BEST OF OUR ABILITIES...
...THAT WE'D BE...
...THE STRONGEST DUO AROUND.
!

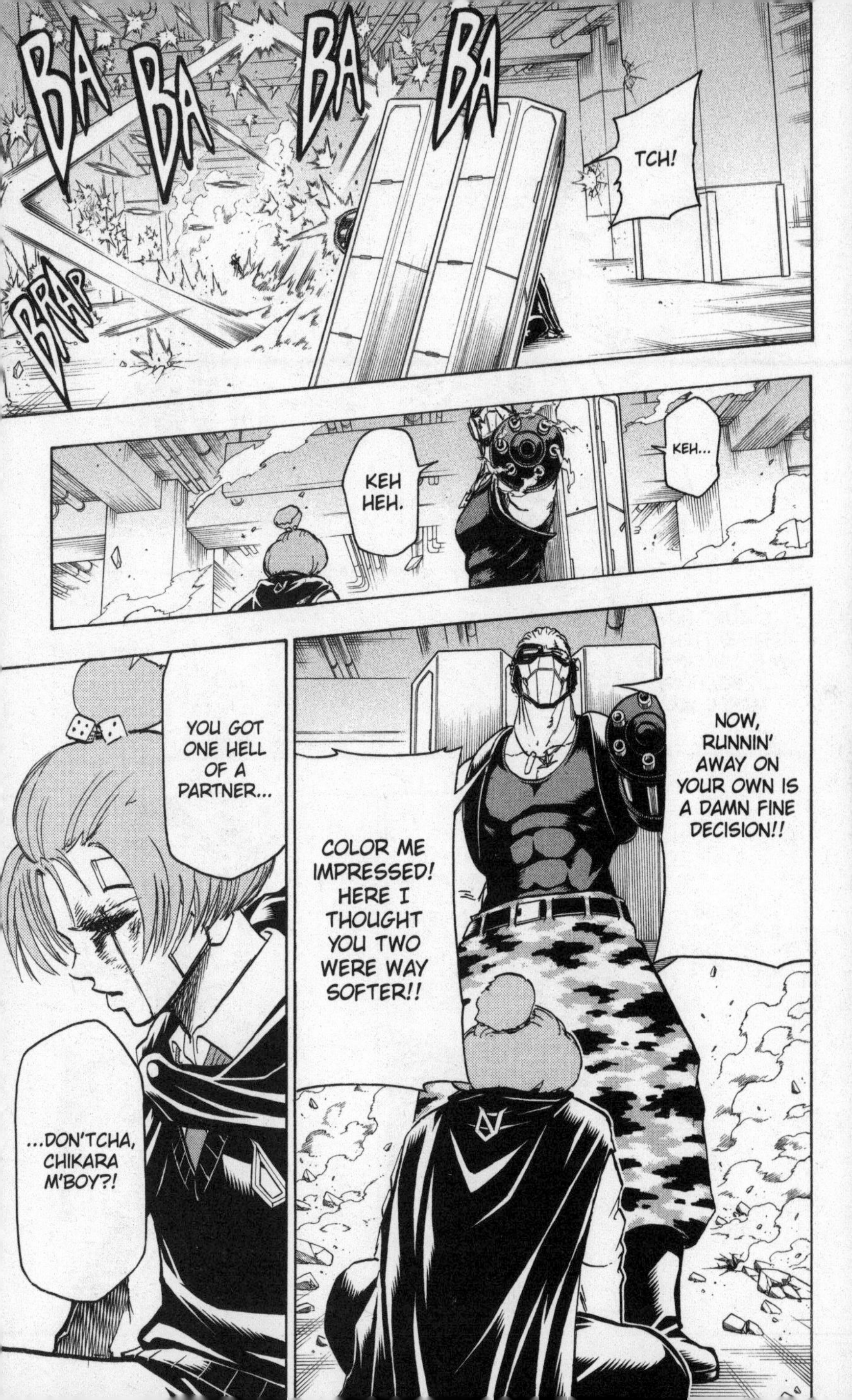
TCH!
BA BA BA BA
BRAP
KEH...
KEH HEH.
NOW, RUNNIN' AWAY ON YOUR OWN IS A DAMN FINE DECISION!!
COLOR ME IMPRESSED! HERE I THOUGHT YOU TWO WERE WAY SOFTER!!
YOU GOT ONE HELL OF A PARTNER...
...DON'TCHA, CHIKARA M'BOY?!

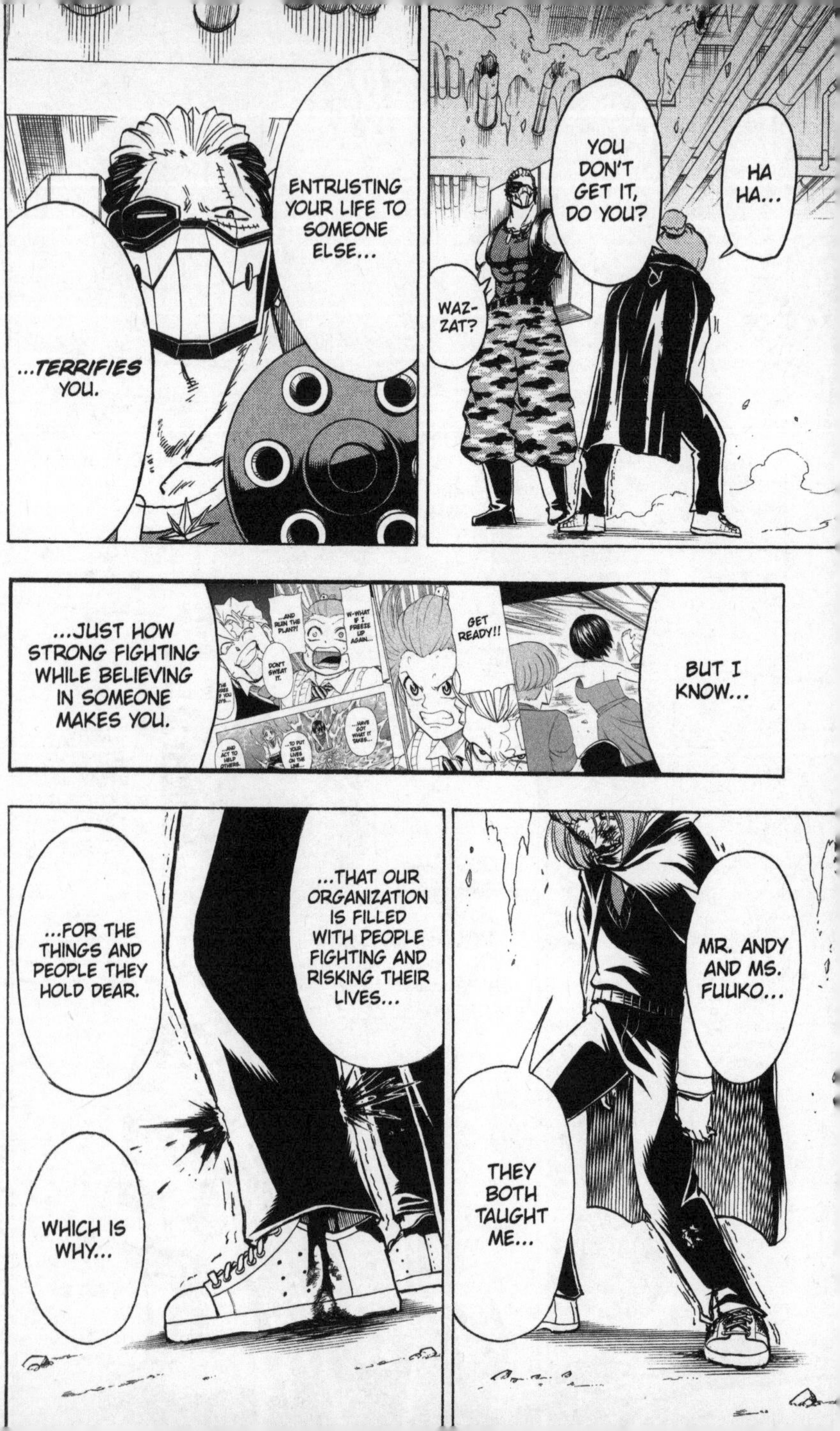
HA HA...
YOU DON'T GET IT, DO YOU?
WAZ-ZAT?
ENTRUSTING YOUR LIFE TO SOMEONE ELSE...
...TERRIFIES YOU.
BUT I KNOW...
GET READY!!
W-WHAT IF I FREEZE UP AGAIN...
...AND RUIN THE PLAN?!
DON'T SWEAT IT.
...HAVE GOT WHAT IT TAKES...
...TO PUT YOUR LIVES ON THE LINE...
...AND ACT TO HELP OTHERS.
...JUST HOW STRONG FIGHTING WHILE BELIEVING IN SOMEONE MAKES YOU.
MR. ANDY AND MS. FUUKO...
THEY BOTH TAUGHT ME...
...THAT OUR ORGANIZATION IS FILLED WITH PEOPLE FIGHTING AND RISKING THEIR LIVES...
...FOR THE THINGS AND PEOPLE THEY HOLD DEAR.
WHICH IS WHY...

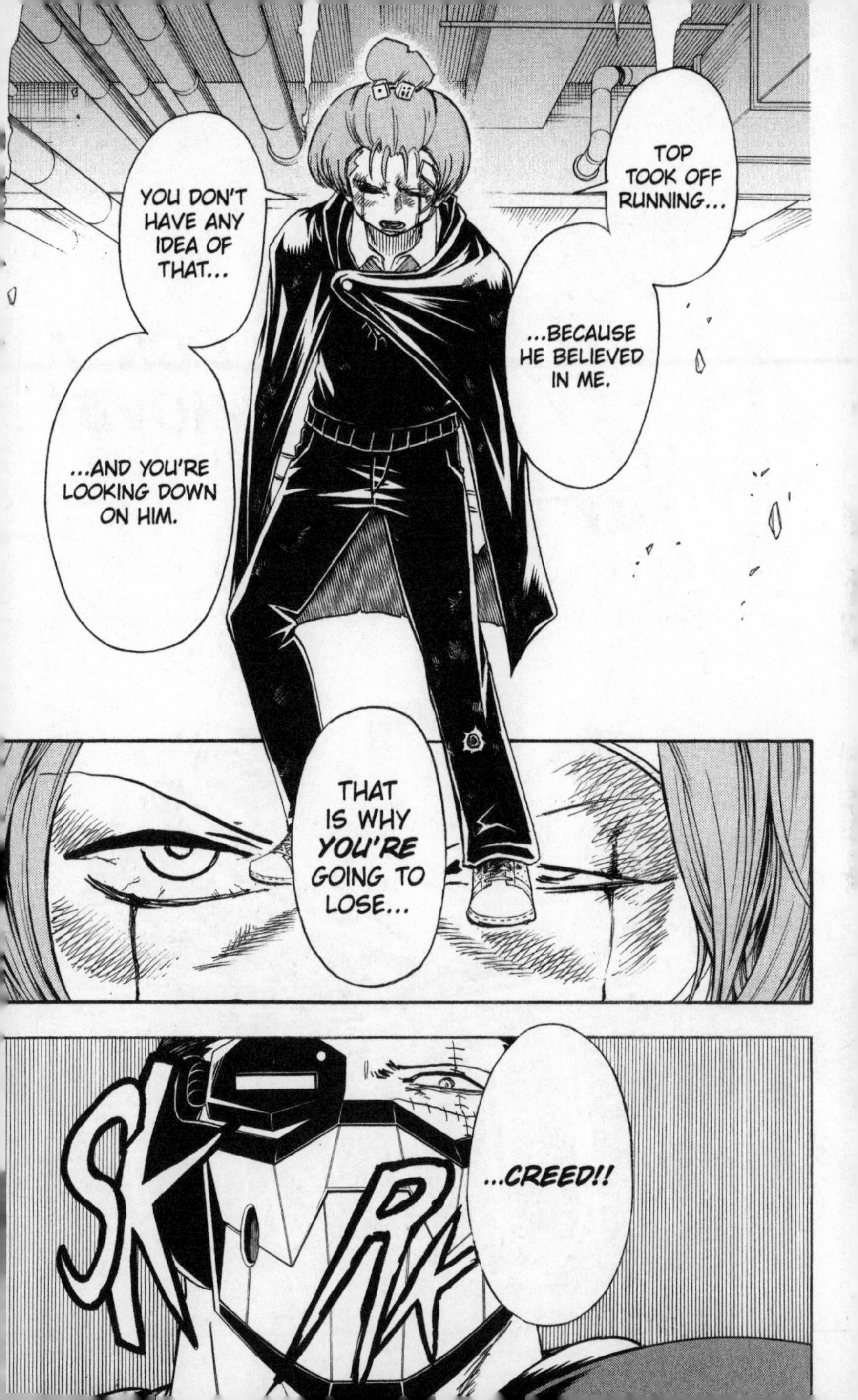
TOP TOOK OFF RUNNING...
...BECAUSE HE BELIEVED IN ME.
YOU DON'T HAVE ANY IDEA OF THAT...
...AND YOU'RE LOOKING DOWN ON HIM.
THAT IS WHY *YOU'RE* GOING TO LOSE...
...CREED!!

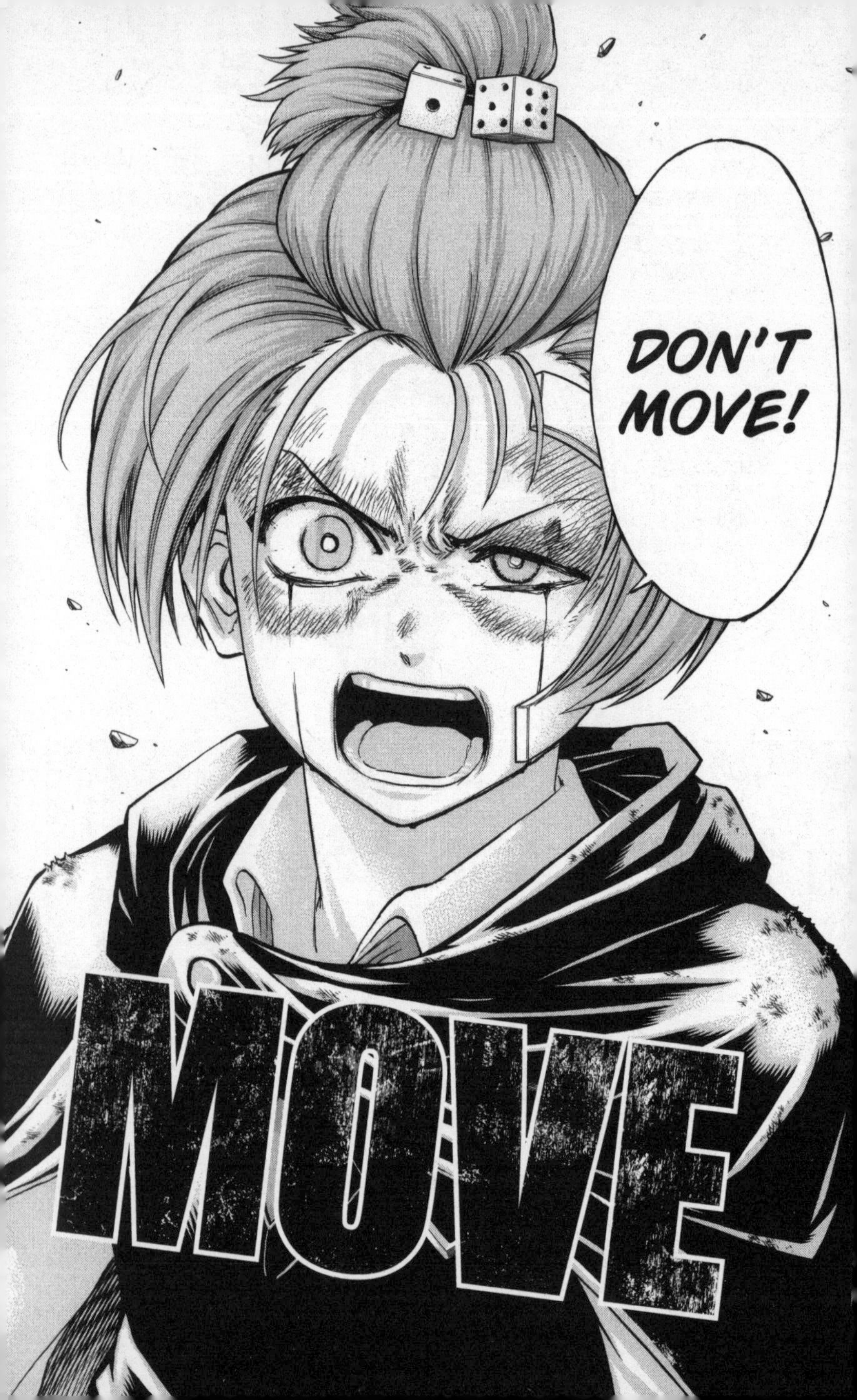
DON'T MOVE!
MOVE

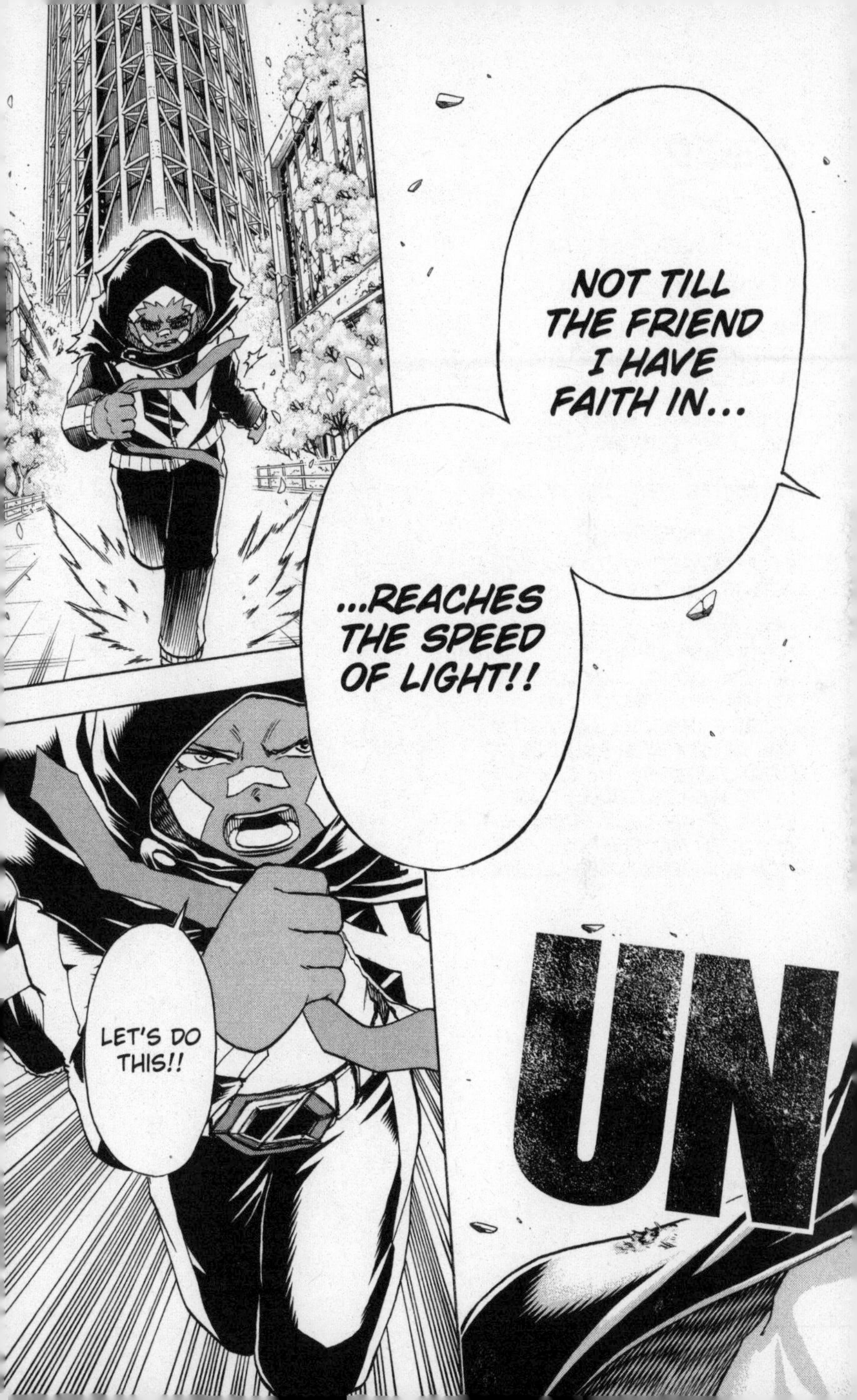
NOT TILL THE FRIEND I HAVE FAITH IN...
...REACHES THE SPEED OF LIGHT!!
UN
LET'S DO THIS!!

CREED

AGE: THIRTIES

HEIGHT: OVER 2 METERS

WEIGHT: AIN'T GOT A CLUE

HOBBIES: CHECKING THE GUN MARKET, COLLECTING HANDGUNS

SPECIAL SKILL: STRICTLY EDUCATING SUBORDINATES

FAVORITES: BEEF JERKY, BEER

ABILITY: UNDECREASE

SELF-TARGETING COMPULSORY ACTIVATION-TYPE

NEGATES THE CONSUMPTION OR "DECREASE" OF ANYTHING THAT HE CONSCIOUSLY RECOGNIZES AS HIS OWN WEAPON. IN CREED'S CASE, HE CAN ACTIVATE THE ABILITY WITH BULLETS OR HAND GRENADES. HE CAN FIRE UP TO HIS LAST BULLET OR BLOW UP HIS LAST GRENADE AND THEN MANIFEST THE SAME ITEM IN A DESIGNATED LOCATION.

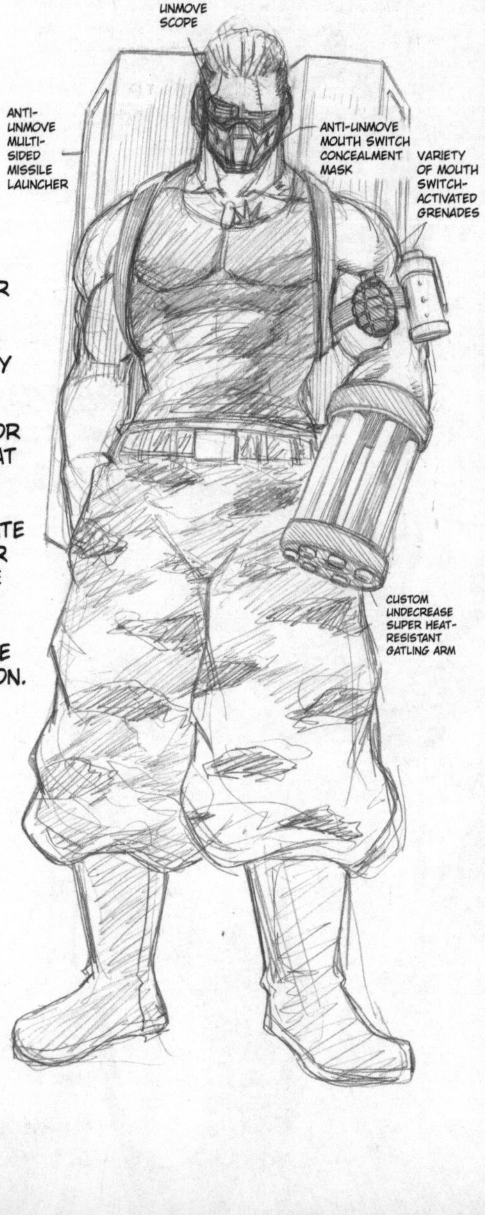

ANTI-UNMOVE SCOPE
ANTI-UNMOVE MULTI-SIDED MISSILE LAUNCHER
ANTI-UNMOVE MOUTH SWITCH CONCEALMENT MASK
VARIETY OF MOUTH SWITCH-ACTIVATED GRENADES
CUSTOM UNDECREASE SUPER HEAT-RESISTANT GATLING ARM

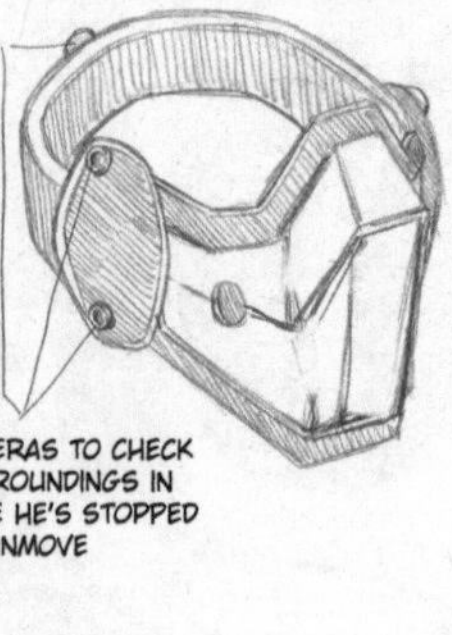

CAMERAS TO CHECK SURROUNDINGS IN CASE HE'S STOPPED BY UNMOVE

No. 077 On Your Mark

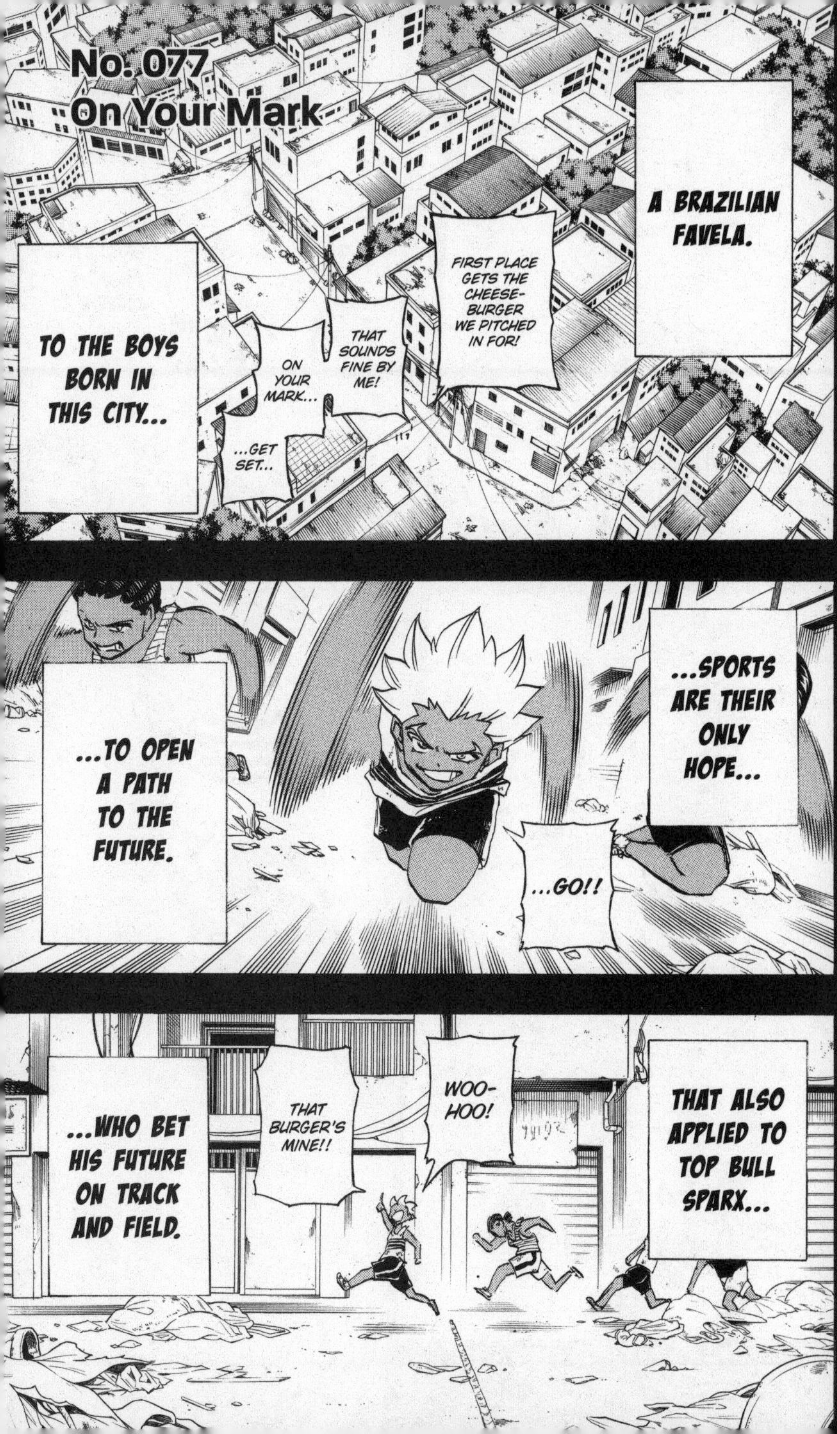
A BRAZILIAN FAVELA.
FIRST PLACE GETS THE CHEESE-BURGER WE PITCHED IN FOR!
THAT SOUNDS FINE BY ME!
ON YOUR MARK...
...GET SET...
TO THE BOYS BORN IN THIS CITY...
...SPORTS ARE THEIR ONLY HOPE...
...GO!!
...TO OPEN A PATH TO THE FUTURE.
THAT ALSO APPLIED TO TOP BULL SPARX...
WOO-HOO!
THAT BURGER'S MINE!!
...WHO BET HIS FUTURE ON TRACK AND FIELD.

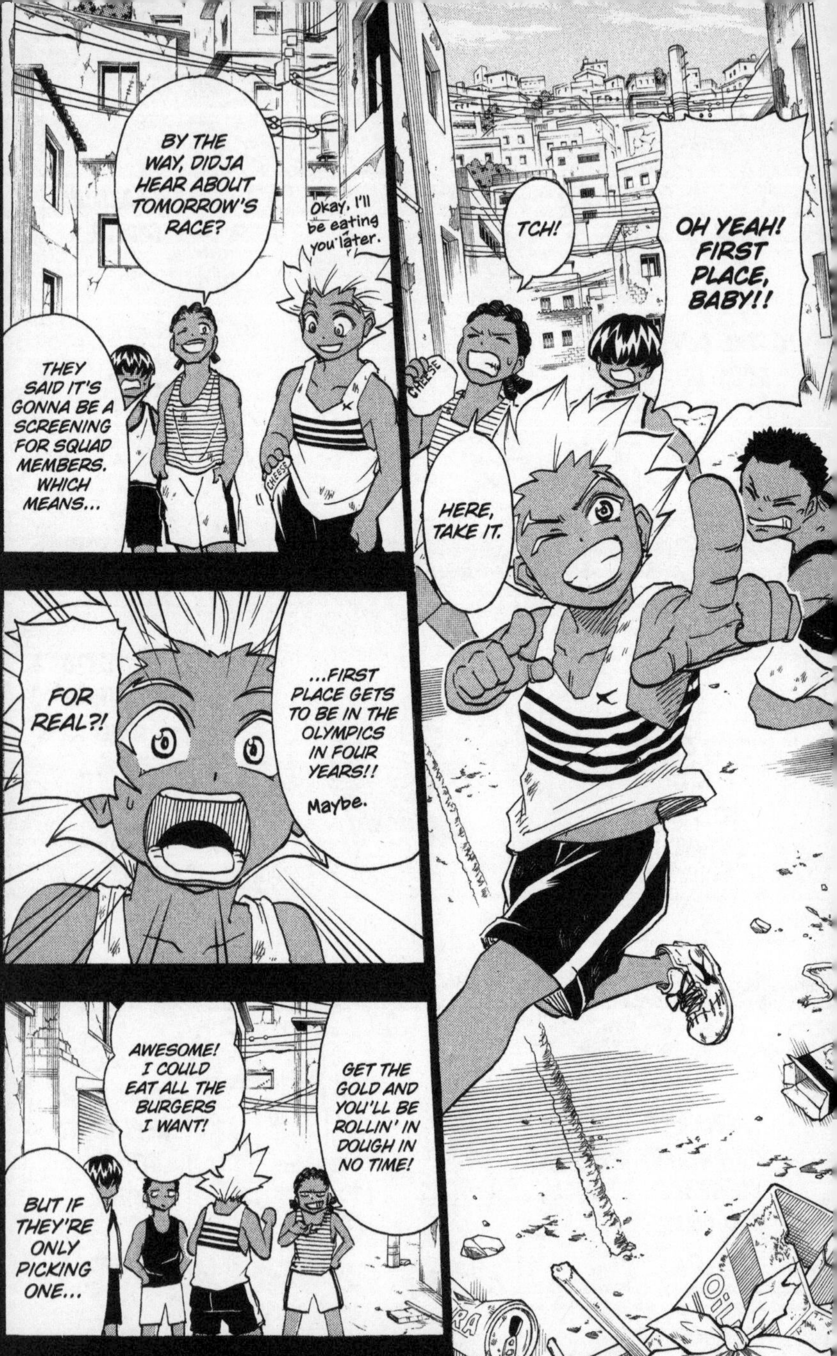
OH YEAH! FIRST PLACE, BABY!!
TCH!
HERE, TAKE IT.
CHEESE
Okay, I'll be eating you later.
BY THE WAY, DIDJA HEAR ABOUT TOMORROW'S RACE?
THEY SAID IT'S GONNA BE A SCREENING FOR SQUAD MEMBERS. WHICH MEANS...
CHEESE
...FIRST PLACE GETS TO BE IN THE OLYMPICS IN FOUR YEARS!!
Maybe.
FOR REAL?!
GET THE GOLD AND YOU'LL BE ROLLIN' IN DOUGH IN NO TIME!
AWESOME! I COULD EAT ALL THE BURGERS I WANT!
BUT IF THEY'RE ONLY PICKING ONE...

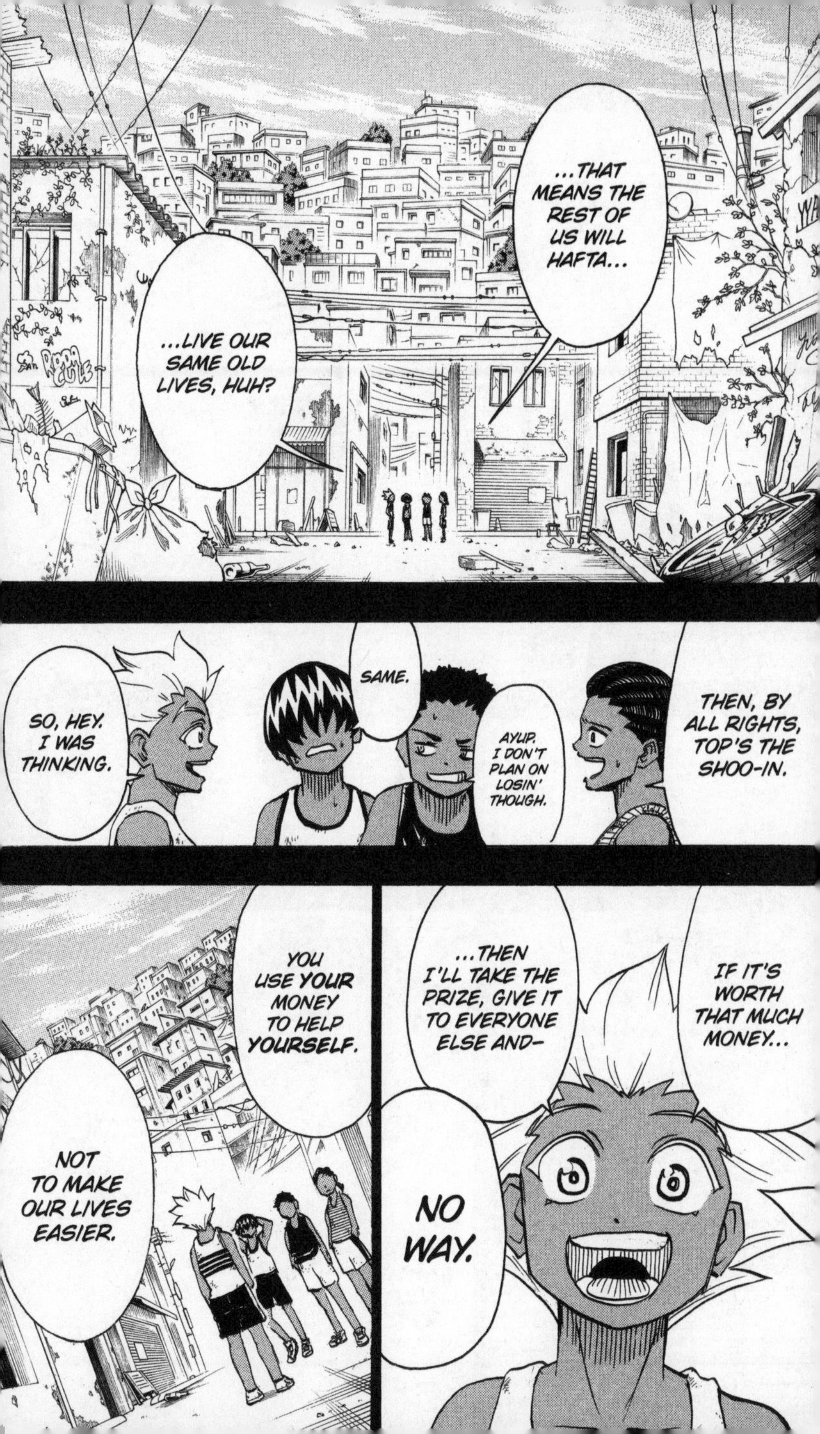
...THAT MEANS THE REST OF US WILL HAFTA...
...LIVE OUR SAME OLD LIVES, HUH?
THEN, BY ALL RIGHTS, TOP'S THE SHOO-IN.
AYUP. I DON'T PLAN ON LOSIN' THOUGH.
SAME.
SO, HEY. I WAS THINKING.
IF IT'S WORTH THAT MUCH MONEY...
...THEN I'LL TAKE THE PRIZE, GIVE IT TO EVERYONE ELSE AND-
NO WAY.
YOU USE YOUR MONEY TO HELP YOURSELF.
NOT TO MAKE OUR LIVES EASIER.

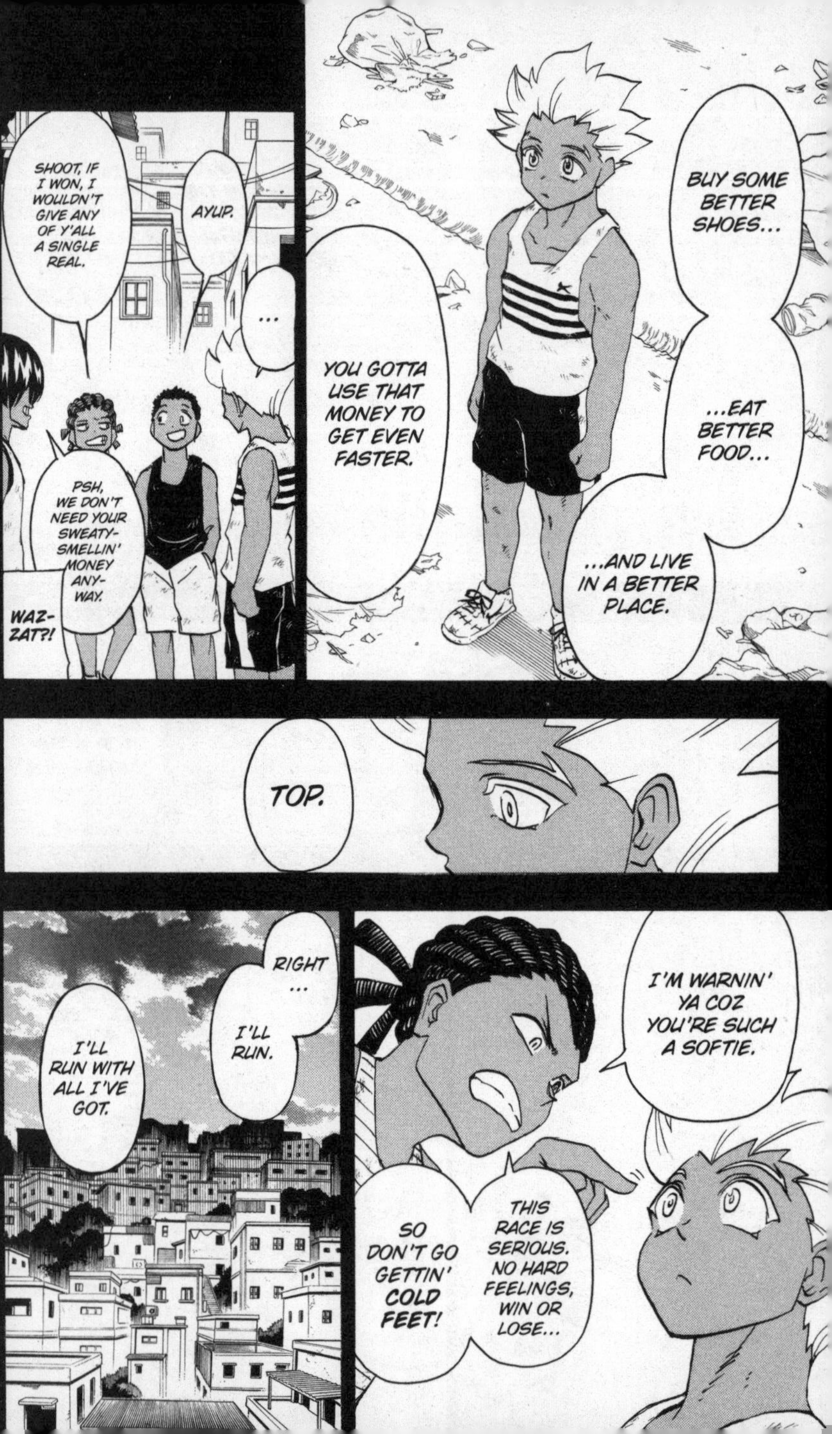

BUY SOME BETTER SHOES...
...EAT BETTER FOOD...
...AND LIVE IN A BETTER PLACE.
YOU GOTTA USE THAT MONEY TO GET EVEN FASTER.
...
AYUP.
SHOOT, IF I WON, I WOULDN'T GIVE ANY OF Y'ALL A SINGLE REAL.
PSH, WE DON'T NEED YOUR SWEATY-SMELLIN' MONEY ANYWAY.
WAZ-ZAT?!
TOP.
I'M WARNIN' YA COZ YOU'RE SUCH A SOFTIE.
THIS RACE IS SERIOUS. NO HARD FEELINGS, WIN OR LOSE...
SO DON'T GO GETTIN' COLD FEET!
RIGHT...
I'LL RUN.
I'LL RUN WITH ALL I'VE GOT.

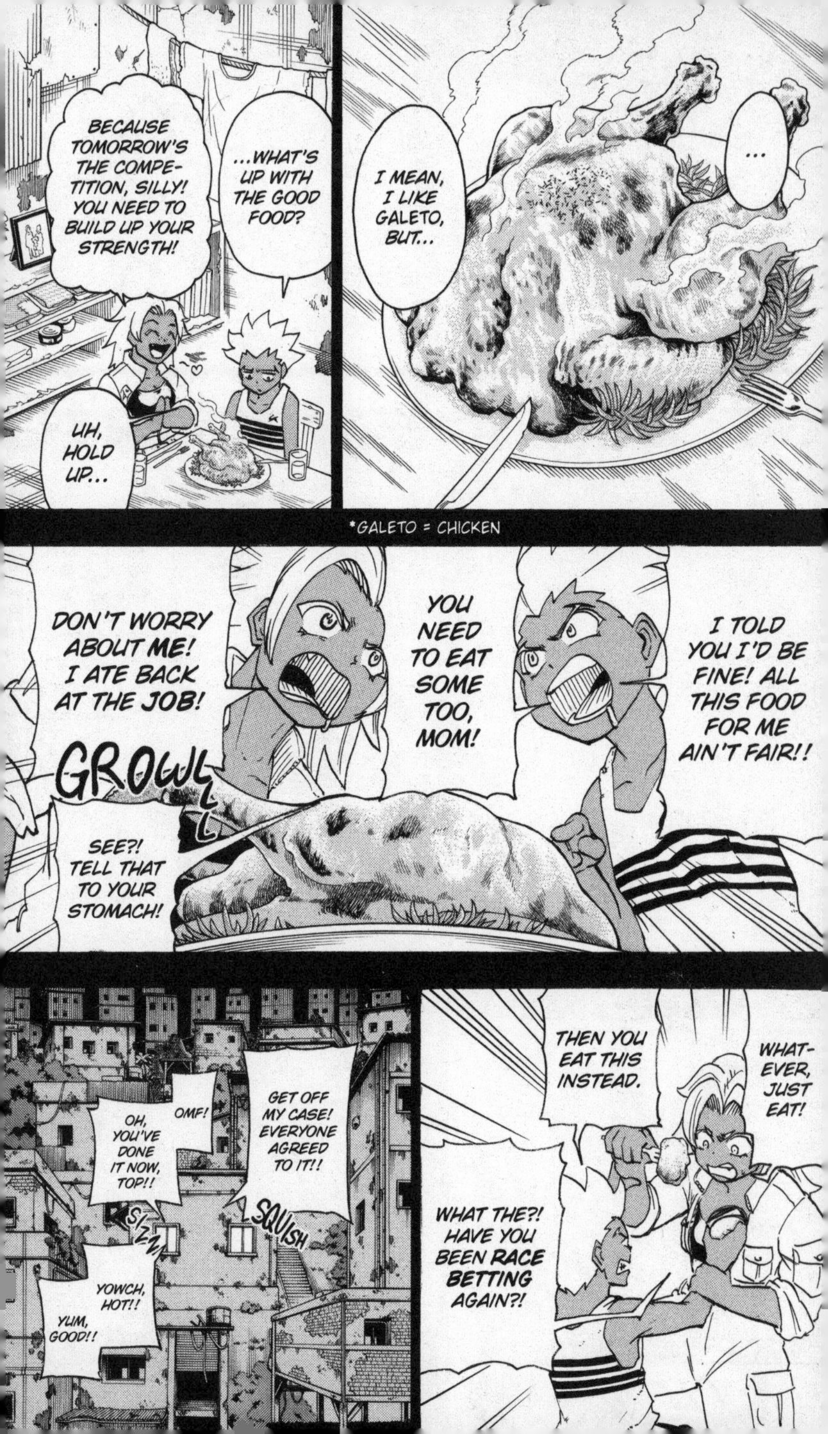
...
I MEAN, I LIKE GALETO, BUT...
...WHAT'S UP WITH THE GOOD FOOD?
BECAUSE TOMORROW'S THE COMPETITION, SILLY! YOU NEED TO BUILD UP YOUR STRENGTH!
UH, HOLD UP...
*GALETO = CHICKEN
I TOLD YOU I'D BE FINE! ALL THIS FOOD FOR ME AIN'T FAIR!!
YOU NEED TO EAT SOME TOO, MOM!
DON'T WORRY ABOUT ME! I ATE BACK AT THE JOB!
GROWL
SEE?! TELL THAT TO YOUR STOMACH!
WHATEVER, JUST EAT!
THEN YOU EAT THIS INSTEAD.
WHAT THE?! HAVE YOU BEEN RACE BETTING AGAIN?!
GET OFF MY CASE! EVERYONE AGREED TO IT!!
OMF!
OH, YOU'VE DONE IT NOW, TOP!!
SQUISH
SIZZ
YOWCH, HOT!!
YUM, GOOD!!

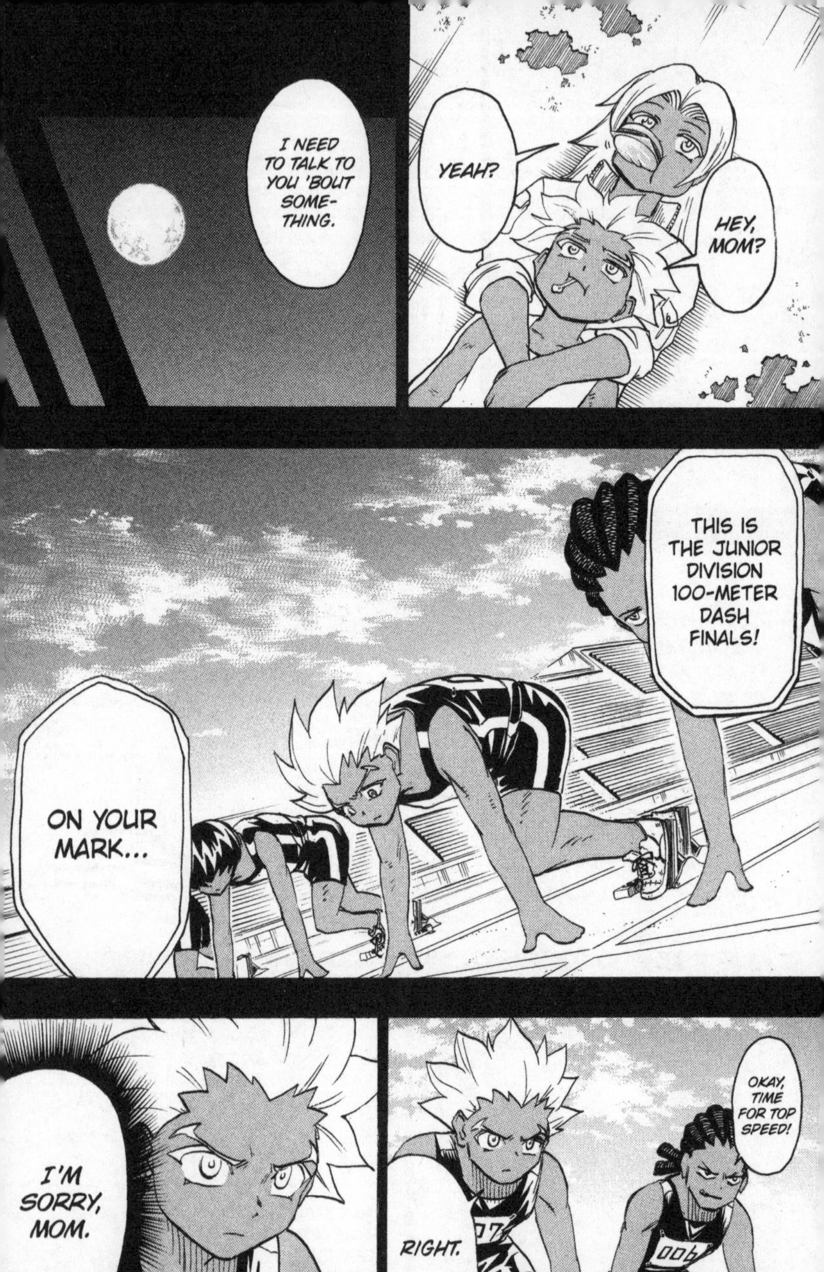
HEY, MOM?
YEAH?
I NEED TO TALK TO YOU 'BOUT SOMETHING.
THIS IS THE JUNIOR DIVISION 100-METER DASH FINALS!
ON YOUR MARK...
OKAY, TIME FOR TOP SPEED!
RIGHT.
I'M SORRY, MOM.

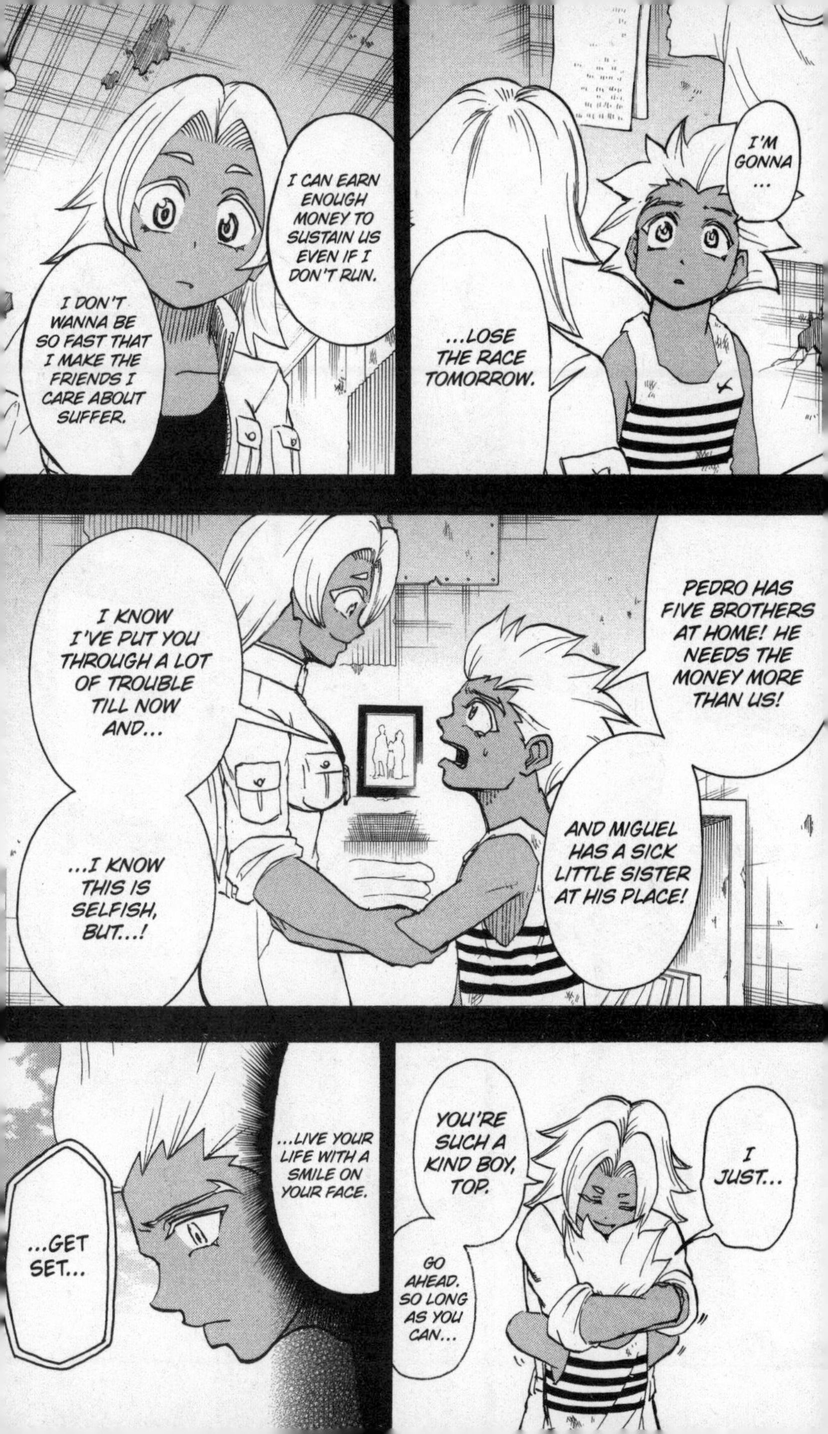
I'M GONNA ...
...LOSE THE RACE TOMORROW.
I CAN EARN ENOUGH MONEY TO SUSTAIN US EVEN IF I DON'T RUN.
I DON'T WANNA BE SO FAST THAT I MAKE THE FRIENDS I CARE ABOUT SUFFER.
PEDRO HAS FIVE BROTHERS AT HOME! HE NEEDS THE MONEY MORE THAN US!
AND MIGUEL HAS A SICK LITTLE SISTER AT HIS PLACE!
I KNOW I'VE PUT YOU THROUGH A LOT OF TROUBLE TILL NOW AND...
...I KNOW THIS IS SELFISH, BUT...!
I JUST...
YOU'RE SUCH A KIND BOY, TOP.
GO AHEAD. SO LONG AS YOU CAN...
...LIVE YOUR LIFE WITH A SMILE ON YOUR FACE.
...GET SET...

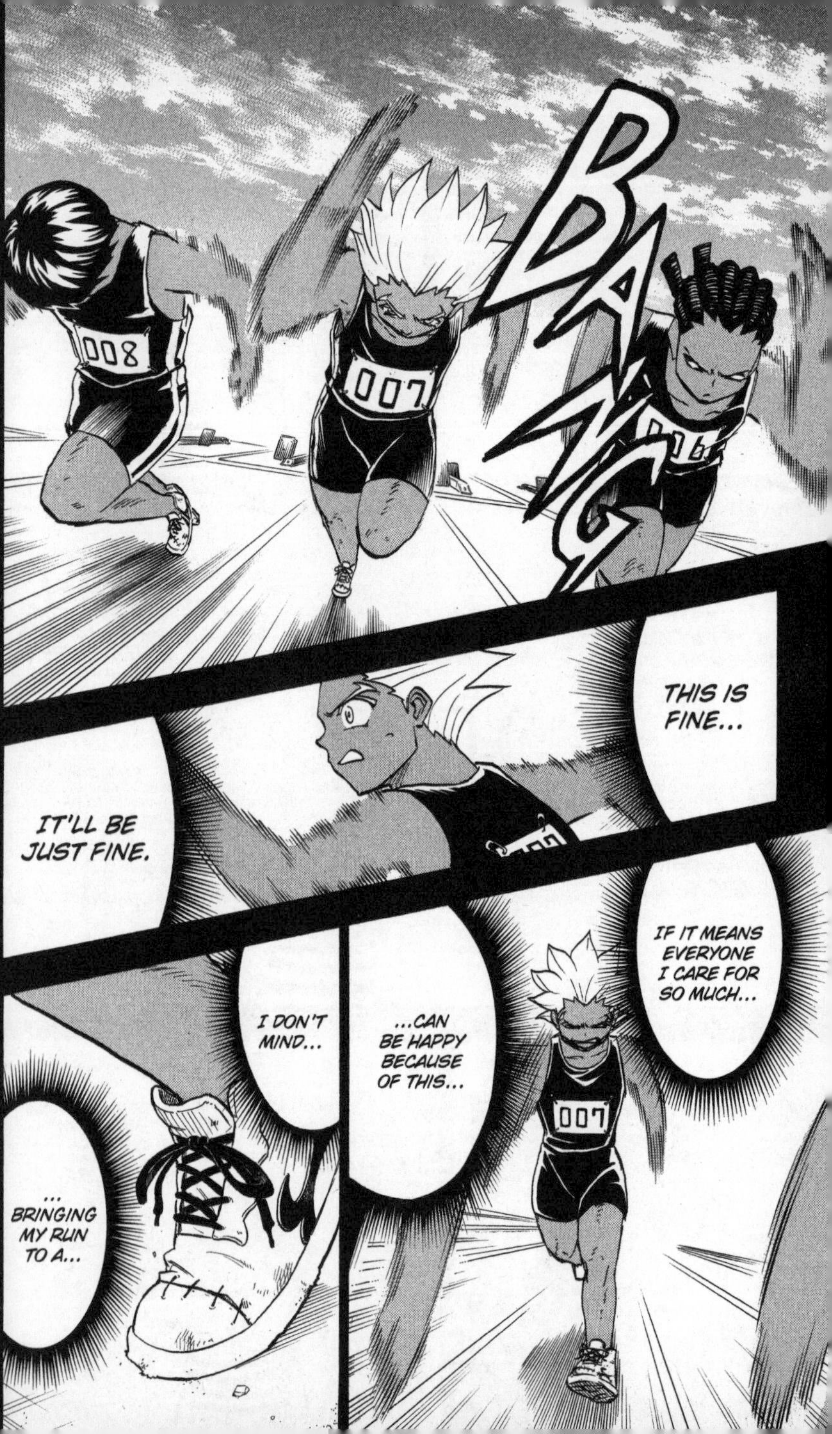
BANG
THIS IS FINE...
IT'LL BE JUST FINE.
IF IT MEANS EVERYONE I CARE FOR SO MUCH...
...CAN BE HAPPY BECAUSE OF THIS...
I DON'T MIND...
... BRINGING MY RUN TO A...

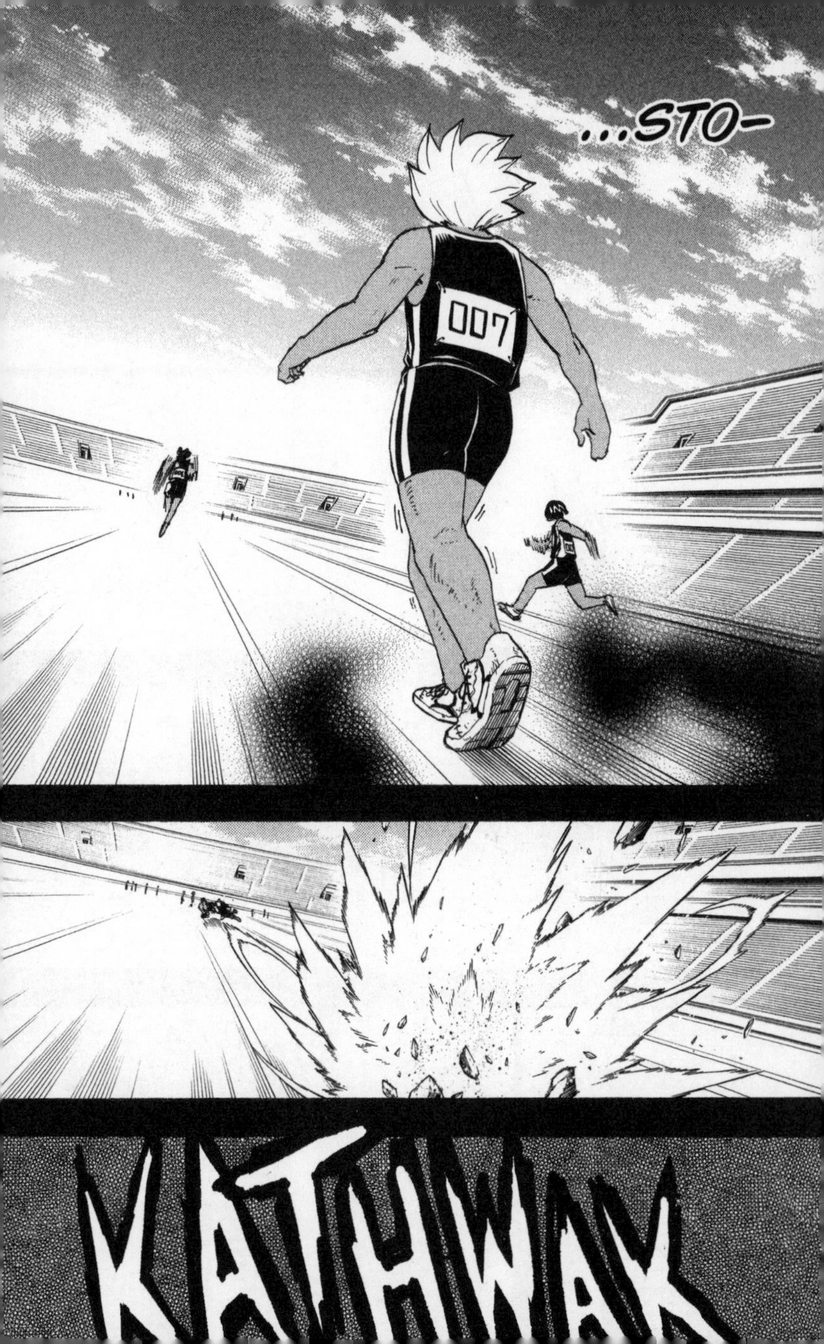
...STO-
007
KATHWAK

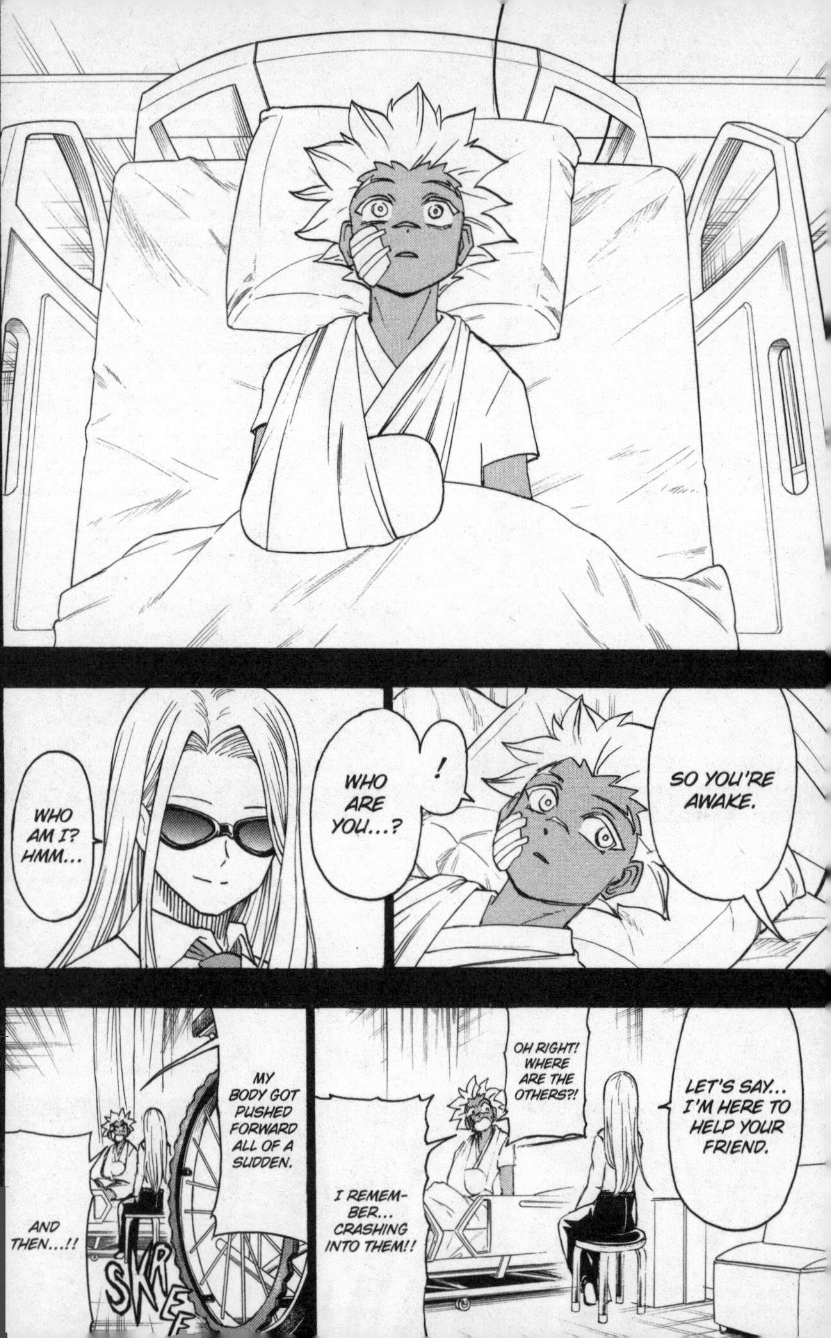
SO YOU'RE AWAKE.
!
WHO ARE YOU...?
WHO AM I? HMM...
LET'S SAY... I'M HERE TO HELP YOUR FRIEND.
OH RIGHT! WHERE ARE THE OTHERS?!
I REMEMBER... CRASHING INTO THEM!!
MY BODY GOT PUSHED FORWARD ALL OF A SUDDEN.
AND THEN...!!
SKREE

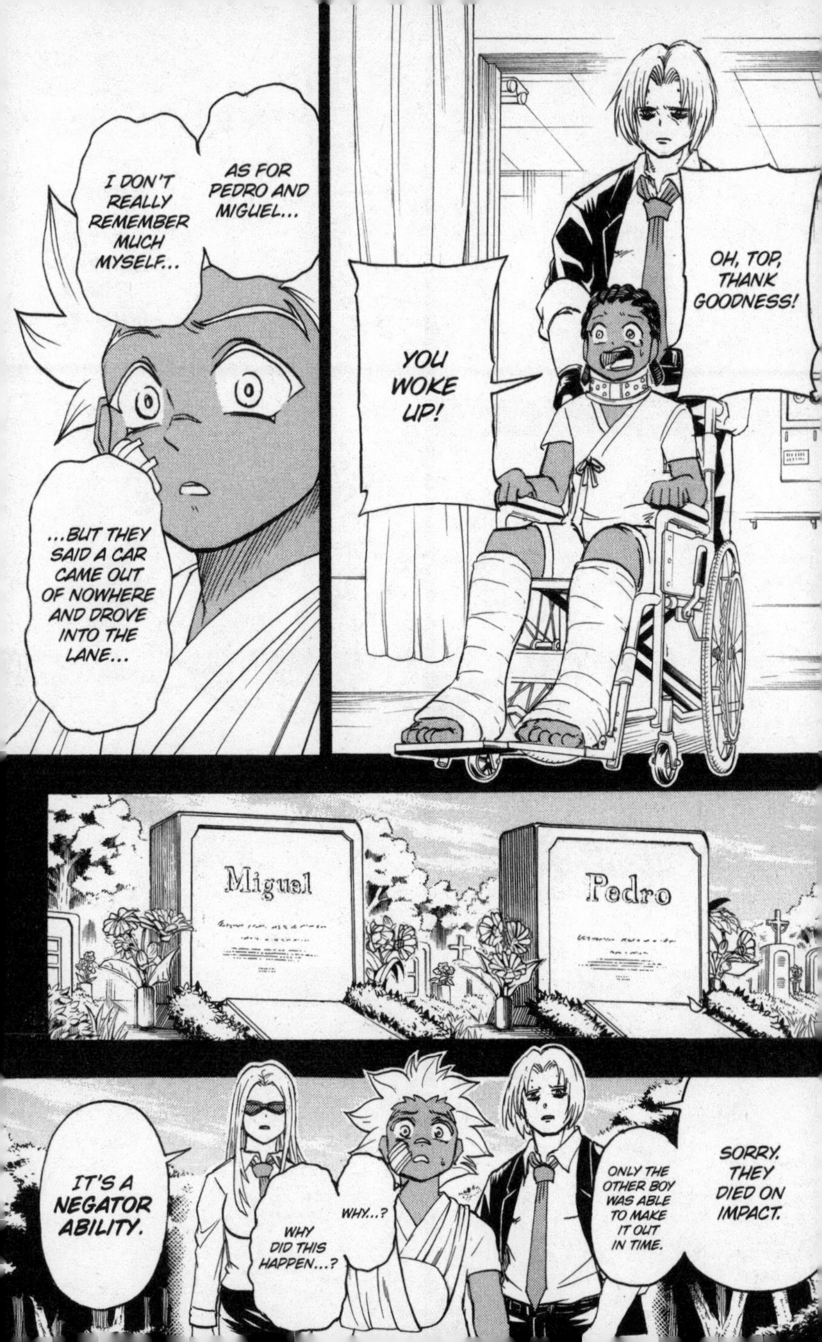
OH, TOP, THANK GOODNESS!
YOU WOKE UP!
AS FOR PEDRO AND MIGUEL...
I DON'T REALLY REMEMBER MUCH MYSELF...
...BUT THEY SAID A CAR CAME OUT OF NOWHERE AND DROVE INTO THE LANE...
Pedro
Miguel
SORRY. THEY DIED ON IMPACT.
ONLY THE OTHER BOY WAS ABLE TO MAKE IT OUT IN TIME.
WHY...?
WHY DID THIS HAPPEN...?
IT'S A NEGATOR ABILITY.

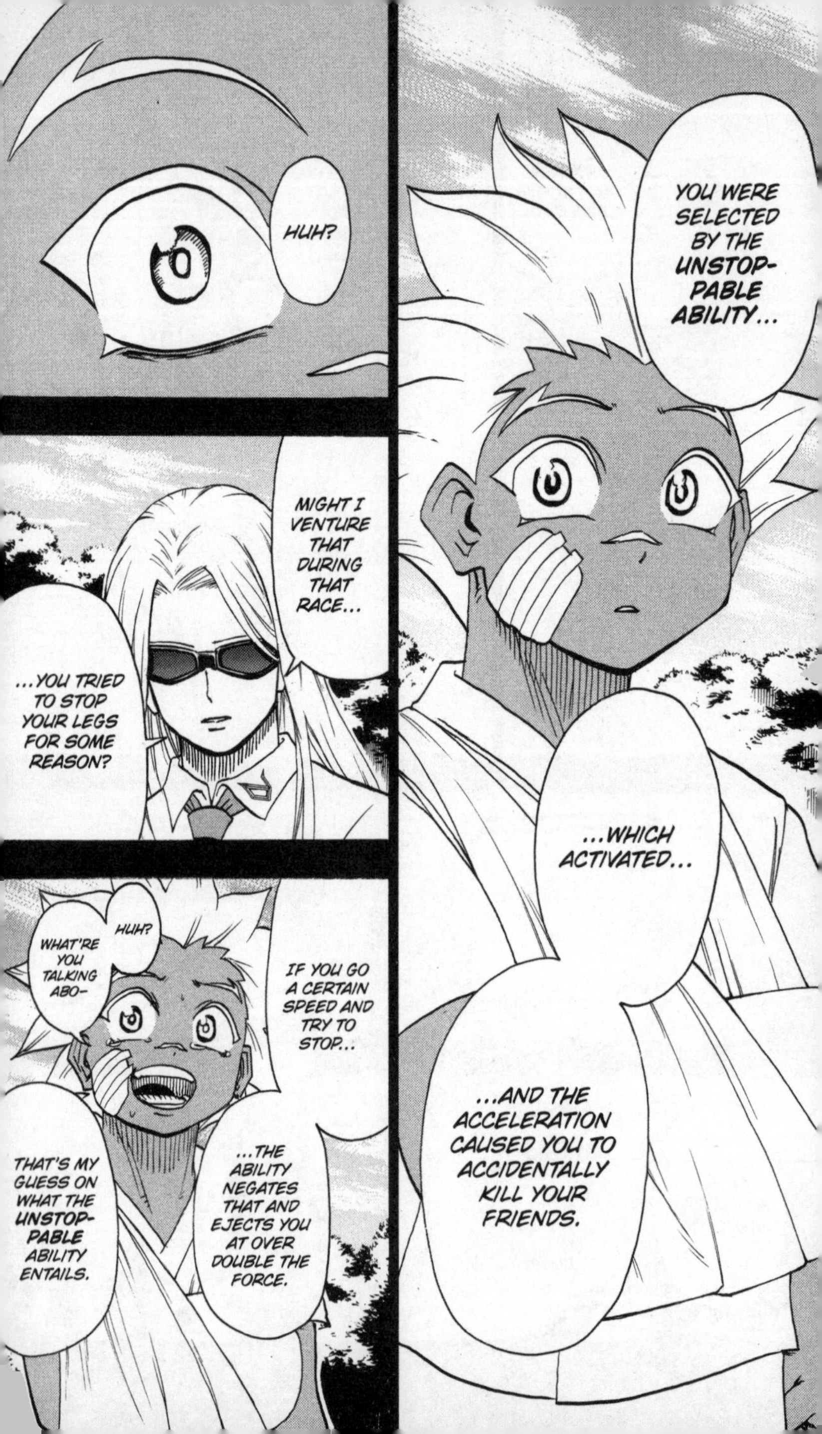
YOU WERE SELECTED BY THE UNSTOP-PABLE ABILITY...
...WHICH ACTIVATED...
...AND THE ACCELERATION CAUSED YOU TO ACCIDENTALLY KILL YOUR FRIENDS.
HUH?
MIGHT I VENTURE THAT DURING THAT RACE...
...YOU TRIED TO STOP YOUR LEGS FOR SOME REASON?
HUH?
WHAT'RE YOU TALKING ABO-
IF YOU GO A CERTAIN SPEED AND TRY TO STOP...
...THE ABILITY NEGATES THAT AND EJECTS YOU AT OVER DOUBLE THE FORCE.
THAT'S MY GUESS ON WHAT THE UNSTOP-PABLE ABILITY ENTAILS.

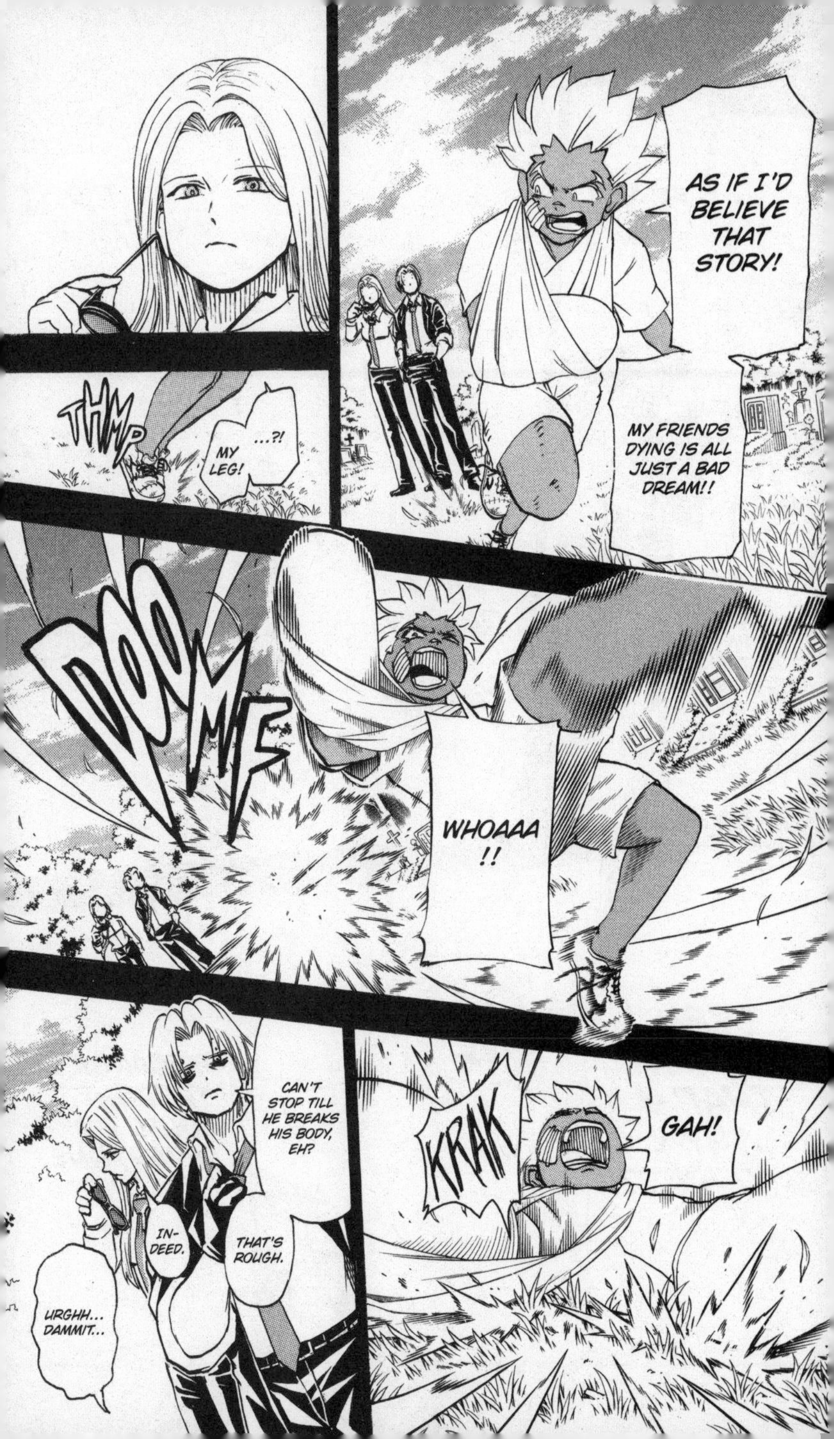
AS IF I'D BELIEVE THAT STORY!
MY FRIENDS DYING IS ALL JUST A BAD DREAM!!
...?!
MY LEG!
THMP
WHOAAA!!
DOOMF
GAH!
KRAK
CAN'T STOP TILL HE BREAKS HIS BODY, EH?
THAT'S ROUGH.
IN-DEED.
URGHH... DAMMIT...

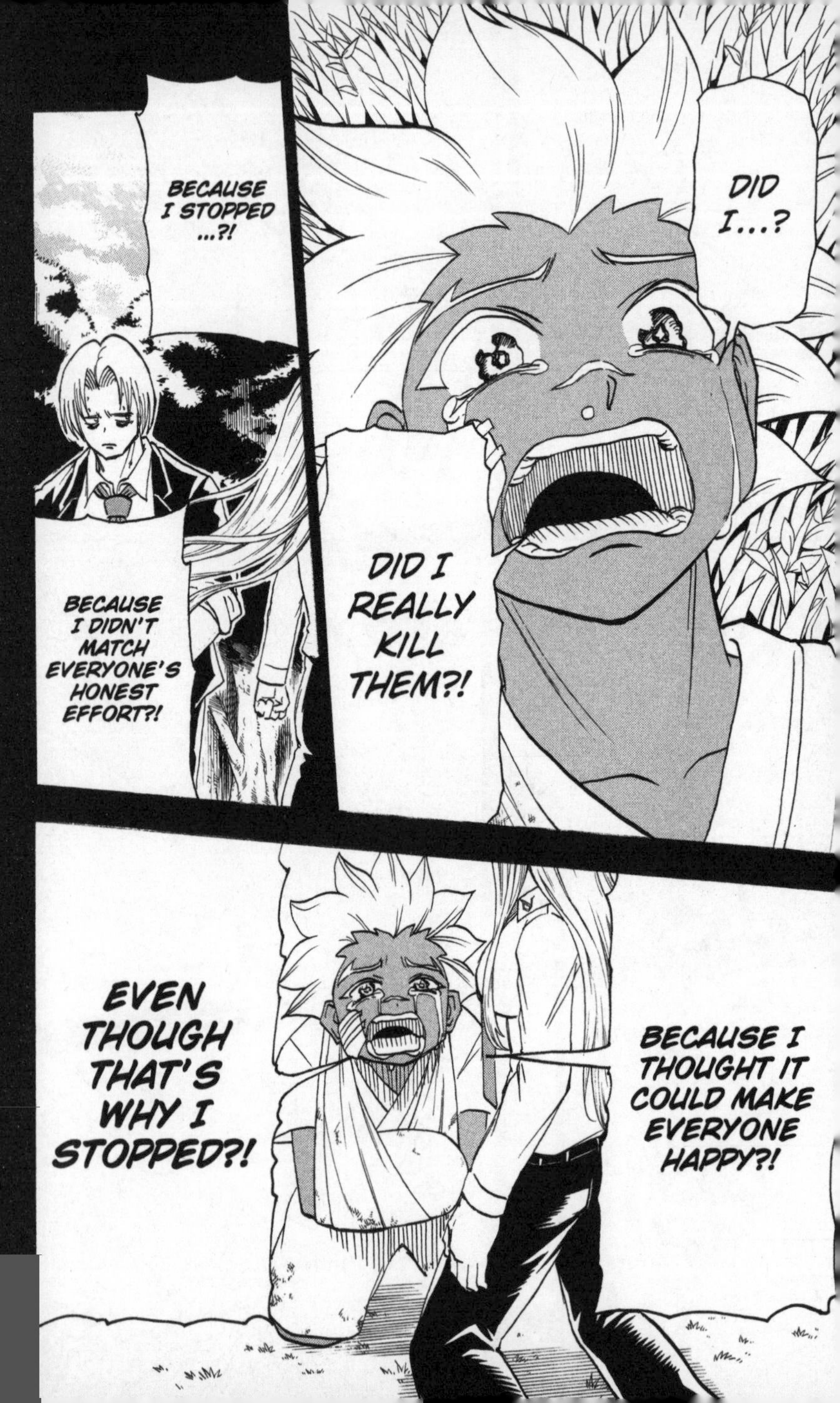
DID I...?
DID I REALLY KILL THEM?!
BECAUSE I STOPPED ...?!
BECAUSE I DIDN'T MATCH EVERYONE'S HONEST EFFORT?!
BECAUSE I THOUGHT IT COULD MAKE EVERYONE HAPPY?!
EVEN THOUGH THAT'S WHY I STOPPED?!

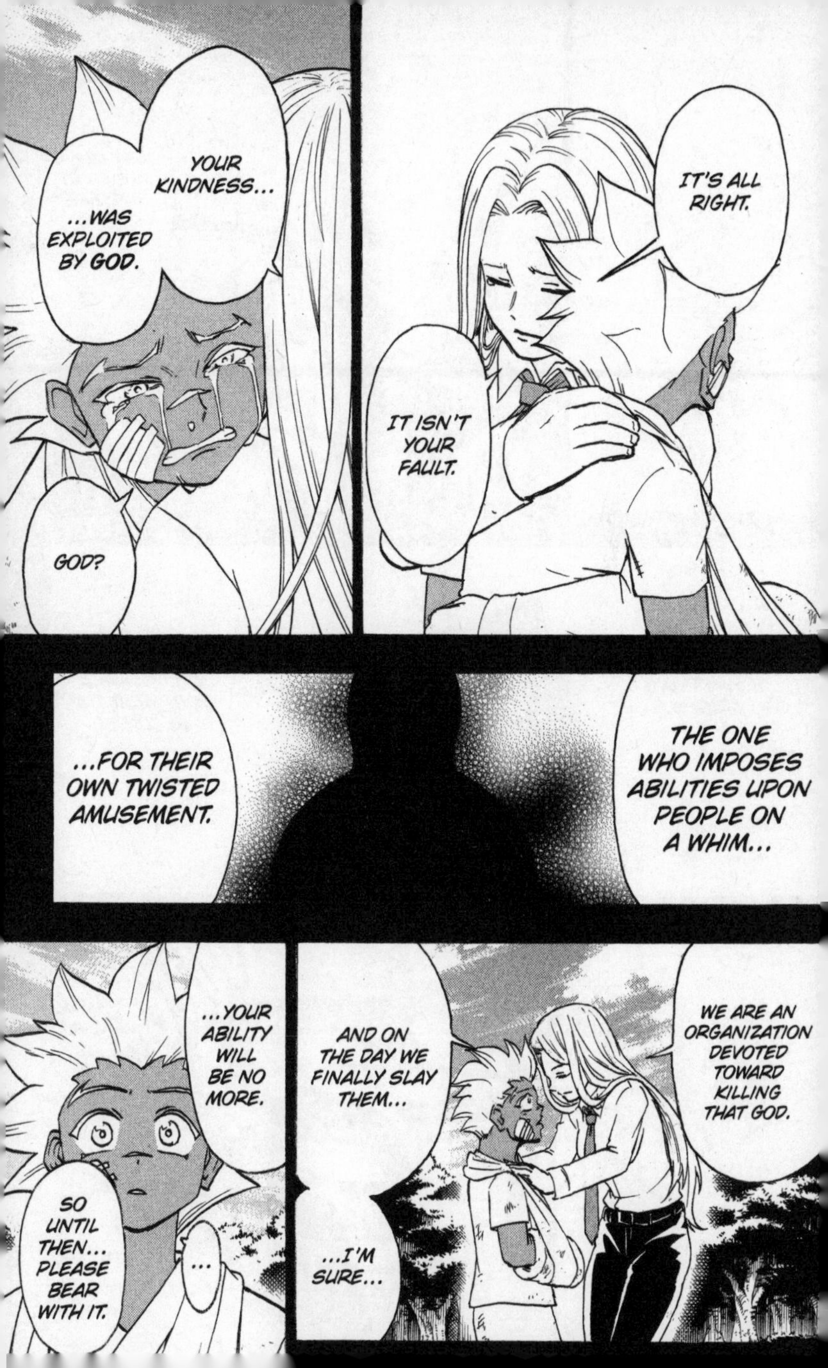
IT'S ALL RIGHT.
IT ISN'T YOUR FAULT.
YOUR KINDNESS...
...WAS EXPLOITED BY GOD.
GOD?
THE ONE WHO IMPOSES ABILITIES UPON PEOPLE ON A WHIM...
...FOR THEIR OWN TWISTED AMUSEMENT.
WE ARE AN ORGANIZATION DEVOTED TOWARD KILLING THAT GOD.
AND ON THE DAY WE FINALLY SLAY THEM...
...I'M SURE...
...YOUR ABILITY WILL BE NO MORE.
SO UNTIL THEN... PLEASE BEAR WITH IT.
...

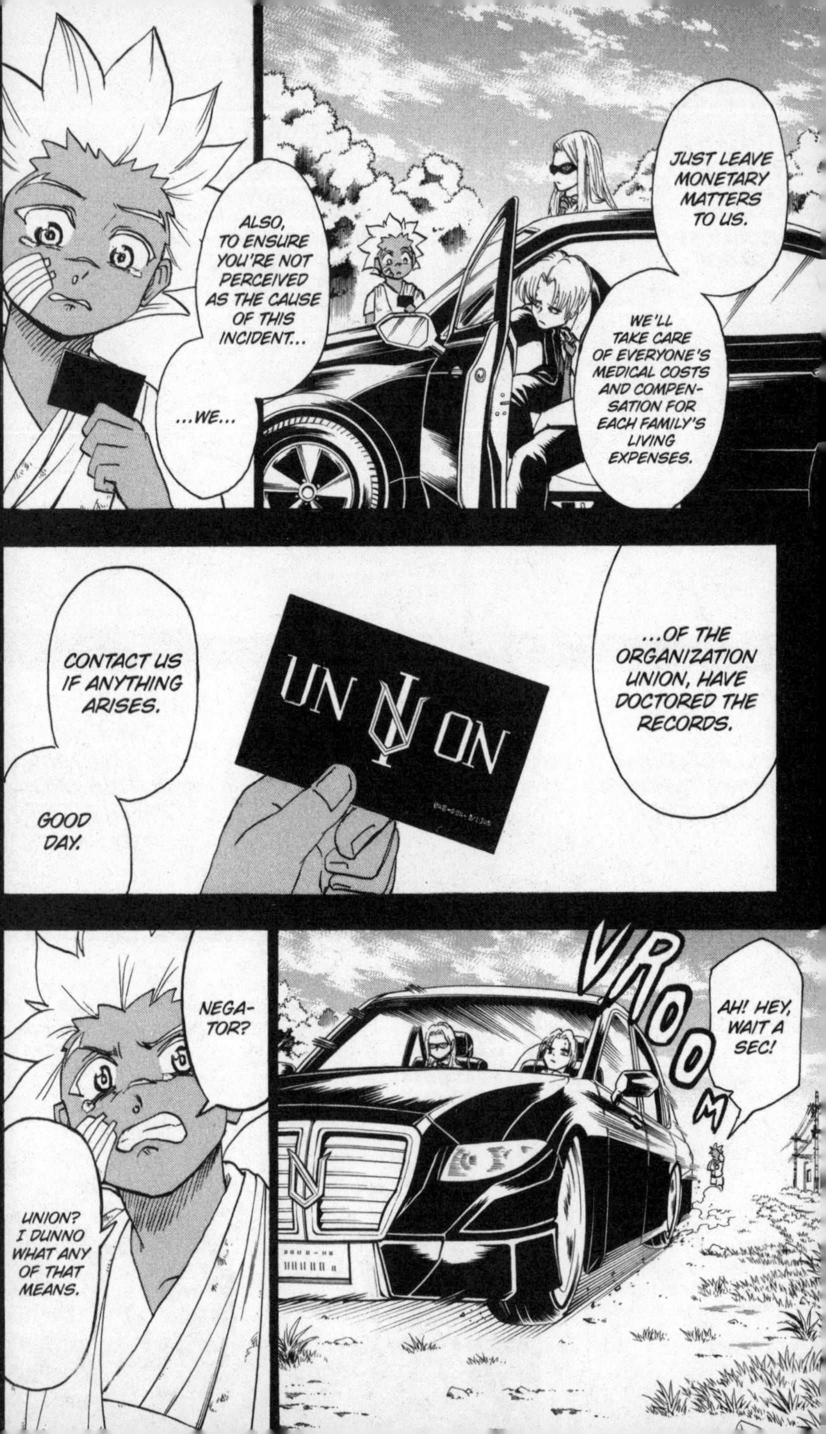
JUST LEAVE MONETARY MATTERS TO US.
WE'LL TAKE CARE OF EVERYONE'S MEDICAL COSTS AND COMPENSATION FOR EACH FAMILY'S LIVING EXPENSES.
ALSO, TO ENSURE YOU'RE NOT PERCEIVED AS THE CAUSE OF THIS INCIDENT...
...WE...
...OF THE ORGANIZATION UNION, HAVE DOCTORED THE RECORDS.
UNION
CONTACT US IF ANYTHING ARISES.
GOOD DAY.
VROOM
AH! HEY, WAIT A SEC!
NEGATOR?
UNION? I DUNNO WHAT ANY OF THAT MEANS.

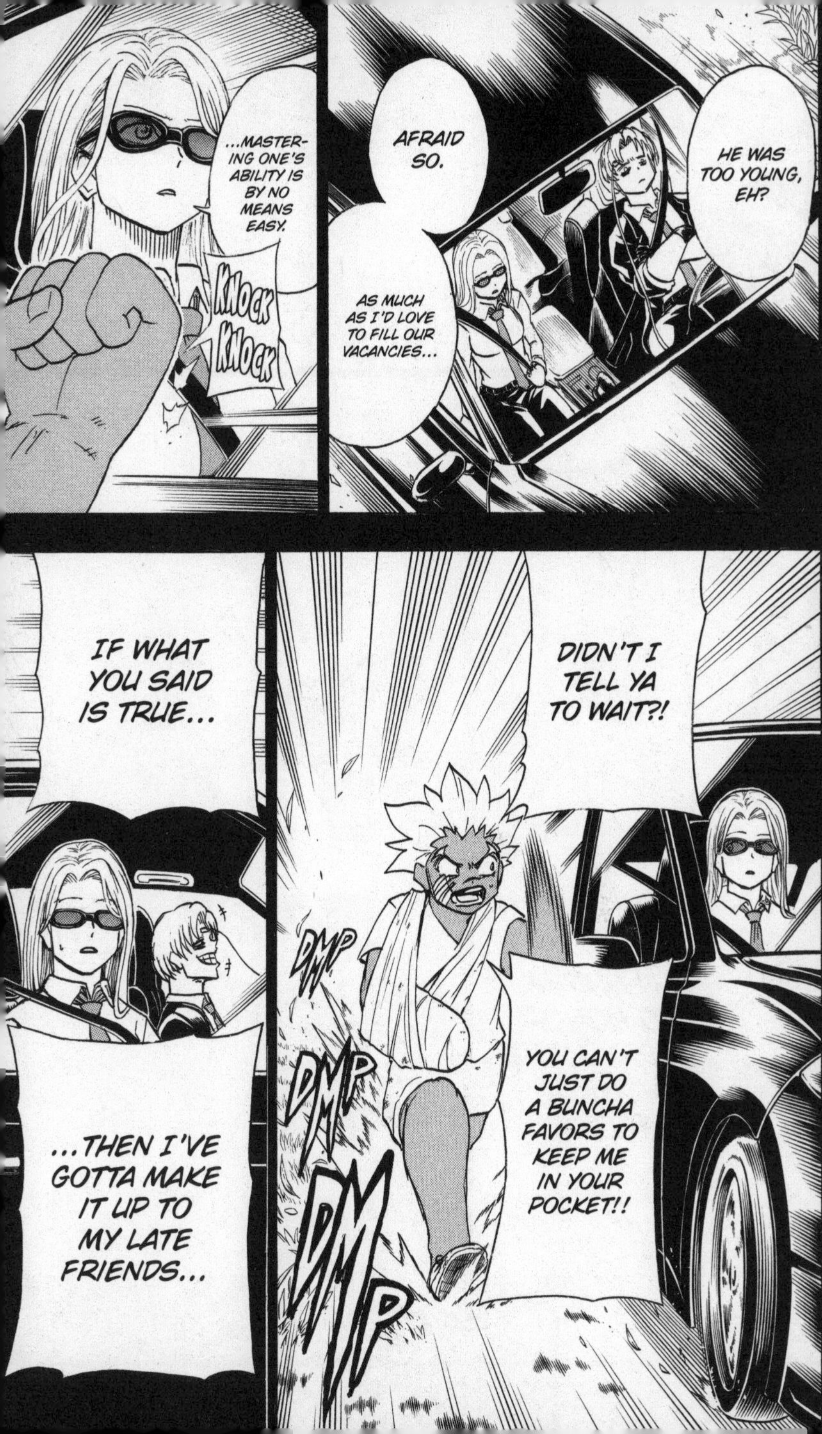
HE WAS TOO YOUNG, EH?
AFRAID SO.
AS MUCH AS I'D LOVE TO FILL OUR VACANCIES...
...MASTERING ONE'S ABILITY IS BY NO MEANS EASY.
KNOCK KNOCK
DIDN'T I TELL YA TO WAIT?!
YOU CAN'T JUST DO A BUNCHA FAVORS TO KEEP ME IN YOUR POCKET!!
DMP DMP DMP
IF WHAT YOU SAID IS TRUE...
...THEN I'VE GOTTA MAKE IT UP TO MY LATE FRIENDS...

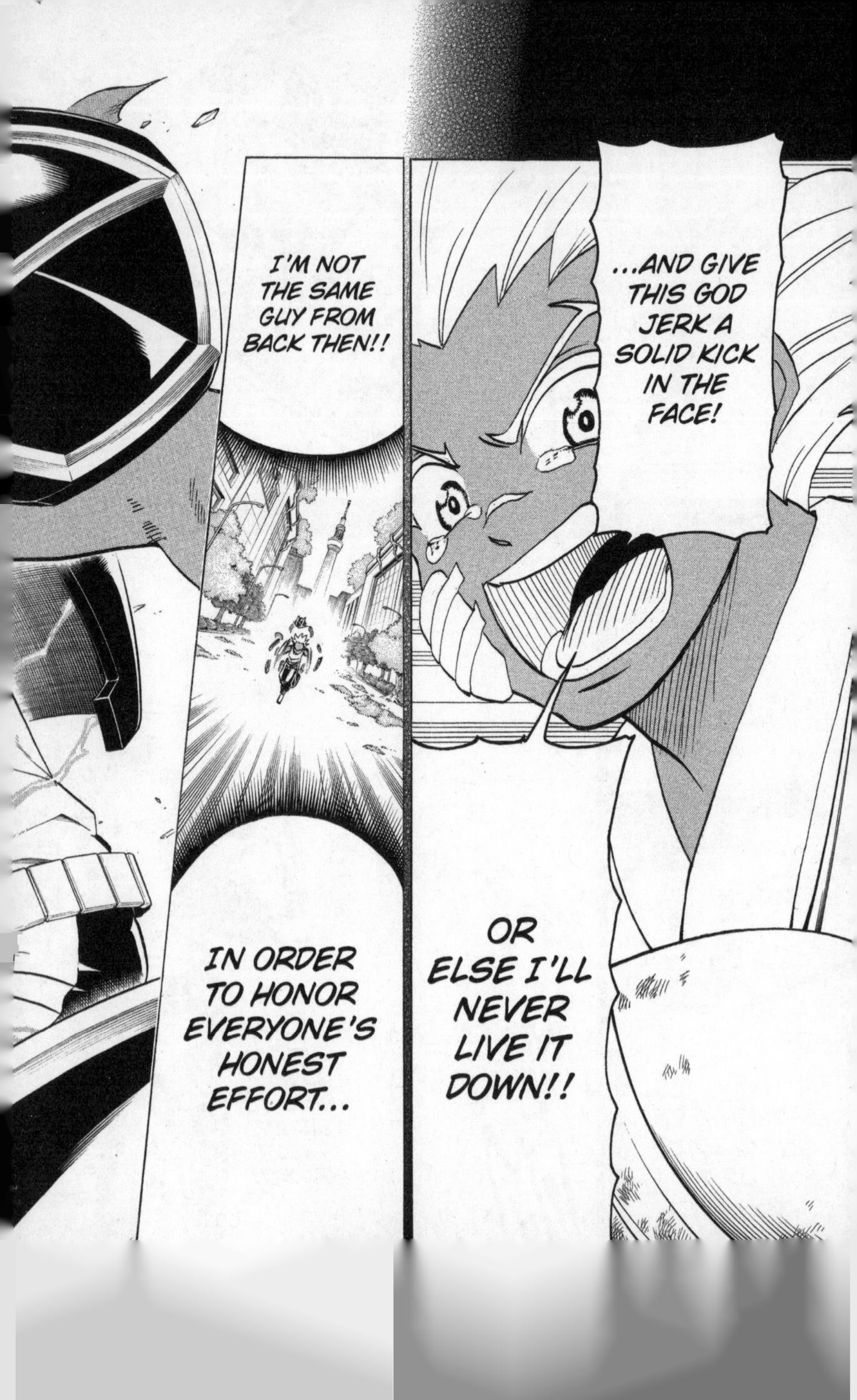
I'M NOT THE SAME GUY FROM BACK THEN!!
IN ORDER TO HONOR EVERYONE'S HONEST EFFORT...
...AND GIVE THIS GOD JERK A SOLID KICK IN THE FACE!
OR ELSE I'LL NEVER LIVE IT DOWN!!

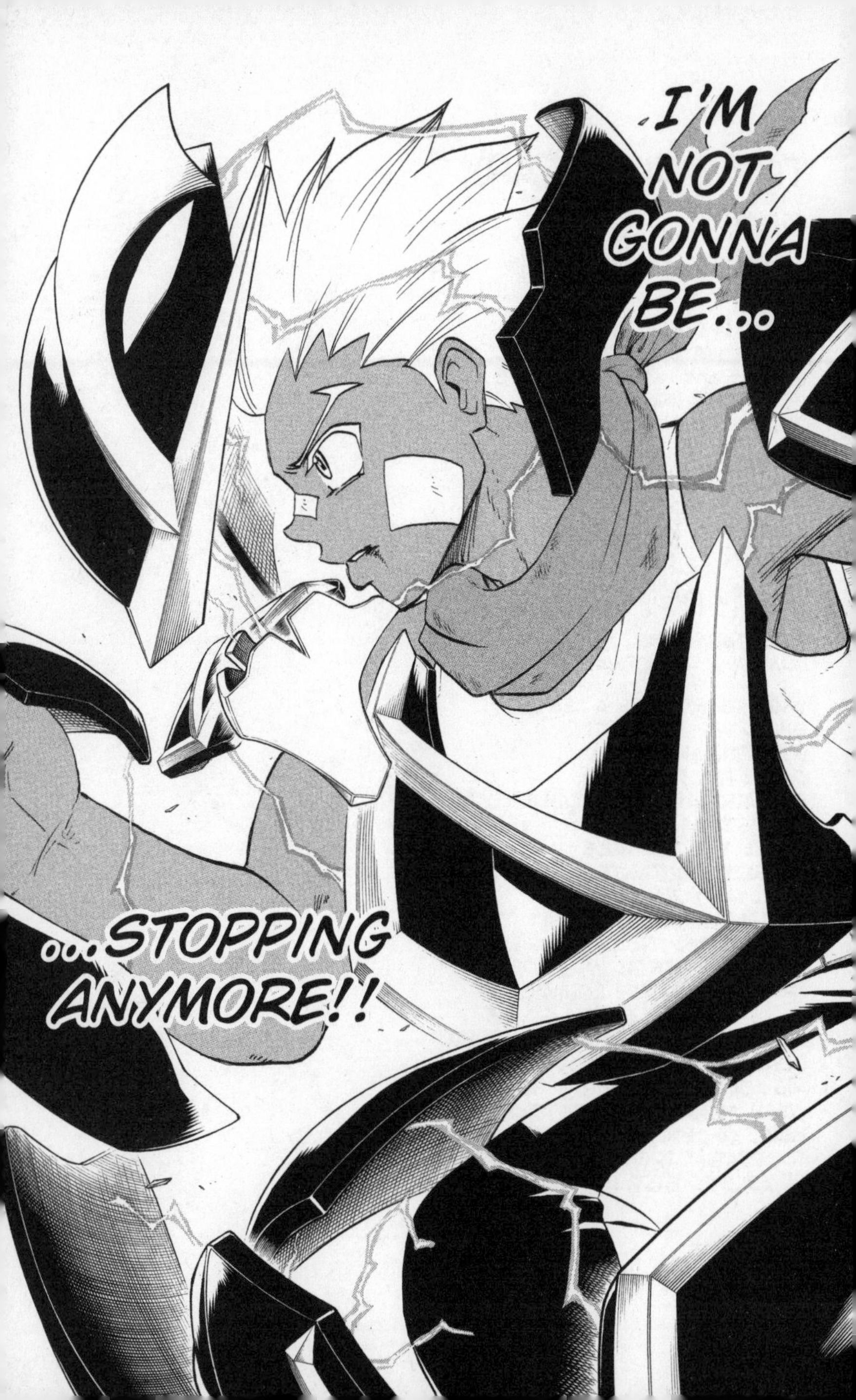
I'M NOT GONNA BE...
...STOPPING ANYMORE!!

TOP BULL SPARX

AGE: 15

HEIGHT: TALLER THAN TATIANA! MAYBE...

HOBBIES: COLLECTING RUNNING SHOES, WATCHING *TOKUSATSU* HERO SHOWS (RECENTLY, HE'S BEEN WATCHING THEM WITH THE CHILDREN FROM LONGING)

SPECIAL SKILLS: RUNNING FAST, ENDURING PAIN

FAVORITES: MOM'S GALETO CHICKEN

ABILITIES: UNSTOPPABLE

SELF-TARGETING COMPULSORY ACTIVATION-TYPE

WHEN HE EXCEEDS A CERTAIN SPEED WHILE SPRINTING, STOPPING HIS LEGS WILL CAUSE HIM TO PROPEL FORWARD AT OVER DOUBLE THE SPEED HE WAS TRAVELING. THE RULE DOESN'T DEACTIVATE UNTIL HIS BODY BREAKS. PERHAPS THIS IS A RESULT OF HIM DOING TRACK AND FIELD, BUT TOP'S MENTAL IMAGE OF "BREAKING" IS THE EQUIVALENT OF "BREAKING A BONE." SO, HE WILL INTENTIONALLY BREAK HIS BONES TO PUT THE BRAKES ON HIS ABILITY. HOWEVER, IF SOMEONE ELSE WERE TO HAVE UNSTOPPABLE AND THEIR IMAGE OF "BREAKING" WERE DIRECTLY LINKED TO "DEATH," THEN THAT PERSON WOULDN'T BE ABLE TO STOP UNTIL THEY DIED.

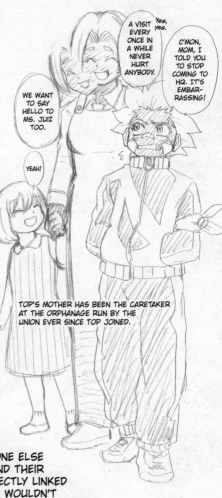

C'MON, MOM, I TOLD YOU TO STOP COMING TO HQ. IT'S EMBAR-RASSING!
Yes, yes.
A VISIT EVERY ONCE IN A WHILE NEVER HURT ANYBODY.
WE WANT TO SAY HELLO TO MS. JUIZ TOO.
YEAH!
TOP'S MOTHER HAS BEEN THE CARETAKER AT THE ORPHANAGE RUN BY THE UNION EVER SINCE TOP JOINED.

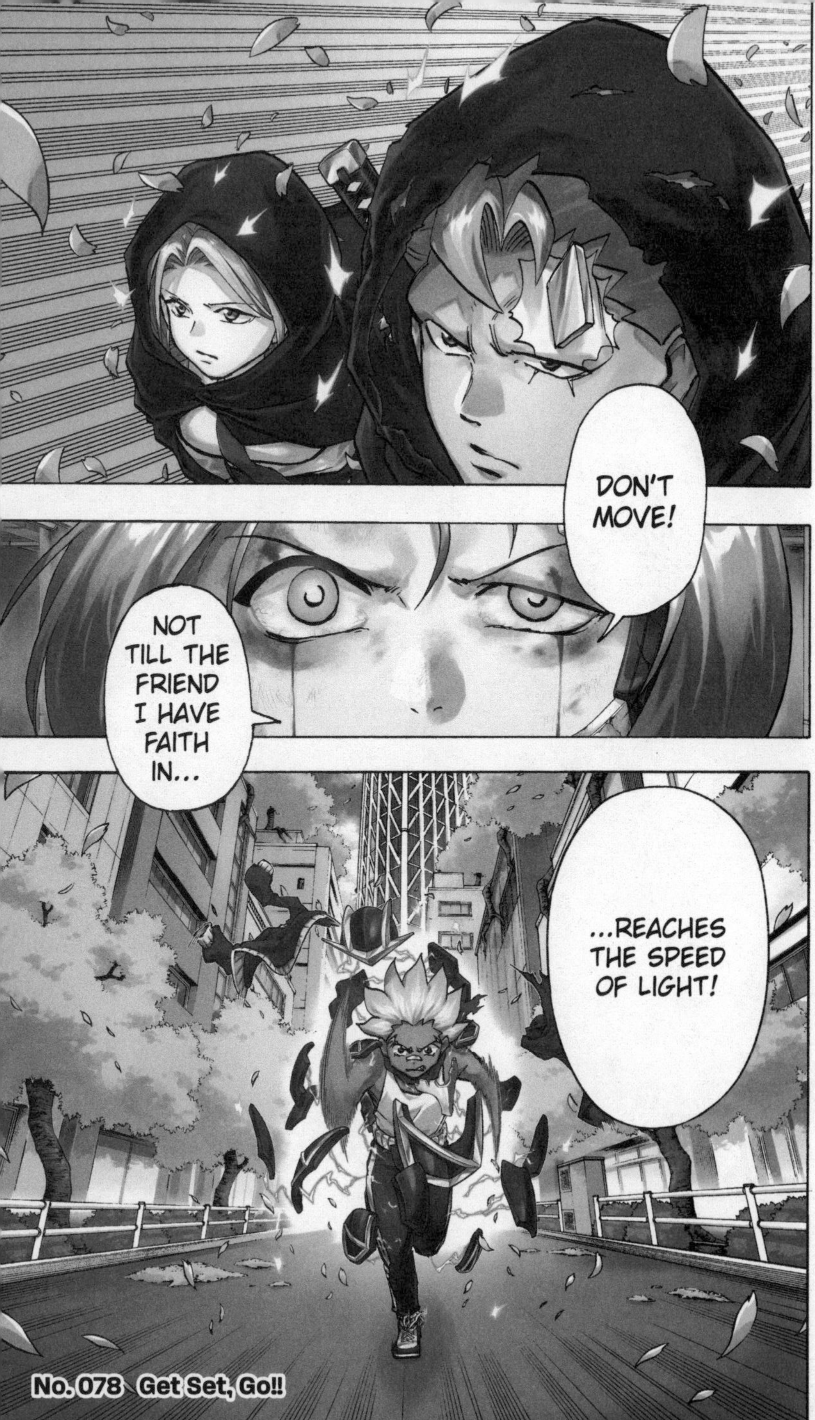
DON'T MOVE!
NOT TILL THE FRIEND I HAVE FAITH IN...
...REACHES THE SPEED OF LIGHT!

No. 078 Get Set, Go!!

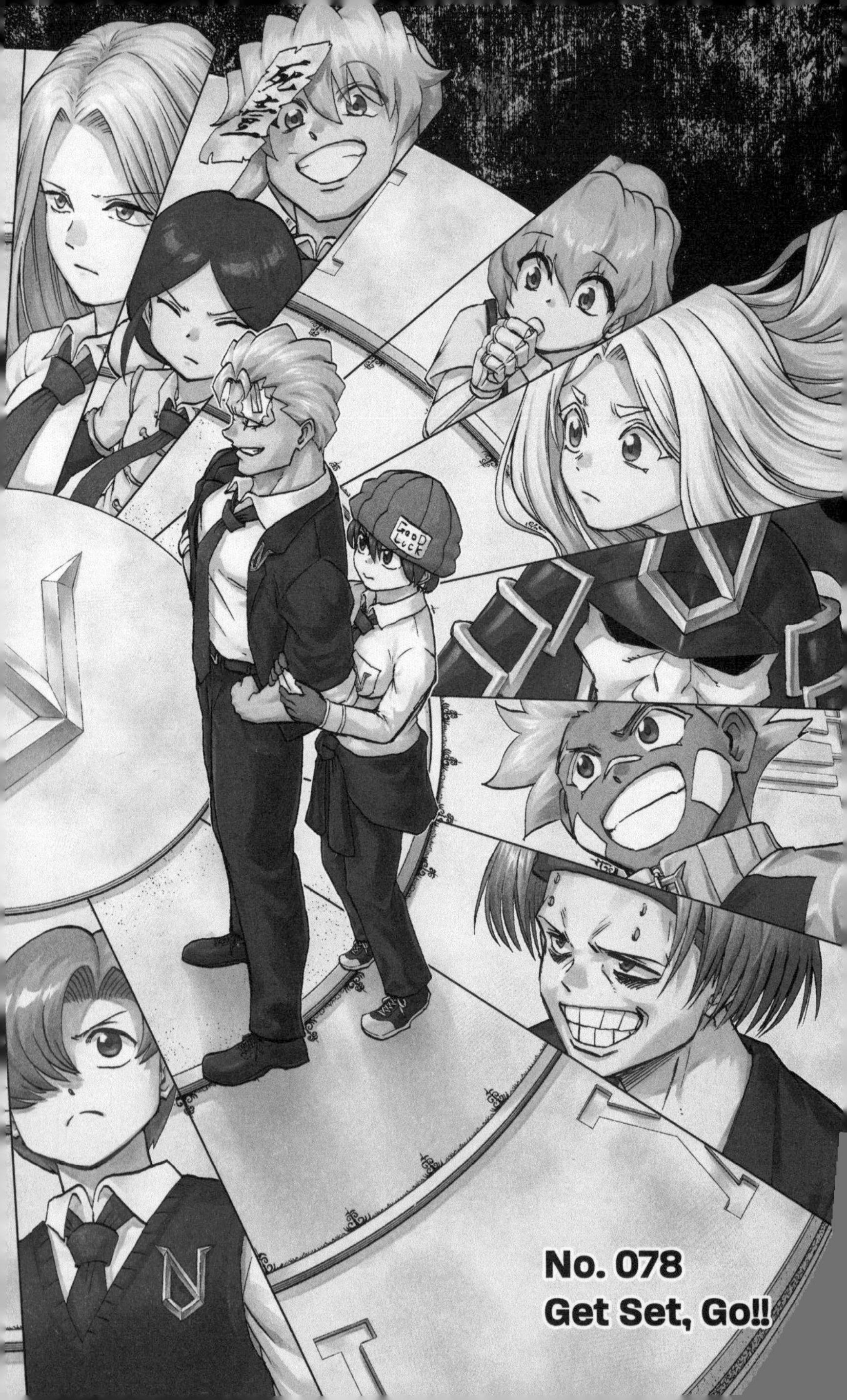
Good Luck

No. 078
Get Set, Go!!

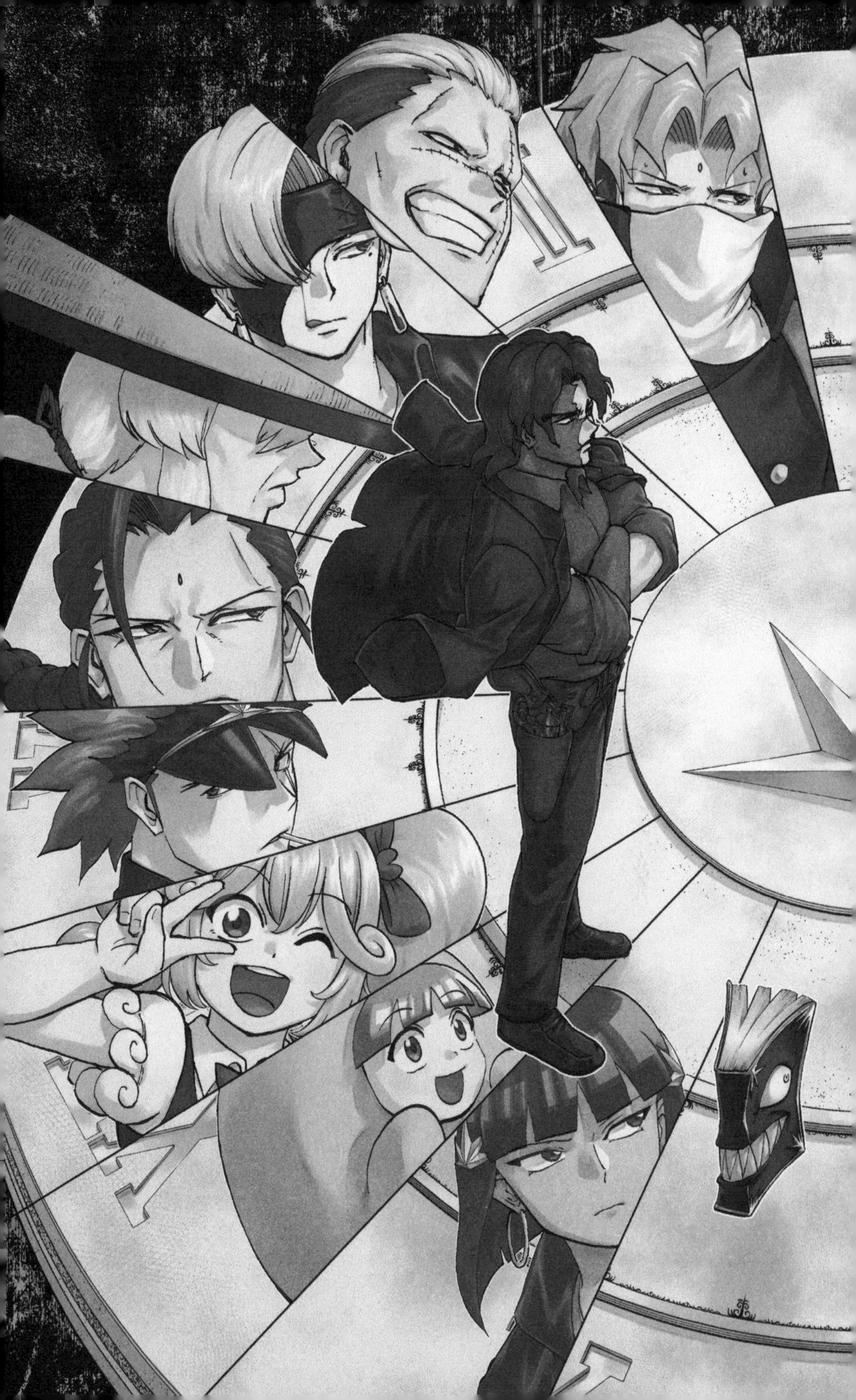

WEEKLY SHONEN JUMP 2021 #41 COVER

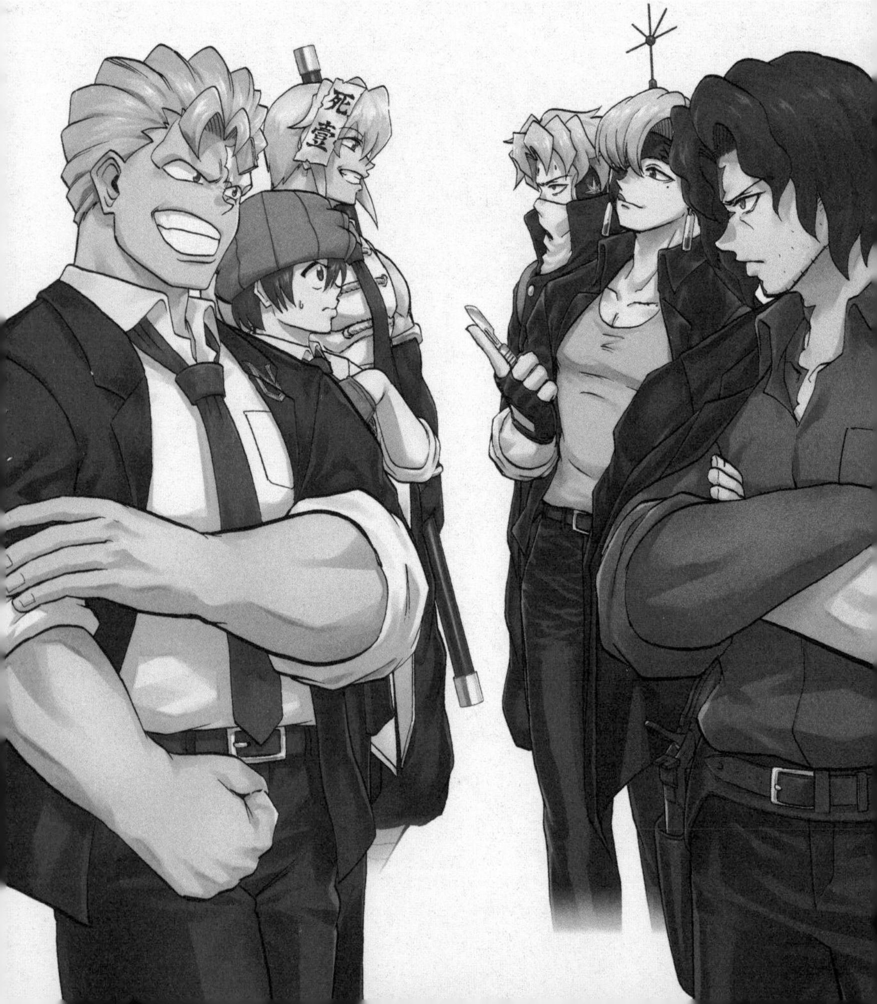

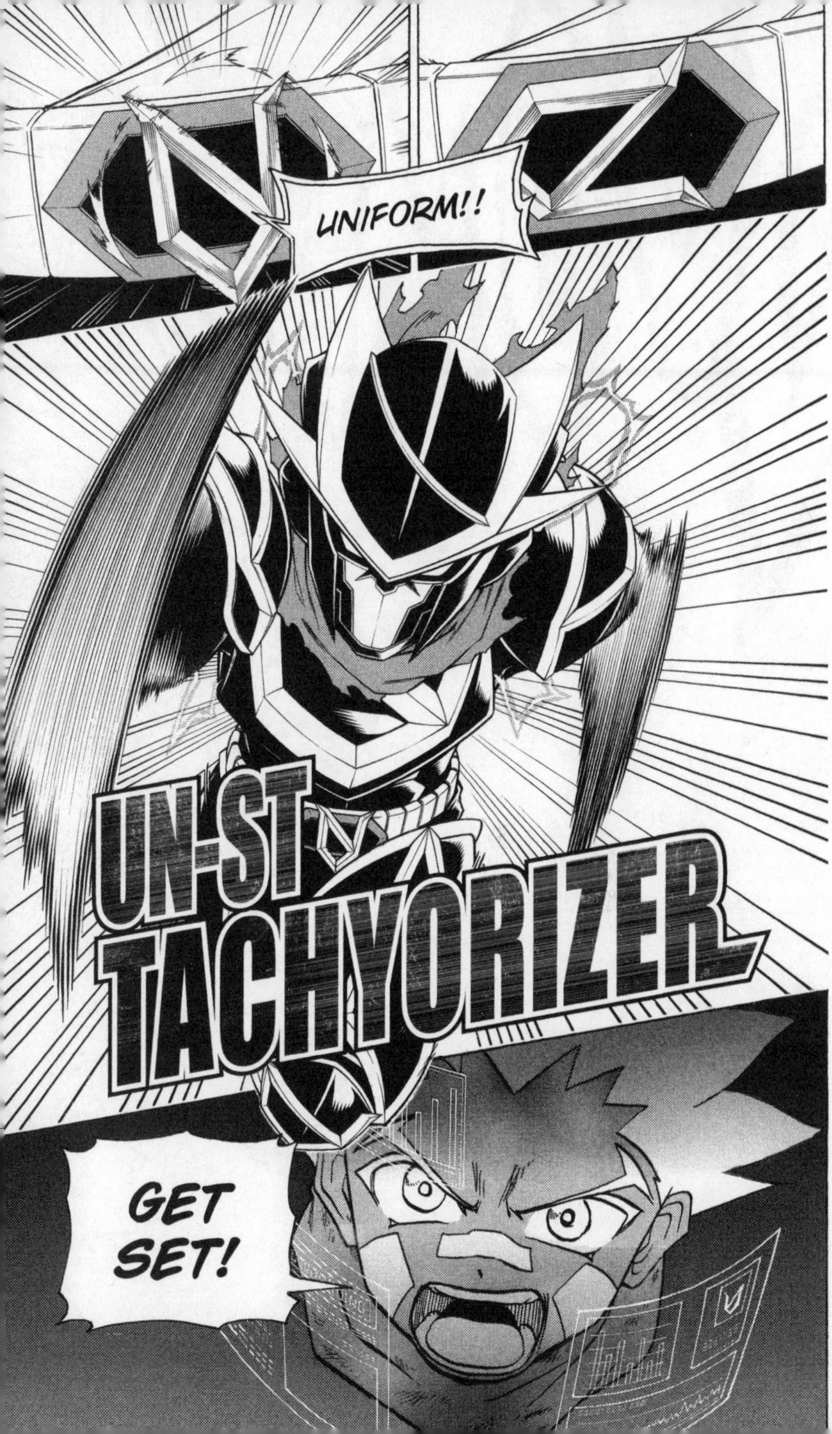
UNIFORM!!
UN-ST TACHYORIZER
GET SET!

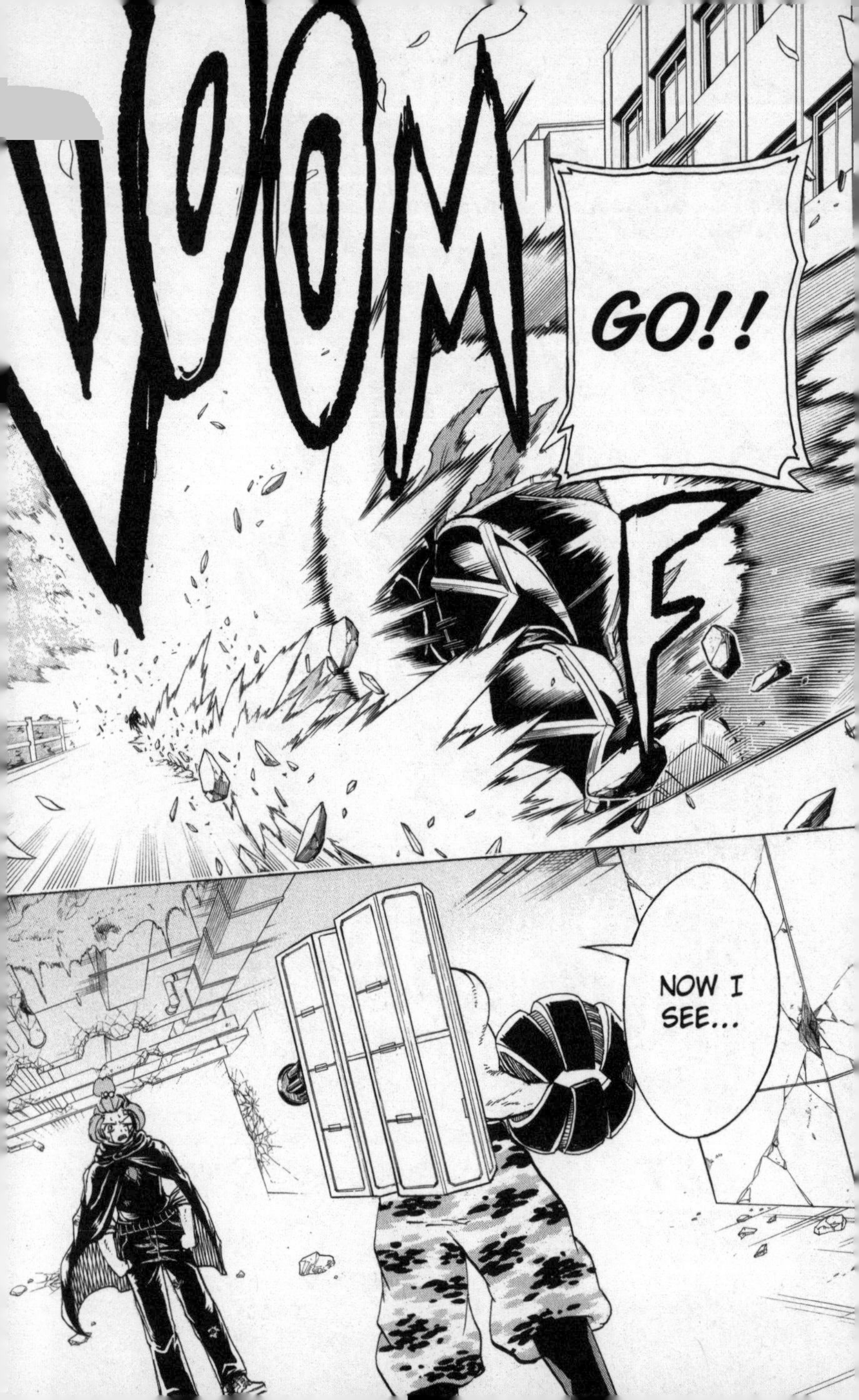
GO!!
VOOOM
NOW I SEE...

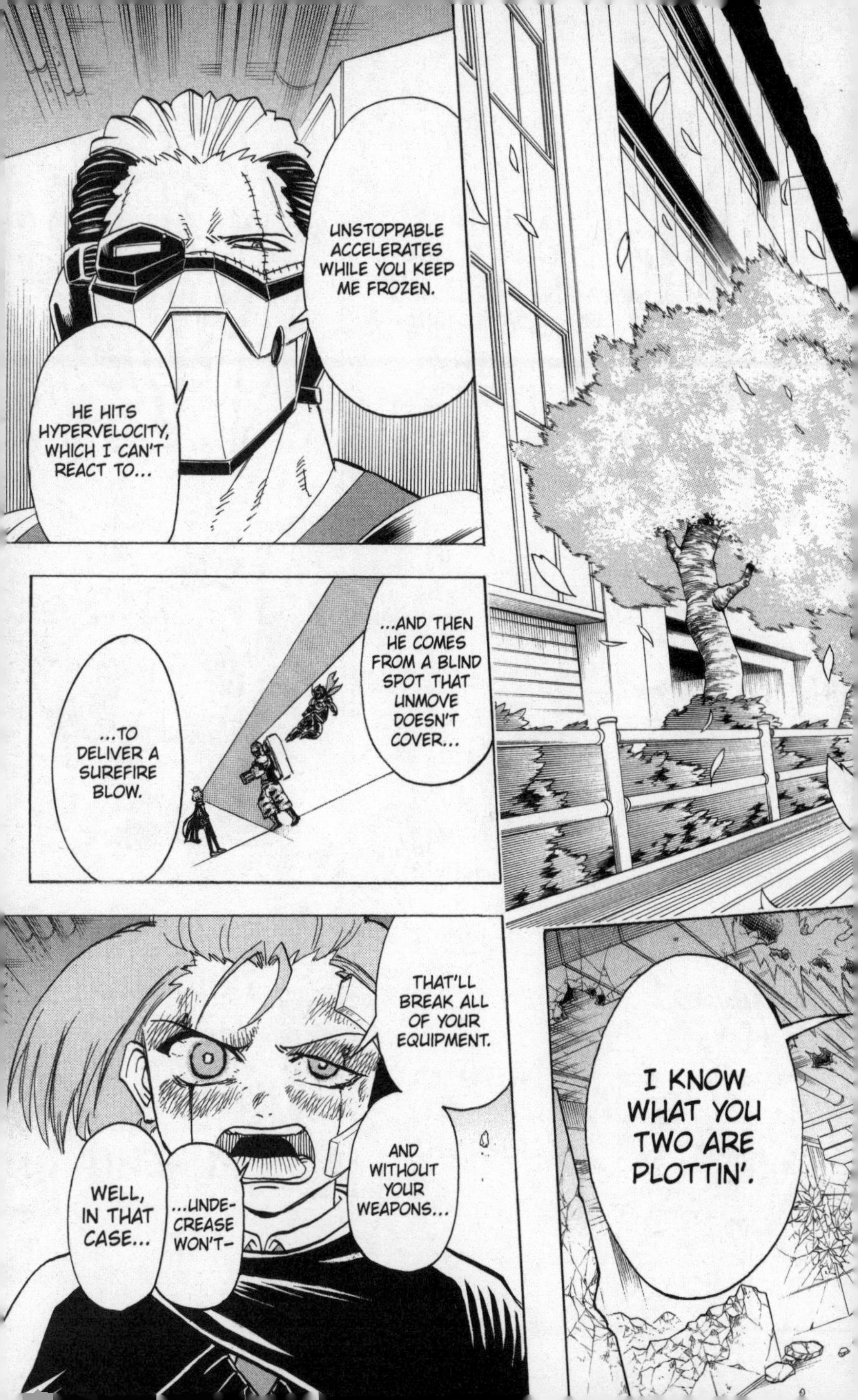
UNSTOPPABLE ACCELERATES WHILE YOU KEEP ME FROZEN.
HE HITS HYPERVELOCITY, WHICH I CAN'T REACT TO...
...AND THEN HE COMES FROM A BLIND SPOT THAT UNMOVE DOESN'T COVER...
...TO DELIVER A SUREFIRE BLOW.
I KNOW WHAT YOU TWO ARE PLOTTIN'.
THAT'LL BREAK ALL OF YOUR EQUIPMENT.
AND WITHOUT YOUR WEAPONS...
...UNDE-CREASE WON'T-
WELL, IN THAT CASE...

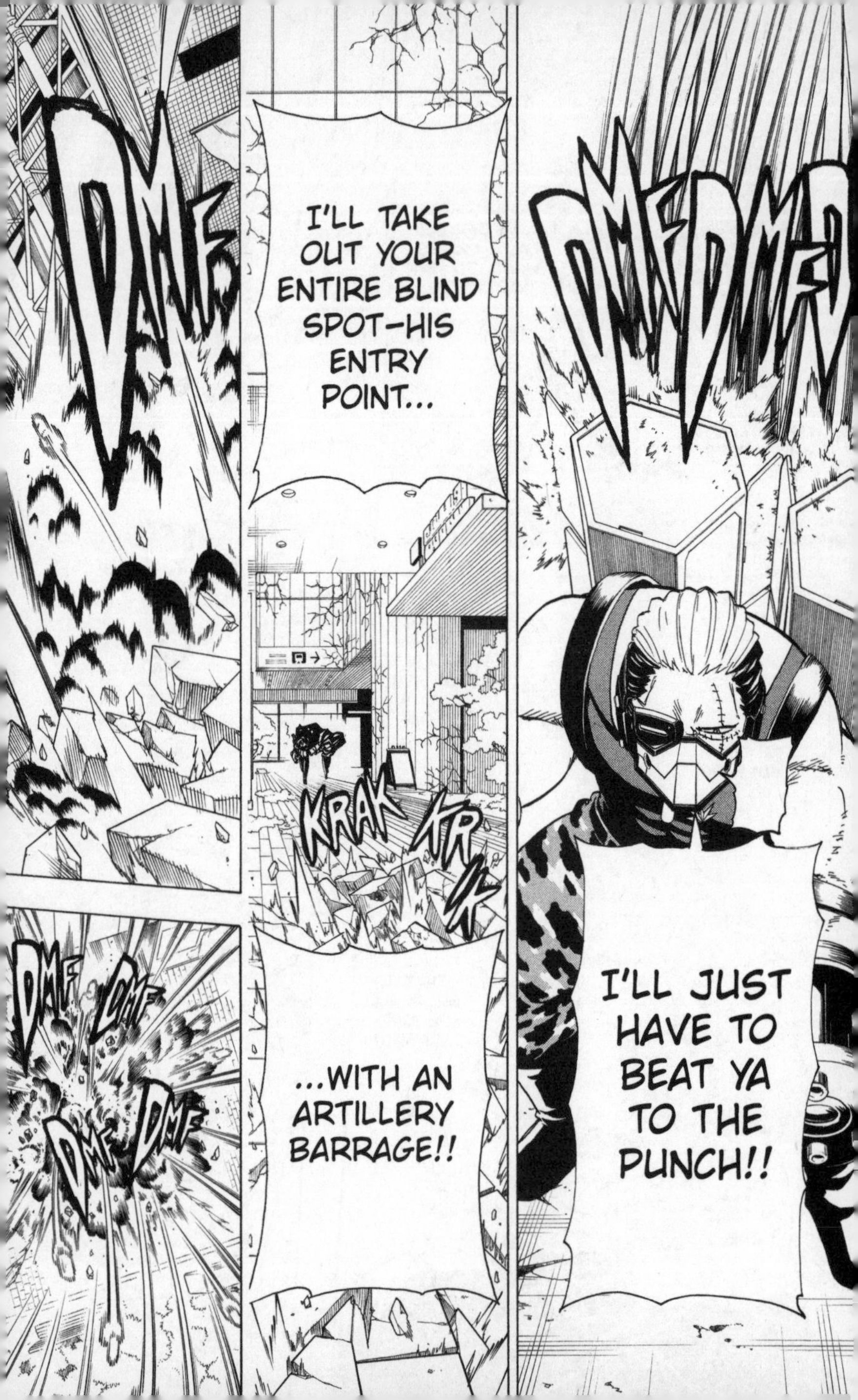
I'LL JUST HAVE TO BEAT YA TO THE PUNCH!!
I'LL TAKE OUT YOUR ENTIRE BLIND SPOT—HIS ENTRY POINT...
KRAK
...WITH AN ARTILLERY BARRAGE!!
DMF
DMF
DMF
DMF
DMF

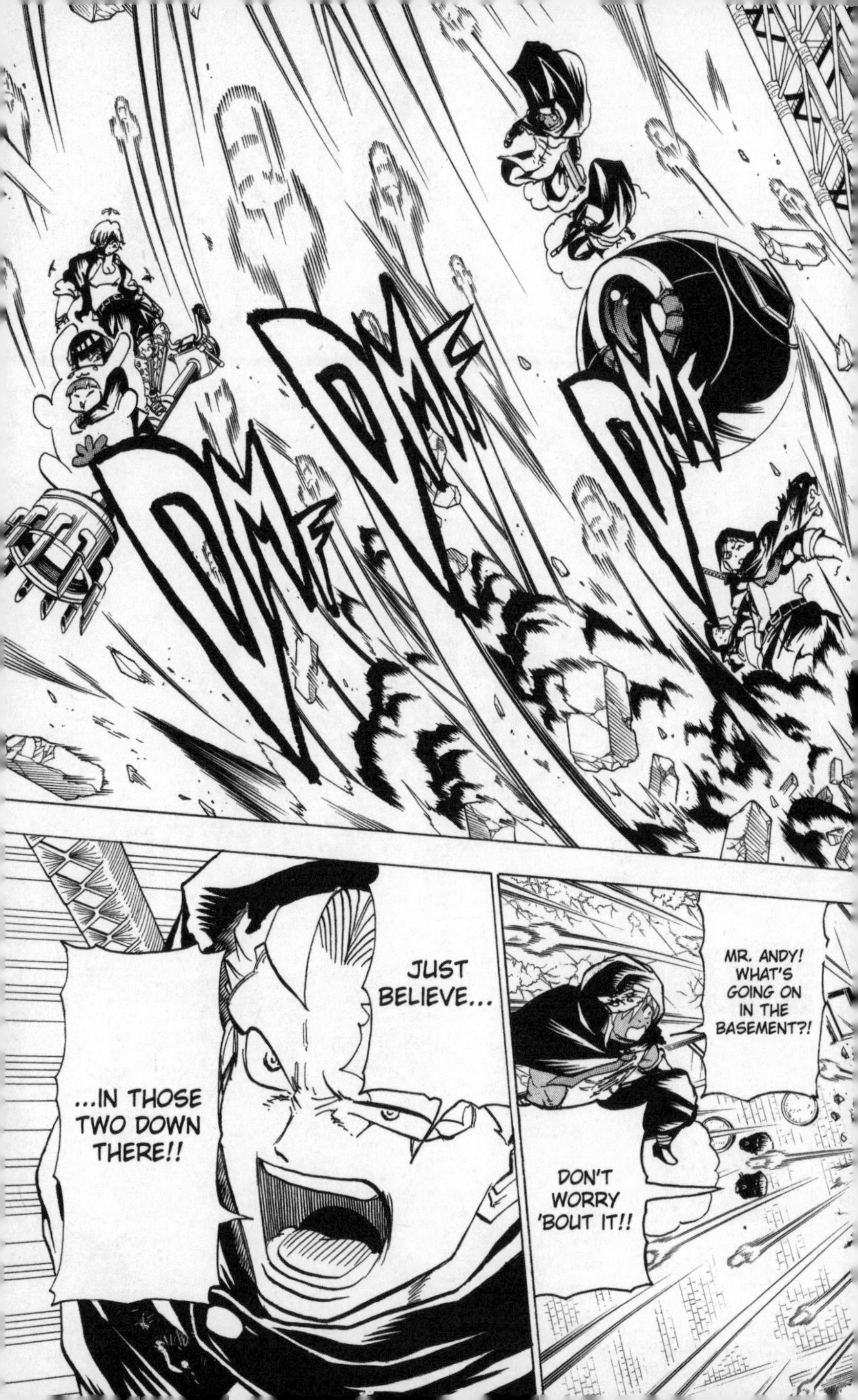
DMF
DMF
DMF
MR. ANDY! WHAT'S GOING ON IN THE BASEMENT?!
DON'T WORRY 'BOUT IT!!
JUST BELIEVE...
...IN THOSE TWO DOWN THERE!!

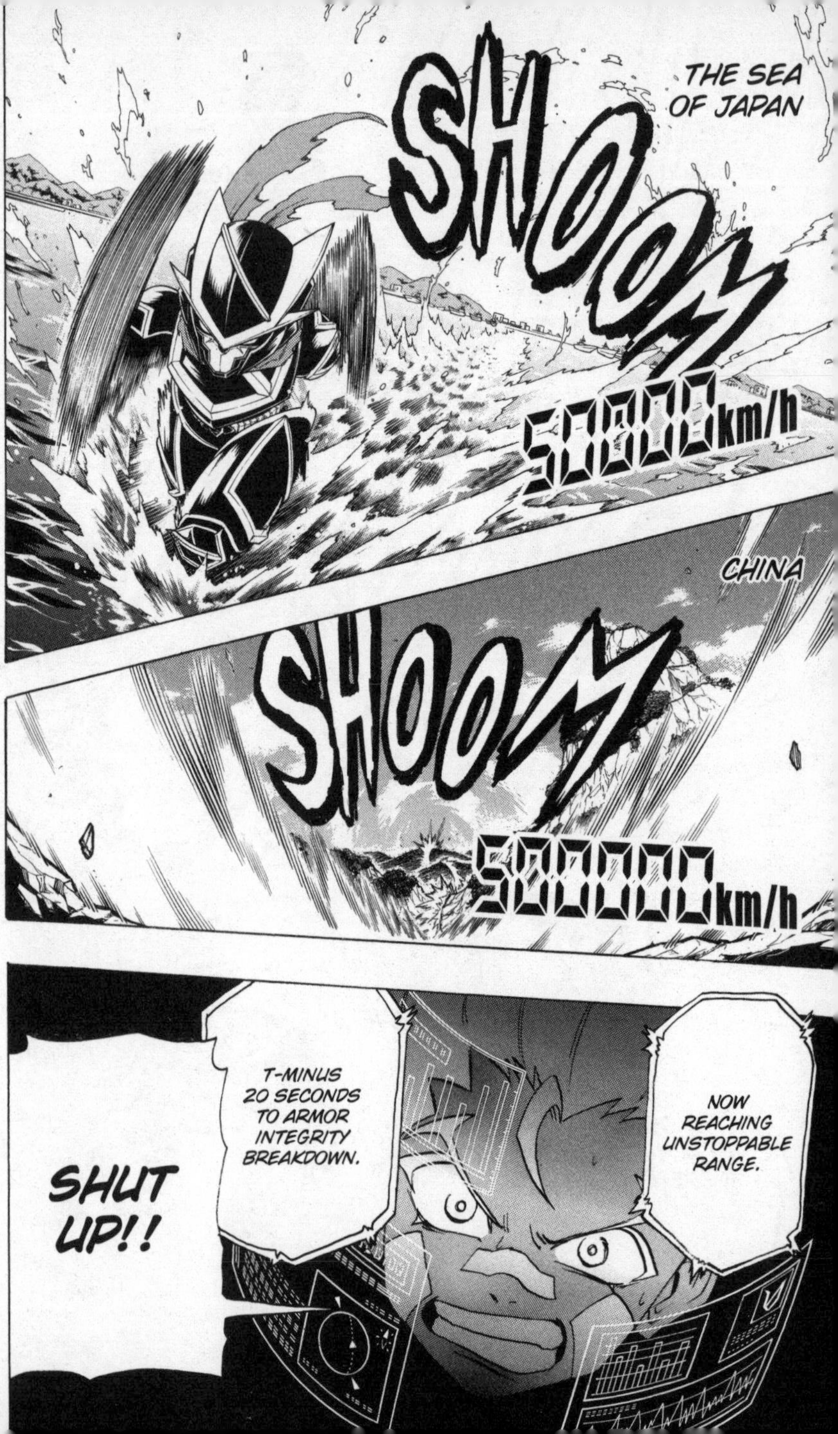
THE SEA OF JAPAN
SHOOM
50800km/h
CHINA
SHOOM
500000km/h
NOW REACHING UNSTOPPABLE RANGE.
T-MINUS 20 SECONDS TO ARMOR INTEGRITY BREAKDOWN.
SHUT UP!!

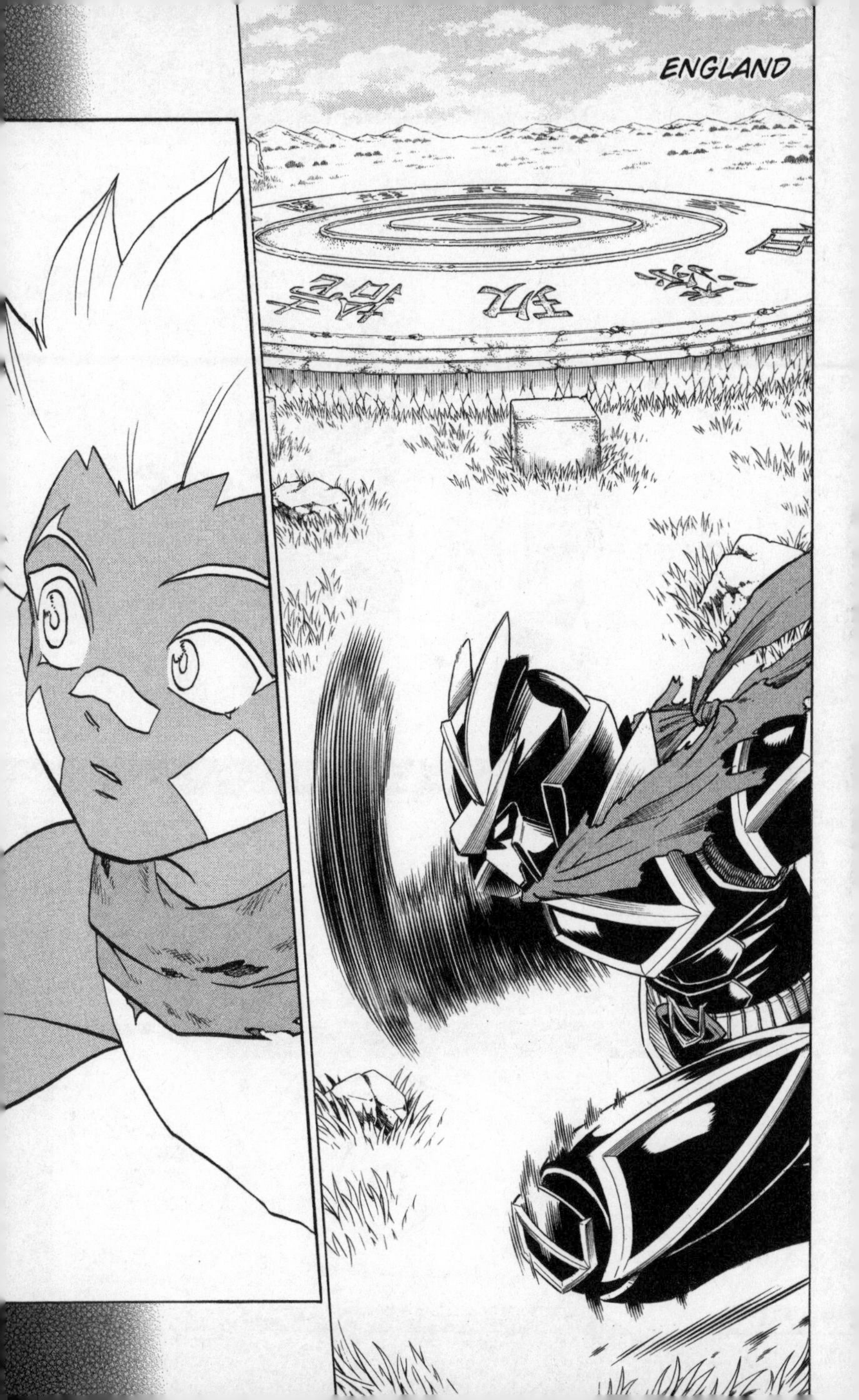
ENGLAND

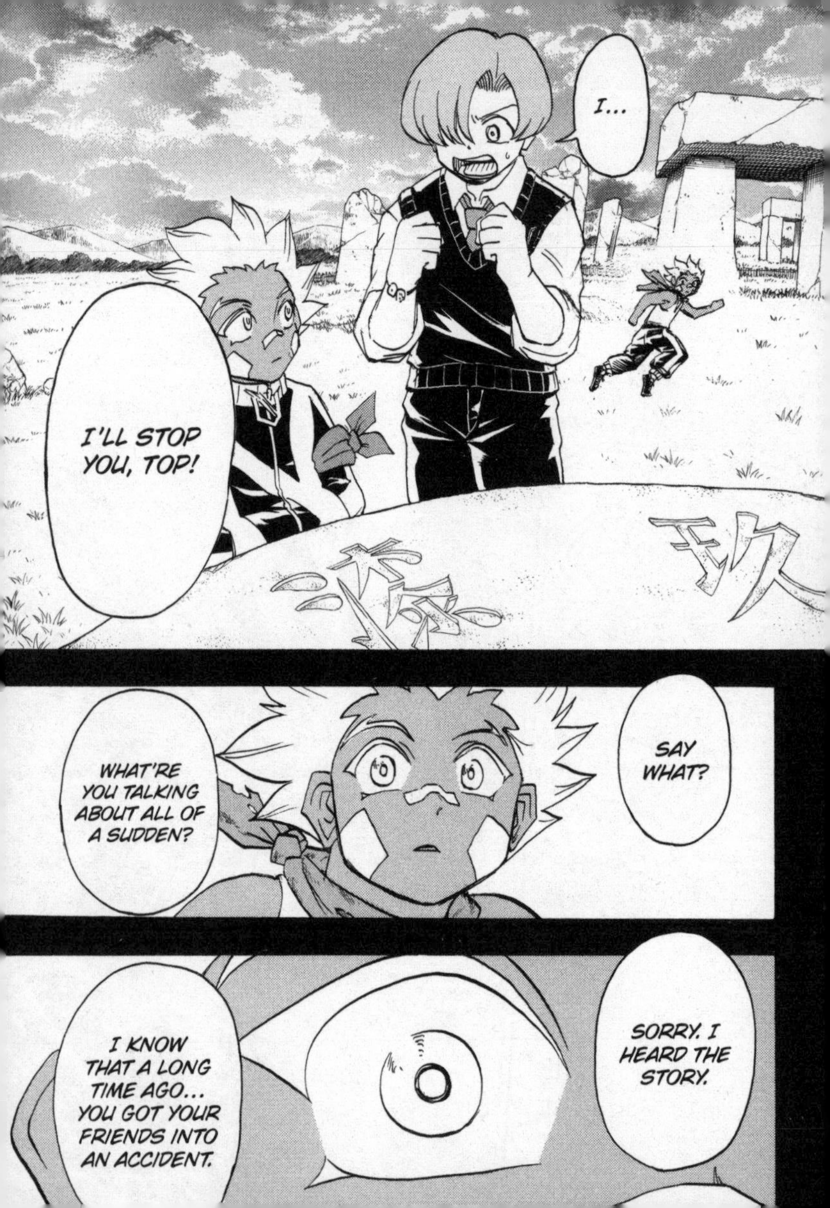
I...
I'LL STOP YOU, TOP!
SAY WHAT?
WHAT'RE YOU TALKING ABOUT ALL OF A SUDDEN?
SORRY. I HEARD THE STORY.
I KNOW THAT A LONG TIME AGO... YOU GOT YOUR FRIENDS INTO AN ACCIDENT.

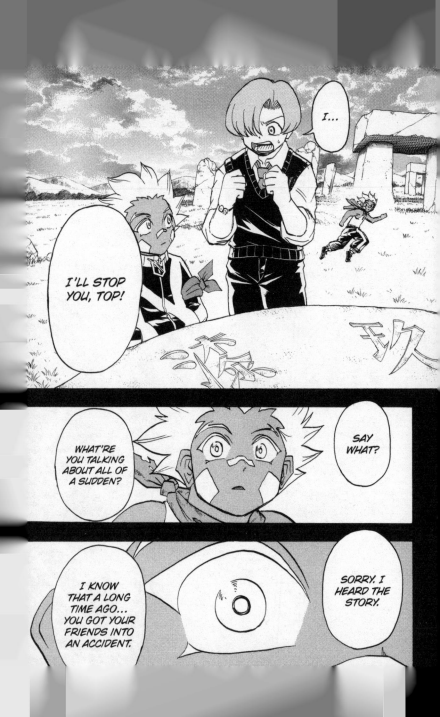

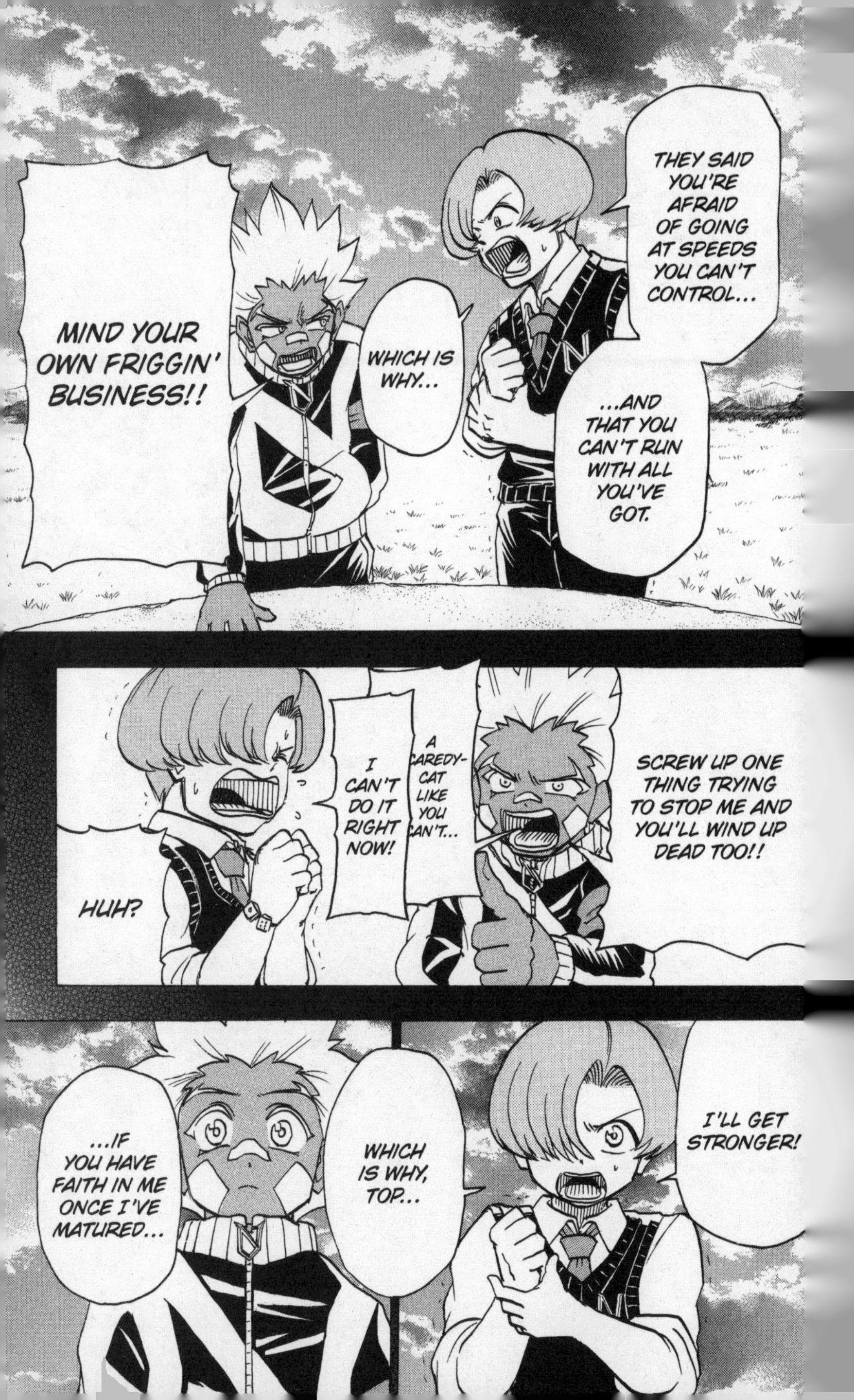
THEY SAID YOU'RE AFRAID OF GOING AT SPEEDS YOU CAN'T CONTROL...
...AND THAT YOU CAN'T RUN WITH ALL YOU'VE GOT.
WHICH IS WHY...
MIND YOUR OWN FRIGGIN' BUSINESS!!
SCREW UP ONE THING TRYING TO STOP ME AND YOU'LL WIND UP DEAD TOO!!
A CAREDY-CAT LIKE YOU CAN'T...
I CAN'T DO IT RIGHT NOW!
HUH?
I'LL GET STRONGER!
WHICH IS WHY, TOP...
...IF YOU HAVE FAITH IN ME ONCE I'VE MATURED...

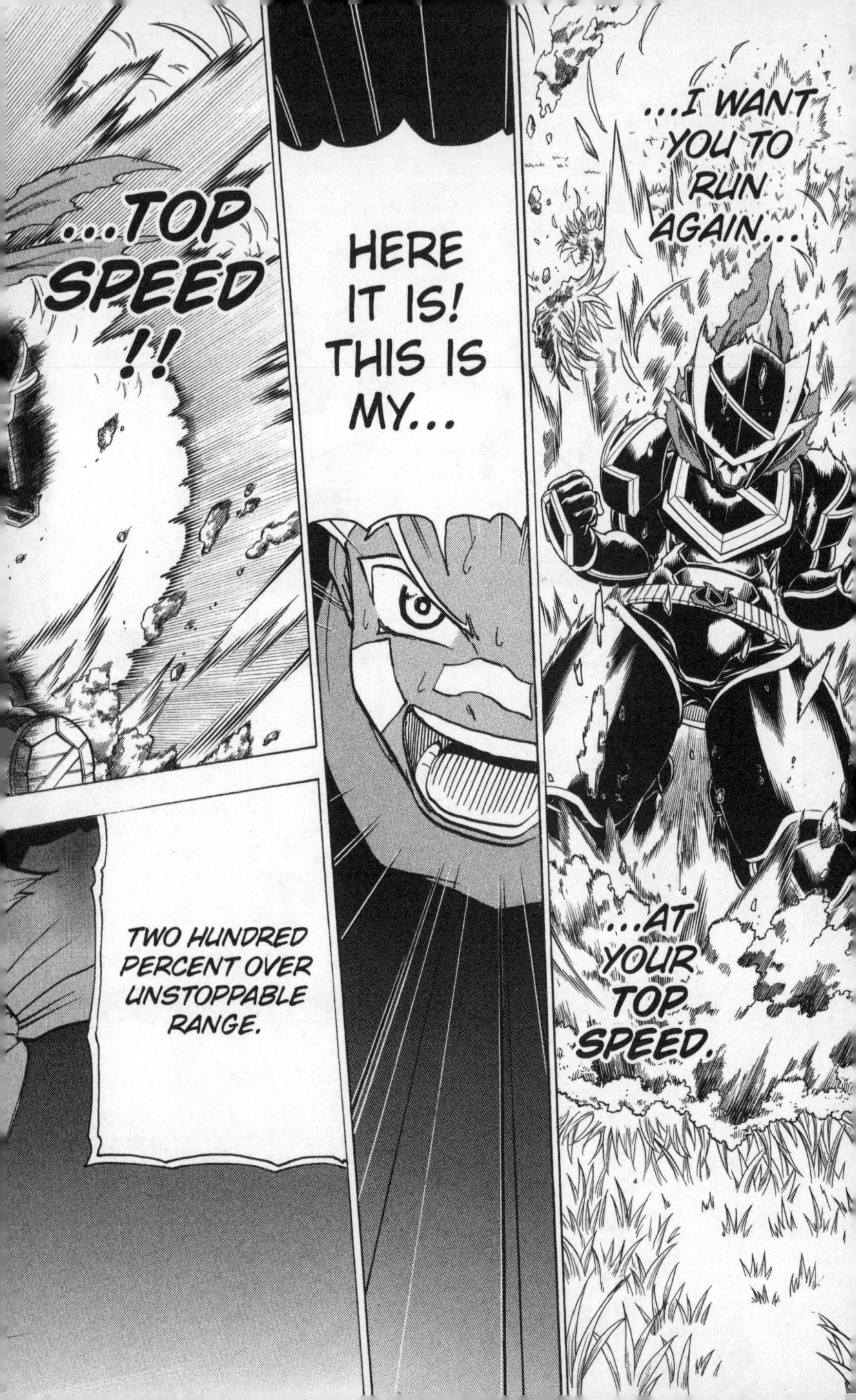
...I WANT YOU TO RUN AGAIN...
...AT YOUR TOP SPEED.
HERE IT IS! THIS IS MY...
...TOP SPEED!!
TWO HUNDRED PERCENT OVER UNSTOPPABLE RANGE.

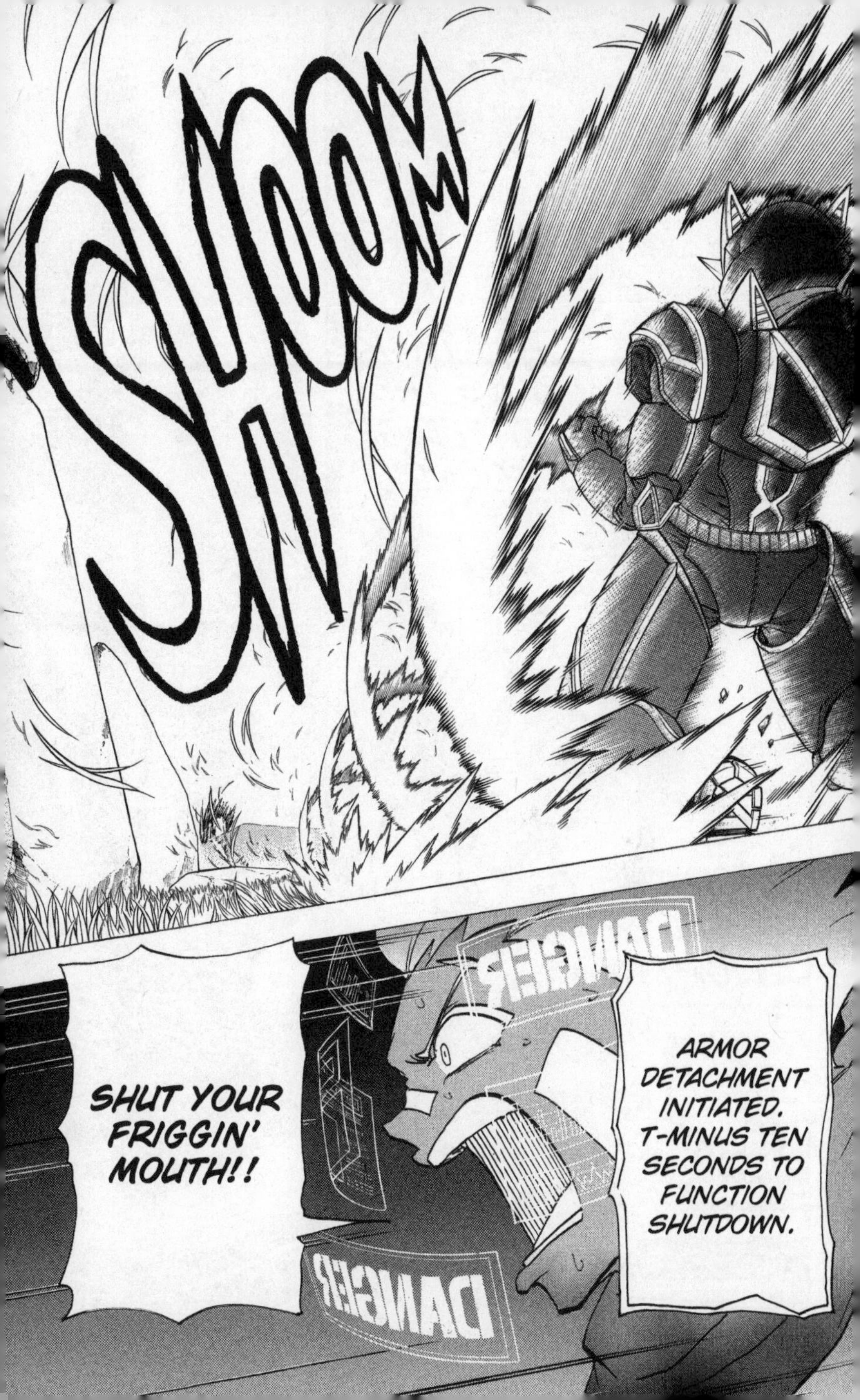
SHOOM
DANGER
ARMOR DETACHMENT INITIATED. T-MINUS TEN SECONDS TO FUNCTION SHUTDOWN.
SHUT YOUR FRIGGIN' MOUTH!!
DANGER

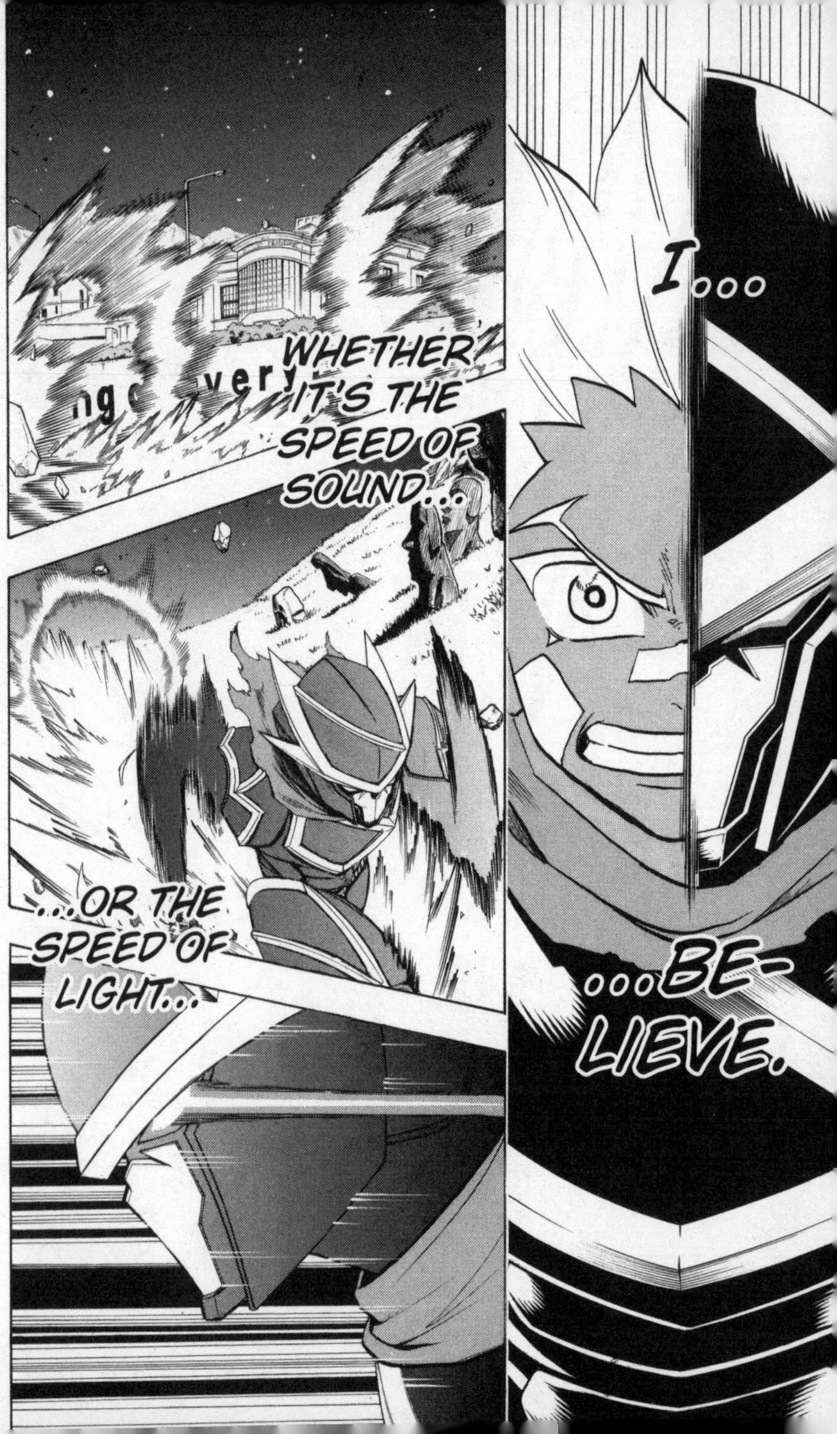
I...
...BE-LIEVE.
WHETHER IT'S THE SPEED OF SOUND...
...OR THE SPEED OF LIGHT...

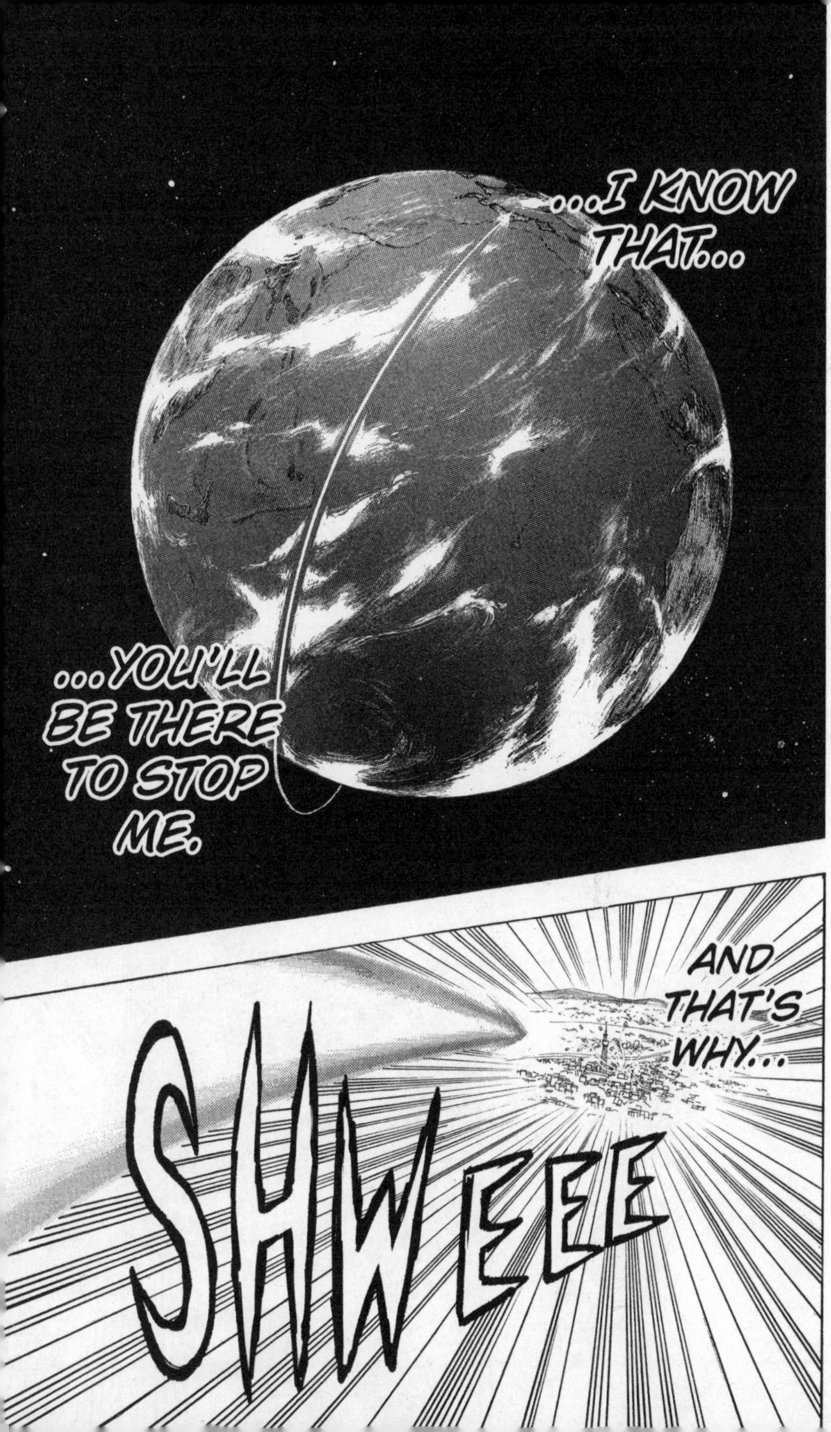
...I KNOW THAT...
...YOU'LL BE THERE TO STOP ME.
AND THAT'S WHY...
SHWEEE

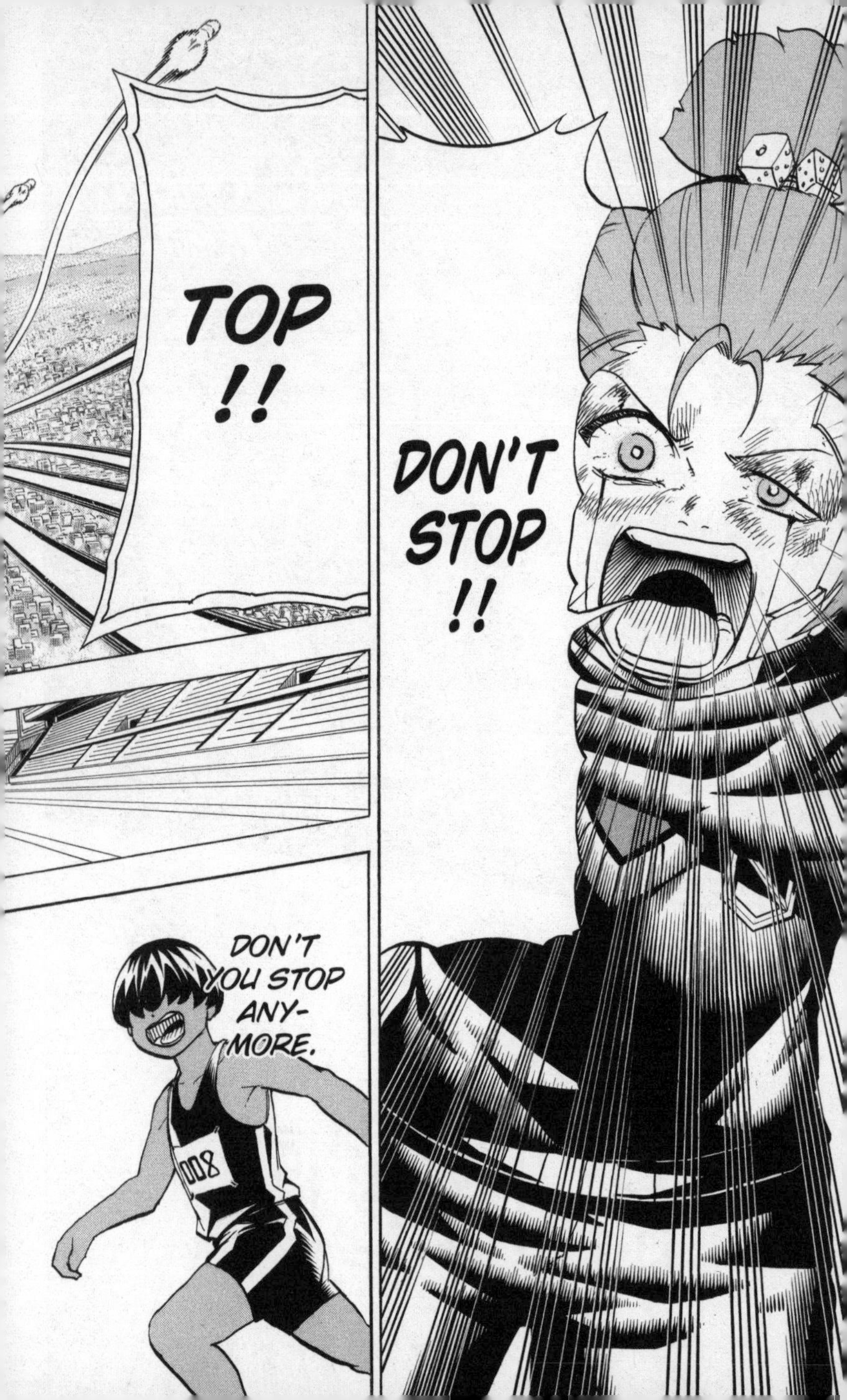
DON'T STOP !!
TOP !!
DON'T YOU STOP ANY-MORE.

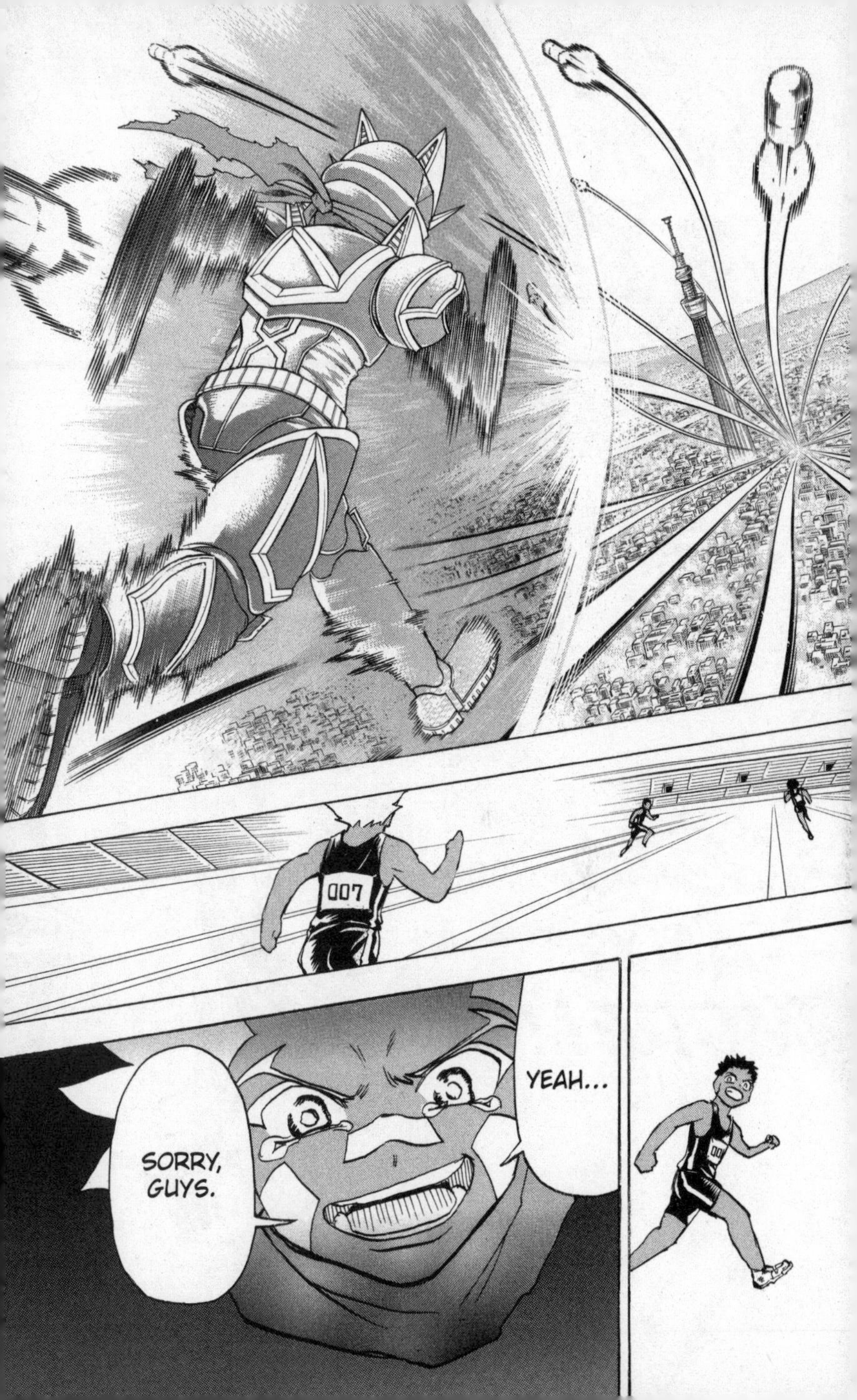
007
YEAH...
SORRY, GUYS.

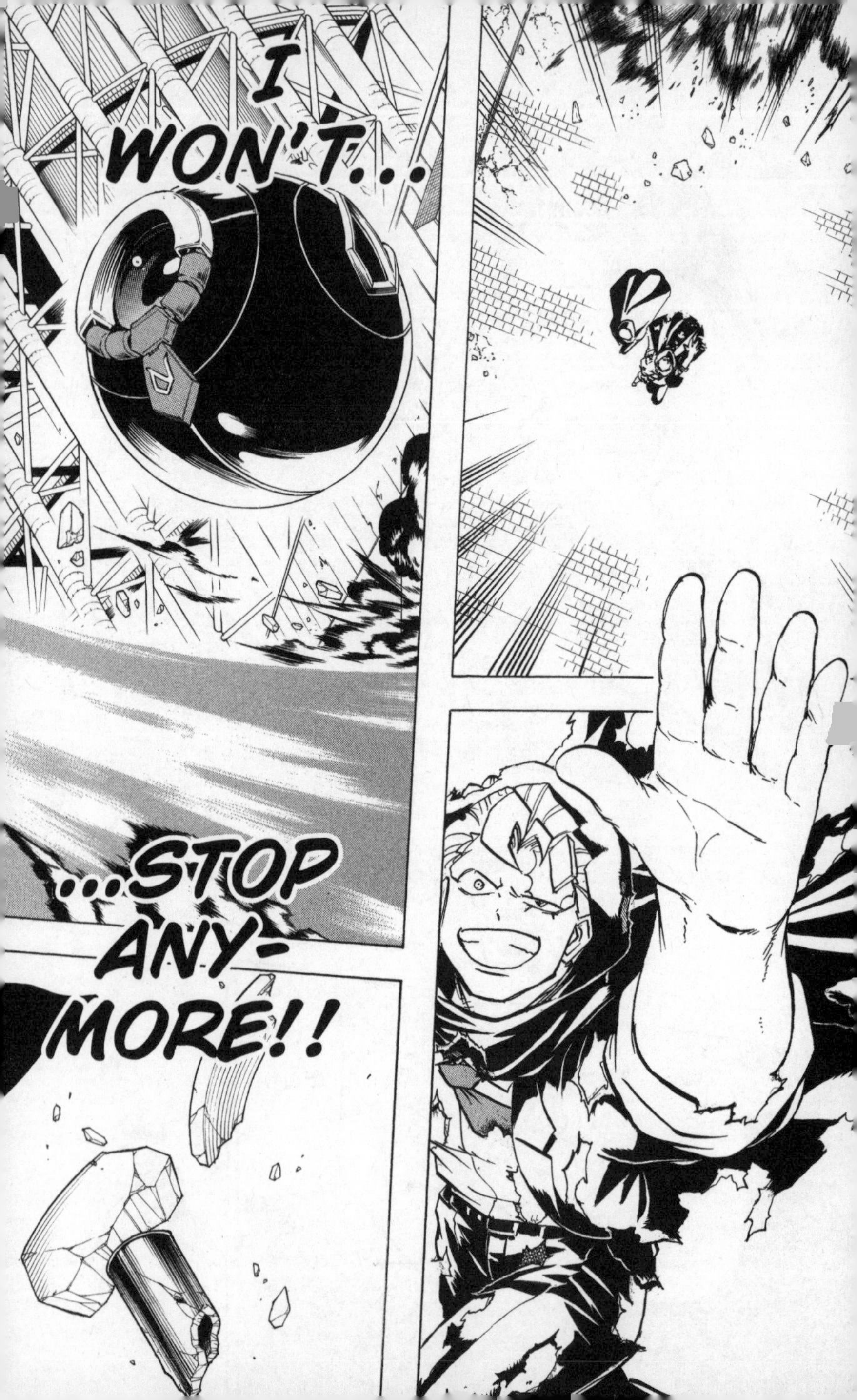
I WON'T...
...STOP ANY-MORE!!

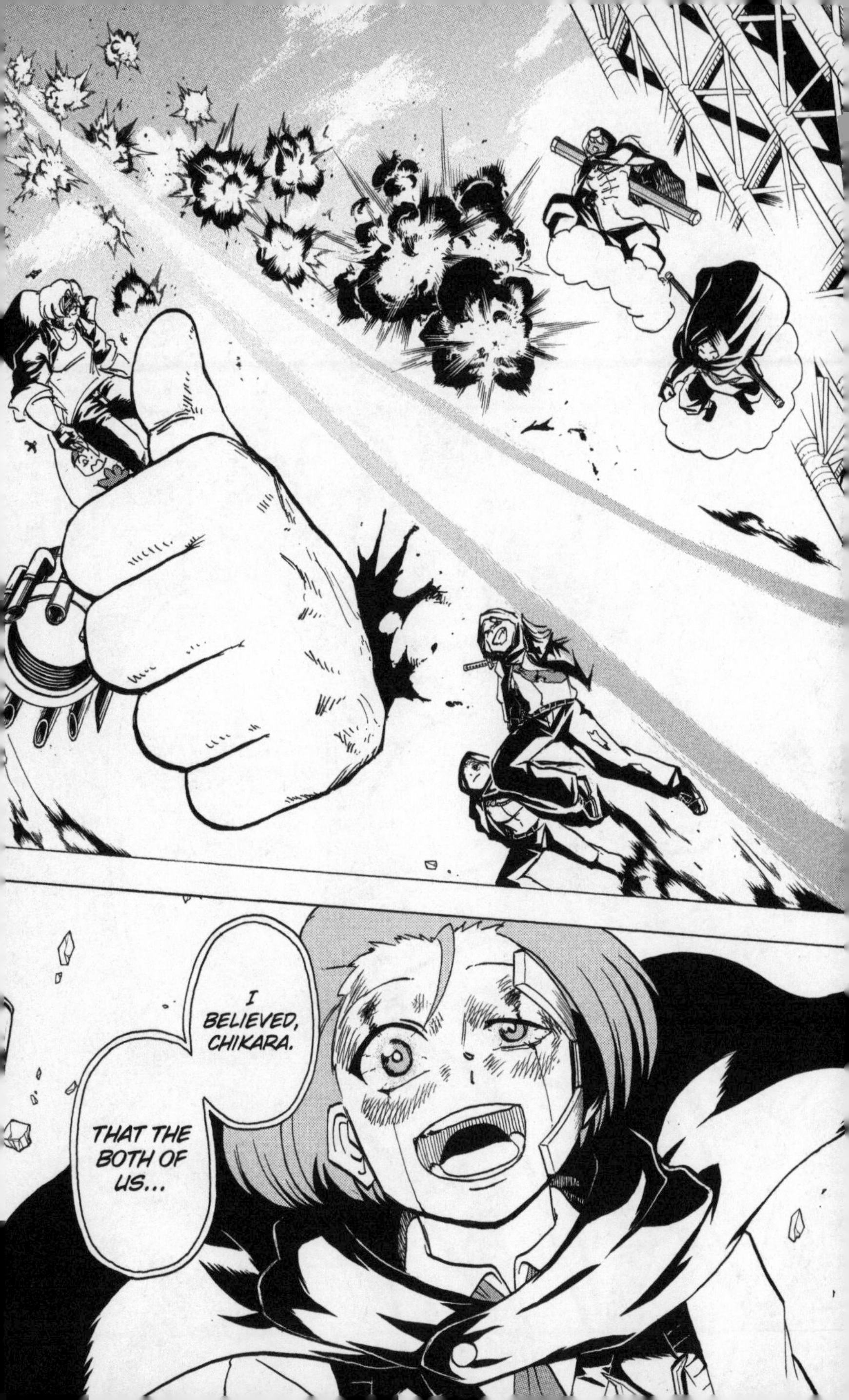
I BELIEVED, CHIKARA.
THAT THE BOTH OF US...

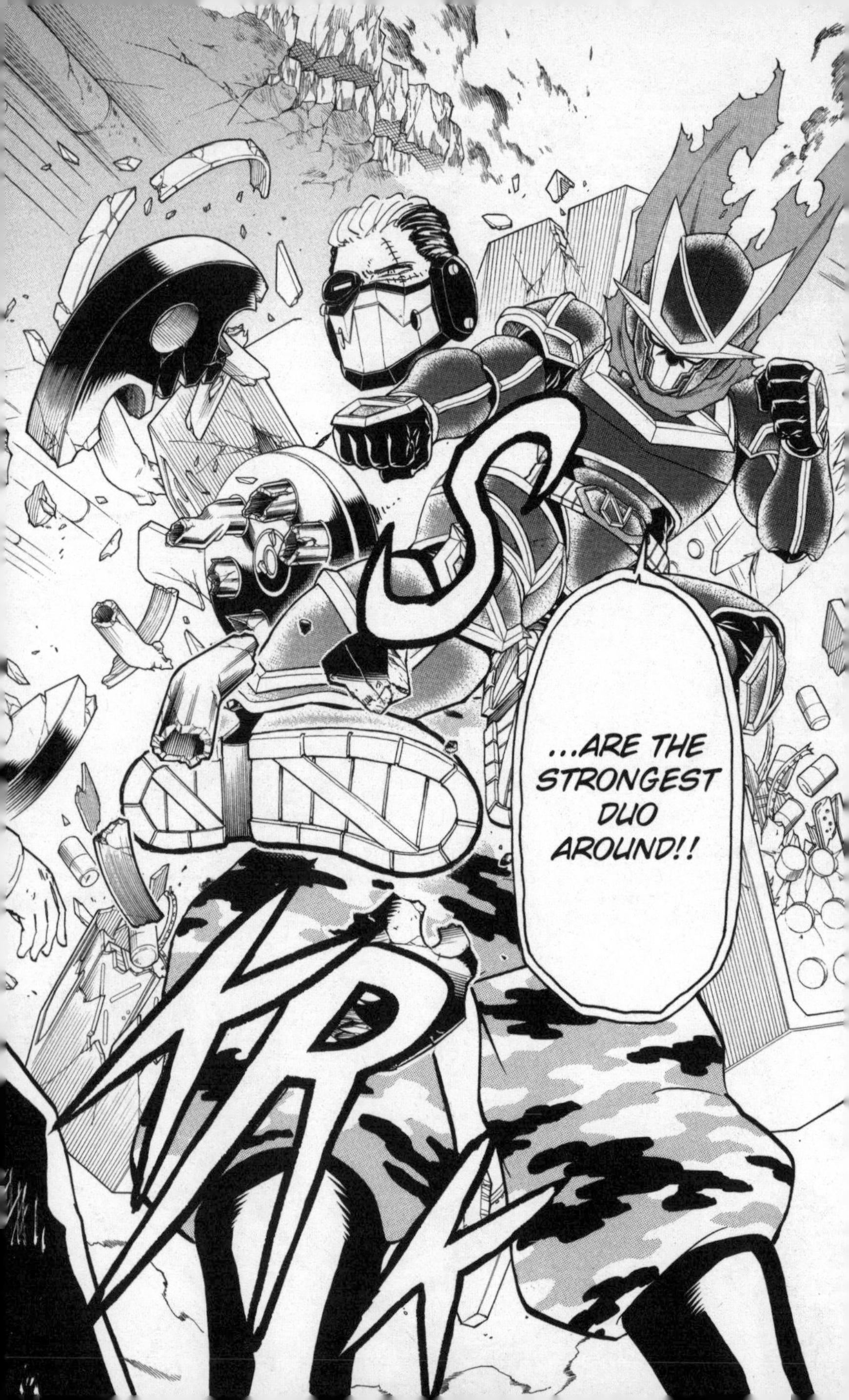
...ARE THE STRONGEST DUO AROUND!!

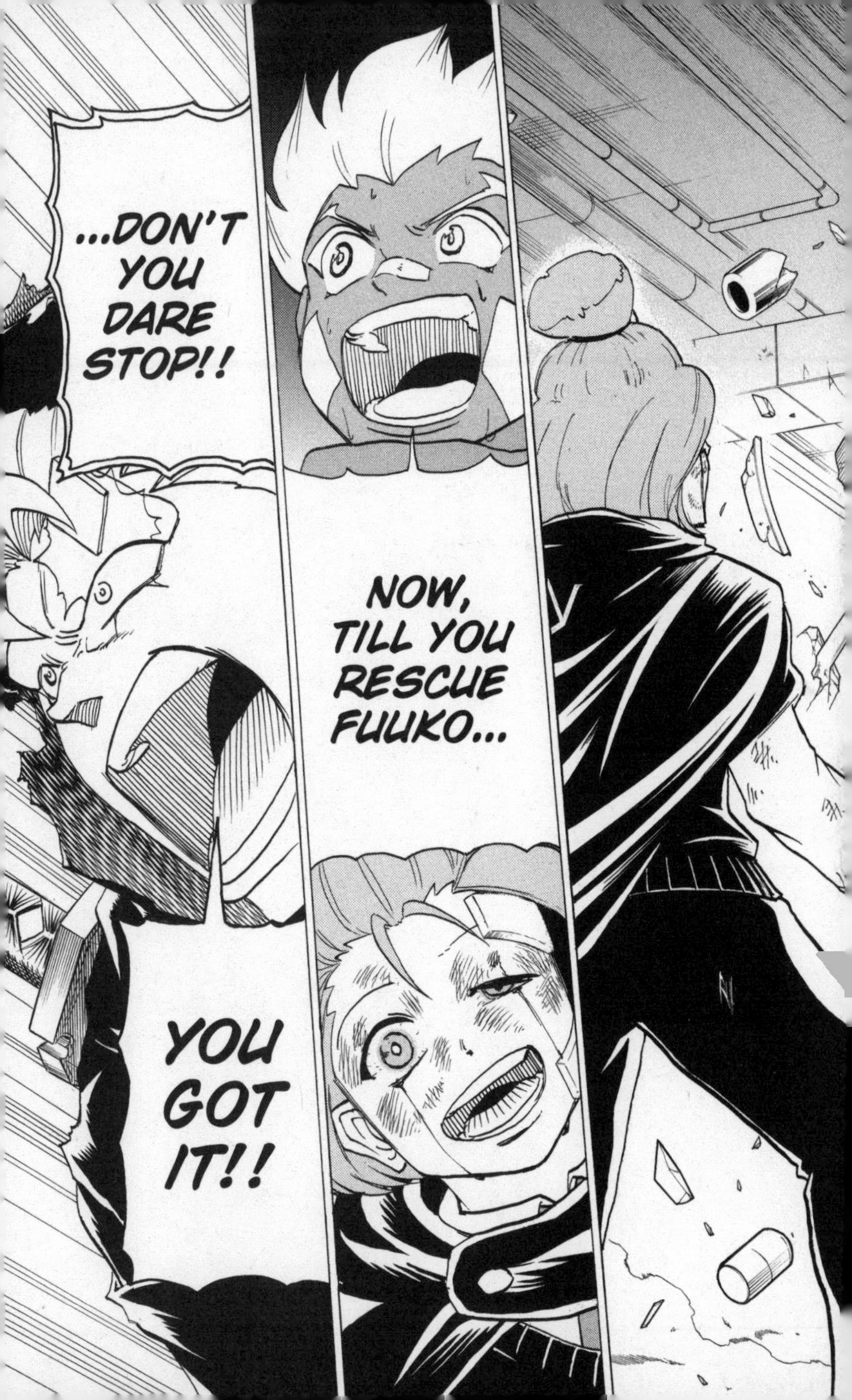
NOW, TILL YOU RESCUE FUUKO...
...DON'T YOU DARE STOP!!
YOU GOT IT!!

UN-ST
TACHYORIZER

A POWER SUIT DESIGNED BY NICO
FOR TOP'S USE. HE CAN CHANGE
INTO IT BY SWITCHING ON THE
"TACHYODRIVER" WRAPPED AROUND
HIS WAIST. AS IT'S STILL IN THE
PROTOTYPE STAGE, IT HASN'T YET
BEEN IMBUED WITH ISSHIN'S
UNBREAKABLE ABILITY. HOWEVER,
IT HAS A NUMBER OF DIFFERENT
FUNCTIONS SUCH AS: ABSORBING
THE SHOCK WAVES EMITTED BY HIS
SUPER ACCELERATION AND CONVERTING
THEM INTO ENERGY FOR FURTHER
ACCELERATION; EXTENDING
FUNCTIONALITY BY AUTOMATICALLY
REMOVING OUTER PARTS OF THE
ARMOR THAT HAVE OVERHEATED
DUE TO FRICTION; BREAKING A LIMB
IN ORDER TO DEACTIVATE THE
UNSTOPPABLE ABILITY; AND
OFFSETTING ANY KINETIC ENERGY
AFTER BEING STOPPED BY UNMOVE.

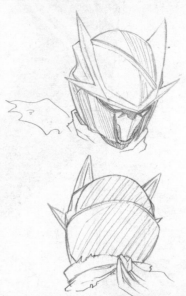

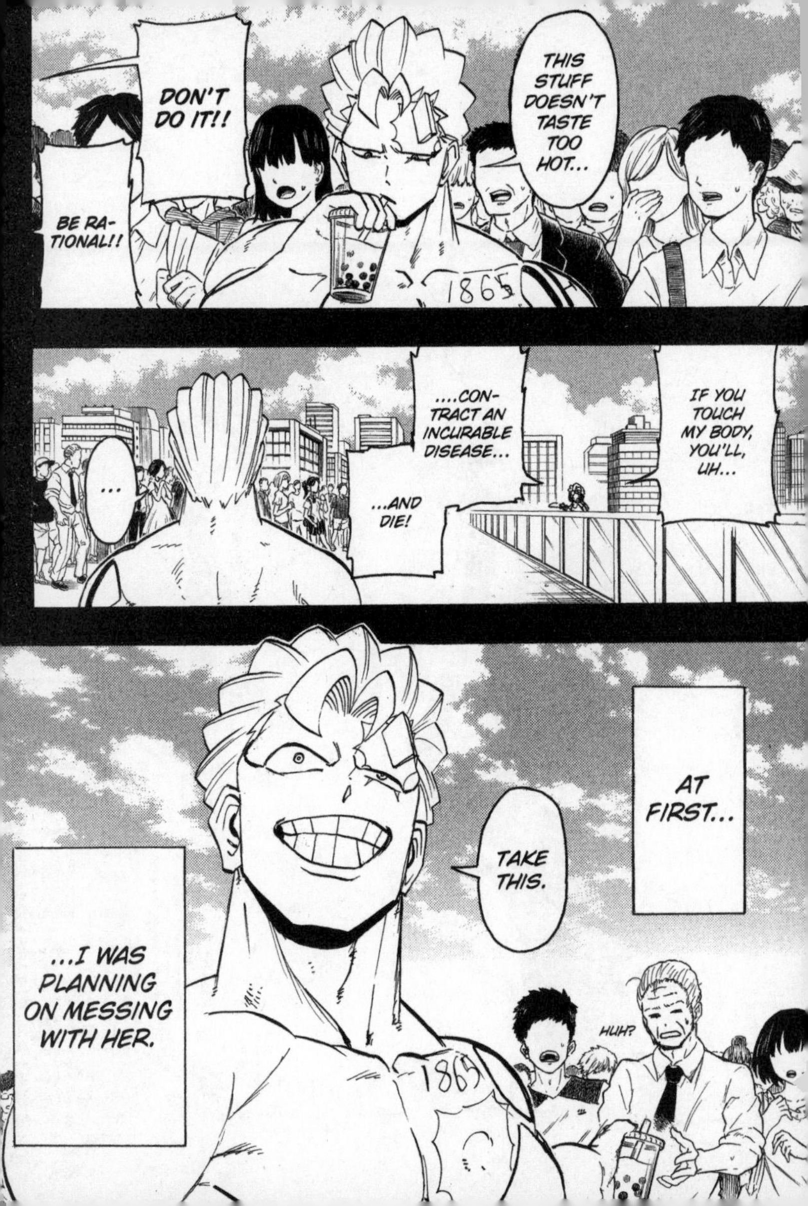
THIS STUFF DOESN'T TASTE TOO HOT...
DON'T DO IT!!
BE RA-TIONAL!!
1865
IF YOU TOUCH MY BODY, YOU'LL, UH...
....CON-TRACT AN INCURABLE DISEASE...
...AND DIE!
...
AT FIRST...
TAKE THIS.
HUH?
1865
...I WAS PLANNING ON MESSING WITH HER.

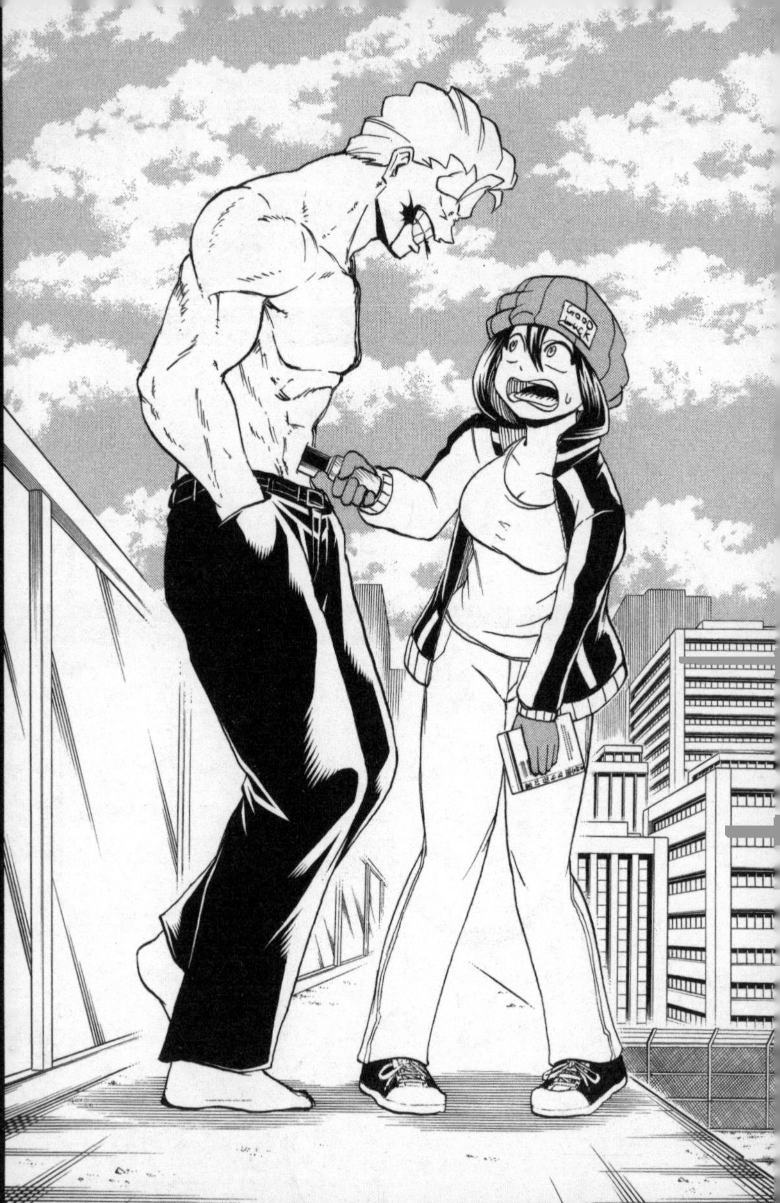
GOOD LUCK

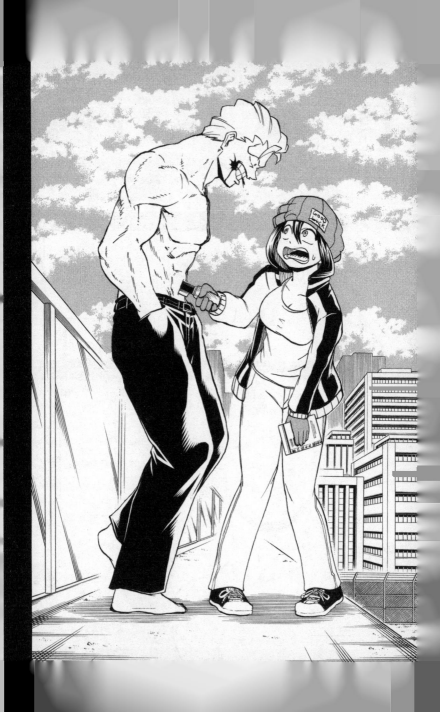

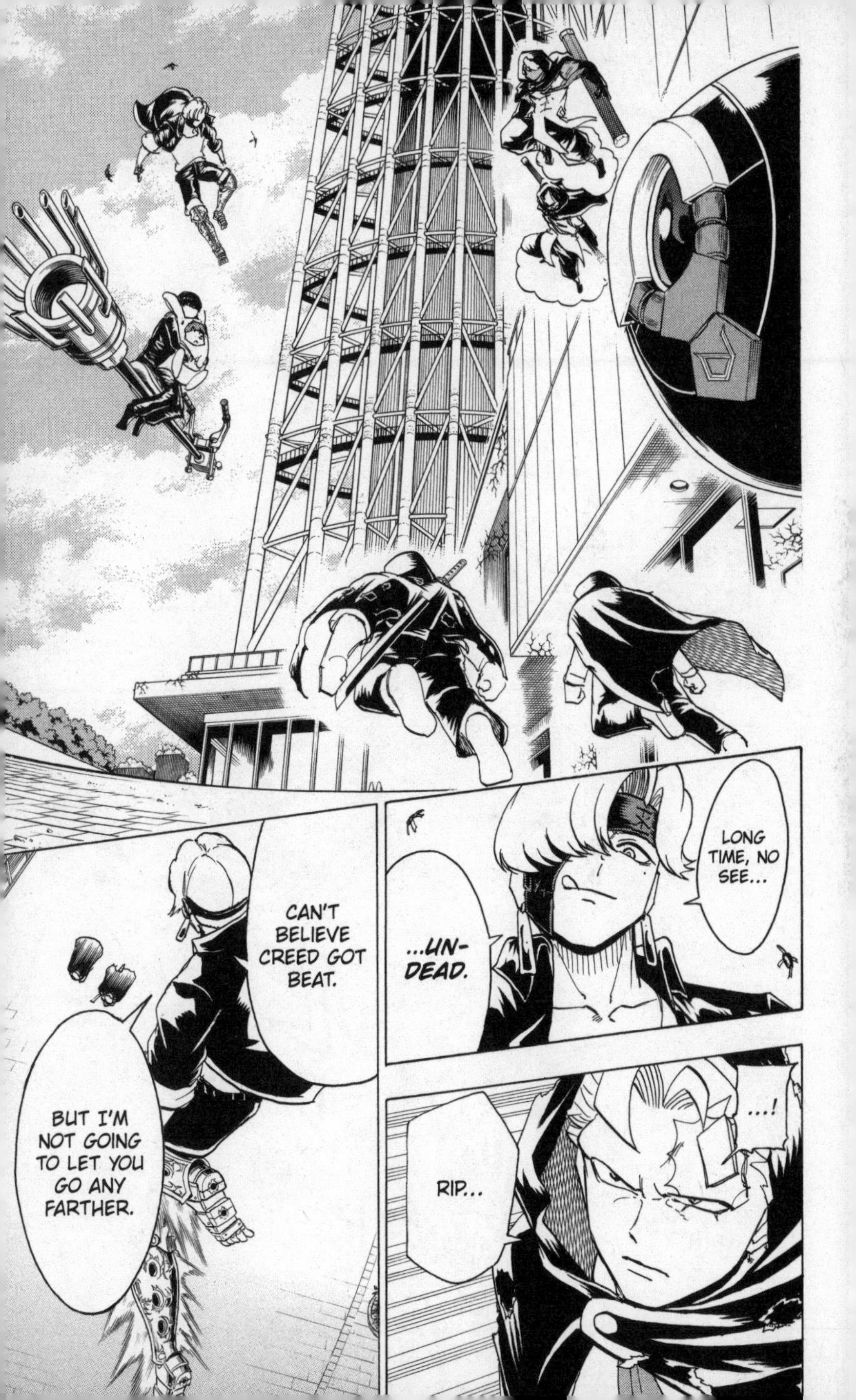

LONG TIME, NO SEE...
...UN-DEAD.
...!
RIP...
CAN'T BELIEVE CREED GOT BEAT.
BUT I'M NOT GOING TO LET YOU GO ANY FARTHER.

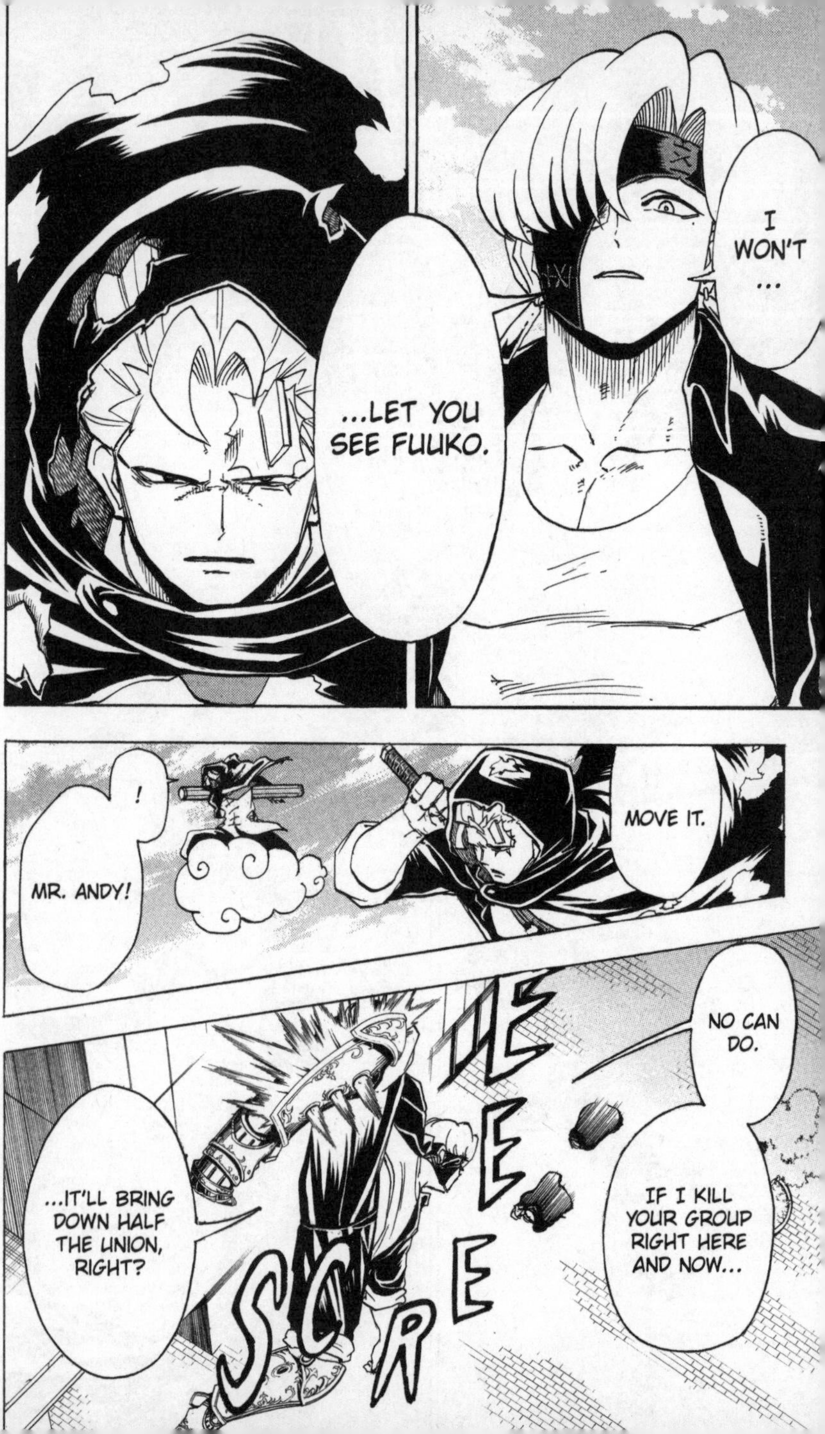
I WON'T ...
...LET YOU SEE FUUKO.
MOVE IT.
!
MR. ANDY!
NO CAN DO.
IF I KILL YOUR GROUP RIGHT HERE AND NOW...
...IT'LL BRING DOWN HALF THE UNION, RIGHT?
SCREEE

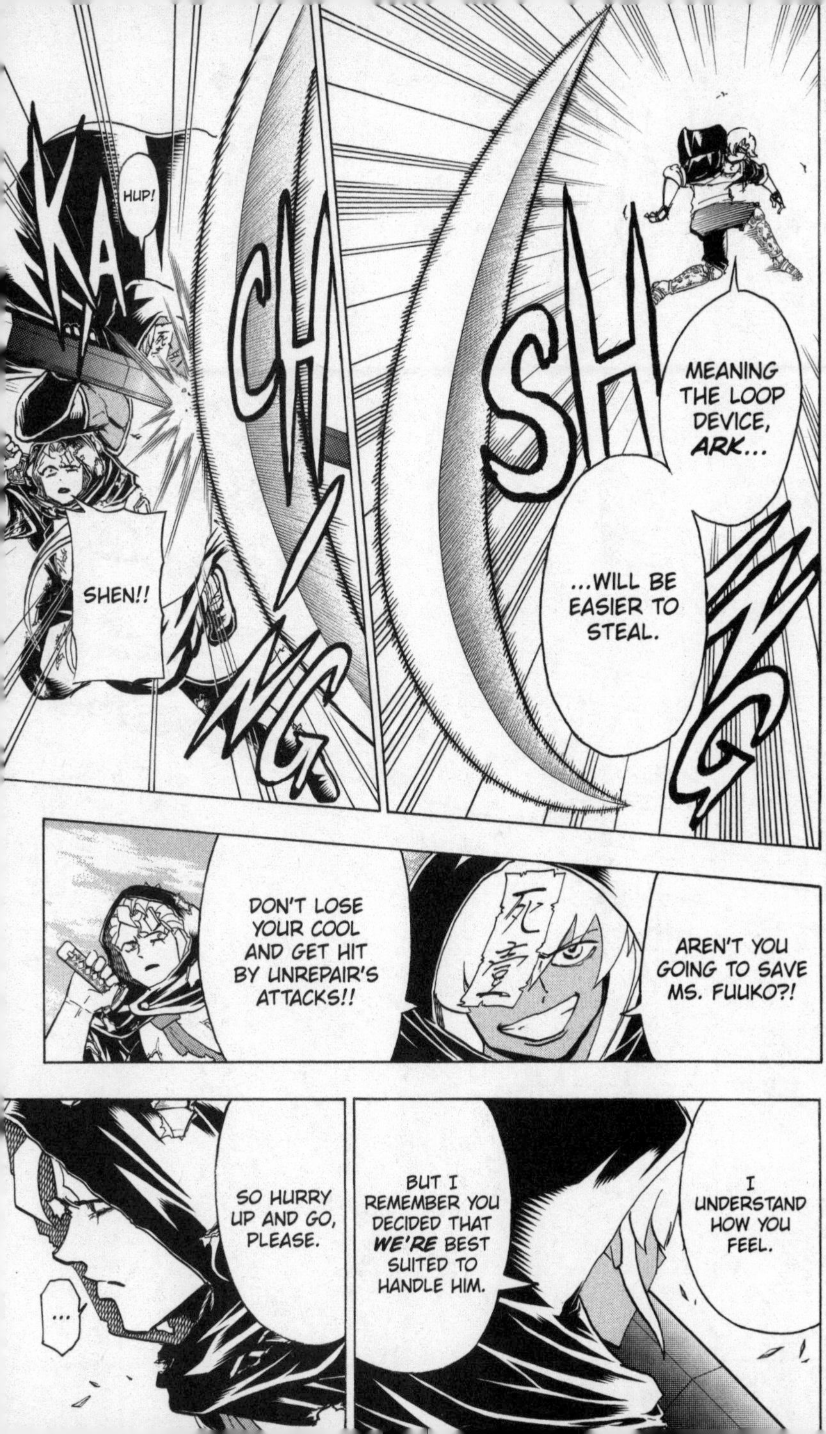
MEANING THE LOOP DEVICE, ***ARK***...
...WILL BE EASIER TO STEAL.
SHING
CHING
HUP!
KA
SHEN!!
AREN'T YOU GOING TO SAVE MS. FUUKO?!
DON'T LOSE YOUR COOL AND GET HIT BY UNREPAIR'S ATTACKS!!
I UNDERSTAND HOW YOU FEEL.
BUT I REMEMBER YOU DECIDED THAT ***WE'RE*** BEST SUITED TO HANDLE HIM.
SO HURRY UP AND GO, PLEASE.
...

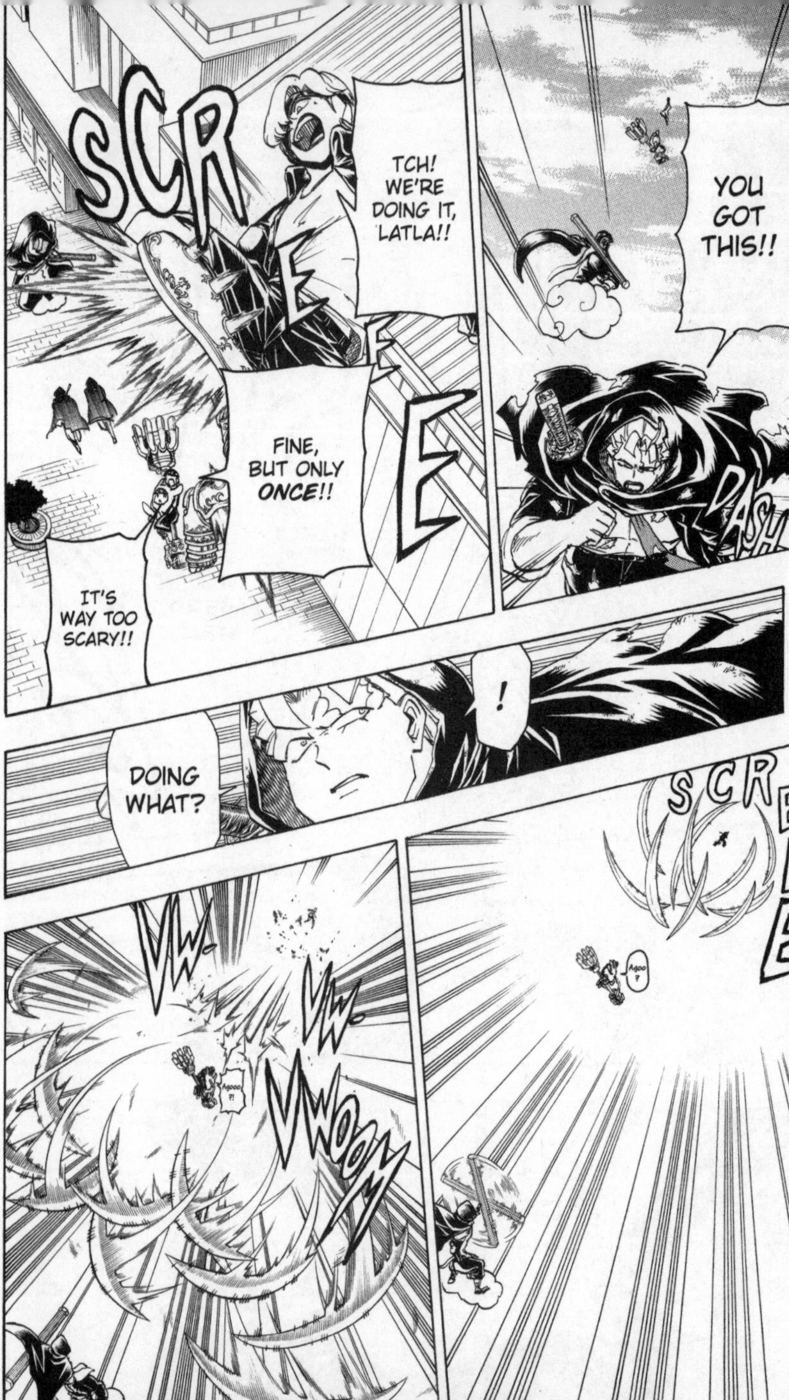
YOU GOT THIS!!
DASH
SCREEE
TCH! WE'RE DOING IT, LATLA!!
FINE, BUT ONLY *ONCE*!!
IT'S WAY TOO SCARY!!
!
DOING WHAT?
SCREEEE
Agoo?
VW-
VW-
VWOOM
Agooo?!

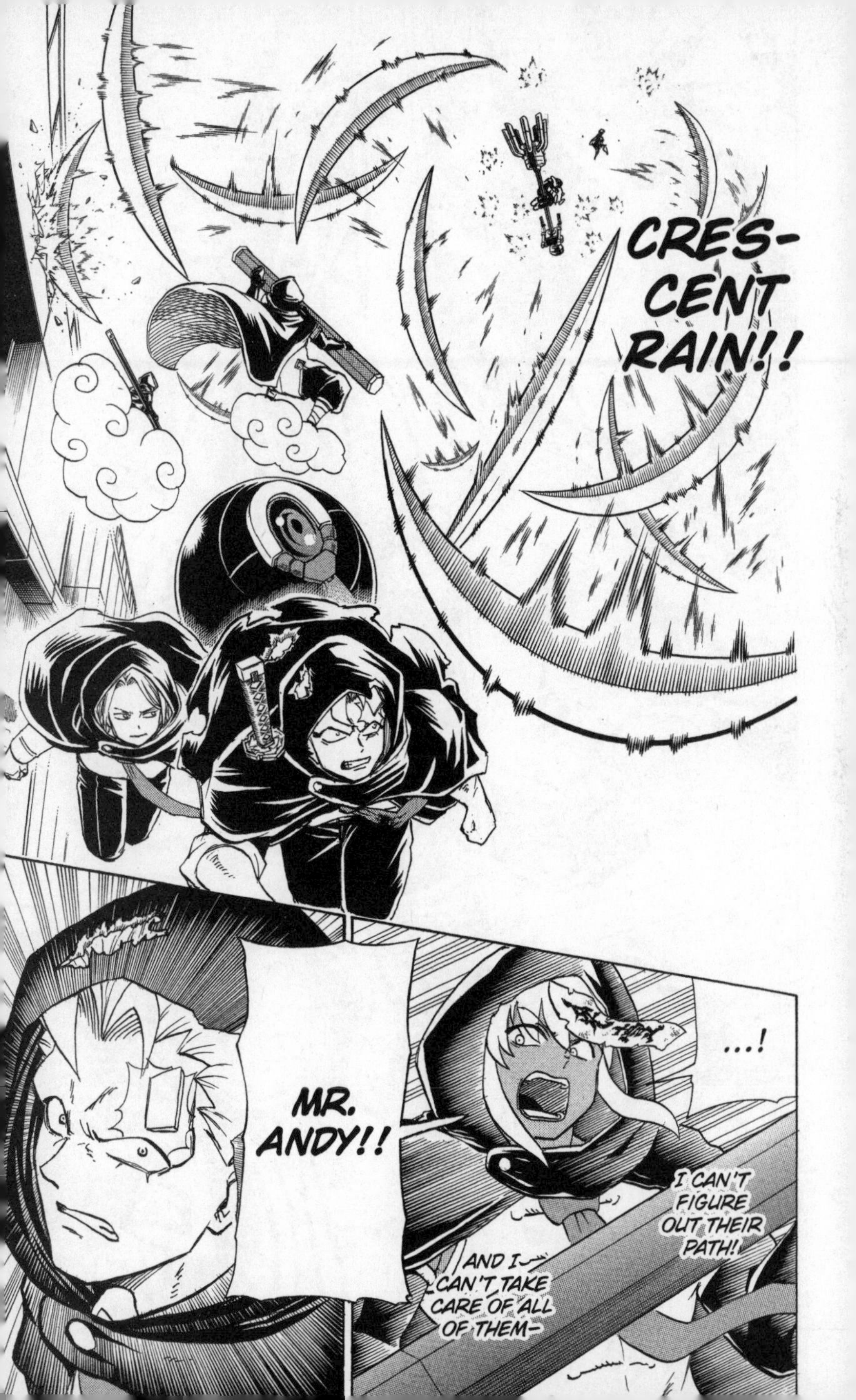
CRES-
CENT
RAIN!!
...!
I CAN'T FIGURE OUT THEIR PATH!
AND I— CAN'T TAKE CARE OF ALL OF THEM—
MR. ANDY!!

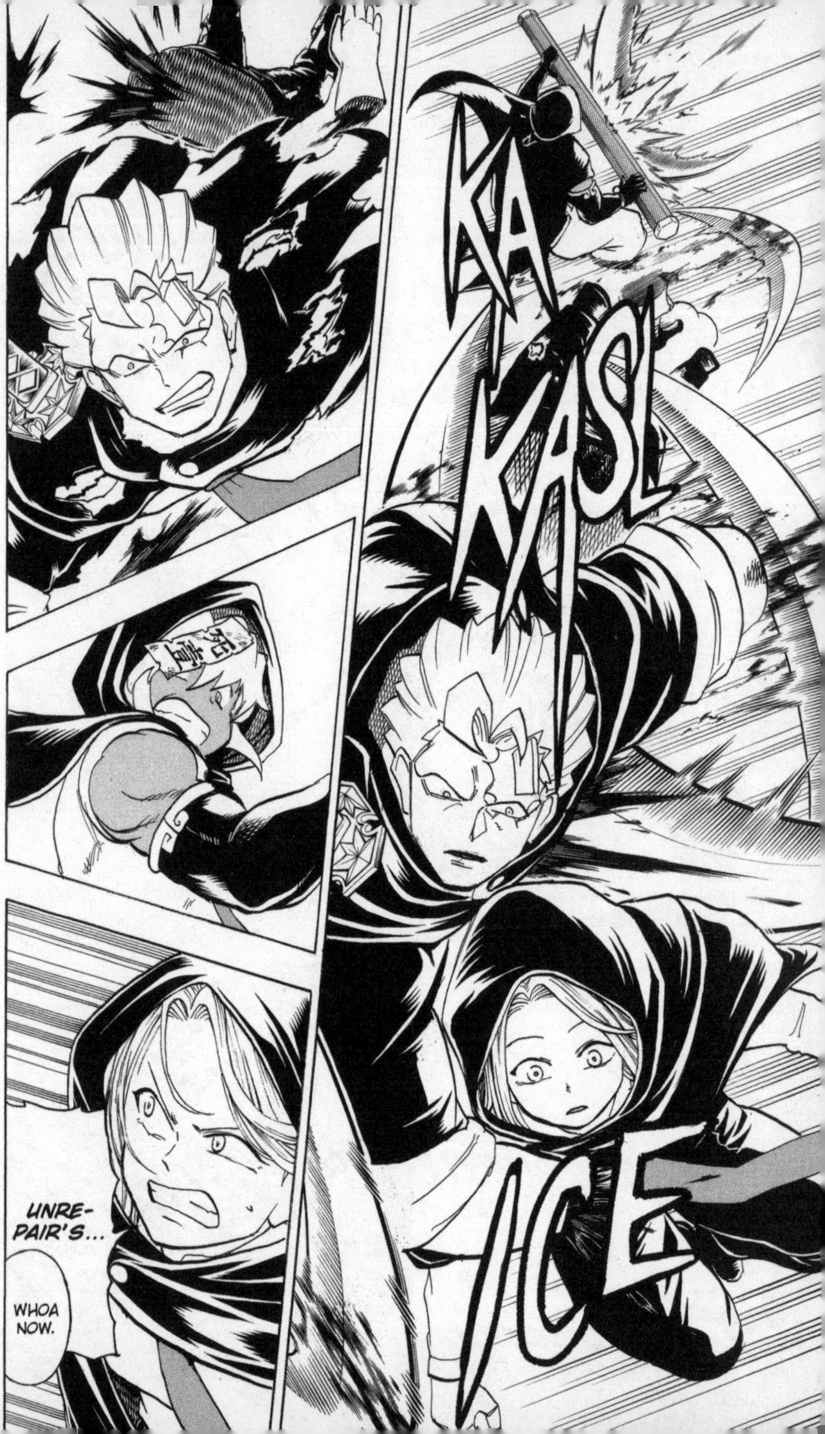
KA
KASL
ICE
UNRE-PAIR'S...
WHOA NOW.

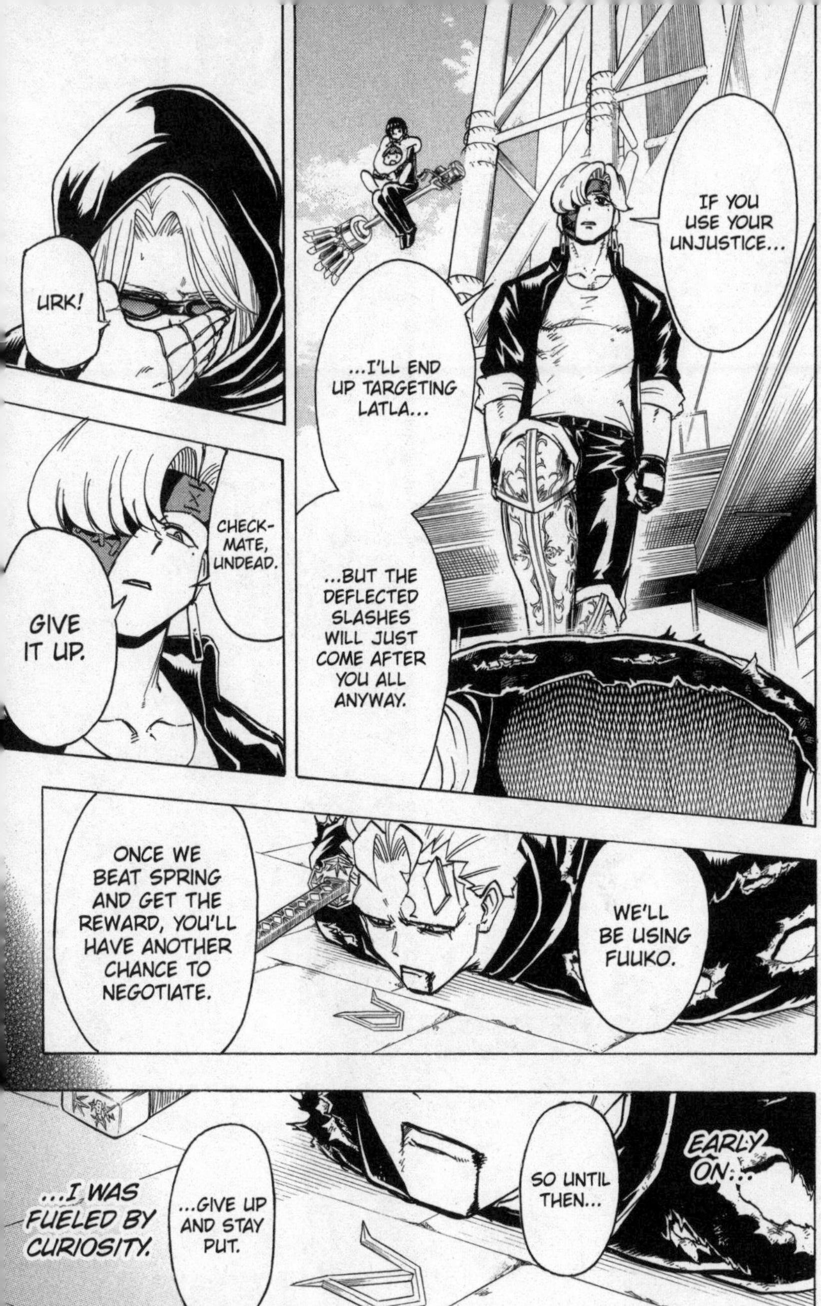
IF YOU USE YOUR UNJUSTICE...
...I'LL END UP TARGETING LATLA...
...BUT THE DEFLECTED SLASHES WILL JUST COME AFTER YOU ALL ANYWAY.
URK!
CHECK-MATE, UNDEAD.
GIVE IT UP.
WE'LL BE USING FUUKO.
ONCE WE BEAT SPRING AND GET THE REWARD, YOU'LL HAVE ANOTHER CHANCE TO NEGOTIATE.
EARLY ON...
SO UNTIL THEN...
...GIVE UP AND STAY PUT.
...I WAS FUELED BY CURIOSITY.

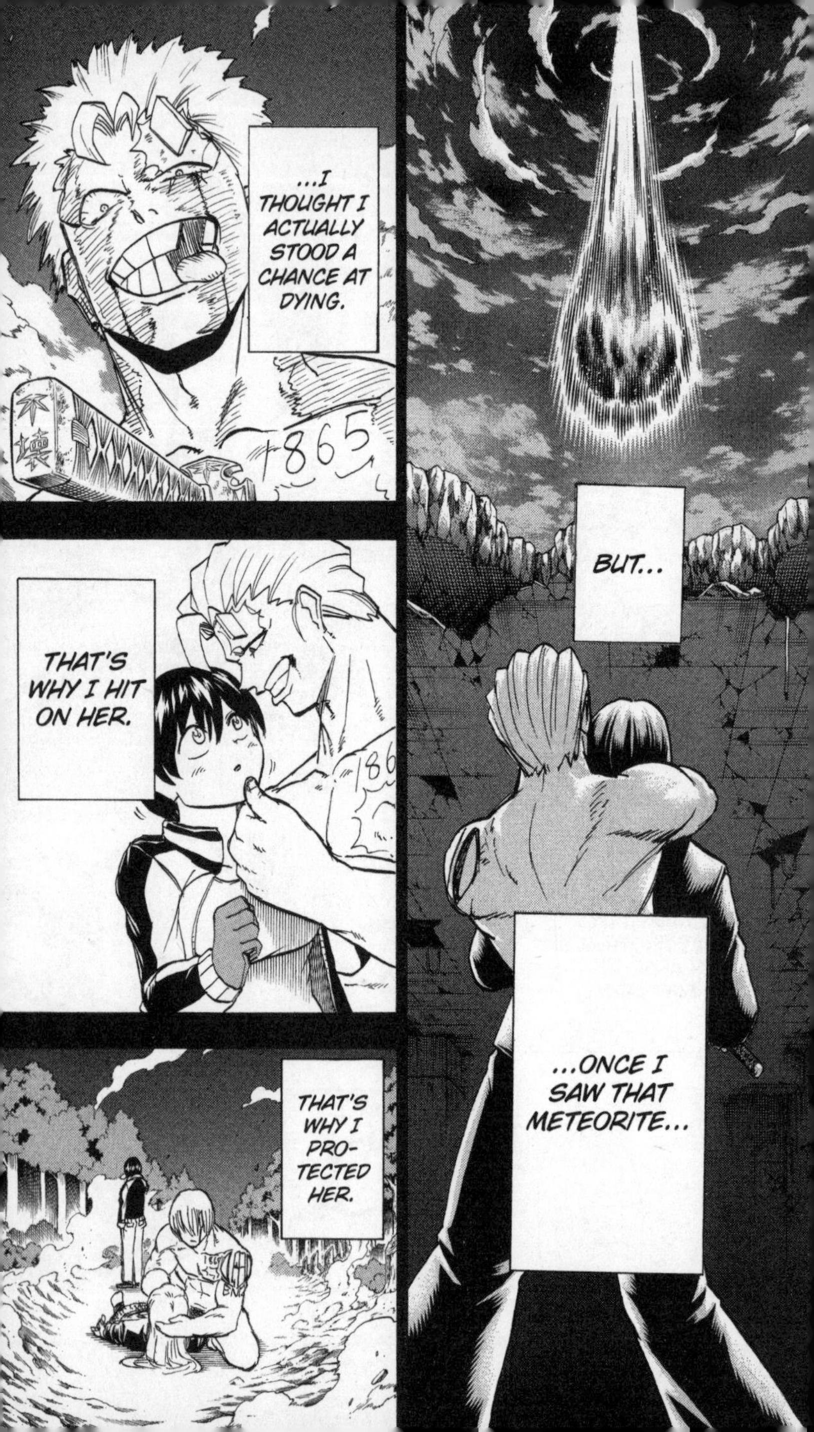
BUT...
...ONCE I SAW THAT METEORITE...
...I THOUGHT I ACTUALLY STOOD A CHANCE AT DYING.
1865
THAT'S WHY I HIT ON HER.
THAT'S WHY I PRO-TECTED HER.

I WAS SURE THAT...
...NOT EVEN YOU COULD KILL ME.
BUT I SOON REALIZED.
YOU WON'T BE ABLE TO KILL ME.
IN SPITE OF THAT...
WESTERN SALOON

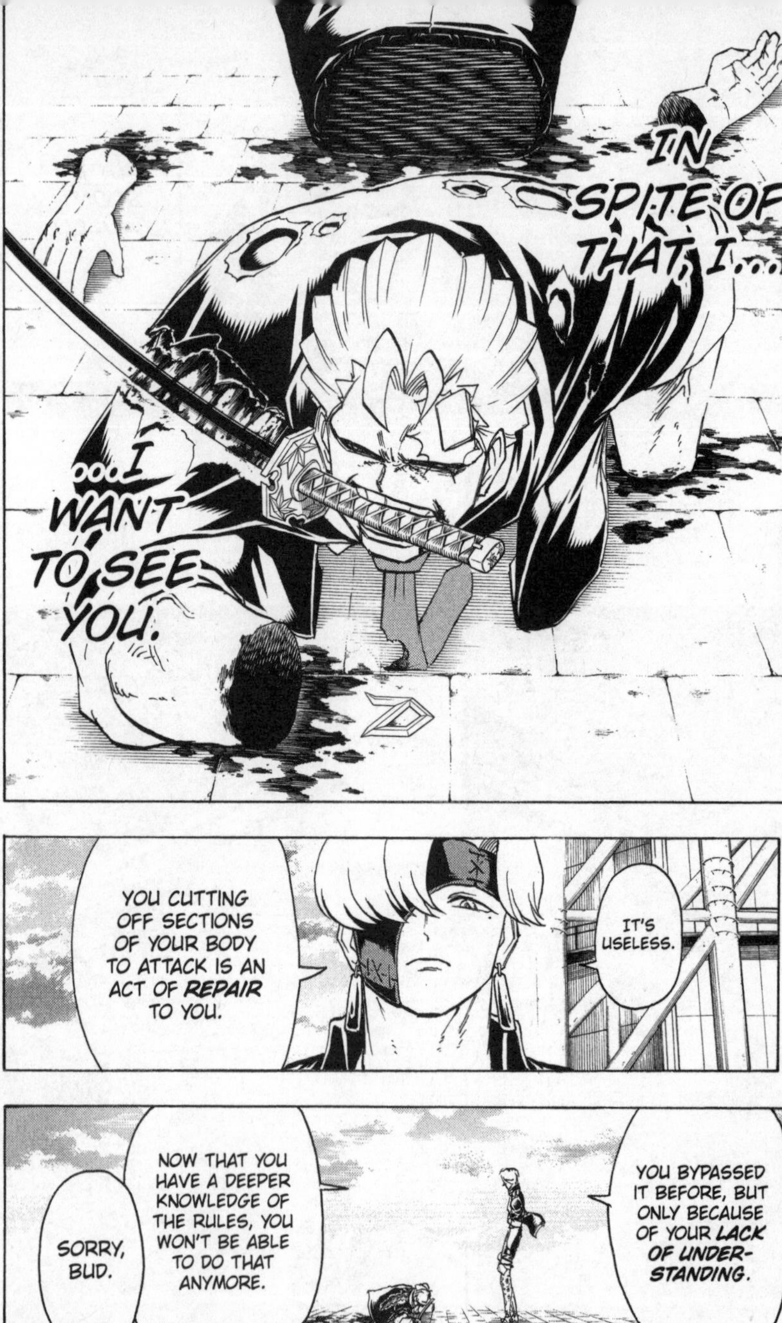
IN SPITE OF THAT, I...
...I WANT TO SEE YOU.
IT'S USELESS.
YOU CUTTING OFF SECTIONS OF YOUR BODY TO ATTACK IS AN ACT OF *REPAIR* TO YOU.
YOU BYPASSED IT BEFORE, BUT ONLY BECAUSE OF YOUR *LACK OF UNDER-STANDING*.
NOW THAT YOU HAVE A DEEPER KNOWLEDGE OF THE RULES, YOU WON'T BE ABLE TO DO THAT ANYMORE.
SORRY, BUD.

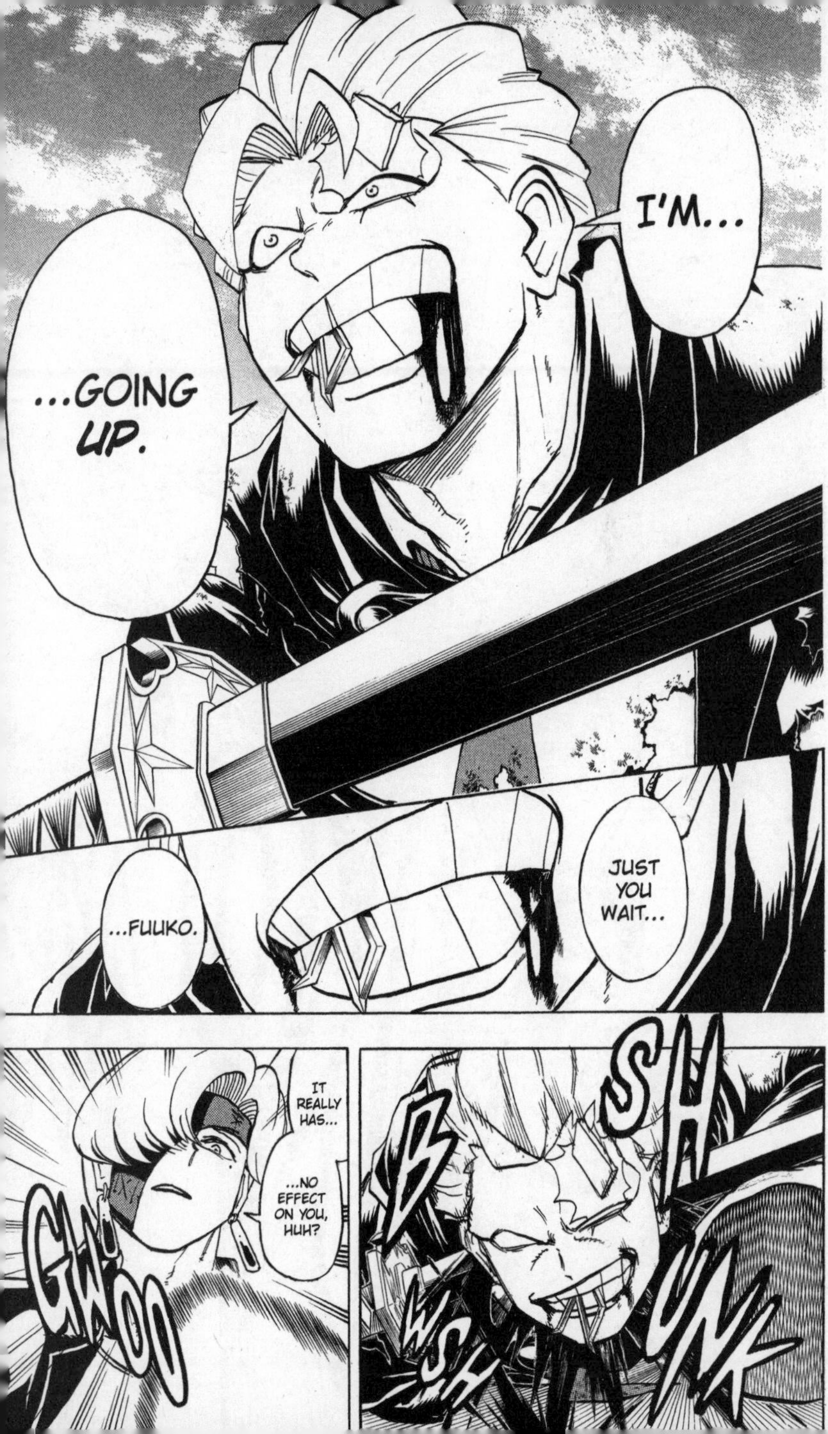
I'M...
...GOING UP.
JUST YOU WAIT...
...FUUKO.
BWSH
IT REALLY HAS...
...NO EFFECT ON YOU, HUH?
GWOOO

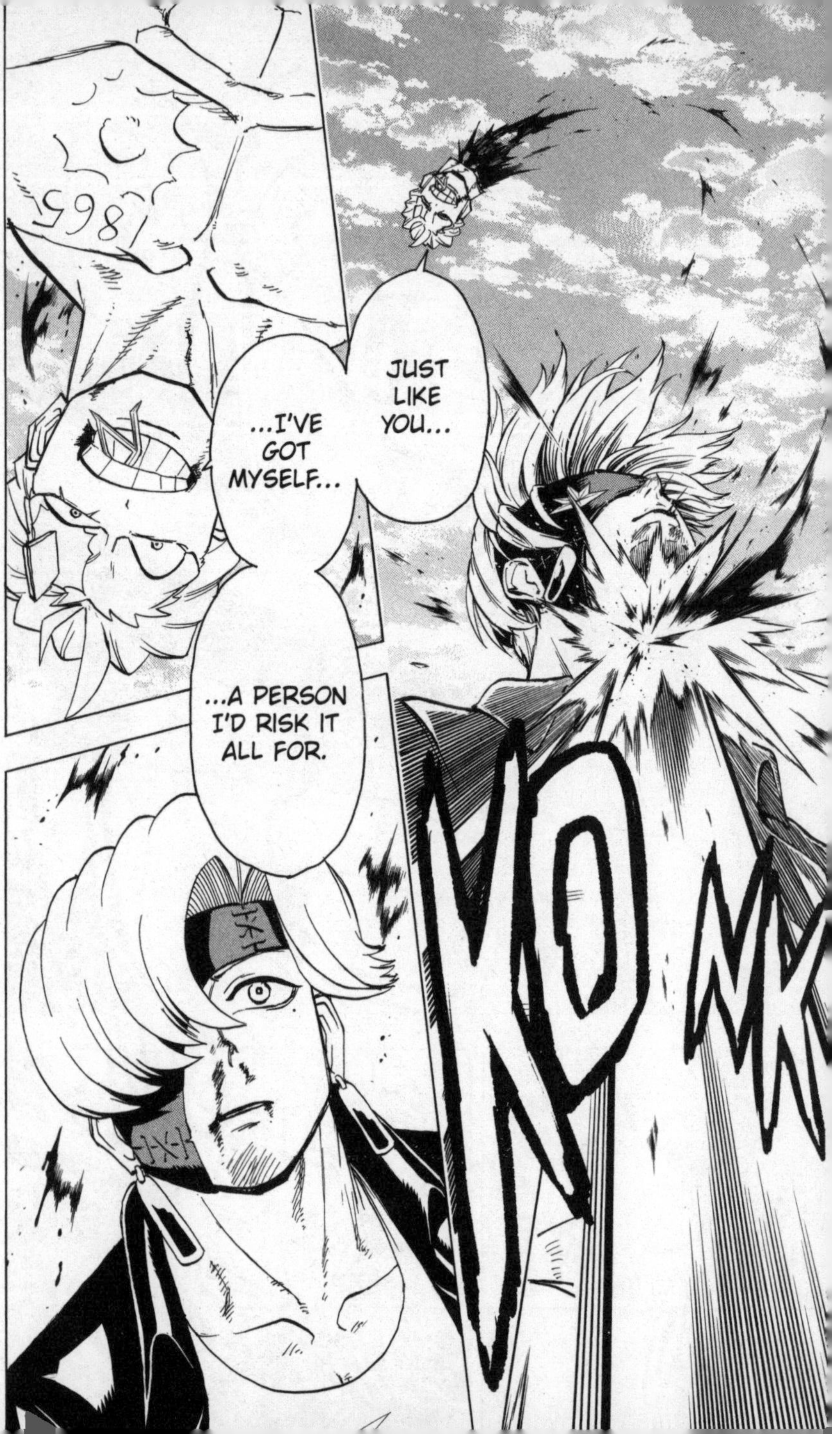
JUST LIKE YOU...
...I'VE GOT MYSELF...
...A PERSON I'D RISK IT ALL FOR.
KONK

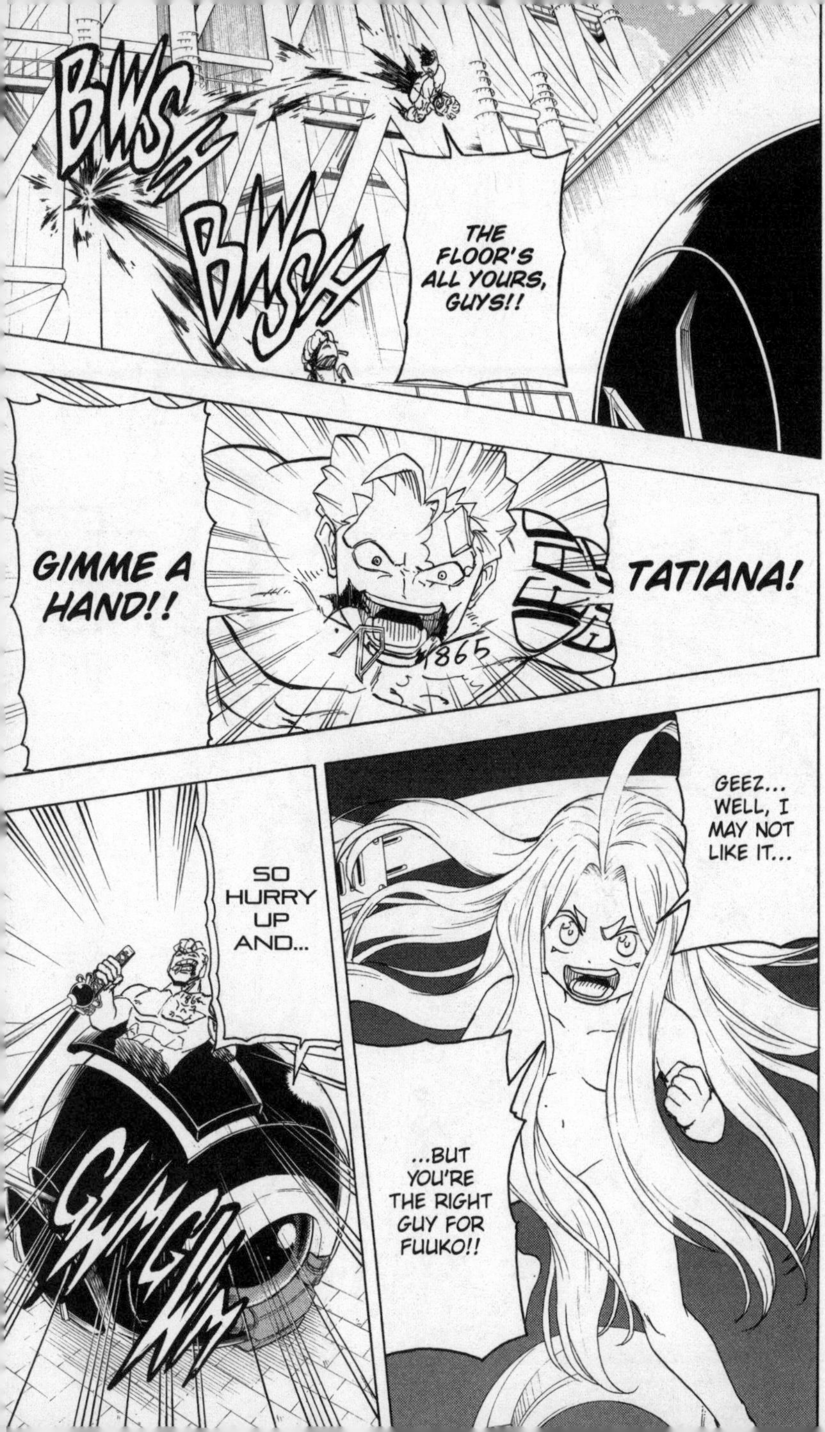

THE FLOOR'S ALL YOURS, GUYS!!
BWSH
BWSH
TATIANA!
GIMME A HAND!!
GEEZ... WELL, I MAY NOT LIKE IT...
...BUT YOU'RE THE RIGHT GUY FOR FUUKO!!
SO HURRY UP AND...

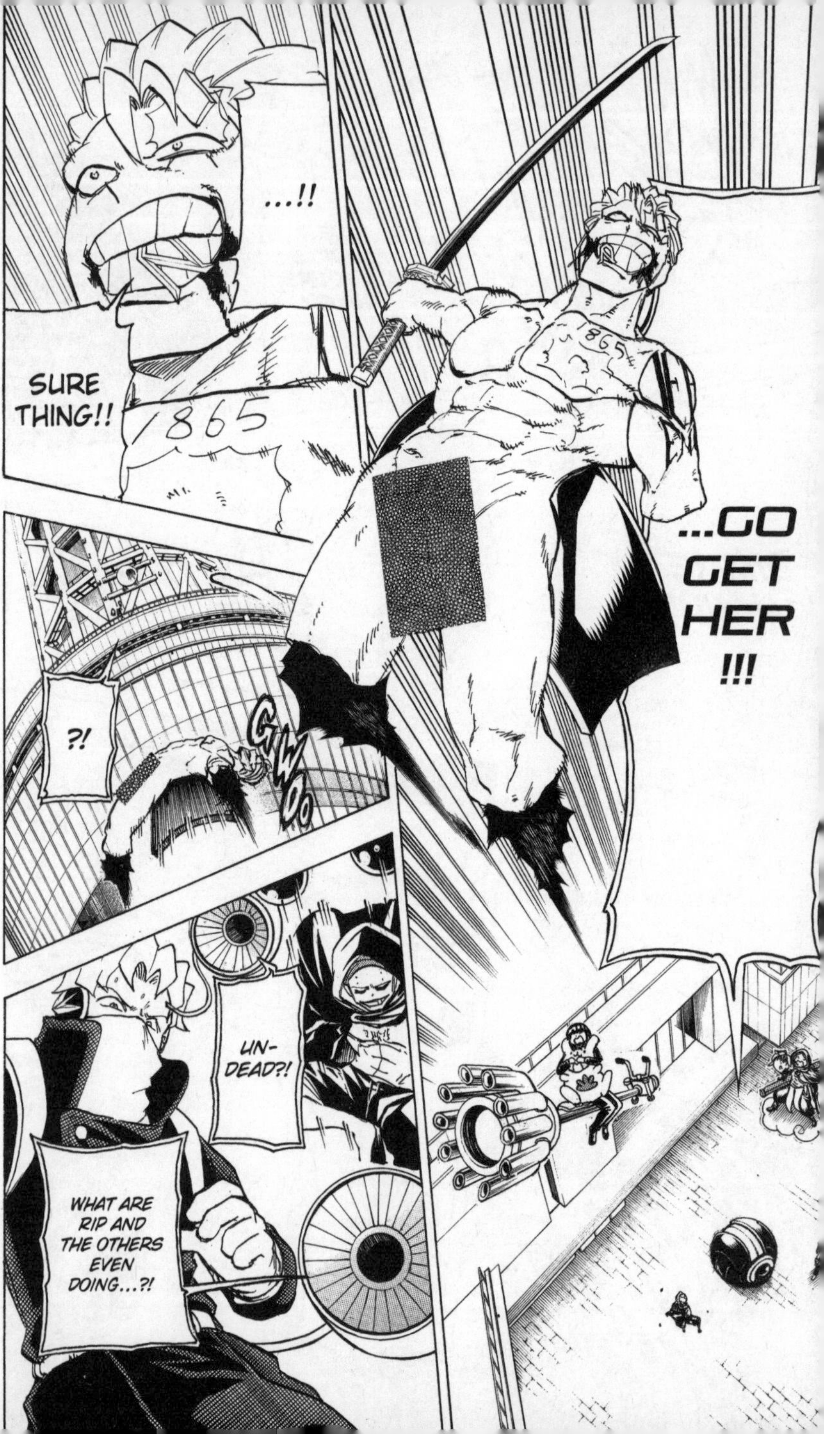
...GO GET HER!!!
...!!
SURE THING!!
1865
?!
GWOO
UN-DEAD?!
WHAT ARE RIP AND THE OTHERS EVEN DOING...?!

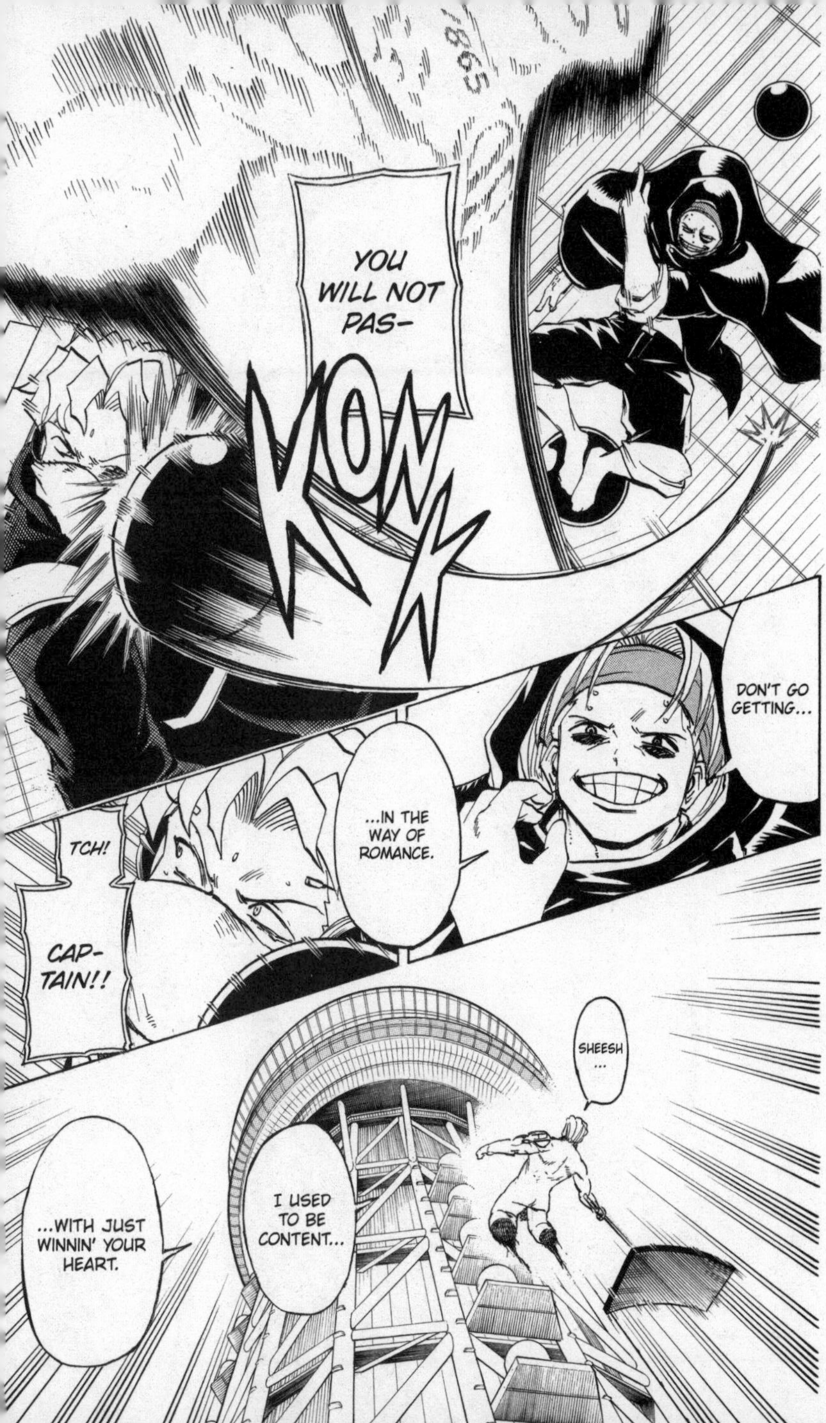
YOU WILL NOT PAS-
KON
DON'T GO GETTING...
...IN THE WAY OF ROMANCE.
TCH!
CAP-TAIN!!
SHEESH ...
I USED TO BE CONTENT...
...WITH JUST WINNIN' YOUR HEART.

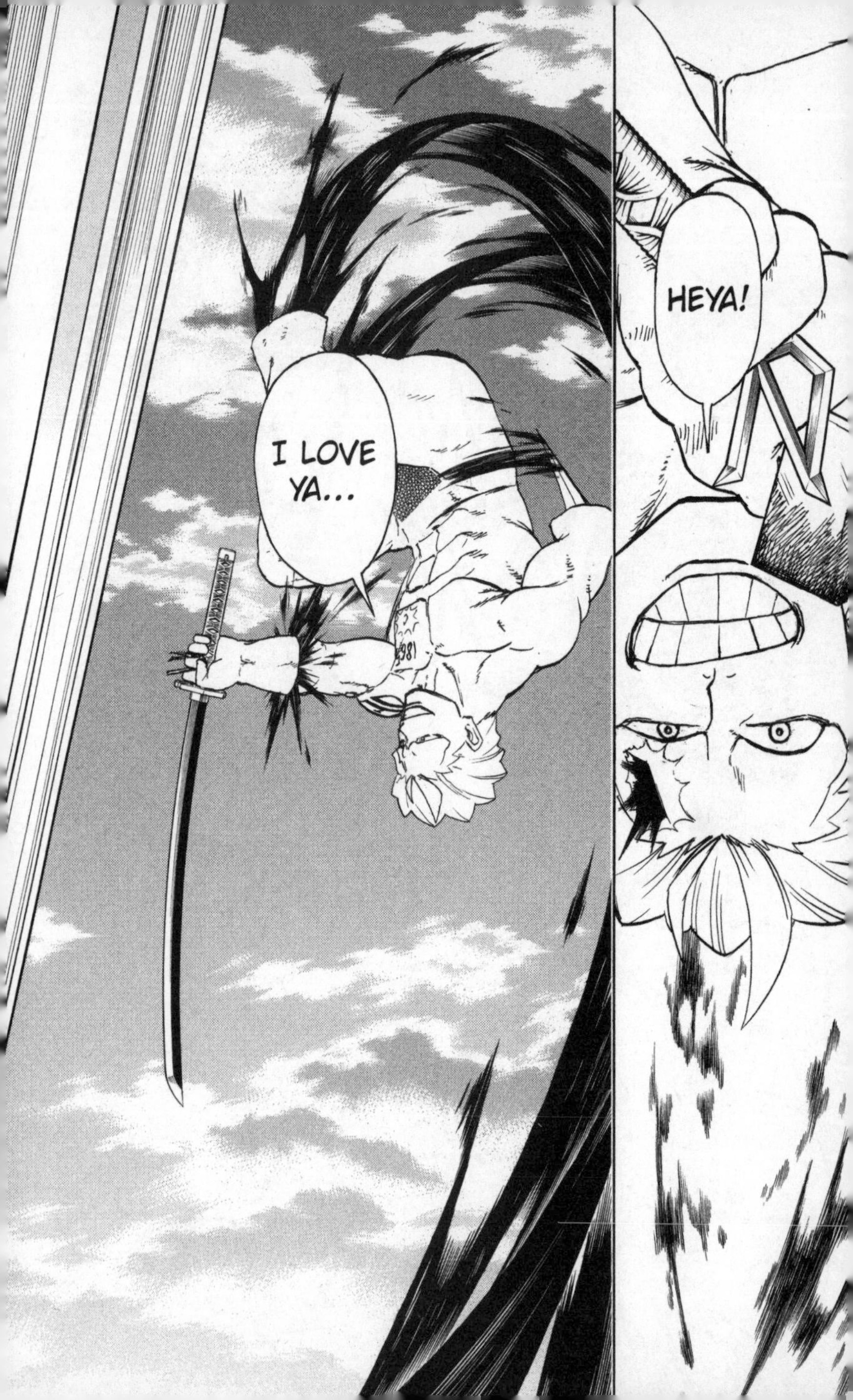
HEYA!
I LOVE YA...

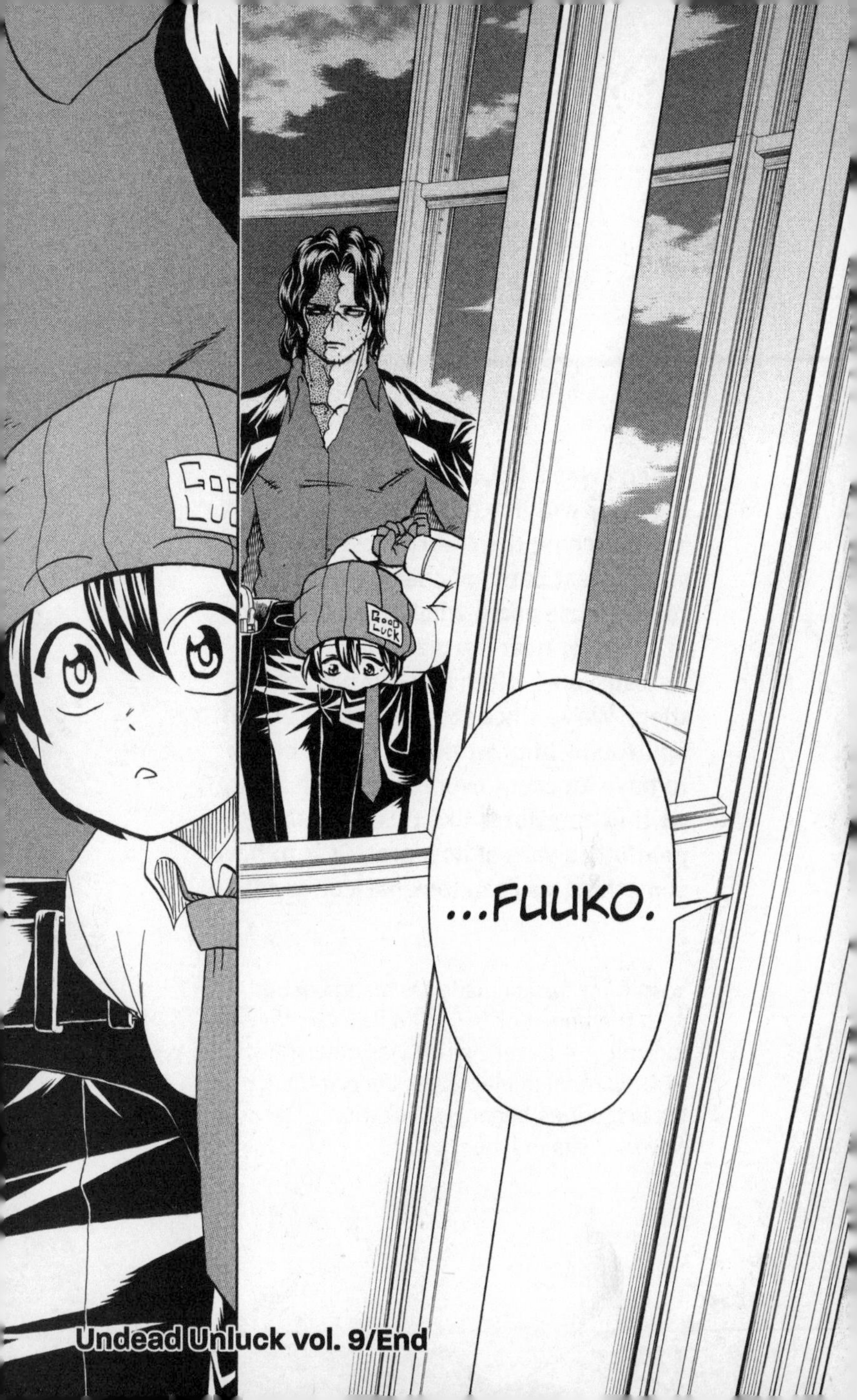

GOOD LUCK
GOOD LUCK
...FUUKO.

Undead Unluck vol. 9/End

When I was a kid, I remember getting together with my relatives every year and watching the cherry blossoms. There was a great patch of cherry trees close to my house and a whole bunch of them at the river near my grandpa's house as well, so we often had our picnics there. We've since stopped doing that in adulthood, but I wonder if it'd be better to have an event every season. After all, writing anecdotes like this makes me painfully aware of how great it is to have something you can look back on fondly.

Yoshifumi Tozuka made his manga debut with the one-shot *Uchuu Kankou C-Arc* (Cosmic Arc Travel), which was published in *Jump Next!* in May 2014. *Undead Unluck*, his first series, began serialization in *Weekly Shonen Jump* in January 2020.

UNDEAD UNLUCK

Volume 9
Shonen Jump Edition

STORY AND ART BY
Yoshifumi Tozuka

Translation: **David Evelyn**
Touch-Up Art & Lettering: **Michelle Pang**
Design: **Kam Li**
Editor: **Karla Clark**

The stories, characters, and incidents mentioned in this
publication are entirely fictional.

Printed in the U.S.A.

Published by VIZ Media, LLC
P.O. Box 77010
San Francisco, CA 94107

10 9 8 7 6 5 4 3 2 1
First printing, October 2022

PARENTAL ADVISORY
UNDEAD UNLUCK is rated T+ for Older Teen
and is recommended for ages 16 and up. This
volume contains suggestive themes, crude
humor, and violence.

viz.com

This is the LAST PAGE!

You're reading THE WRONG WAY!

UNDEAD UNLUCK reads from right to left, starting in the upper-right corner. Japanese is read from right to left, meaning that action, sound effects, and word-balloon order are completely reversed from English order.

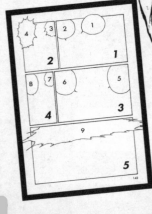